Introduction to t¹
Theory of Compl

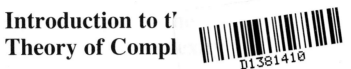

D1381410

C. A. R. Hoare, Series Editor

Introduction to the Theory of Complexity

Daniel Pierre Bovet
and
Pierluigi Crescenzi

Prentice Hall
New York   London   Toronto   Sydney   Tokyo   Singapore

First published 1994 by
Prentice Hall International (UK) Limited
Campus 400, Maylands Avenue
Hemel Hempstead
Hertfordshire, HP2 7EZ
A division of
Simon & Schuster International Group

Printed and bound in Great Britain by
Bookcraft, Midsomer Norton.

Library of Congress Cataloging-in-Publication Data

Bovet, D. (Daniel)
    Introduction to the theory of complexity / Daniel Pierre Bovet and
Pierluigi Crescenzi.
        p.   cm.
    Includes bibliographical references and index.
    ISBN 0-13-915380-2
    1. Computational complexity.   I. Crescenzi, Pierluigi.
II. Title.
QA267.7.B68   1993
511.3–dc20   93–31138
                                        CIP

British Library Cataloguing in Publication Data

A catalogue record for this book is available from
the British Library

ISBN 0-13-915380-2 (pbk)

---

  2 3 4 5   98 97 96 95 94

Contents

Preface

The birth of the theory of computational complexity can be set in the early 1960s when the first users of electronic computers started to pay increasing attention to the performances of their programs. As in the theory of computation, where the concept of a model of computation had led to that of an algorithm and of an algorithmically solvable problem, similarly, in the theory of computational complexity, the concept of resource used by a computation led to that of an efficient algorithm and of a computationally feasible problem.

Since these preliminary stages, many more results have been obtained and, as stated by Hartmanis (1989), 'the systematic study of computational complexity theory has developed into one of the central and most active research areas of computer science. It has grown into a rich and exciting mathematical theory whose development is motivated and guided by computer science needs and technological advances.'

The aim of this introductory book is to review in a systematic way the most significant results obtained in this new research area. The main goals of computational complexity theory are to introduce classes of problems which have similar complexity with respect to a specific computation model and complexity measure, and to study the intrinsic properties of such classes.

In this book, we will follow a balanced approach which is partly algorithmic and partly structuralist. From an algorithmic point of view, we will first present some 'natural' problems and then illustrate algorithms which solve them. Since the aim is merely to prove that the problem belongs to a specific class, we will not always give the most efficient algorithm and we will occasionally give preference to an algorithm which is simpler to describe and analyse.

From a structural point of view, we will be concerned with intrinsic properties of complexity classes, including relationships between classes, implications between several hypotheses about complexity classes, and identification of structural properties of sets that affect their computational complexity.

The reader is assumed to have some basic knowledge of theory of computation (as taught in an undergraduate course on Automata Theory, Logic, Formal Languages Theory, or Theory of Computation) and of programming languages and techniques. Some mathematical knowledge is also required.

The first eight chapters of the book can be taught on a senior undergraduate course. The whole book together with an exhaustive discussion of the problems should be suitable for a postgraduate course.

Let us now briefly review the contents of the book and the choices made in selecting the material.

The first part (Chapters 1-3) provide the basic tools which will enable us to study topics in complexity theory. Chapter 1 includes a series of definitions and notations related to classic mathematical concepts such as sets, relationships and languages (this chapter can be skipped and referred to when needed). Chapter 2 reviews some important results of computability theory. Chapter 3 provides the basic tool of complexity theory: dynamic complexity measures are introduced, the concept of classes of languages is presented, the strict correspondence between such classes and decision problems is established, and techniques used to study the properties of such classes are formulated.

The second part (Chapters 4-8) studies, in a detailed way, the properties of some of the most significant complexity classes. Those chapters represent the 'heart' of complexity theory: by placing suitable restrictions on the power of the computation model, and thus on the amount of resources allowed for the computation, it becomes possible to define a few fundamental complexity classes and to develop a series of tools enabling us to identify, for most computational problems, the complexity class to which they belong.

The third part (Chapters 9-10) deals with probabilistic algorithms and with the corresponding complexity classes. Probabilistic Turing machines are introduced in Chapter 9 and a few probabilistic algorithms for such machines are analysed. In Chapter 10, a more elaborate computation model denoted as interactive proof system is considered and a new complexity class based on such a model is studied.

The last part (Chapters 11 and 12) is dedicated to the complexity of parallel computations. As a result of advances in hardware technology, computers with thousands of processors are now available; it thus becomes important, not only from a theoretical point of view but also from a practical one, to be able to specify which problems are best suited to be run on parallel machines. Chapter 11 describes in detail a few important and widely differing models of parallel computers and shows how their performance can be considered roughly equivalent. Chapter 12 introduces the concept of a problem solvable by a fast parallel algorithm and the complementary one of a problem with no fast parallel algorithm, and illustrates examples of both types of problems.

While selecting material to be included in the book, we followed a few guidelines. First, we have focused our attention on results obtained in the past two decades, mentioning without proof or leaving as problems some well-known results obtained in the 1960s. Second, whenever a proof of a theorem uses a technique described in a previous proof, we have provided an outline, leaving the complete proof as a problem for the reader. Finally, we have systematically avoided stating without proof specialistic results in other fields in order to make the book as self-contained as possible.

Acknowledgements

This book originated from a course on Algorithms and Complexity given at the University of Rome 'La Sapienza' by D.P. Bovet and P. Crescenzi since 1986. We would like to thank the students who were exposed to the preliminary versions of the chapters and who contributed their observations to improve the quality of the presentation. We also would like to thank R. Silvestri for pointing out many corrections and for suggesting simpler and clearer proofs of some results.

Chapter 1

Mathematical preliminaries

In this chapter some preliminary definitions, notations and proof techniques which are going to be used in the rest of the book will be introduced.

1.1 Sets, relations and functions

Intuitively, a *set* A is any collection of elements. If a, b and c are arbitrary elements, then the set A consisting of elements a, b and c is represented as $A = \{a, b, c\}$.

A set cannot contain more than one copy or instance of the same element; furthermore, the order in which the elements of the set appear is irrelevant. Thus we define two sets A and B as *equal* (in symbols, $A = B$) if every element of A is also an element of B and vice versa. Two sets A and B are *not equal* (in symbols, $A \neq B$) when $A = B$ does not hold true.

The symbols $\in$ and $\notin$ denote, respectively, the fact that an element belongs or does not belong to a set. Referring to the previous example, it is clear that $a \in A$ and that $d \notin A$.

A set is a *singleton* if it includes a single element; it is important to distinguish the singleton set $\{x\}$ from the element x. A set is *empty* (in symbols, $X = \emptyset$) if it includes no element, otherwise it is *non-empty*. A set is *finite* if it includes a finite number of elements, otherwise it is *infinite*.[1]

Typical examples of infinite sets are the sets of *natural numbers* N, of *integer numbers* Z, and of *real numbers* R.

Since an infinite set cannot be described by listing all its elements, other approaches are used: one of these consists of defining new sets relying on the definition of a few basic ones which are assumed to be already known. More precisely, given a set X and a property π, we write $Y = \{y : y \in X \text{ and } y \text{ satisfies } \pi\}$ to express in a compact way the fact that Y consists of all elements y which belong

---

[1]Since the previous concepts are rather intuitive, we only give informal definitions here. A branch of logic called axiomatic set theory deals with formal definitions.

to X and which satisfy property π.

Example 1.1 Using the approach just mentioned, it is easy to verify that $A = \{x : x \in N$ and $(x \equiv 0 \pmod 3)\}$ denotes the set of natural numbers which are multiples of 3.

A set A is a *subset* of B (in symbols, $A \subseteq B$) if each element of A is also an element of B. A set A is a *proper subset* of B (in symbols, $A \subset B$) if $A \subseteq B$ and $A \neq B$. If $A = B$, then both $A \subseteq B$ and $B \subseteq A$ hold.

1.1.1   Connectives and quantifiers

We shall make use of notations from elementary logic: 'and' will be abbreviated to '$\wedge$'; 'or' to '$\vee$'; 'only if' to '$\rightarrow$'; and 'not' to '$\neg$'. All these symbols are called *connectives*.

'$\forall$' and '$\exists$' are called *universal* and *existential quantifiers*, respectively. '$\forall x$' is read as 'for all x' and '$\exists x$' as 'an x exists such that'.

The logical symbols above serve as convenient abbreviations of ordinary mathematical language. For example, $A \subseteq B$ can be expressed as $\forall x[x \in A \rightarrow x \in B]$.

1.1.2   Operations on sets

Given two sets A and B, their *union* denoted as $A \cup B$ is the set of all elements which belong either to A or to B: $A \cup B = \{x : x \in A \vee x \in B\}$; their *intersection* denoted as $A \cap B$ is the set of all elements common to A and B: $A \cap B = \{x : x \in A \wedge x \in B\}$; the *difference* set of A from B denoted as $A - B$ is defined as the set of all elements which belong to A but not to B: $A - B = \{x : x \in A \wedge x \notin B\}$; finally, the *symmetric difference* set of A and B denoted as $A \triangle B$ is the set of all elements which belong to A but not to B or which belong to B but not to A: $A \triangle B = (A - B) \cup (B - A)$.

Two sets A and B are *disjoint* if they do not include common elements, that is, if $A \cap B = \emptyset$.

The *power set* of A (in symbols, 2^A) is a set whose elements are all possible subsets of A, including the empty set and the set A. If A is finite and consists of n elements, then the power set of A consists of 2^n elements, thus the notation 2^A.

Example 1.2 Consider the finite set $A = \{x, y\}$. The corresponding power set is $2^A = \{\emptyset, \{x\}, \{y\}, \{x, y\}\}$.

Given a non-empty set A, a *partition* of A is a subset P of 2^A such that

1. every element of P is non-empty;
2. the elements of P are pairwise disjoint;

3. the union of the elements of P is equal to A.

Example 1.3 Let $A = \{1, 3, 5, 8, 12, 16, 25, 50\}$. A partition P of A is given by $P = \{\{1, 3, 8\}, \{5, 16, 50\}, \{12, 25\}\}$.

1.1.3   Pairs, n-tuples and relations

Given two elements x and y, let us denote the *ordered pair* of x and y with $\langle x, y \rangle$. Notice that $\langle x, y \rangle$ is distinct from the two-element set $\{x, y\}$ because the order in which the two elements appear in the pair is significant and because the same element may appear twice in the pair. Two pairs $\langle x, y \rangle$ and $\langle z, w \rangle$ are equal if and only if $x = z$ and $y = w$.

The *Cartesian product* of two sets A and B, denoted as $A \times B$, is the set of all ordered pairs $\langle x, y \rangle$ with $x \in A$ and $y \in B$.

Any subset R of $A \times B$ is called a *binary relation* between A and B. Given a binary relation R, we can associate with it a predicate $R(x, y)$ which assumes the value **true** if and only if $\langle x, y \rangle \in R$. In the following chapters, we shall use the term 'relation' to denote both the set of ordered pairs R and the predicate associated with it.

The *domain* of R is the set of all x such that $\langle x, y \rangle \in R$ for some y; the *codomain* or *range* of R is the set of all y such that $\langle x, y \rangle \in R$ for some x.

Example 1.4 Given two sets $A = \{1, 2, 3\}$ and $B = \{a, b, c\}$, their Cartesian product is

$$A \times B = \{\langle 1, a \rangle, \langle 1, b \rangle, \langle 1, c \rangle, \langle 2, a \rangle, \langle 2, b \rangle, \langle 2, c \rangle, \langle 3, a \rangle, \langle 3, b \rangle, \langle 3, c \rangle\}.$$

The set $R = \{\langle 1, a \rangle, \langle 2, b \rangle, \langle 3, c \rangle\}$ is a binary relation between A and B. The corresponding predicate is such that $R(1, a) = $ **true** and $R(3, b) = $ **false**.

We can easily extend the concept of ordered pairs to sequences of n elements with n finite. Such sequences, called *ordered n-tuples*, are denoted as $\langle x_1, \ldots, x_n \rangle$. Two n-tuples $\langle x_1, \ldots, x_n \rangle$ and $\langle y_1, \ldots, y_m \rangle$ are *equal* if and only if $m = n$ and $x_i = y_i$ for $i = 1, 2, \ldots, n$.

The *Cartesian product of n sets* $A_1, \ldots, A_n$ is defined as $A_1 \times A_2 \times \ldots \times A_n = \{\langle a_1, a_2, \ldots, a_n \rangle : (a_1 \in A_1) \wedge (a_2 \in A_2) \wedge \ldots \wedge (a_n \in A_n)\}$.

Sometimes it is convenient to consider the Cartesian product of n sets coinciding with A: in such cases we shall use the shorthand notation $A^n = A \times A \times \ldots \times A$.

Any subset R of $A_1 \times A_2 \times \ldots \times A_n$ is called an *n-ary relation* between the n sets $A_1, \ldots, A_n$. Given an n-ary relation R we can associate with it a predicate $R(x_1, \ldots, x_n)$ which assumes the value **true** if and only if $\langle x_1, \ldots, x_n \rangle \in R$.

1.1.4   Set closure

Given a set A, a natural number $n > 0$ and an $(n+1)$-ary relation $R \subseteq A^{n+1}$, a set $B \subseteq A$ is said to be *closed with respect to* R if, for all $(n+1)$-tuple $\langle b_1, \ldots, b_{n+1} \rangle$ of R, $(b_1 \in B \land b_2 \in B \land \ldots \land b_n \in B) \to b_{n+1} \in B$.

Example 1.5 Consider the relation $R_{dif} \subseteq Z^3$ corresponding to the difference between two integer numbers. It can immediately be verified that Z is closed with respect to R_{dif}, while N is not.

1.1.5   Equivalence relations

A binary relation between A and A is called a *binary relation in* A. Let R be a binary relation in A. R is called *reflexive* if $R(x, x) = \textbf{true}$ for all x, while it is called *antireflexive* if $R(x, x) = \textbf{false}$ for all x. R is called *symmetric* if, for all pairs of elements x and y, $R(x, y)$ implies $R(y, x)$, while it is called *antisymmetric* if, for all pairs of elements x and y, $R(x, y)$ and $R(y, x)$ imply $x = y$. R is called *transitive* if, for all triples of elements x, y and z, $R(x, y)$ and $R(y, z)$ imply $R(x, z)$.

A binary relation in A which is reflexive, symmetric and transitive is called an *equivalence* relation.

1.1.6   Functions

Given two sets A and B, a *function* f from A to B (in symbols, $f : A \to B$) is a binary relation between A and B which includes, at most, one pair $\langle a, b \rangle$ for any $a \in A$. The definitions of domain and codomain introduced for relations can be easily extended to functions. A function with domain A' and codomain B' is called a function *from* A' *onto* B'. When referring to functions we prefer to say that the value of f in a is b (in symbols, $f(a) = b$) instead of the pair $\langle a, b \rangle$ belongs to f.

If $f : A \to B$ is a function and $f(a) = b$ with $a \in A$ and $b \in B$, then a is called the *argument* and b the *value* of f.

A function $f : A \to B$ is *total* if its domain coincides with A and is *partial* when the opposite is true.

A function $f : A \to B$ is *injective* if, for all $a, a' \in A$ with $a \neq a'$, $f(a) \neq f(a')$. A function is *surjective* if B coincides with the codomain of f. A function is *bijective* if it is both injective and surjective. A bijective function is also called a *bijection*.

1.1.7 Inverse relations and inverse functions

Given a binary relation $R \subseteq A \times B$, the *inverse relation* of R is defined as $R^{-1} = \{\langle y, x \rangle : \langle x, y \rangle \in R\}$. It follows from the definition that $(R^{-1})^{-1} = R$.

Similarly, given a function $f : A \rightarrow B$, we say that it admits an *inverse function* $f^{-1} : B \rightarrow A$ if the following identity holds true: $f(a) = b \leftrightarrow f^{-1}(b) = a$.

Note that a binary relation R always admits a unique inverse relation R^{-1} while only the injective functions admit an inverse function.

Example 1.6 The sum function $f : N \times N \rightarrow N$, defined as $f(x, y) = x + y$, is not invertible because, given z, in general several pairs of numbers $\langle x, y \rangle$ exist such that $x + y = z$.

1.2 Set cardinality

Given a finite set X, its *cardinality* is equal to the number n of its elements. In order to extend the definition of cardinality to infinite sets, we shall make use of the following definitions. Two sets (finite or infinite) X and Y are *equinumerous* or *equivalent* (in symbols, $X \equiv Y$) if a bijection between the two sets exists. Note how this definition is inherently 'non-constructive': two sets are considered equinumerous even if we are unable to compute the bijection, but are only certain that one exists.

The *cardinality* of a set X (in symbols, $|X|$) is introduced as an object which is only associated with those sets (including X itself) that are equinumerous to X. By this definition $|X| = |Y| \leftrightarrow X \equiv Y$. In particular, if the set includes a finite number of elements, a more concrete definition of cardinality can be given (see Theorem 1.1).

Not all infinite sets are equinumerous. A set is said to be *countable* or *enumerable* or *denumerable* if it is finite or if it is equinumerous with the set of natural numbers N.

Example 1.7 The set Z is countable since its elements can be counted by listing them in the following order:
$$0,1,-1,2,-2,3,-3,...$$

A set that is not countable is *uncountable*. In the next section we shall give examples of countable and uncountable sets.

1.3 Three proof techniques

The act of proving a theorem is often considered an art which may never be fully automated. Some techniques, however, have been useful so often in proving theorems that it is certainly worth mastering them. In this section we present three proof techniques that will be widely used in the rest of the book.

1.3.1   The induction technique

Suppose that you want to prove that, for any natural number n, the sum of the first n odd natural numbers is equal to n^2. If you have a computer you can easily write a program that, for any n, generates the first n odd natural numbers, sums them and checks that the sum is equal to n^2. But there is one problem: the previous proof is 'infinite' since there is an infinity of natural numbers. This book mostly deals with the efficiency of algorithms and it does not give a good impression to start with an algorithm that will run for ever!

Fortunately, mathematicians have developed a technique that allows them to give finite proofs for statements like the one above. This is based on the *induction principle*.

Let R be a unary relation in the set of natural numbers, that is, a subset of N. The induction principle states that if $R(0) = \mathbf{true}$ and, for any n, $R(n) = \mathbf{true}$ implies that $R(n + 1) = \mathbf{true}$, then, for any natural number n, $R(n) = \mathbf{true}$. Applying such a principle yields the following proof technique.

> *The induction technique.* Given a unary relation R in the set of natural numbers, to prove that, for any n, $R(n) = \mathbf{true}$ carry out the following.
>
> **Basis.** Prove that $R(0) = \mathbf{true}$.
>
> **Inductive step.** Assuming that $R(n) = \mathbf{true}$, prove that $R(n + 1) = \mathbf{true}$. The assumption $R(n) = \mathbf{true}$ is also called the *induction hypothesis*.

The reader should try to apply the above technique to prove that, for any n, $\sum_{i=1}^{n}(2i - 1) = n^2$ (the practitioner may still prefer the computer method, but we cannot wait for his or her answer!). As a second example, we shall apply the induction technique to prove the following result.

Theorem 1.1 For any finite set A, $|2^A| = 2^{|A|}$.

Proof. The proof is by induction on $n = |A|$.

Basis. If $n = 0$, that is, $A = \emptyset$, then $2^A = \{\emptyset\}$ and $|2^A| = 1 = 2^n$.

Inductive step. Assume that, for any set of n elements, the cardinality of its power set is equal to 2^n. Let A be a finite set of $n+1$ elements and let x be any of its elements. By the induction hypothesis, $|2^{A-\{x\}}| = 2^n$. Corresponding to any subset B of $A - \{x\}$ there are two subsets of A, that is, B itself and $B \cup \{x\}$. Then $|2^A| = 2|2^{A-\{x\}}| = 2^{n+1}$.

The assertion then follows.   □

1.3.2 The breadth-first technique

Let us consider the following problem. Given a countable set of infinite countable sets $A_0, A_1, \ldots, A_n, \ldots$ and an element x, does x belong to at least one A_i? An enthusiastic reader might say: 'OK, it's easy! First of all, note that, for any i, we can check whether $x \in A_i$ in the following way. For $j = 1, 2, 3, \ldots$, compare x with the jth element of A_i. Now, check if $x \in A_0$; if so, we have finished. Otherwise, check if $x \in A_1$; if it is, we have finished. Otherwise ...'. Wait, wait! We agree that if $x \in A_0$, then the previous procedure will find it. But what happens if $x \notin A_0$? We will be deadlocked inside A_0 without being able to explore the other sets further. Once again, we have to contend with infinity!

The breadth-first technique allows us to solve the previous problem because we will either discover that $x \in A_i$, for some i, or we will never end our search (should none of the A_i's include x).

> *The breadth-first technique.* Given a countable set of infinite countable sets $A_0, A_1, \ldots, A_n, \ldots$ and an element x, to check whether, for some i, $x \in A_i$ carry out the following.
>
> **Step 1.** Check whether x is the first element of A_0.
>
> **Step k.** Check whether x is the first element of A_{k-1}, the second element of A_{k-2}, $\ldots$, or the kth element of A_0.

A curious reader might ask: 'Why is this technique called breadth-first?' In order to answer this question, let us write the sets A_n as shown in Figure 1.1, where the pair (i, j) denotes the $(i+1)$th element of A_j. The sequence of elements checked by the breadth-first technique is then represented by the arrows, so that the entire picture looks like visiting a tree by means of a breadth-first search algorithm.

An immediate consequence of this search technique is that the set $N \times N$ is countable. More generally, the following result (whose proof is left to the reader) holds true.

Theorem 1.2 Given n countable sets $A_1, A_2, \ldots A_n$, the set $A = A_1 \times A_2 \times \ldots \times A_n$ is also countable.

1.3.3 The diagonalization technique

Given any countable set A of subsets of a countable set X, we wish to show that $A \neq 2^X$, in other words, 2^X is not countable unless X is finite. In order to prove such a statement, we shall derive a subset of X which does not belong to A.

> *The diagonalization technique.* Given a countable set $A = \{A_i : i \geq 0\}$ of subsets of a countable set $X = \{x_0, x_1, \ldots, x_n, \ldots\}$, the diagonal set D is defined as
> $$D = \{x_i : x_i \notin A_i\}.$$

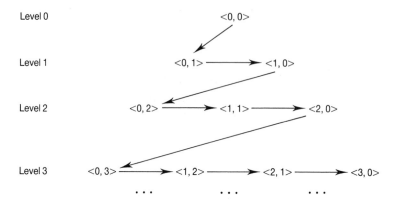

Figure 1.1 A representation of the breadth-first technique

It is easy to verify that $D \subseteq X$ and, for any i, $D \neq A_i$.

Once again, to justify the name of the technique let us provide a different interpretation. Let M be a binary infinite matrix such that $M_{ij} = 0$ if $x_i \in A_j$, otherwise $M_{ij} = 1$. The diagonal of such a matrix represents the set D since $M_{ii} = 1$ if and only if $x_i \in D$.

Wide use of the diagonalization technique will be made in the rest of this book. We give the following result, whose proof is based on different interpretations of the previously defined matrix M, as a first example.

Theorem 1.3 The set 2^N, the set R and the set of all functions $f : N \to \{0, 1\}$ are not countable.

1.4   Graphs

A *graph* G is a pair of finite sets (N, E) such that E is a binary symmetric relation[2] in N. The set N is the set of *nodes* and E is the set of *edges*. If $\langle x, y \rangle \in E$, then x and y are said to be *adjacent* and they are the *end-points* of that edge (see Figure 1.2(a)). The number of nodes adjacent to a given node x is called the *degree* of x. The degree of G is the maximum over all node degrees.

We say that $G' = (N', E')$ is a subgraph of $G = (N, E)$ if $N' \subseteq N$ and $E' \subseteq \{\langle n_i, n_j \rangle : n_i, n_j \in N' \wedge \langle n_i, n_j \rangle \in E\}$.

---

[2]In a few examples, we shall also consider *directed graphs*, that is, graphs $G = (N, E)$ where E is not symmetric.

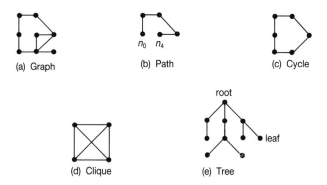

Figure 1.2 Some example graphs

A *weighted graph* is a graph $G = (N, E)$ together with a function $w : E \rightarrow N$ which associates a weight with any edge so that $w(n_i, n_j) = w(n_j, n_i)$.

A graph $G = (N, E)$ is called a *complete graph* or a *clique* if $E = N \times N$, that is, if every two nodes are adjacent (see Figure 1.2(d)).

Given a graph G and two nodes n_0 and n_k, a *path from n_0 to n_k of length k* is a sequence of edges $\langle n_0, n_1 \rangle, \langle n_1, n_2 \rangle, \ldots, \langle n_{k-1}, n_k \rangle$ such that, for $0 \le i < j \le k$, $n_i \ne n_j$ (see Figure 1.2(b)). If $n_0 = n_k$, then such a sequence is said to be a *cycle* (see Figure 1.2(c)).

A graph is *connected* if, for every two distinct nodes x and y, there is a path from x to y. A *tree* is a connected graph with no cycles. Equivalently, a tree is a graph one of whose nodes is distinguished as a *root*, together with a relation that creates a hierarchical structure among the nodes. Formally, a tree can be defined recursively in the following alternative manner:

1. A single node by itself is a tree. This node is also the root of the tree.
2. Suppose n is a node and $T_1, T_2, \ldots, T_k$ are trees with roots $n_1, n_2, \ldots, n_k$. A new tree is obtained by joining n with nodes $n_1, n_2, \ldots, n_k$. In this tree n is the root and $T_1, T_2, \ldots, T_k$ are the *subtrees* of the root. Nodes $n_1, n_2, \ldots, n_k$ are called the *children* of node n.

The *height of a node* in a tree is the length of the path from the root to the node itself. Figure 1.2(e) shows a tree with three height-one nodes, four height-two nodes, and two height-three nodes. The *height of a tree* is the maximum among the node heights.

In a tree, a node with no children is called a *leaf*. A tree is a *binary tree* (respectively, a *complete binary tree*) if every node that is not a leaf has at most (respectively, exactly) two children. A complete binary tree is *perfect* if all leaves have the same height. It is easy to prove by induction that the number of nodes of a perfect binary tree whose leaves have a height h is equal to $2^{h+1} - 1$.

1.5   Alphabets, words and languages

An *alphabet* is any non-empty finite set $\Sigma = \{\sigma_1, \ldots, \sigma_k\}$. A *symbol* is an element of an alphabet. A *word* is a finite tuple $x = \langle \sigma_{i_1}, \sigma_{i_2}, \ldots, \sigma_{i_n} \rangle$ of symbols from Σ; the *empty word* is denoted by e. For the sake of brevity, the word $\langle \sigma_{i_1}, \sigma_{i_2}, \ldots, \sigma_{i_n} \rangle$ will be denoted by $\sigma_{i_1} \sigma_{i_2} \ldots \sigma_{i_n}$. The infinite set of all words over an alphabet Σ will be denoted by Σ^*.

The *length* $|x|$ of a word $x = \sigma_{i_1} \sigma_{i_2} \ldots \sigma_{i_n}$ is the number n of symbols that x contains. The empty word has a length 0. Clearly, the number of words of length n over a k-symbol alphabet is equal to k^n. Given two words x and y, the *concatenation* of x and y (in symbols, xy) is defined as the word z consisting of all symbols of x followed by all symbols of y, thus $|z| = |x| + |y|$. In particular, the concatenation of a word x with itself k times will be denoted as x^k. Given two words x and y, x is said to be a *prefix* of y if a word z exists such that $y = xz$.

Given an alphabet Σ, a *language* over Σ is a subset of Σ^*. The *complement* of a language L, in symbols L^c, is defined as $L^c = \Sigma^* - L$.

Let $\Sigma = \{0, 1\}$. The *join* of two languages L_1 and L_2 over Σ is defined as

$$L_1 \oplus L_2 = \{x : (x = 1y \wedge y \in L_1) \vee (x = 0y \wedge y \in L_2)\}.$$

Given an alphabet Σ, any order among the symbols of Σ induces an order among the words in Σ^* in the following way:

1. For any n, the words of length n precede the words of length $n + 1$.
2. For each length, the order is alphabetical.

Such an order is called a *lexicographic order*. As a consequence, any language over Σ is a countable set.

Example 1.8 Let $\Sigma = \{a, b, c\}$. The lexicographic order of Σ^* is the following:
$$e, a, b, c, aa, ab, ac, ba, bb, bc, ca, cb, cc, aaa, aab, \ldots$$

Given a language L, we shall denote by L_n the set of all words of L having length n, and by $L_{\leq n}$ the set of all words having a length not greater than n.

The *census function* of a language L, in symbols c_L, is a function which yields, for any n, the number of words of length not greater than n included in L, thus $c_L(n) = |L_{\leq n}|$.

The 'density' of a language is determined by the rate of growth of its census function according to the following classification:

1. Finite languages are the least dense since their census function is constant for sufficiently large n.
2. Languages whose census function is bounded above by a polynomial in n are called *sparse*. It is easy to verify that a language L is sparse if and only if a polynomial p exists such that $\forall n[|L_n| \leq p(n)]$. Languages included in $\{\sigma\}^*$, that is, languages over singleton sets, are called *tally* languages. Clearly, the census function of a tally language grows at most as n, thus tally languages are sparse.
3. The most dense languages are those whose census function grows exponentially with n. It can immediately be verified that the census function of Σ^* is equal to $\sum_{i=0}^{n} k^i = (k^{n+1} - 1)/(k - 1)$ where $k \geq 2$ denotes the cardinality of Σ.

Example 1.9 Let $\Sigma = \{0, 1\}$ and let $b(n)$ denote the binary encoding of the natural number n. The language L defined as

$$L = \{b(n) : n \text{ is a power of 2}\}$$

is sparse since its census function is linear.

Conversely, it is easy to verify that, for any natural number k, the language $L(k)$ defined as

$$L(k) = \{b(n) : n \text{ is divisible by } 2^k\}$$

is not sparse.

Chapter 2

Elements of computability theory

This chapter briefly reviews some important concepts and results of computability theory which will be used in the remaining chapters. As stated in the Preface, complexity theory may be considered as a refinement of computability theory. In fact, in several cases the same proof technique, initially developed for the first theory, has been adapted for the second.

Intuitively, computing means being able to specify a finite sequence of actions which will lead to the result. What do we mean by action? A precise answer to this question can only be given after having defined a model of computation, that is, a formal system which allows us to unambiguously express the actions to be performed.

Mathematical logicians have developed many distinct models of computation. General recursive functions, unrestricted rewriting systems (also called type 0 grammars), Post systems, Markov systems, and Turing machines are only a few examples of the many formal systems that may be used to perform basically the same set of computations and which are referred to as *unrestricted models of computation*.

All efforts in trying to produce a model of computation more powerful than those just mentioned have not yielded any results, even if it has never been proved that such a model cannot exist. We are thus left with a conjecture called *Church's thesis*, which states that all 'solvable' problems can be solved by using any one of the previously mentioned unrestricted models of computation.

Since Church's thesis has valiantly resisted logicians' attacks for over 50 years, we feel entitled to focus our attention in Section 2.1 on a specific model called the Turing machine and to refer to it in order to introduce the concept of computable function in a precise way. In fact, we shall not restrict ourselves to standard Turing machines and we shall also consider a few extensions of the basic model which will be found to be quite useful in studying the complexity of some problems. We shall also consider a different model of computation called the random access machine in order to convince the reader that Turing machines are as powerful as an 'almost' real computer.

Next, in Section 2.2 we provide a first rough classification of languages. More precisely, given a language, we shall study to what extent Turing machines succeed in discriminating whether a word belongs to that language or not.

Finally, we present in Section 2.3 a basic tool which will be used repeatedly in the remaining chapters to compare the complexity of languages, namely the concept of reducibility between pairs of languages.

2.1   Turing machines

The Turing machine is an unrestricted model of computation developed by the great logician Alan Turing in 1935. We may consider it an idealized computer: the role of memory is played by semi-infinite tapes subdivided into cells, each cell containing a symbol of a given alphabet; the control consists of read/write tape heads which can be positioned on any cell of the tapes and of a set of instructions called tuples which determine the actions to be performed.

2.1.1   Deterministic Turing machines

A *k-tape deterministic Turing machine* T with $k \geq 1$ is a tuple $\langle Q, \Sigma, I, q_0, F \rangle$ where

1. Q is a finite set called the *set of states*.
2. Σ is a finite set called the *tape alphabet* which is always assumed to contain a special symbol called *blank* and is denoted by $\square$.
3. I is a finite set of quintuples $\langle q, \mathbf{s}, \mathbf{s}', \mathbf{m}, q' \rangle$ with $q, q' \in Q$, $\mathbf{s} \in \Sigma^k$, $\mathbf{s}' \in (\Sigma - \{\square\})^k$, and $\mathbf{m} \in \{L, R, S\}^k$ such that no pair of quintuples in the set has the same first two elements.[1]   *Instruction set*
4. $q_0 \in Q$ is a special state called the *initial state*.
5. $F \subseteq Q$ is a set of special states called *final states*.

Each of the k read/write semi-infinite tapes, in turn, consists of an infinite number of cells labeled as $0, 1, \ldots$ and each cell can store precisely one of the tape alphabet symbols.

As stated earlier, the quintuples correspond, in a certain sense, to a computer's machine language instructions. The meaning of a quintuple is described below and illustrated in Figure 2.1 (for simplicity, the figure refers to a one-tape Turing machine).

1. The first element q denotes the current (internal) state of T and the second element $\mathbf{s} = \langle s_1, \ldots, s_k \rangle$ denotes the k symbols contained in the cells currently scanned by the k tape heads.

---

[1] Note that, by definition, I includes, at most, $|Q||\Sigma|^k$ elements.

q & q' are states

s & s' area words with k letters

m is k instructions to the tape

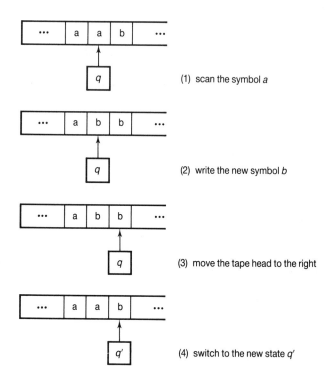

Figure 2.1 Execution of the quintuple $\langle q, a, b, R, q' \rangle$

2. The third element $\mathbf{s}' = \langle s'_1, \ldots, s'_k \rangle$ denotes the new k symbols which will replace those currently being scanned.
3. The vector $\mathbf{m} = \langle m_1, \ldots, m_k \rangle$ describes the type of motion m_i of each of the k tape heads after the rewriting has taken place: L denotes a one-cell leftward move (an L move when the tape head is positioned on cell 0 is ignored by T and replaced by an S move), R denotes a one-cell rightward move and S denotes a no-move.
4. The last element q' of the quintuple denotes the new state reached by the machine after the rewriting of symbols and the tape head moves have taken place.

The execution of a quintuple by the Turing machine is also called a *step*.

A *global state* S of a Turing machine T consists of the current state of T, the current contents of the k tapes and the current positions of the corresponding tape heads. Intuitively, the global state contains the information which needs to be saved if one wants to interrupt the machine at any time and then restart it later. At first, such an amount of information seems infinite. However, note that, according to the definition of the set of quintuples, the symbol $\Box$ can never be written. Thus, after a finite number of steps, only the contents of the cells containing a non-blank symbol have to be specified. More precisely, a global state can be thought of as a word of a length proportional to the number of steps executed (see Problem 2.7).

We must now define some conventions for how the machine starts to operate and how it ends.

Initial global state

When the machine starts executing the first step, it is in the initial state q_0 and all tape cells, except those used to store symbols of the input x, contain the symbol $\Box$. By convention, the input x does not include $\Box$ symbols, thus the first $\Box$ symbol to the right of x plays the role of delimiter of the input word.

The *initial global state* $\mathcal{S}_0$ can then be specified by stating that input x consisting of n symbols is contained in the leftmost n cells of tape 1 and that machine T is in state q_0 with the read/write heads positioned on cell 0 (there are obviously many other possible conventions which lead to other definitions of $\mathcal{S}_0$).

Deterministic computations

Each step causes a transition from one global state to another. We say that a global state $\mathcal{S}_1$ *yields* a global state $\mathcal{S}_2$ if a step exists causing the transition from $\mathcal{S}_1$ to $\mathcal{S}_2$. Notice that if $\mathcal{S}_1$ yields $\mathcal{S}_2$, then the two global states differ by a finite number of symbols.

A *(deterministic) computation* for machine T on input x, in symbols $T(x)$, is a (possibly infinite) sequence of global states starting with the initial global state of T with input x and such that each global state in the sequence yields the next.

Final global states for acceptor machines

We still have to define a *halting computation*. For that purpose, we say that a computation $T(x)$ halts whenever it is finite and its last global state is a *final global state*. Two types of Turing machines will be considered, respectively called transducers and acceptors, which differ mainly in their definition of final global states.

Acceptor machines include two final states called *accepting state* and *rejecting state* and are denoted as q_A and q_R, respectively. All finite computations of T must halt in one of those final states.

In later proofs it will be found to be useful to assume that only two final global states, the *accepting* and the *rejecting* ones, exist. This can easily be achieved by allowing the machine to 'clean the tapes', that is, to write $\Box$ symbols in all cells used by the computation and to position the k tape heads on 0 cells before reaching a final state. This clearly requires a slight modification of our definition of Turing machines (see Problem 2.5).

An input x is *accepted* by T if the computation $T(x)$ ends in the accepting global state. The set of inputs accepted by T, in symbols $L(T)$, is called the *language accepted* by T.

Example 2.1 Table 2.1 shows in detail the quintuples of a two-tape machine T which accepts the language $L = \{x : x = 0^n 1^n \text{ with } n = 0, 1, \ldots\}$. The machine is assumed initially in state q_0 with the first tape head positioned on the leftmost input symbol of x (if any).

For clarity, the same table has been redrawn in Figure 2.2 as a state transition diagram: nodes denote internal states while labelled edges of the form $x_1 x_2 / y_1 y_2$ from node q_i to node q_j express the fact that the machine in state q_i reading symbols x_1 and x_2 from the two tapes rewrites symbols y_1 and y_2 and switches to state q_j.

Table 2.1 An example of a two-tape
Turing machine

	q	$\langle s_1, s_2 \rangle$	$\langle s_1', s_2' \rangle$	$\langle m_1, m_2 \rangle$	q'
1	q_0	$\langle \square, \square \rangle$	$\langle \#, \# \rangle$	$\langle S, S \rangle$	q_1
2	q_0	$\langle 1, \square \rangle$	$\langle 1, \# \rangle$	$\langle S, S \rangle$	q_2
3	q_0	$\langle 0, \square \rangle$	$\langle 0, 0 \rangle$	$\langle R, R \rangle$	q_3
4	q_3	$\langle 0, \square \rangle$	$\langle 0, 1 \rangle$	$\langle R, R \rangle$	q_3
5	q_3	$\langle \square, \square \rangle$	$\langle \#, \# \rangle$	$\langle S, S \rangle$	q_2
6	q_3	$\langle 1, \square \rangle$	$\langle 1, \# \rangle$	$\langle R, L \rangle$	q_4
7	q_4	$\langle 0, \square \rangle$	$\langle 0, \# \rangle$	$\langle S, S \rangle$	q_2
8	q_4	$\langle 1, 1 \rangle$	$\langle 1, 1 \rangle$	$\langle R, L \rangle$	q_4
9	q_4	$\langle \square, 1 \rangle$	$\langle \#, 1 \rangle$	$\langle S, S \rangle$	q_2
10	q_4	$\langle 1, 0 \rangle$	$\langle 1, 0 \rangle$	$\langle S, S \rangle$	q_2
11	q_4	$\langle \square, 0 \rangle$	$\langle \#, 0 \rangle$	$\langle S, S \rangle$	q_1

In the table, q_1 and q_2 denote, respectively, the accepting and the rejecting states. The meaning of the quintuples is as follows:

1. $e = 0^0 1^0$ belongs to L.

2. If input starts with a 1, then reject it.

3. The first 0 has been read, write a 0 on tape 2 to delimit the sequence of 0s read on tape 1 and switch to q_3.

4. Write a 1 on tape 2 for each 0 read on tape 1.

5. Input of the form $x = 0^h$, reject it.

6. The first 1 has been read, move rightward on tape 1 looking for other 1s and leftward on tape 2 to check whether a corresponding 0 has been encountered, switch to q_4.

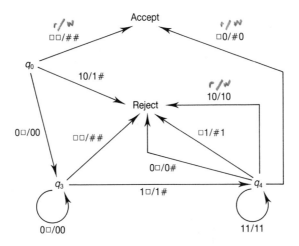

Figure 2.2 State diagram for the example two-tape Turing machine

7. Input read is $x = 0^h 1^k 0$, reject it.

8. Continue checking for other matchings.

9. Input has more 0s than 1s, reject it.

10. Input has more 1s than 0s, reject it.

11. Input $x = 0^n 1^n$, accept it.

Final global state for transducer machines

A *transducer* machine T is used to compute functions. It receives a word x as input and produces on a special tape called the *output tape* another word, say y, as output. A transducer T includes a single final state denoted as q_f and is said to be in the final global state if it has reached state q_f and if the k tape heads are positioned on 0 cells. The first $|y|$ cells of the output tape contain the *output* of the computation. As for the input x, it will be assumed that y consists of symbols of $\Sigma - \{\square\}$ so that the first $\square$ symbol to the right of y plays the role of output delimiter.

Given a function f, a transducer machine T *computes* f if the computation $T(x)$ reaches a final global state containing $f(x)$ as output whenever $f(x)$ is defined. In the opposite case, $T(x)$ is infinite, that is, it never reaches a final global state. A function is *computable* if a Turing machine T exists capable of computing it.

Universal Turing machines

Turing machines can be considered as fixed program machines: the set of quintuples implement a specific algorithm and the resulting machine is only capable of applying that algorithm to distinct input values.

Existing computers, on the other hand, are programmable machines able to execute any program on any set of input data. We will now demonstrate that even Turing machines are in some sense programmable since it is possible to define a *universal Turing machine U* which acts on an input consisting of a Turing machine T description and of a datum x and which simulates the corresponding computation $T(x)$. We shall assume, for simplicity, that T is a one-tape machine. This is not a restriction since we will show in Section 4.2 how to transform k-tape machines into equivalent one-tape machines. Thus, we are not limiting the power of U.

Before defining the characteristics of the universal machine, let us resolve the alphabet problem. Like any other Turing machine, U consists of a finite set of quintuples which refer to a finite alphabet Σ_U and a finite set of states Q_U. On the other hand, U is assumed to simulate all possible Turing machines T and those machines may make use of an alphabet Σ_T and of a set of states Q_T much larger than the ones used by U. We overcome this problem by encoding in Σ_U both Σ_T and Q_T. The following example illustrates a possible encoding which will perform the task. We shall return in Section 3.3 to the encoding problem.

Example 2.2 We choose to encode the symbols of Σ_T (respectively, the states of Q_T) as the binary representation of the natural numbers so that the ith symbol of Σ_T (respectively, the ith state of Q_T) will be encoded as the binary representation of i (eventually filled by leading 0s in order to ensure that all the encodings have the same length). The three types of tape head moves L, R, S are encoded, respectively, as 00, 01, 10. We then use two new characters ',' and ';' as delimiters between the components of a quintuple and between quintuples. Similarly, the input $x = \sigma_{i_1} \ldots \sigma_{i_n}$ on Σ_T will be encoded as $b(i_1), \ldots, b(i_n)$ where $b(i_j)$ is the binary representation of the integer i_j.

The description of T is then separated from the encoding of the input x by a third new character, say '.'.

Now that it is clear how to represent the quintuples of T and the input x, let us provide a few more details on the required data structures. Machine U makes use of three tapes: the first will contain the description of T and of the input x, the second will be used to simulate the tape of T and the last tape will contain the description of the current state of T along with the description of the symbol scanned by the tape head of T.

In the initialization phase, U copies the word x onto the second tape and writes a suitable number of 0's into the third tape (since q_0 is the initial state of T) followed by the description of the first symbol of x (since that symbol is initially scanned by T). The simulation of a quintuple of T by U is straightforward: depending on the value of the current state of T and on that of the scanned symbol, U selects the proper quintuple of T and executes it. As a result, a new binary sequence corresponding to the new symbol is rewritten onto the old one, the values of the current state and of the scanned symbol are updated and the appropriate moves are performed.

Whenever T halts, U halts according to the final state of T. If the input is not a valid description of a Turing machine along with its input, U is assumed never to halt.

2.1.2   Nondeterministic Turing machines

Deterministic Turing machines owe their name to the fact that each computation can be viewed as a sequence (finite or infinite) of global states whose first element is the initial global state. The uniqueness of such a computation is in turn due to the fact that a deterministic Turing machine cannot include two or more quintuples with the same first two elements.

Nondeterministic Turing machines, denoted as NT, are not constricted by such a limitation. Let us denote by Q the set of states and with Σ the tape alphabet of a k-tape nondeterministic machine NT. NT can include up to $3^k |Q|^2 |\Sigma|^k (|\Sigma| - 1)^k$ quintuples.

Suppose that NT is in global state $\mathcal{S}$ and let q and $\mathbf{s}$ be, respectively, the current state and the set of currently scanned symbols. Then, if NT includes p quintuples $(1 \leq p \leq 3^k |Q| (|\Sigma| - 1)^k)$ whose first two elements are q and $\mathbf{s}$, any of the p global states yielded by $\mathcal{S}$ can be the next global state.

A nondeterministic computation $NT(x)$ can then be viewed as a tree called a *computation tree*; the nodes correspond to global states while the edges between nodes correspond to transitions between global states caused by a single step. Each of the (finite or infinite) paths of the tree starting from the root is said to be a *computation path*. Figure 2.3 shows the first three steps of an example of a computation tree.

The highest number r of quintuples of NT having the same first two elements is called the *degree of nondeterminism* of NT.

As in the case of deterministic machines, it is possible to define both nondeterministic acceptors and nondeterministic transducers.

Let NT be a nondeterministic acceptor machine which includes two final states: an accepting (q_A) and a rejecting one (q_R). An input x is *accepted* by NT if the computation tree associated with $NT(x)$ includes at least one *accepting computation path*, i.e. a finite computation path whose leaf is an accepting global state. The set of inputs accepted by NT is called the *language accepted by NT* and is denoted as $L(NT)$.

Defining a nondeterministic transducer machine requires some imagination. Let NT be a nondeterministic transducer machine which includes a single final state q_f. Let x be a given input and assume that $NT(x)$ computes several distinct values: how do we know which is correct? The only way to overcome this problem is by placing suitable restrictions on NT: for example, it can be assumed that all finite

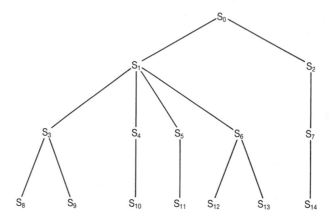

Figure 2.3 The first three levels of an example of a computation tree

computation paths of $NT(x)$ compute the same value $f(x)$.

In this book, only acceptor nondeterministic machines will be considered.

Determinism versus nondeterminism

Since the purpose of acceptor machines, whether deterministic or nondeterministic, is the same, namely to accept languages, we shall consider two acceptor Turing machines as *equivalent* if they accept the same language.

The following theorem shows that the class of languages accepted by nondeterministic Turing machine coincides with the class of languages accepted by deterministic machines. It may be considered as a first corroboration of Church's thesis.

Theorem 2.1 Given a nondeterministic Turing machine NT, it is always possible to derive an equivalent corresponding deterministic machine T. Furthermore, a constant c exists such that, for any input x, if NT accepts x in t steps, T will accept x in, at most, c^t steps.

Proof. For any input x, the aim of T is to systematically visit the computation tree associated with $NT(x)$ until it finds an accepting computation path, if it exists. However, the fact that the computation tree may include computation paths of an infinite length poses a problem for us since we do not know how to detect them. A depth-first visit of the tree must be ruled out since the visit might proceed for ever following one of those infinite paths, overlooking other finite accepting paths. We already encountered a similar problem in Section 1.3.2 and we were able to solve it by making use of the breadth-first technique.

We rely again on the same technique and explore the computation tree as follows. Visit all the computation paths for, at most, one step and if an accepting global state is found then accept x; otherwise visit all the computation paths for, at most, two steps, and so on. If NT accepts x, sooner or later T will find an accepting global state and accept the input.

We must still specify how to visit all the computation paths for, at most, i steps, for $i = 1, 2, \ldots$ Observe that we are now dealing with a finite tree and a depth-first search proves to be a good technique for visiting such a tree. More formally, denote by r the degree of nondeterminism of NT. The computation tree of depth i of $NT(x)$ includes, at most, r^i 'partial' computation paths.

We can associate a word over the alphabet $\Gamma = \{1, 2, \ldots, r\}$ with a maximum length i with each of these paths. Intuitively, such a word represents the sequence of choices that have been made along that path.

We can then successively generate all such words in lexicographic order and execute the corresponding computation path for each, starting from the initial global state. As soon as a new word w is generated, we start simulating p_w, the sequence of steps of NT represented by w. Three situations may occur:

1. If p_w does not represent a valid sequence of steps by NT (this happens when a symbol of w specifies the choice of the jth quintuple among those with the same first two elements while NT includes less than j such quintuples), then T moves to the next word in Γ^i.
2. If the first j symbols of w $(0 \leq j \leq i)$ induce a sequence of steps causing NT to accept x, then T also accepts x.
3. If the first j symbols of w $(0 \leq j \leq i)$ induce a sequence of steps causing NT to reject x, then T moves to the next word in Γ^i.

The details of the simulation are left as a problem (you may consider introducing a few additional tapes).

It is easy to verify that in order to derive the next word $w \in \Gamma^i$ and simulate the corresponding p_w a linear number of steps with respect to i is required. Thus all the computation paths for, at most, i steps can be visited by executing, at most, c_1^i steps with c_1 constant. If NT accepts x in t steps, then the total time spent in simulating it is bounded by $\sum_{i=1}^{t} c_1^i \leq c^t$ where c is a suitable constant.   □

2.1.3   Oracle Turing machines

Let us now consider a further variation of the Turing machine model which plays an important part in complexity theory.

An *oracle deterministic (nondeterministic) Turing machine* is a k-tape machine with an additional special-purpose tape called an *oracle tape* and three additional special-purpose states called *query state*, *yes state*, and *no state*. Whenever an oracle Turing machine enters the query state after having written a given word on the oracle tape, the next state will be the yes or the no state, depending on whether that word belongs to the oracle language or not.

Both acceptor and transducer oracle machines will be considered. Notice how the same basic machine T (respectively, NT) may be combined with any oracle L. Oracle machines will thus be denoted as T^L (respectively, NT^L).

Clearly, the behavior of an oracle Turing machine is established once the language to be used as an oracle has been determined. Intuitively, the oracle may be viewed as a 'supercomputer' capable of deciding *in a single step* whether a word belongs to the oracle language.

Powerful oracle languages may significantly enhance the power of the basic machine. Conversely, very simple ones do not enhance its power at all since the basic machine is able to answer the query efficiently without making use of the oracle (we do not need a supercomputer to decide that a number is even!).

2.1.4   Alternating Turing machines

The computation tree associated with a nondeterministic computation $NT(x)$ may be considered a tree of 'existential' nodes. Assume that a given node of the tree corresponding to global state S has been reached. NT will only accept x starting from S if the computation tree includes a path from S to an accepting global state.

Alternating Turing machines, denoted as AT, are a natural extension of nondeterministic ones where both 'existential' and 'universal' branching is allowed. Let us refer to the previous example. Informally, if S is a 'universal' global state, then *all* paths from S must end in an accepting global state. Thus, the definition of AT is similar to that of NT except that an AT has two types of state called existential and universal.

We shall limit our attention to acceptor alternating Turing machines. The definition of the acceptance of a word x by AT is more involved since it depends on the existence in the computation tree of finite subtrees, called alternating trees, with specific properties.

Let $AT(x)$ denote a (possibly infinite) computation tree of AT on input x. An *alternating tree* A included in $AT(x)$ is a finite subtree defined as follows:[2]

1. A consists of a finite subset of nodes of $AT(x)$.
2. The root of A coincides with the root of $AT(x)$.
3. If A includes an existential node S, then it must include exactly one child of S.
4. If A includes a universal node S, then it must include all children of S.
5. The leaf nodes of A must be final nodes.

---

[2]For simplicity, we say that a node of the tree is existential (respectively, universal or final) if the state corresponding to that node is an existential (respectively, universal or final) one.

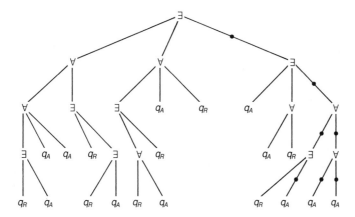

Figure 2.4 An example of an alternating tree

The (Boolean) *value* of an alternating tree A is **true** if and only if all the leaves of A are accepting final nodes.

An alternating machine AT *accepts* x if the corresponding computation tree includes at least one alternating tree whose value is **true**.

Figure 2.4 shows a simple example of a computation tree for an alternating machine. The marked edges form an alternating tree whose value is **true**.

Let us restrict our attention to machines AT which only induce finite computation trees. It is then possible to give the following definitions.[3]

A path from the root to a leaf of an alternating tree A includes k alternations if the number of alternations between existential and universal nodes (or vice versa) along that path is exactly k.

An alternating tree includes k alternations if the largest number of alternations among all paths from the root to a leaf is exactly k.

The number of alternations of a computation $AT(x)$ is defined as the largest number of alternations among all possible alternating trees included in $AT(x)$. If we refer to the example shown in Figure 2.4, it is easy to verify that the marked alternating tree includes two alternations while the computation tree includes three.

Finally, a machine AT is said to be k-*alternating* if, for all x, the number of alternations of $AT(x)$ is, at most, k .

---

[3]The same definition has been extended to infinite computation trees (see Notes).

2.1.5   Random access machines

Let us now turn to another unrestricted model of computation called a *random access machine* (RAM) which will be the basis for a parallel model of computation to be presented in the last part of this book. As the name suggests, RAMs make use of a random access memory, thus overcoming the limitation of Turing machines which use a sequential access tape as a memory component.

A RAM consists of a *processor* and of a *memory* composed of a potentially unlimited number of *cells* denoted as M_i ($i = 0, 1, \ldots$). Each cell M_i is identified by an *index i*.

The processor can execute a limited set of distinct instructions which cause, in general, random accesses to memory cells. Each cell can contain any finite number (even a very large one!) expressed in binary and the time spent reading (respectively, writing) a number from (respectively, in) cell M_i is assumed to be constant.[4] A RAM is controlled by a *program* consisting of a sequence of instructions; each instruction has a unique *sequencing number*. The *state* of a RAM is defined as the sequencing number of the instruction which is being executed; the *initial state* is 1 (program execution starts with the first instruction). As in the case of Turing machines, the RAM program is not stored in memory but is encoded in the machine's control. RAM *instructions* are quite simple and are similar to those of existing computers:

1. $M_i \leftarrow 1$ (write constant 1 in memory cell M_i).
2. $M_i \leftarrow M_j + M_k$ (write in M_i the sum of the numbers contained in M_j and in M_k).
3. $M_i \leftarrow M_j - M_k$ (write in M_i the difference of the numbers contained in M_j and in M_k).
4. $M_i \leftarrow \lfloor M_i/2 \rfloor$ (divide by 2 the number contained in M_i and leave the result in M_i).
5. $M_i \leftarrow M_{M_j}$ (indirect addressing: write in M_i the number contained in the cell whose index is contained in M_j).
6. $M_{M_i} \leftarrow M_j$ (indirect addressing: write the number contained in M_j in the cell whose index is contained in M_i).
7. **go to** m **if** $M_i > 0$ (conditional branching: if the number contained in M_i is greater than 0, then set the RAM state to m; otherwise add one to the current RAM state).
8. **halt** (end the computation of the RAM).

The first six instructions modify the state of the RAM in the same way. After the instruction has been executed, the current state of the RAM is increased by one.

----

[4]A variation of the model in which the access time depends on the value of the number x to be transferred has also been considered (see Notes).

For simplicity, it is assumed that each instruction requires the same constant time in order to be executed. It is also assumed that input x consists of m integers $x_1, x_2, \ldots, x_m$ which are contained, respectively, in memory cells $M_1, \ldots, M_m$. The length n of input x is defined as the sum of the lengths of all numbers x_i ($1 \le i \le m$).

Both acceptor and transducer RAM models will be considere here. In the first case, the RAM writes 1 or 0 in cell M_0, depending on whether it accepts or rejects input x. In the second case, the RAM writes the value $f(x)$ of the computed function in cell M_0.

Is it possible to transform a Turing machine T into an equivalent RAM? To do this, we simply map the ith tape cell ($i = 0, 1, 2, \ldots$) of T into memory cell M_{i+c} of the corresponding RAM (the first c cells are reserved for RAM internal use). Then all we have to do is to write a RAM program which simulates the set of quintuples of T and this turns out to be quite easy (see Problem 2.13).

How can a RAM be transformed into an equivalent Turing machine T? This task, which will provide further evidence for Church's thesis, is more difficult since the memory cells of a RAM are much more flexible than the tape cells of T. The following theorem shows how to transform a RAM into a deterministic Turing machine.

Theorem 2.2 Given a RAM, it is always possible to derive a corresponding three-tape deterministic Turing machine T equivalent to the RAM. Furthermore, the number of steps executed by T to simulate the execution of the first t instructions ($t > n$) of the RAM on input x of length n is, at most, $ct^2(t + n)$ where c denotes a constant.

Proof. Machine T uses the first tape to describe the contents of the RAM memory and the remaining two as working tapes. The RAM program is encoded into the quintuples.

We can observe that the RAM can modify the contents of, at most, t distinct cells while executing t instructions. Each of these cells is represented on the tape as a pair $\langle i, m_i \rangle$ where i denotes the index and m_i the contents of the cell.

How many cells of tape 1 do we have to set aside for storing a value m_i? Note that, in general, of the eight types of instructions available, only addition may increase the value of an operand. In particular, an addition instruction with the form $M_i \leftarrow M_i + M_i$ succeeds in doubling the value m_i initially contained in M_i. Since the numbers are expressed in binary, the length in bits of the new value $2m_i$ is equal to the length of m_i plus one. In other words, each instruction execution may, at most, increase the length of an operand by one bit.

Initially, all memory cells are empty, except the cells used to store the input x. Denote by n the total length of the input. Clearly, n tape cells are sufficient to store any of the values x_i of the input x. To be certain, we agree to set aside $c_1(t + n)$ consecutive tape cells for each of the t RAM cells with $c_1 > 1$ constant; hence, the portion of tape 1 used by T has length $c_1 t(t + n)$.

The cost of simulating a RAM instruction depends on the type of instruction. Let us consider the case of addition which may involve three distinct operands. To save time, we use tapes 2 and 3 as working tapes. We scan tape 1 looking for the cells corresponding to M_j and M_k, copy their contents, respectively, into tape 2 and tape 3, and add them into tape 2 (this can be done in linear time when the operands are on distinct tapes). Next we scan tape 1 looking for M_i and we write into that cell the result contained in tape 2. It should be clear that the number of steps required by T to perform such a simulation is, at most, $ct(t + n)$. Thus, the time required to simulate t RAM instructions is, at most, $ct^2(t + n)$ with c constant.   □

2.2   Machines and languages

Now let us study how well Turing machines succeed in discriminating whether a word belongs to a given language. As we shall see in Section 3.3, we may restrict our attention, without loss of generality, to languages L based on a common alphabet Σ ($L \subseteq \Sigma^*$).

2.2.1   Acceptability and decidability

A language L_1 is *acceptable* if a Turing machine T exists which accepts L_1, that is, a machine T such that $L(T) = L_1$. In Example 2.1 we have already seen a first acceptable language. [Are all languages acceptable or do *non-acceptable* languages exist,] i.e. languages L such that, for all T, $L(T) \neq L$? Since the class of all languages over Σ, that is, 2^{Σ^*}, is not countable while the set of Turing machines is countable (remember how we can encode a Turing machine as a word in a given alphabet), the answer is that non-acceptable languages must exist. Indeed, the diagonalization technique allows us to define one of them. [For any i, let T_i be the ith Turing machine and x_i be the ith word over Σ. The diagonal language thus contains all words x_i such that $x_i \notin L(T_i)$ and it is obviously not acceptable.]

Notice how the behavior of a machine which accepts a given language is left partly unspecified for words not included in that language. For such words, the computation can either halt in the rejecting state or continue for ever. The next definition constricts the machine to a somewhat greater extent.

A language L is *decidable* if an acceptor Turing machine T exists such that, for all $x \in \Sigma^*$, $T(x)$ halts and it accepts x if and only if $x \in L$ (that is, if $x \notin L$ then $T(x)$ halts in the rejecting state). We shall also state that such a T *decides L*.

The next lemmas and theorems illustrate the relation between acceptability and decidability.

Lemma 2.1 If a language is decidable then it is acceptable.

Proof. It follows from the definition.   □

Lemma 2.2 If a language L is decidable then L^c is also decidable.

Proof. Let T be the machine which decides L. Derive T' from T by inverting the accepting state q_A with the rejecting state q_R and vice versa for all quintuples of T. It can immediately be verified that such T' decides L^c.   □

Theorem 2.3 Languages exist which are acceptable but not decidable.

Proof. Consider the language

$$L_{\text{halt}} = \{\langle T, x\rangle : T(x) \text{ terminates}\}$$

(Observe that we use the symbol T to denote both the machine T and its description. However, the correct interpretation should always be clear from the context.)

1. L_{halt} is acceptable: we make use of a universal Turing machine U (see Section 2.1) which receives the pair $\langle T, x\rangle$ as input and simulates the computation $T(x)$. We slightly modify U so that it accepts all pairs $\langle T, x\rangle$ such that $T(x)$ halts either in state q_A or in state q_R (in the original definition, U accepts $\langle T, x\rangle$ only if T accepts x).

2. L_{halt} is not decidable: in the opposite case, a Turing machine T_{halt} exists which decides L_{halt}. Let us define the following Turing machine T based on T_{halt}. For input x, T simulates $T_{\text{halt}}(x, x)$; if T_{halt} accepts $\langle x, x\rangle$, then $T(x)$ does not halt, otherwise it accepts x. What is the computation $T(T)$ supposed to do? Assume it halts. This implies that T_{halt} does not accept $\langle T, T\rangle$, that is, that $T(T)$ does not halt. Now assume that $T(T)$ does not halt. This implies that T_{halt} accepts $\langle T, T\rangle$, that is, that $T(T)$ does halt. In both cases, we encounter a contradiction and we conclude that T_{halt} cannot exist.

We have thus shown that L_{halt} is acceptable but not decidable.   □

Theorem 2.4 A language L is decidable if and only if both L and L^c are acceptable.

Proof. If L is decidable, then L^c is also decidable (see Lemma 2.2) and both L and L^c are acceptable. Conversely, if L and L^c are acceptable, then two machines T and T^c exist which accept such languages. We can then combine T and T^c into a single machine T' which alternatively executes quintuples of T and of T^c using the breadth-first technique. T' terminates for all possible inputs x and decides L.   □

2.3   Reducibility between languages

Reducibility is a powerful tool whose first two main applications in the field of computability theory were to classify acceptable languages according to their degree of unsolvability and to prove that some important languages are not decidable. In this section we shall concentrate on the second application, namely how to prove, via a suitable reduction, that a given language is not decidable. First, however, we must clarify the terms 'reducibility' and 'reduction'.

2.3.1   m-reducibility

Informally, a language A is reducible to a second language B if the existence of an algorithm to decide whether a word belongs to B induces the existence of another algorithm to decide whether a word belongs to A. Even though several definitions of reducibility have been proposed (see Notes), it will be sufficient for our purpose to consider only one.

A language A is *many-one reducible* or *m-reducible* to a second language B, in symbols $A \leq_m B$, if a total and computable function f exists such that, for all $x \in \Sigma^*$,

$$x \in A \leftrightarrow f(x) \in B.$$

The function f is called an *m-reduction* between A and B.

Many proofs of non-decidability can easily be obtained by making use of suitable m-reductions. Suppose we want to prove that a given language, say L_2, is not decidable. The following lemma shows us how to proceed.

Lemma 2.3 If $L_1 \leq_m L_2$ and L_1 is not decidable, then L_2 is not decidable either.

Proof. Assume a Turing machine T_2 exists which decides L_2 and denote by f the reduction from L_1 to L_2. Whether $x \in L_1$ or not could then be decided by first computing $f(x)$ and then by using T_2 to check whether $f(x) \in L_2$. Thus T_2 cannot exist and L_2 is not decidable.   □

A simple example will show how to apply the previous lemma.

Example 2.3 We want to prove that the language $L_{\text{halt}-e} = \{T : T(e) \text{ halts}\}$, that is, the language corresponding to the halting computations of Turing machines applied to the empty word e, is not decidable. This can be done by showing that the language L_{halt}, which is known to be not decidable (see Theorem 2.3), is m-reducible to the language $L_{\text{halt}-e}$.

In order to do this, we notice that, given any machine T and any input x, it is always possible to derive a machine T' which acts on an empty word and such that $T'(e)$ terminates if and only if $T(x)$ terminates. This can be done as follows. T', which has the value x stored in its internal states (since x is finite, this is always possible), first writes x on the tape and then proceeds to simulate T. Clearly, such a transformation from $\langle T, x \rangle$ to T' is an m-reduction.

2.3.2 Properties of m-reducibility

It can immediately be verified that $\leq_m$ is both reflexive and transitive, that is, for all languages $A, B, C \subseteq \Sigma^*$,

$$A \leq_m A \quad \text{and} \quad A \leq_m B \wedge B \leq_m C \rightarrow A \leq_m C.$$

A second property of $\leq_m$ is that, for all pairs of languages $A, B \subseteq \Sigma^*$,

$$A \leq_m B \quad \rightarrow \quad A^c \leq_m B^c.$$

A third property of $\leq_m$, expressed in the following lemma, shows that such a reducibility is of limited interest when dealing with decidable languages.

Lemma 2.4 Let B be any language such that $B \neq \emptyset$ and $B \neq \Sigma^*$. Then, for any decidable language A, $A \leq_m B$.

Proof. Denote a word of B with y and a word of B^c with z (according to the definition of B, y and z must exist). Define the function f as

$$f(x) = \begin{cases} y & \text{if } x \in A, \\ z & \text{otherwise.} \end{cases}$$

The function f is total and computable since A is decidable. Furthermore, $x \in A \leftrightarrow f(x) \in B$, thus f is an m-reduction between A and B. $\qquad\square$

Since complexity theory deals mostly with decidable languages, in the following chapters we shall consider reducibilities enhanced with quantitative refinements for which the previous lemma does not hold true.

Problems

2.1. How is it possible to detect whether the tape head of a given tape is currently positioned on cell 0?

2.2. Define a one-tape acceptor deterministic Turing machine T with tape alphabet $\Sigma = \{0, 1, \square\}$ which accepts all words including an even number of 1s and rejects all remaining words.

2.3. Define a two-tape acceptor deterministic Turing machine T with tape alphabet $\Sigma = \{0, 1, \square\}$ which decides whether a given word of the form $1^m 0 1^n$ is such that m is a multiple of n.

2.4. Define a two-tape transducer deterministic Turing machine T with tape alphabet $\Sigma = \{0, 1, \#, \square\}$ which computes the number of 1s included in input x. The value computed by $T(x)$ must be written on the tape as a binary number. How many additional tapes are needed to compute the same function if the marker symbol '$\#$' is no longer available?

2.5. Supply an alternative definition of acceptor Turing machines satisfying the following two properties:

1. After a finite number of steps, only the contents of the cells containing a non-blank symbol have to be specified in a global state.

2. Only two final global states, the accepting and the rejecting ones, exist.

2.6. Define one-tape Turing machines by means of triples $(q_i, \sigma, ?)$ where $?$ denotes either a symbol to be rewritten in the cell, a read/write head move to be performed, or a new state. Show how to transform a standard one-tape Turing machine into an equivalent machine which uses triples. [Hint: mark the symbols scanned by the former machine by making use of additional symbols.]

2.7. Show that, for any t greater than the input length, the global state of a k-tape Turing machine after executing t steps can be encoded by a word of length kt. [Hint: make use of a suitable alphabet which enables scanned and unscanned symbols to be distinguished and the internal state of the machine to be encoded.]

2.8. Given a nondeterministic machine, derive an equivalent nondeterministic machine whose computation trees are binary trees.

2.9. Illustrate a RAM program which on input x and i computes the ith bit of the binary representation of x.

2.10. Define a RAM program which on input x and y computes the product xy by executing a total number of instructions proportional to the length of the input.

2.11. Define a RAM program which on input x and y computes the integer division $x \div y$ by executing a total number of instructions proportional to the length of the input.

2.12. Consider a *Random Access Stored Program* machine (RASP) which is similar to RAM except that the program is stored in memory and can thus modify itself, and that indirect addressing is not allowed. Show that a RAM can be simulated by a RASP with a constant overhead and vice versa. [Aho, Hopcroft, and Ullman (1974)]

2.13. Describe a RAM program which simulates t steps of a one-tape deterministic Turing machine T in $c_1 t + c_2$ steps with c_1, c_2 constant. [Hint: for each state q of T, define a block of $|\Sigma|$ groups of instructions, each group simulating the quintuple having $\langle q, \sigma \rangle$ as prefix.]

2.14. Show that any language accepted by a RAM can be accepted by a RAM without indirect addressing. [Hint: make use of Theorem 2.2 and of the solution of the previous problem.]

2.15. Show that the set of acceptable languages is closed under union and intersection.

2.16. A non-empty language L is *recursively enumerable*, in short r.e., if a transducer deterministic Turing machine T exists such that

$$L = \{y : \exists x[T(x) \text{ outputs } y]\},$$

that is, L is the codomain of the function computed by T.

Show that L is r.e. if and only if L is acceptable. [Hint: make use of the breadth-first technique in order to prove the necessity.]

2.17. An infinite language L is r.e. *without repetitions* if L is the codomain of an injective computable function. Prove that L is r.e. without repetitions if and only if L is infinite and r.e. [Hint: derive a transducer deterministic machine which reads x and outputs x if and only if $x \in L$.]

2.18. Prove that a language L is r.e. if and only if L is the domain of a partial computable function. [Rogers (1967)]

2.19. Consider the language

$$L = \{x : \text{ the decimal expression of } \pi \text{ includes at least } |x| \text{ consecutive 5s}\}.$$

Prove that L is decidable even if the decimal expression of π is found to be not computable. [Hint: the definition of decidability is inherently non-constructive.]

2.20. Show that the class of decidable languages is closed under union, complementation, intersection, and concatenation.

2.21. A language L is r.e. in *increasing order* if L is the codomain of an increasing total computable function (a function f is increasing if, for any x and y, $x < y$ implies $f(x) < f(y)$). Prove that L is r.e. in increasing order if and only if L is infinite and decidable. [Rogers (1967)]

2.22. Show that any acceptable language admits a decidable infinite subset. [Rogers (1967)]

2.23. Consider the language $L_{\exists-\text{halt}} = \{T : \exists x[T(x) \text{ halts}]\}$. Prove that this language is not decidable. [Hint: supply an m-reduction from $L_{\text{halt}-e}$ to $L_{\exists-\text{halt}}$.]

Notes

Turing machines were introduced in Turing (1936) in order to formally define the concept of computable numbers (equivalently, that of computable functions or predicates): a number is computable if its digits can be written down by such a machine. In particular, it is shown that certain large classes of numbers are computable although definable numbers exist which are not computable. Furthermore, it is shown that there is no general method for ascertaining whether a given formula is provable in Hilbert's functional calculus.

An interesting introduction to Turing machines can be found in Minsky (1967). More advanced treatments of such machines and of computability theory in general are included in Kleene (1962), Davis (1958), Rogers (1967), and Hermes (1969). We also recommend the book edited by Davis (1965) which is an anthology of fundamental papers dealing with undecidability and unsolvability.

As pointed out in Spaan, Torenvliet, and van Emde Boas (1989), the concept of nondeterministic machines was inspired by automata theory and computational complexity theory rather than by computability theory and it was not introduced before the end of the 1950s. In the original Turing paper, nondeterministic quintuples are viewed in some respects as an abberation of the concept of computability.

A first reference to oracle Turing machines appeared in Turing (1939) in studying systems of logic based on ordinals. Such machines played an important part both in computability theory and, as we shall see in the following chapters, in the theory of computational complexity.

Alternating Turing machines were introduced in Chandra, Kozen, and Stockmeyer (1981). Although few results based on such machines will be explicitly described in the text, the concept of alternation impacts on several topics in computer science, including time and space complexity, logic, games, and parallelism.

The RAM model was considered in Shepherdson and Sturgis (1963) and in Elgot and Robinson (1964). Two cost criteria for RAM programs have been proposed in those papers: the *uniform* cost criterion, according to which each RAM instruction requires one unit of time, and the *logarithmic* cost criterion where the time varies roughly as $\lfloor \log(|x|) \rfloor$ where x denotes the value of an operand. Notice also that the basic set of instructions may be defined in several ways. If additional instructions, such as multiplication, are introduced, the second part of Lemma 2.2 must be modified (see Section 4.2). A good introduction to RAMs is provided in Aho, Hopcroft, and Ullman (1974).

The following references deal with the equivalence between Turing machines and other unrestricted models of computation:

- General recursive functions: Kleene (1936).
- Unrestricted rewriting systems: Chomsky (1959).
- Post systems: Post (1943).
- Markov systems: Markov (1954).
- RAM: Shepherdson and Sturgis (1963).

The last two sections of this chapter are a summary of results obtained in the field of computability theory. For further results and additional kinds of reducibilities, the interested reader is referred to many excellent textbooks such as Davis (1965), Rogers (1967), and Lewis and Papadimitriou (1981).

Chapter 3

Complexity classes

Now that we know what a model of computation and a computable function are, the next step is to provide the tools which will allow us to 'measure' the complexity of a problem and to group together problems with a similar complexity.

Discussion of the complexity of a problem implicitly refers to the complexity of an algorithm for solving that problem and to the measure of complexity that allows us to assess the algorithm's performance. Although an infinite number of algorithms exist which solve the same problem, we can clearly identify the complexity of the problem with that of the most efficient with respect to a given measure of complexity.

Observe, however, that the structure of algorithms is so rich and the models of computation so widely different that several definitions of complexity measurement can be given, each taking into account specific aspects of the algorithms and/or of the models of computation.

Two different kinds of complexity measures can be roughly identified: *static* measures that are based only on the structure of the algorithms and *dynamic* measures that take into account both the algorithms and the inputs and are thus based on the behavior of a computation.

A typical example of static measure of complexity is *program size*. Any algorithm can be viewed as a word over a finite alphabet (of course, an algorithm is much more than a word: it has a semantic) and a natural question is: how long is such a word? In this way, a problem has a well-defined minimum complexity, namely, the shortest program that solves it (at least, for a given model of computation).

Although other different static measures of complexity have been defined and interesting results obtained (see Notes), we shall focus our attention on the more familiar dynamic measures. A natural example of such measures is *time*; generally, time is the number of 'elementary steps' of a computation, if such a computation halts, otherwise it is considered to be undefined (observe that a precise definition of an elementary step depends on the characteristics of the model of computation).

In Section 3.1 we present the complexity measures which we are going to use. We

33

then define in Section 3.2 classes of languages and present some general techniques to prove inclusion relations between such classes. In Section 3.3 we show the close connection between combinatorial problems and languages and we investigate how changes in problem encodings and alphabets affect the complexity of a problem. Finally in Section 3.4 we restrict our attention to time-complexity classes, that is, classes defined by means of the time-complexity measure, and present some general properties of such classes.

3.1   Dynamic complexity measures

Before giving specific examples of dynamic measures of complexity, let us provide a general definition applicable to all models of computation.

3.1.1   Model-independent dynamic measures

To define a complexity measure on an arbitrary set $\{P_i\}$ of algorithms, we should be able to assign to each algorithm P_i a 'suitable' resource bound Φ_i. Since neither the model of computation nor the resource are known, we can only put abstract constraints on the Φ_is.

A *dynamic measure of complexity* Φ with respect to the set of algorithms $\{P_i\}$ is a set of computable functions Φ_i such that

1. For each i, the domain of Φ_i coincides with that of P_i and its codomain is a subset of N.
2. A total computable predicate M exists such that, for all i, x and m,

$$M(i, x, m) = \textbf{true} \leftrightarrow \Phi_i(x) = m.$$

Example 3.1 Let us take the Turing machine as a model of computation and let $TIME = \{TIME_i\}$, where $TIME_i(x)$ denotes the number of steps executed by computation $T_i(x)$; if $T_i(x)$ does not halt, then $TIME_i(x)$ has to be considered undefined. Clearly, $TIME$ satisfies the above constraints.

The next two examples show that the two previous constraints are independent, that is, neither of them implies the other.

Example 3.2 Again let us take the Turing machine as a model of computation and let $\Phi_i = T_i$, for each i. In this case, the first constraint is obviously satisfied. If the second is also satisfied, then, for all i, x and m, it can be decided whether $T_i(x) = m$. For any i, let $T_{f(i)}$ be a Turing machine such that $T_{f(i)}(x) = 0$ if and only if $T_i(x)$ halts ($T_{f(i)}$ can be obtained by slightly modifying the program of T_i). Thus asking whether $T_i(x)$ halts is equivalent to asking whether $M(f(i), x, 0) = \textbf{true}$. Since M is computable, it follows that the halting problem is decidable. Thus, constraint 2 cannot be satisfied and the first constraint does not imply the second.

Example 3.3 Let $\Phi_i(x) = k$, for any i and x, with k constant. In this case, it can immediately be verified that the first constraint is not satisfied, while the second is satisfied. Hence constraint 2 does not imply constraint 1.

Although the model-independent approach has yielded some very interesting results (see Notes), we shall proceed within a more specific and practical setting.

3.1.2 Deterministic TIME and SPACE

Complexity theory has developed mainly on the basis of two measures of complexity, namely time and space. In this section we define such measures with respect to deterministic Turing machines.

The measure $TIME$ has been already defined in Example 3.1 and basically consists of counting the number of steps executed by a computation.

The measure $SPACE$ could be defined in a similar way, but it should not be! In fact, if $SPACE_i(x)$ denotes the number of tape cells used by the computation $T_i(x)$, then $SPACE$ does not satisfy the first of the constraints defined in the previous section (think of a machine cycling on the same cell). On the other hand, those constraints are so natural and basic to any concept of complexity measure that they should hold for any such measure.

To overcome this problem we consider $SPACE_i(x)$ as undefined whenever $T_i(x)$ does not halt. We are now faced with a new problem: how can we decide whether $T_i(x)$ halts? We already know that this problem is not decidable in the general case. The following lemma, however, states that the same problem becomes decidable whenever a bound can be put on the number of tape cells used.

Lemma 3.1 Let T be a k-tape Turing machine and let x be an input such that $T(x)$ uses, at most, $h(x)$ cells on any of the k tapes. Then either $T(x)$ halts after $N = |\Sigma|^{h(x)k} h(x)^k |Q|$ steps, where Q and Σ denote the set of the states and the alphabet of T, respectively, or it does not halt at all.

Proof. It suffices to observe that the value N is an upper bound on the number of distinct global states of $T(x)$. In fact, for any of the $|\Sigma|^{h(x)k}$ k-tuples of words of $h(x)$ symbols on alphabet Σ, each of the k heads can be positioned on any of the $h(x)$ symbols and the state can be any of the $|Q|$ states of T. $\qquad\square$

We conclude that the modified definition of $SPACE$ satisfies both the constraints of a dynamic measure of complexity.

To some extent, the previous lemma also states that an upper bound on space implies an upper bound on time. Conversely, it is clear that a bound on time implies a bound on space: in t steps, at most, t tape cells can be scanned! Additional relationships between time and space will be considered in Chapter 8.

3.1.3 Nondeterministic TIME and SPACE

The measure $NTIME$ for nondeterministic Turing machines is the set of functions $NTIME_i$ where, for any x, $NTIME_i(x)$ denotes

1. The number of steps in the shortest accepting computation path of $NT_i(x)$, if such a path exists, and all computation paths of $NT_i(x)$ halt.
2. The number of steps in the shortest computation path of $NT_i(x)$, if all computation paths of $NT_i(x)$ halt and reject.
3. Undefined, otherwise (that is, a non-halting computation path of $NT_i(x)$ exists).

The measure $NSPACE$ is defined similarly.

3.2 Classes of languages

According to the general definition of an infinite set (see Section 1.1), a class of languages $\mathcal{C}$ will be defined referring to the class of all languages over an alphabet Σ and to a predicate π that the members of $\mathcal{C}$ must satisfy. In general, a class $\mathcal{C}$ is defined as $\mathcal{C} = \{L : L \subseteq \Sigma^* \wedge \pi(L)\}$ or, equivalently, as $\mathcal{C} = \{L : \pi(L)\}$ when this does not give rise to confusion.

[handwritten margin note: π is the turing machine that accepts words of the language.]

Example 3.4 The class $\mathcal{T}$ of tally languages (see §1.5) can be defined as $\mathcal{T} = \{L : L \subseteq \Sigma^* \wedge \pi(L)\}$ where $\Sigma = \{0,1\}$ and $\pi(L) = \textbf{true} \leftrightarrow L \subseteq 0^*$.

Example 3.5 The class $\mathcal{S}$ of sparse languages (see Section 1.5) can be defined as $\mathcal{S} = \{L : L \subseteq \Sigma^* \wedge \pi(L)\}$ where $\Sigma = \{0,1\}$ and $\pi(L) = \textbf{true} \leftrightarrow \exists p \forall n [|L_n| \leq p(n)]$ where p is a polynomial.

The *complement* of a class $\mathcal{C} = \{L : \pi(L)\}$ is defined as $co\mathcal{C} = \{L : L^c \in \mathcal{C}\}$ or, equivalently, as $co\mathcal{C} = \{L : \pi(L^c)\}$.

Example 3.6 The complement of the class $\mathcal{T}$ contains all languages L such that L^c is tally. Hence, if $L \in co\mathcal{T}$, then L contains both all words 0^m that do not belong to L and all words in Σ^* which include at least a 1.

3.2.1 Comparing classes of languages

Most of this book is devoted to classifying problems in complexity classes, studying the 'structure' of those classes and proving (or conjecturing) relations between them. In this section we present some general techniques that will be widely used to prove or disprove inclusion results.

In the following we denote by C_i a generic class of languages defined by means of the predicate π_i. Hence, given two classes C_1 and C_2, proving that $C_1 \subseteq C_2$ is equivalent to proving that, for any language L, $\pi_1(L) = \textbf{true}$ implies $\pi_2(L) = \textbf{true}$. Sometimes this implication is quite straightforward (but, unfortunately, life is not always so easy).

Example 3.7 We have already observed that the class T is contained in the class S since if L is a tally language, then, for any n, $|L_n| \leq 1$.

Example 3.8 Let C_1 be the class of languages decidable by deterministic Turing machines and let C_2 be the class of languages decidable by nondeterministic Turing machines. Since the latter machines are an extension of the former, it follows that $C_1 \subseteq C_2$.

In Example 3.8, the predicates π_i specify a property of the Turing machines that decide the members of the class: in the case of C_1 the Turing machines have to be deterministic, while in the case of C_2 they have to be nondeterministic. Most of the complexity classes we will study have similar predicates. In such cases, the inclusion relation between classes can be proved by using a *simulation* technique: given two classes C_1 and C_2, $C_1 \subseteq C_2$ if any machine satisfying predicate π_1 can be simulated by another machine satisfying predicate π_2.

Example 3.9 Theorem 2.1 is an example of simulation: it states that any nondeterministic Turing machine can be simulated by a deterministic one. Hence classes C_1 and C_2 of Example 3.8 coincide.

Once we have proved that a class C_1 is contained in a class C_2, a natural question arises: is this inclusion strict? Intuitively, proving that C_2 is not contained in C_1 consists of finding a *separator* language, that is, a language L such that $L \in C_2$ but $L \notin C_1$. Once again, such a language is sometimes easy to derive.

Example 3.10 We have seen that $T \subseteq S$. It is easy to define a separator language: one of the infinitely many such languages is $L = 0^* \cup 1^*$. $\quad \therefore \; S \subsetneq T$

In complexity theory the few known separation results were not obtained in such an easy way but rather by applying the diagonalization technique (see Section 1.3) in order to derive a language outside of C_1. In those cases, it is also necessary to prove that the diagonal language satisfies predicate π_2 (see Notes and Problems).

If we do not succeed in proving that a class C_1 is strictly contained in a class C_2, we can still hope to obtain a somewhat weaker result along the same lines. Indeed, our next step will be looking for languages that are likely candidates for separator languages.

Formally, let C be a class of languages and let $\leq_r$ be a 'resource-bounded' reducibility, that is, a generalization of the m-reducibility where f can be any function computable within some predefined resource bounds. A language L is C-*complete* with respect to $\leq_r$ if $L \in C$ and for any language $L' \in C$, $L' \leq_r L$.

Example 3.11 Let $\mathcal{R}$ be the class of decidable languages over an alphabet Σ. From Lemma 2.4, it follows that any language $B \in \mathcal{R}$ such that $B \neq \emptyset$ and $B \neq \Sigma^*$ is $\mathcal{R}$-complete with respect to m-reducibility.

A class $\mathcal{C}$ is *closed with respect to reducibility* $\leq_r$ if for any pair of languages L_1 and L_2 such that $L_1 \leq_r L_2$, $L_2 \in \mathcal{C}$ implies $L_1 \in \mathcal{C}$.

Lemma 3.2 Let $\mathcal{C}_1$ and $\mathcal{C}_2$ be two classes of languages such that $\mathcal{C}_1 \subset \mathcal{C}_2$ and $\mathcal{C}_1$ is closed with respect to a reducibility $\leq_r$. Then, any language L that is $\mathcal{C}_2$-complete with respect to $\leq_r$ does not belong to $\mathcal{C}_1$.

Proof. Since $\mathcal{C}_1 \subset \mathcal{C}_2$, then a language $L_1 \in \mathcal{C}_2 - \mathcal{C}_1$ exists. Let L be a $\mathcal{C}_2$-complete language with respect to $\leq_r$; it follows that $L_1 \leq_r L$. If $L \in \mathcal{C}_1$, then $L_1 \in \mathcal{C}_1$ (recall that $\mathcal{C}_1$ is closed with respect to $\leq_r$). This contradicts the hypothesis that $L_1 \in \mathcal{C}_2 - \mathcal{C}_1$. $\square$

The previous lemma has two possible applications: 'as-it-is' and 'as-it-should-be'. In the first case, if we know that $\mathcal{C}_1 \subset \mathcal{C}_2$, the lemma supplies another way, apart from diagonalization, of obtaining separator languages. In the second case, if we are only able to conjecture that $\mathcal{C}_1 \subset \mathcal{C}_2$ (this will happen quite often!), then the lemma states that any $\mathcal{C}_2$-complete language is likely to be in $\mathcal{C}_2 - \mathcal{C}_1$.

Classes which admit complete languages with respect to specific reducibilities are of special interest. On the one hand, it is possible to isolate problems for those classes which capture their computational complexity; on the other, such classes seem to be more useful since they allow us to characterize the complexity of solving specific problems. However, complexity classes which do not have such properties (or at least it is conjectured that they do not) will also be considered, although the lack of complete languages makes a class less useful from a practical point of view, and, in a certain sense, more artificial.

3.3 Decision problems and languages

So far we have defined classes of languages. What of our original goal, that is, to classify the complexity of problems? In this section we can see how the study of a broad class of problems arising in different areas can be led back to the study of languages. To this end we define the class of decision problems and show how an appropriate language can be associated with a specific problem.

Intuitively, a decision problem is one whose instances admit either a 'yes' or a 'no' answer. The basic ingredients of a decision problem are: the set of instances or input objects, the set of possible solutions or output objects and the predicate that decides whether a possible solution is a feasible one. The problem consists of deciding whether, given an instance, a feasible solution exists.

Thus, a *decision problem* Π is a triple $\langle I, S, \pi \rangle$ such that

1. I is a set of words that encode instances of the problem.
2. S is a function that maps an instance $x \in I$ into a finite set $S(x)$ of words that encode possible solutions of x.
3. π is a predicate such that, for any instance x and for any possible solution $y \in S(x)$, $\pi(x, y) =$ **true** if and only if y is a feasible solution.

Solving a decision problem $\langle I, S, \pi \rangle$ consists of deciding, for a given instance $x \in I$, whether the set $\{y : y \in S(x) \wedge \pi(x, y)\}$ is not empty.

Example 3.12 SHORTEST PATH: given a graph $G = (N, E)$, two nodes $n_1, n_2 \in N$ and a natural number k, does a path between n_1 and n_2 exist whose length is, at most, k?

In this case, I is the set of words encoding graphs along with two nodes n_1 and n_2 and a natural number k; given an instance x, $S(x)$ is the set of words encoding subgraphs of G; and, for any instance x and for any possible solution $G' \subseteq G$, $\pi(x, G') =$ **true** if and only if G' is a path between n_1 and n_2 of length, at most, k.

It should be clear that the above definition depends on how a graph is encoded as a sequence of symbols. Even though several different ways to describe a graph are known, they are all interchangeable, namely, given one of them, it is possible to switch quickly to any other. In other words, all those descriptions are 'reasonable' in a sense that we will specify later.

Example 3.13 KNAPSACK: given a finite set U, two functions $c, p : U \to N$ and two natural numbers $k, b \in N$, does a subset $U_1 \subseteq U$ exist such that

$$\sum_{u \in U_1} p(u) \geq k \text{ and } \sum_{u \in U_1} c(u) \leq b?$$

Example 3.14 Game theory has been a rich source of decision problems; the following is a simple example.

CHESS: given an initial configuration on the chessboard and a natural number k, can the white player win in less than k moves independently of the strategy followed by the black player. More precisely, does a white player's first move exist such that, for any black player's move, a white player's second move exists such that, for any black player's move, ..., a white player's hth winning move exists with $h \leq k$?

The above definition of a decision problem did not specify the alphabet over which the words are built. However, since we want to compare problems arising in different areas and using different alphabets, it seems necessary to 'translate' words over an arbitrary alphabet into words over a fixed one. Such a translation has to be 'parsimonious' in the sense that the new word should not be much longer than the original one. For instance, you should avoid translating binary into unary numbers. The unary representation would be exponentially longer than the binary one and the analysis of the algorithms receiving unary numbers as input could result in unrealistically good bounds. Moreover, the translation has to be efficiently computable. We do not want to develop efficient algorithms that solve problems over a fixed alphabet Σ without being sure that representing such problems over Σ is almost without cost.

The next result shows that the unary alphabets, that is, the alphabets consisting of exactly one symbol, are, in practice, the only ones to be discarded.

Lemma 3.3 For any pair of alphabets Σ and Γ such that $|\Gamma| \geq 2$, an injective function $f : \Sigma^* \to \Gamma^*$ exists such that f and f^{-1} are computable in linear time and, for any x, $|f(x)| = \lceil \log_{|\Gamma|} |\Sigma| \rceil |x|$.

Proof. Let k be the smallest natural number such that the number of words on Γ of length k is greater than or equal to $|\Sigma|$. It hence suffices to take $k = \lceil \log_{|\Gamma|} |\Sigma| \rceil$. The function f associates the ith word over Γ of length k to the ith symbol of Σ (in lexicographic order). Finally, for any word $x \in \Sigma^*$, $f(x)$ is the concatenation of the images of the symbols of x. It is clear that, for any x, $|f(x)| = \lceil \log_{|\Gamma|} |\Sigma| \rceil |x|$, f is injective and both f and f^{-1} are computable in linear time. $\square$

Example 3.15 Let $\Sigma = \{0, 1, \ldots, 9\}$ and $\Gamma = \{0, 1\}$. In this case, $k = 4$ and, for any $d \in \Sigma$, $f(d)$ is the binary representation of d itself (eventually filled with some leading 0s). For instance, $f(2) = 0010$, $f(3) = 0011$ and $f(32) = 00110010$.

The previous discussion allows us to fix an alphabet once and for ever. It also enables us to use additional symbols whenever they make the exposition clearer.

Let $\Sigma = \{0, 1\}$ and let Π be a decision problem. Select any *binary encoding of* Π, that is, a function from instances of Π to binary words. With respect to such an encoding, any word $x \in \Sigma^*$ belongs to exactly one of the following three sets:

1. The set R_Π of words that do not encode any instance.
2. The set Y_Π of words that encode yes-instances.
3. The set N_Π of words that encode no-instances.

The *language $L(\Pi)$ associated to* Π is defined as Y_Π. This correspondence will allow us to define complexity classes as classes of languages (instead of problems). Informally, however, we will speak of the complexity of a problem and will say that a problem belongs to a given complexity class. In other words, we will identify the decision problem with its associated language.

Before going further with the definition of time-complexity classes, let us make a final observation on the representation of a decision problem. We have already noticed in Example 3.12 that the instances of a problem can be represented in many different ways. If the fixed representation is 'unreasonable' the complexity of the problem could be hidden in the representation itself. A simple example should clarify this point.

Example 3.16 LONGEST PATH: given a graph $G = (N, E)$, two nodes $n_1, n_2 \in N$ and a natural number k, does a path between n_1 and n_2 exist having a length of at least k?

If an instance of such a problem is represented by listing all the paths in the graph G, then it is easy to derive an efficient algorithm that solves it: we have merely to look for the longest path between n_1 and n_2 and check whether its length is greater than or equal to k.

On the other hand, if the graph G is represented in a more familiar way, for instance, by its adjacency matrix, no subexponential time-complexity algorithm that solves the LONGEST PATH problem is known.

The previous example shows that we have to be careful in selecting the representation of a decision problem. Even though any formal definition of a 'reasonable' representation would be unsatisfiable, some standard rules can be fixed. For instance, we shall make the following assumptions. Numbers are represented in base $k > 1$, sets are represented as sequences of elements delimited by appropriate symbols and, whenever possible, the rules to generate a set will be given instead of the set itself. Using such standard encodings allows us to assume that all reasonable representations of a problem are interchangeable, namely, given one of them, it is possible to quickly switch to any other. In conclusion, we can avoid specifying the representation of a problem, implicitly assuming that it is reasonable.

3.4 Time-complexity classes

We are now ready to define resource-bounded complexity classes. Intuitively, such classes are sets of languages that can be decided within a specific time (or space) bound. In this section, we will focus on time-complexity classes, postponing the study of the space-complexity ones to a later chapter.

To analyse the complexity of solving a specific problem, we must determine the amount of resource that an algorithm requires to solve instances of the problem. It is natural to think that the 'larger' the instances, the more resource units the algorithm requires, that is, the bound on the resource should be an increasing function of the 'size' of the instance. In imposing such bounds, we will not consider additive and multiplicative constants because they depend mostly on the characteristics of the computation model (alphabet size, number of states, number of tapes, and so on), while our goal is to develop a theory as general as possible and capable of capturing the inherent complexity of a problem. For this reason, we shall focus our attention on the 'rate of growth' of the resource requirements rather than on their precise evaluation.

First, however, note that an algorithm with a rapid growth rate could be more efficient, for small instances, than another with a smaller growth rate. For instance, an algorithm whose complexity is $1024n$ is less efficient than one whose complexity is 2^n, for any instance of size n less than 14. In practice, whenever we know that the instances to be solved do not exceed a fixed size, an algorithm with a rapid rate of growth could be preferable to another with a smaller rate of growth. However, we are theoreticians (more than algorithm developers) and our main concern is to study how the complexity of problems increases as the instance sizes become larger.

To formalize the previous discussion, we will define the following notation. Let g be a total function from N to N. The *class* $\mathbf{O}[g(n)]$ (pronounced 'big oh') consists of all functions $f : N \rightarrow N$ for which a constant c exists such that, for any n, $f(n) \leq cg(n)$.

Example 3.17 Let $f(n) = a_0 + a_1 n + a_2 n^2 + \ldots + a_6 n^6$ where $a_0 \ldots, a_6$ are constants. It is easy to verify that $f(n) \notin \mathbf{O}[n^5]$, $f(n) \in \mathbf{O}[n^6]$ and $f(n) \in \mathbf{O}[2^n]$.

All upper bounds on the amount of resource units needed to solve a problem will then be conveniently expressed as $\mathbf{O}[g(|x|)]$ where $|x|$ denotes the length of the word encoding an instance of the problem and $g : N \rightarrow N$. Note that since an instance of a problem is a word over a given alphabet, we have chosen the length of such a word as representative of the 'size' of the instance. Can the reader imagine any more natural measure of size?

To justify further our use of the $\mathbf{O}$-notation, we finally present an intriguing result of the theory of computational complexity which states that, with respect to time, any Turing machine can be 'speeded up' by a constant factor. This rather unintuitive result can be better explained by an example.

Example 3.18 A word x is a *palindrome* if $x = \sigma_1 \sigma_2 \ldots \sigma_n \sigma_n \ldots \sigma_2 \sigma_1$ with $\sigma_i \in \Sigma$. Let $L = \{x : x$ is a palindrome$\}$. To decide whether a word x (for instance, $x = 3726886273$) belongs to L we can devise a one-tape Turing machine T that scans the leftmost symbol of x (3) and erases it, moves to the rightmost symbol (3) and checks whether it is equal to the previously read symbol. If this is not the case, then $T(x)$ rejects, otherwise it erases the rightmost symbol, moves to the leftmost one and starts the cycle again. If there are no more symbols, then $T(x)$ accepts.

A more efficient one-tape Turing machine is based on reading pairs of symbols instead of single symbols. The machine scans simultaneously the two leftmost symbols (3 and 7) and erases them, moves to the two rightmost symbols (3 and 7) and checks whether they are equal to the previously read symbols. The time-complexity of the new machine is approximately half that of the original, for almost all inputs.

The basic idea of the previous example is that of memorizing two symbols instead of one. Let us extend it to all possible algorithms, that is, all possible Turing machines. Proving that any arbitrary machine can be 'speeded up' consists of showing that another machine exists which simulates the first and executes half the number of steps. The technique of the previous example is based on the characteristic of the algorithm in hand (for instance, that the algorithm erases a symbol once it has been read). To generalize, we can think of a 'preprocessor' phase that compresses the input by substituting any pair of symbols with a symbol of a richer alphabet. Hence, the faster machine (with a suitable larger set of states) is able to simulate in one step the original machine's two steps. Note that if only one tape is available, then the input compression takes quadratic time, while if at least two tapes are available, then the compression can be realized in linear time. (Can the reader imagine the consequences of this observation?)

The reader should now be in a position to prove the following *speed-up theorem* (see Problem 3.8).

Theorem 3.1 Let L be a language decided by a k-tape Turing machine operating in $TIME(x) \leq t(|x|)$. Then, for any natural m, a $(k+1)$-tape Turing machine exists that decides L in $TIME(x) \leq \lceil \frac{1}{2^m} t(|x|) \rceil + |x|$.

In conclusion, the *asymptotic complexity* seems to be the correct basis on which we can build our theory of complexity.

3.4.1 Time-constructible functions

To prevent the complexity classes behaving unintuitively, we will impose some constraints on the functions that bound the resource units. First, it is reasonable to assume that such functions are at least total and computable. But this is not enough: strange situations can still be found (see Problem 3.12).

Intuitively, the definition of 'step-counting' functions we are going to give is motivated by the following. Whenever we know that a Turing machine *accepts* a language in a given time, it should be desirable to have another machine that simulates the former machine and is able to *decide* the same language. In order to obtain this, we need a 'clock' that informs the latter machine when it has to halt the simulation (otherwise, how could it avoid simulating an infinite computation?). Clearly, the number of steps made for managing the clock should be negligible with respect to the number of simulated steps. This brief discussion leads to the following definition.

A *time-constructible function t* is a function mapping natural numbers onto natural numbers such that a multitape Turing machine exists which, for any input x, halts after exactly $t(|x|)$ steps. It is easy to verify that any time-constructible function is total and computable (see Problem 3.10). Using such functions makes setting a 'timer' on Turing machines very easy and some hierarchical inclusion results have been proved between complexity classes defined by means of time-constructible functions (see Notes and Problems). Even though we do not present such results, we will still make use only of time-constructible functions. In fact, all the complexity classes we shall define use either a polynomial function or an exponential one and, as we shall see in the next example, such functions are time-constructible ones.

Originally, the time-constructible functions were defined in a slightly different way. t is a time-constructible function if a multitape Turing transducer T exists such that, for any natural number n, $T(1^n)$ outputs $1^{t(n)}$ in no more than $ct(n)$ steps, where c is a constant. It can be shown that the two definitions are equivalent for a broad class of functions, namely, for all functions f for which an $\epsilon > 0$ exists such that $f(n) > (1 + \epsilon)n$ almost everywhere. The second definition is found to be an easier tool for proving that a function is a time-constructible one.

Example 3.19 For any constant $k \geq 1$, the following functions are time-constructible:

1. $t(n) = n^k$.

2. $t(n) = 2^{kn}$.

3. $t(n) = 2^{n^k}$.

The proof is based on the above discussion and is left as a problem (see Problem 3.11).

We conclude this section with a lemma showing that time-constructible functions can grow as fast as any other total computable function (this lemma will also be used in a later chapter).

Lemma 3.4 For any total computable function $f : N \to N$, a time-constructible function t exists such that, for any n, $t(n) > f(n)$.

Proof. Let T be a Turing transducer that computes f. Without loss of generality, we assume that T computes f in unary notation, that is, for any n, $T(1^n)$ outputs $1^{f(n)}$. Let T_1 be a Turing transducer that, for any input x, produces the word $y = 1^{|x|}$ and then simulates $T(y)$. Obviously, for any input x of length n, the number of steps executed by the computation $T_1(x)$ is always the same. Furthermore, such a number is greater than $f(n)$ since at least $f(n)$ steps are necessary to output $1^{f(n)}$. Thus the function $t = TIME_1$ is a time-constructible function such that, for any n, $t(n) > f(n)$. □

3.4.2 Deterministic time-complexity classes

Given a time-constructible function t, the *time-complexity class* DTIME$[t(n)]$ is defined as

$$\text{DTIME}[t(n)] = \{L : \exists T_i[L = L(T_i) \land TIME_i(x) \in \mathbf{O}[t(|x|)]]\}$$

(Note that since the number of steps is bounded by a time-constructible function, we can assume that T_i halts for every input.)

The first three lemmas of this section show three properties of deterministic time-complexity classes. The first states that such classes are *closed with respect to the complement operation*.

Lemma 3.5 For any time-constructible function t,

$$\text{DTIME}[t(n)] = co\text{DTIME}[t(n)].$$

Proof. It suffices to observe that, for any deterministic Turing machine which decides a language L within a given time, a deterministic Turing machine deciding L^c within the same time can be obtained by simply reversing the roles of the accepting and rejecting states. □

The next lemma states that deterministic time-complexity classes are *closed under finite variations* and it will be widely used (either explicitly or implicitly) in the rest of the book.

Lemma 3.6 For any time-constructible function t such that $t(n) \geq n$ and for any pair of languages L_1 and L_2 which differ for finitely many words, $L_1 \in \text{DTIME}[t(n)]$ if and only if $L_2 \in \text{DTIME}[t(n)]$.

Proof. Since $L_1 \Delta L_2$ is finite, we can use the hardware of a machine, that is, a finite number of quintuples to decide words in that set. More precisely, given a deterministic Turing machine T_1 which decides L_1, we derive a deterministic Turing machine T_2 which decides L_2 within the same time as the former machine by adding a finite number of states specialized in deciding words in $L_1 \Delta L_2$. Initially, T_2 scans the input x to check whether either $x \in L_1 - L_2$ (and thus rejects x) or $x \in L_2 - L_1$ (and thus accepts x). If this is not the case, then T_2 merely simulates T_1. Since the pre-simulation phase can be executed in linear time and by our assumption on t, it follows that if $L_1 \in \text{DTIME}[t(n)]$, then $L_2 \in \text{DTIME}[t(n)]$.

By a similar argument, we can prove that if $L_2 \in \text{DTIME}[t(n)]$, then $L_1 \in \text{DTIME}[t(n)]$. □

An immediate consequence of the previous lemma is the following corollary.

Corollary 3.1 For any finite language L and for any time-constructible function t such that $t(n) \geq n$, $L \in \text{DTIME}[t(n)]$.

Proof. It is clear that, for any time-constructible function t, the empty set belongs to $\text{DTIME}[t(n)]$. Since, for any finite language L, $L \Delta \emptyset$ is finite, the corollary follows from the previous lemma. □

The third and last lemma shows that deterministic time-complexity classes are *constructively enumerable*.

Lemma 3.7 For any time-constructible function t, an enumerable set $\{T_i : i \geq 1\}$ of deterministic Turing machines exists such that

1. $\text{DTIME}[t(n)] = \{L : \exists i[L = L(T_i)]\}$.
2. A Turing machine T exists such that, for any i and x, $T(i, x) = T_i(x)$, that is, the enumeration is effective.

Proof. Let $T_1', T_2', \ldots$ be any enumeration of all deterministic Turing machines and let T_t be a deterministic Turing machine witnessing the time-constructibility of t, that is, for any input x, $T_t(x)$ halts after exactly $t(|x|)$ steps.

For any pair of natural numbers j and c, let $T_{\langle j,c \rangle}$ be the Turing machine operating as follows. For any x, simulate $ct(|x|)$ steps of $T'_j(x)$; if $T'_j(x)$ does not halt in such a time, then halt in the rejecting state, otherwise halt according to $T'_j(x)$. Note that since t is time-constructible, $T_{\langle j,c \rangle}$ can be implemented so that it works in time $\mathbf{O}[t(|x|)]$. The following is a general description of the machine:

1. Initialize a counter to c (even in unary, if that is more convenient).
2. Simulate one step of $T'_j(x)$ and if $T'_j(x)$ halts, then halt accordingly.
3. Simulate one step of $T_t(x)$. If $T_t(x)$ does not halt, then go to step 2. Otherwise if the counter is equal to 1, reject; otherwise decrement the counter, 'restart' T_t and go to step 2.

The ith machine of the effective enumeration is then defined as $T_i = T_{\langle j,c \rangle}$ where j and c are the numbers encoded by i (see Section 1.3.2).

If a language L belongs to DTIME$[t(n)]$, then a pair of natural numbers j and c exists such that L is decided by T'_j and, for any x, $T'_j(x)$ halts in a time of, at most, $ct(|x|)$. It follows that $L = L(T_i)$ where i is the natural number associated to j and c. Hence, DTIME$[t(n)] \subseteq \{L : \exists i[L = L(T_i)]\}$.

Conversely, let $L = L(T_i)$ for some i. Since T_i works in time $\mathbf{O}[t(|x|)]$, it follows that $L \in$ DTIME$[t(n)]$. Hence, $\{L : \exists i[L = L(T_i)]\} \subseteq$ DTIME$[t(n)]$ and condition 1 is satisfied.

Finally, it is easy to derive a Turing machine such that, for any i and x, $T(i, x) = T_i(x)$. Indeed, such a machine has to extract from i the two numbers j and c and by making use of the universal Turing machine as a subroutine (see Section 2.1.1) it has to simulate $T'_j(x)$ for, at most, $ct(|x|)$ steps. $\qquad \square$

Note that while Lemmas 3.5 and 3.6 do not rely on the time-constructibility of function t, Lemma 3.7 depends heavily on it. However, it is possible to obtain the same result even if t is assumed to be merely total and computable (see Problem 3.15).

Note also that in the hypothesis of Lemma 3.6 we have assumed that the bounding function grows at least linearly. But let us consider the following question: which are the most elementary time-complexity classes? It should be clear that, according to the reasonable encoding assumption (see Section 3.3), all machines must read *all* input symbols since systematically ignoring some of them would imply an unreasonable encoding of the input. Thus the smallest class consists of languages decidable in linear time and the hypothesis of the lemma is not at all restrictive (this result is no longer valid for other models of computation such as RAMs for which sublinear time-complexity classes can be defined).

3.4.3 Nondeterministic time-complexity classes

Since the nondeterministic Turing machines are an extension of the deterministic ones, it seems reasonable to extend our definition of the time-complexity class by replacing the decidability by deterministic Turing machines with the decidability by nondeterministic Turing machines.

Given a time-constructible function t, the *time-complexity class NTIME[t(n)]* is defined as

$$\text{NTIME}[t(n)] = \{L : \exists NT_i[L = L(NT_i) \wedge NTIME_i(x) \in \mathbf{O}[t(|x|)]]\}$$

(Note that, since the number of steps in a computation is bounded by a time-constructible function, we can assume that, for any input x, all computation paths of $NT_i(x)$ halt.)

The reader can easily verify that Lemmas 3.6 and 3.7 still hold true in the case of nondeterministic time-complexity classes. One of the main open questions in complexity theory, however, is whether Lemma 3.5 holds true in the nondeterministic case. The reader should try to understand why the proof of that lemma cannot be generalized for nondeterministic Turing machines.

3.4.4 Relativized time-complexity classes

In the following, given a complexity class $\mathcal{C}$ (either deterministic or nondeterministic), $\mathcal{C}^X$ denotes the complexity class defined by making use of Turing machines with oracle X. For instance, the class $\text{DTIME}^X[t(n)]$ denotes the set of languages L for which a deterministic Turing machine with oracle X exists such that T^X decides L in $TIME(x) \in \mathbf{O}[t(|x|)]$. The importance of such classes will be clarified in later chapters.

3.5 The pseudo-Pascal language

Although our basic model of computation is the Turing machine, we do not want to describe our algorithms in terms of such primitive machines but we shall prefer to make use of a high-level programming language, called *pseudo-Pascal*. Such a language uses such familiar programming language constructs as **if-then-else** or **while-do**. It also makes use of two special 'halt' instructions, that is, **accept** and **reject**. Moreover, plain English sentences or familiar mathematical notations will often be used inside statements and that is why we call such a language pseudo-Pascal. The goal of this informal notation is only to provide a more succinct description of algorithms. All pseudo-Pascal programs which will be introduced can be translated into RAM programs.

Assuming that the size of the numbers to be dealt with is polynomially related to the length of the input, from Theorem 2.2 it follows that any RAM program can be translated into a Turing machine with only a polynomial loss of efficiency (that is, t steps executed by the RAM can be simulated with ct^k steps of the Turing machine, where c and k are constants).

Finally, to describe nondeterministic algorithms we will make use of an additional construct:

guess variable **in** finite set.

Intuitively, this statement causes a nondeterministic algorithm to branch into as many computation paths as the cardinality of the finite set, with the value of the variable along the ith computation path being equal to the ith element of the finite set. Once again, if for any i, the ith element of the finite set can be generated in polynomial time, such a statement can be simulated by a nondeterministic Turing machine with a polynomial loss of efficiency.

Problems

3.1. Given a dynamic measure Φ, consider a new measure Φ' defined as $\Phi'_i(x) = \Phi_i(x)f(i,x)$ where f is any total computable function. Is Φ' a dynamic measure?

3.2. Given a deterministic one-tape Turing machine T_i, let m_i denote the function which computes, for any x, the maximum number of consecutive moves of the head in the same direction during the computation $T_i(x)$. Furthermore, let s_i denote the function which computes, for any x, the maximum number of times a cell has been scanned during the computation $T_i(x)$. Is the set $\Phi = \{\Phi_i\}$ a dynamic measure, where, for any x, $\Phi_i(x) = \max\{m_i(x), s_i(x)\}$?

3.3. Define m_i and s_i as in the previous problem and let r_i denote the function which computes, for any x, the reversals of the computation $T_i(x)$ (the reversals associated with a computation correspond to the number of times the tape heads changes direction). Is $\Phi = \{\Phi_i\}$ a dynamic measure, where, for any x, $\Phi_i(x) = \max\{m_i(x), s_i(x), r_i(x)\}$?

3.4. Show that dynamic measures do not differ greatly from each other. In particular, prove that, for any two dynamic measures Φ and Φ', a total computable function f exists such that $f(x, \Phi'_i(x)) \geq \Phi_i(x)$ and $f(x, \Phi_i(x)) \geq \Phi'_i(x)$ for all i and almost all n. [Blum (1967a)]

3.5. Given two classes of languages C_1 and C_2, prove that $C_1 \subseteq C_2$ if and only if $coC_1 \subseteq coC_2$.

3.6. Show that, for any class C, if L is any C-complete language with respect to m-reducibility, then L^c is coC-complete.

3.7. Given two alphabets Σ and Γ, derive an injective function f which maps pairs of words over Σ onto words over Γ and such that both f and f^{-1} are linear-time computable. [Hint: Consider a symbol not in Σ in order to associate a single word of the enriched alphabet with each pair of words over Σ, and then make use of Lemma 3.3.] Further, generalize the previous pairing function in order to encode tuples of fixed length. [Hint: define the encoding of k-tuples by means of the encoding of $(k-1)$-tuples.] Finally, derive an encoding for tuples of varying length. [Hint: note that, in this case, it is also necessary to know the length of the sequence.]

3.8. Prove Theorem 3.1.

3.9. Prove the *tape compression theorem*. Let L be a language decided by a k-tape Turing machine operating in $SPACE(x) \leq s(|x|)$. Then, for any natural m, a k-tape Turing machine exists that decides L in $SPACE(x) \leq \lceil \frac{1}{2m} s(|x|) \rceil$.

3.10. Show that any time-constructible function is total and computable.

3.11. Given two time-constructible functions t_1 and t_2, prove that functions $t_1 + t_2$, $t_1 t_2$ and 2^{t_1} are also time-constructible. [Hint: compute the constituent functions first and then compose the results in a suitable way.] By making use of this result, prove that all functions in Example 3.19 are time-constructible. [Hint: prove that $t(n) = n$ is time-constructible.]

3.12. Prove that a computable function $f : N \to N$ exists such that DTIME$[f(n)] =$ DTIME$[2^{f(n)}]$. This result, called the gap theorem, shows that whenever the complexity classes are not defined by means of time-constructible functions, very unintuitive phenomena can occur. [Hint: define f so that no Turing machine with an input of a length n halts after a number of steps between $f(n)$ and $2^{f(n)}$.]

3.13. Given a time-constructible function t_1, derive a time-constructible function t_2 such that DTIME$[t_1(n)] \subset$ DTIME$[t_2(n)]$. [Hint: consider the language $L_{\text{halt}-f} = \{\langle i, x \rangle : T_i(x) \text{ accepts in, at most, } f(|x|) \text{ steps}\}$ where f is a time-constructible function.] Two immediate consequences of this result are: (a) an infinite hierarchy of deterministic time-complexity classes exists and (b) no time-constructible function t exists such that any decidable language belongs to DTIME$[t(n)]$.

3.14. Show that no algorithm exists which, for any time-constructible function t and for any language L, decides whether $L \in$ DTIME$[t(n)]$. [Hint: derive a reduction from L_{halt} by associating a language L to any pair $\langle i, x \rangle$ such that $L \in$ DTIME$[t(n)]$ if and only if $T_i(x)$ halts. Make use of the previous problem and of Lemma 3.6.]

3.15. In the text it is stated that Lemma 3.7 still holds if the bounding function is only total and computable. Prove that statement. [Hint: derive an enumeration of languages which either are finite or belong to the complexity class. This exercise is not a waste of time: similar proof techniques will be used in the rest of the book.]

3.16. Prove that, for any time-constructible function t, NTIME$[t(n)] \subseteq$ DTIME$[2^{t(n)}]$.

Notes

At the very beginning of the 1960s it was clear that a general theory that studied the difficulty of computing functions had to be developed. Indeed, the first attempt to make a systematic approach to computational complexity was made by Rabin

(1960). Since then this area of research has been an essential part of the theoretical work in computer science. It would be impossible to mention all the papers and results that have influenced this discipline during the last thirty years. Our choices will inevitably be incomplete and unsatisfactory. Hence, whenever possible, we will mention surveys and reviews which can be used for further references.

The size of programs was studied in Blum (1967b). For other examples of static measures of complexity, the reader should also see Li and Vitany (1990).

The axiomatic study of model-independent dynamic measures of complexity (as presented in this book) was formulated by Blum (1967a). In this work, influenced by Rabin (1960), the two constraints that a dynamic measure must satisfy were defined, and on the basis of these constraints some interesting results were obtained. Hartmanis and Hopcroft (1971) and Machtey and Young (1978) provide two good overviews of the results obtained using this line of research. A more recent presentation of machine-independent complexity theory is contained in Seiferas (1990) which is also a good pointer to the literature to date.

The discussion on reasonable representations and, in general, on the relation between decision problems and languages was partly influenced by the pioneering textbook of Garey and Johnson (1979).

The **O**-notation was proposed by Knuth (1968) in his 'bible' on the design and analysis of algorithms and is based on well-known mathematical notations.

The first systematic analysis of specific complexity measures, namely time and space, is due to Hartmanis and Stearns (1965) and to Stearns, Hartmanis and Lewis (1965). But almost at the same time the papers by Cobham (1964) and Edmonds (1965) appeared which were both concerned with the study of quantitative aspects of computation.

The paper by Hartmanis and Stearns (1965) contains almost all we know about inclusion relations between time-complexity classes (see the problems section). Most of these results have already appeared in textbooks on theoretical computer science and for this reason, we have decided not to present them here, leaving the choice of the preferred presentation to the reader.

The main grounds for considering time-constructible functions instead of total computable ones is the so-called Gap Theorem mentioned in Problem 3.12. Intuitively such a theorem states that a total computable function f exists such that an arbitrarily large gap exists beyond f in which no function's complexity can lie. This rather unintuitive phenomenon was proved in Borodin (1972) and in a slightly weaker form in Constable (1972) and Young (1973). The equivalence between the two definitions of time-constructibility appeared in Kobayashi (1985).

Chapter 4

The class P

In this chapter we shall consider a first complexity class, called P, which includes all problems solvable in polynomial time. The importance of such a class derives from the fact that it includes all 'simple' problems, that is, those that are computationally tractable. Let us try to understand why this is so. In practice, we are saying that all problems solvable by algorithms requiring an hyperpolynomial[1] number of steps must be considered, in the general case, to be computationally untractable.

The following example which compares the performance of polynomial-time and exponential-time algorithms makes the difference quite clear.

Example 4.1 Consider a problem and assume that five algorithms A_1 through A_5 exist to solve it whose complexity are illustrated in Table 4.1. Assume also that the machine running them requires 10^{-9} seconds to execute a single step. The execution times of the five algorithms are represented in the table in terms of increasing instance sizes.

Table 4.1 An example of polynomial and exponential times versus instance sizes

Instance	Algorithm/complexity				
size n	A_1/n^2	A_2/n^3	A_3/n^5	$A_4/2^n$	$A_5/3^n$
10	0.1 μs	1 μs	0.01 ms	1 μs	59 μs
30	0.9 μs	27 μs	24.3 ms	1 s	2.4 days
50	2.5 μs	0.125 ms	0.31 s	13 days	2.3×10^5 centuries

By choosing a somewhat more favorable time bound, for instance a subexponential one such as $k^{log^h(n)}$ with h and k constant, the differences would be less

---

[1]A function is hyperpolynomial if it grows faster than n^k for any fixed k.

51

significant for small values of n but they would reappear as n becomes larger. We can then conclude that, if our objective is to use a computer to solve a problem whose description includes relatively many elements, a necessary condition for obtaining an acceptable computation time is to solve the problem by making use of a polynomial-time algorithm. We shall see in Section 4.1.1 that this condition is necessary albeit not sufficient.

A formal definition of the class P is given in Section 4.1 with some significant examples of problems included in such a class. In Section 4.2 it is shown how the definition of P is relatively invariant with respect to the model of computation considered. Next, we introduce a restriction of the m-reducibility called polynomial-time reducibility which will be a basic tool in studying the properties of complexity classes. Finally, in Section 4.4, we will extend the diagonalization technique introduced in Section 1.3.3 to more than one class. More precisely, we will show how a diagonal language which does not belong to the union of two classes can be obtained and still be polynomially reducible to two languages known *a priori* not to be included in those classes.

4.1   The class P

Let $p_k(n) = n^k$ and let $\mathrm{DTIME}[p_k(n)]$ be the corresponding deterministic time-complexity class. The *class* P is defined as

$$P = \bigcup_{k \geq 0} \mathrm{DTIME}[p_k(n)]$$

Since polynomials $q(n) = a_0 + a_1 n + a_2 n^2 + \ldots + a_k n^k$ of degree k belong to $\mathbf{O}[n^k]$, class P coincides with the infinite union of all time-complexity classes $\mathrm{DTIME}[t(n)]$ where t is a polynomial having a finite degree.

Informally, we shall say that an algorithm requires *polynomial time* if it runs in $\mathbf{O}[n^k]$ steps where n denotes the problem size and k is a constant. Similarly, we shall define the *class FP* as the class of all functions computable in polynomial-time by a deterministic transducer Turing machine.

Let us introduce a few initial members of P and FP. Tens of thousands of fascinating polynomial-time algorithms have been designed to solve problems arising in many different areas. We refer the reader to appropriate texts on algorithmics (see Notes) for an exhaustive treatment and we shall content ourselves with describing three significant problems.

Example 4.2 The greatest common divisor (GCD) of two integers a and b is defined to be the largest integer that divides both a and b. For example, the GCD of 24 and 30 is 6. We may derive an algorithm for GCD by observing that, if r is the remainder of a divided by b ($a \geq b$), then the common divisors of a and b coincide with the common divisors of b and r. In symbols, $GCD(a, b) = GCD(b, r)$ with $r = a \bmod b$.

The algorithm can then be stated as follows:

```
function GCD(a, b): integer;
begin
    if b = 0 then GCD := a else GCD := GCD(b, a mod b)
end;
```

We have to show that GCD halts for all pairs a, b. In fact, we shall prove that, at most, $\log(b)$ recursive calls are needed.

Let $\langle a_{k-1}, b_{k-1} \rangle, \langle a_k, b_k \rangle, \langle a_{k+1}, b_{k+1} \rangle$ be three successive pairs in the reduction process; let us show that $b_{k-1} \geq b_k + b_{k+1}$. First note that $a_k = qb_k + b_{k+1}$ for some integer $q \geq 1$. Thus, $a_k \geq b_k + b_{k+1}$. Since $b_{k-1} = a_k$, then $b_{k-1} \geq b_k + b_{k+1}$. From this last inequality it is easy to see that $b = b_0 \geq 2^{k/2} b_k$ for any even $k \geq 2$ (see Problem 4.8). Therefore, the number of steps k must be less than the logarithm of b. Hence, the time complexity of GCD is logarithmic with respect to the *value* of the numbers and *linear* with respect to the input length. This concludes the proof that GCD belongs to FP.

The next example refers to a problem introduced in Example 3.12.

Example 4.3 Recall that the SHORTEST PATH problem consists of determining whether a path of length, at most, k exists between a pair of nodes n_1 and n_2 of an input graph G. We are now able to prove that this problem belongs to P.

The proposed algorithm makes use of a dynamic programming technique. Denote by n the number of nodes of G and let $A^h(i, j)$ be the length of the shortest path from node i to node j going through no node with an index greater than h. We then obtain

$$A^{h+1}(i, j) = \min\{A^h(i, h+1) + A^h(h+1, j), A^h(i, j)\},$$

that is, either a shortest path from i to j going through no node of index greater than $h + 1$ passes through node $h + 1$ or it does not. By construction, the entry $A^n(n_1, n_2)$ yields the value of the shortest path between n_1 and n_2. If the value is not greater than k, then the SHORTEST PATH instance admits a yes answer. The algorithm can then be described as follows:

```
begin {input:G, n_1, n_2, k}
    n := number of nodes of G;
    {derive adjacency matrix A^1 from G}
    for all i, j ≤ n do
        if G includes an edge ⟨i, j⟩ then A^1[i, j] := 1 else A^1[i, j] := ∞;
    for h := 2 to n do
        for all i, j ≤ n do
            A^h[i, j] := min(A^{h-1}[i, h] + A^{h-1}[h, j], A^{h-1}[i, j]);
    if A^n(n_1, n_2) ≤ k then accept else reject;
end.
```

Clearly, the number of steps required by the algorithm is $\mathbf{O}[n^3]$.

The last example is a decision problem related to a basic property of Boolean formulas called *satisfiability*.

Example 4.4 Let $U = \{u_1, u_2, \ldots, u_n\}$ be a set of n Boolean variables. A Boolean formula f is said to be in *conjunctive normal form* if it can be expressed as a conjunction of m *clauses* C_i such as

$$f = C_1 \wedge C_2 \wedge \ldots \wedge C_m$$

where each clause C_i, in turn, is a disjunction of *literals* such as

$$C_i = (l_{i_1} \vee l_{i_2} \vee \ldots \vee l_{i_k}).$$

Finally, each literal l_{i_j} denotes either a Boolean variable or a negated Boolean variable in U.

An *assignment of values* for U is a function $t : U \to \{\textbf{true}, \textbf{false}\}$ which assigns to each variable the Boolean value **true** or **false**. A literal l is **true** if either $l = u_h$ and $t(u_h) = \textbf{true}$ or $l = \neg u_h$ and $t(u_h) = \textbf{false}$. A clause is satisfied by an assignment if at least one literal included in it is **true**. The formula f is *satisfied* if all the m clauses are satisfied.

We are now ready to define the 2-SATISFIABILITY problem. Given a Boolean formula f in conjunctive normal form such that each clause contains exactly two literals, does an assignment of values satisfying f exist? The objective is to guess the value of an arbitrary variable and to deduce the consequences of this guess for other variables of f.

Initially, all clauses are declared unsatisfied. A starting variable x is selected arbitrarily and x and $\neg x$ receive the values **true** and **false**, respectively. The assignment is then extended to as many variables as possible by repeated applications of the following elementary step:

> Take an arbitrary unsatisfied clause $(l_h \vee l_k)$. If one of the two literals has the value **true**, then declare the clause satisfied. Otherwise, if one of the literals, say l_h, has the value **false**, then assign to l_k and $\neg l_k$ the values **true** and **false**, respectively. Declare the clause $(l_h \vee l_k)$ satisfied.

Three exclusive cases may occur:

1. During the execution of any step, a conflict takes place while the algorithm attempts to assign the value **true** to a literal which is already **false**. This means that the initial guess of the value of the starting variable was wrong. Thus all the steps starting from the assignment of the value **true** to x are cancelled. This time x and $\neg x$ receive the values **false** and **true**, respectively, and the assignment procedure starts again. If a second conflict occurs, the algorithm stops and f is declared unsatisfiable.

2. No conflict occurs and all variables receive a value. Then the formula is satisfiable.

3. No conflict occurs but some variables remain unassigned. This may only happen when, for every unsatisfied clause, literals appearing in that clause are unassigned. In this case, we may ignore the clauses already satisfied and work on the reduced formula consisting only of the remaining unsatisfied clauses. Clearly, the reduced formula is satisfiable if and only if the previous one is also satisfiable. A guess is then made for an arbitrary variable, and the assignment procedure is again applied to the reduced formula.

The algorithm can then be stated as follows:

begin {input: f}
  C := set of clauses of f;
  declare the clauses of C unsatisfied;
  V := set of variables of f;
  declare the variables of V unassigned;
  while V contains a variable x **do**
  begin
    assign the value **true** to x;
    $firstguess$:= **true**;
    while C contains an unsatisfied clause $c = (l_1 \vee l_2)$ with
    at least one assigned literal **do**
    begin
      if $l_1 = $ **true** $\vee l_2 = $ **true then**
        declare c satisfied
      else if $l_1 = $ **false** $\wedge l_2 = $ **false then**
      begin
        if not $firstguess$ **then** reject
        else
        begin
          declare the clauses of C unsatisfied;
          declare the variables of V unassigned;
          assign the value **false** to x;
          $firstguess$:= **false**;
        end
      end
      else if $l_1 = $ **false then** assign the value **true** to l_2
      else assign the value **true** to l_1;
    end;
    delete from C the satisfied clauses;
    delete from V the assigned variables;
  end;
  accept;
end.

It is easy to verify that the previous algorithm decides 2-SATISFIABILITY in $\mathbf{O}[nm]$ steps. The 2-SATISFIABILITY problem may be considered to be the simplest of a series of satisfiability problems which will be considered in the following chapters.

4.1.1   Polynomial-time untractable problems

Although the class P is usually associated with the class of computationally tractable problems, it also includes many 'natural' problems which cannot in practice be solved by computers. Let us examine why this occurs.

The first reason is the high degree of the polynomial. While it is correct to state that the majority of the existing polynomial-time algorithms are characterized by a low degree (not higher than 5 or 6), it is also true that many problems exist for which the only known algorithms run in $\mathbf{O}[n^k]$ steps with k constant but arbitrarily large.

Example 4.5 Given a graph $G = (N, E)$, the problem k-CLIQUE consists of deciding whether G admits a complete k-node subgraph, that is, a clique of size k with k constant.

The only algorithm known to solve this type of problem consists of considering exhaustively all possible k-node subsets of G, checking, for each subset, whether the induced subgraph is a clique. The running time of the algorithm grows with the number of distinct subsets to be considered and is $\mathbf{O}[n^k]$ where n denotes the number of nodes of G.

Thus, for a sufficiently large k, this problem must be considered computationally untractable.

The second reason is the high values of the constants. Remember that the exact number of steps of a polynomial-time algorithm is bounded by $c_1 n^k$ with c_1 and k constants. On the other hand, it is true that the great majority of such algorithms make use of relatively small constants so that the dominant time-complexity factor is n^k, but we cannot rule out *a priori* the existence of algorithms with very large constants.

The third and even more important reason why not all problems in P can be considered computationally tractable is now briefly outlined. Remember that, according to the definition of time-complexity classes introduced in Section 3.4, a language belongs to a given class if a Turing machine *exists* which decides that language within the given time bounds. In most cases it is possible to prove in a *constructive way* that a language belongs to that class, that is, we can describe the characteristics of the Turing machine which decides it.

Could there be occurrences where we are only able to state that such a machine must exist although we are unable to describe it? In other words, do languages exist for which it is only possible to prove that they belong to a given class in a *non-constructive way* ? The answer is yes, although we will not be able to present the lengthy proofs of the series of fascinating theorems which establish the above results. The interested reader will find in this chapter's Notes an exhaustive bibliography for this research field.

For the sake of curiosity, we limit ourselves in the next example to presenting a decision problem which can be shown to belong to P in a non-constructive way, although no constructive algorithm, no matter how time consuming, is currently known to solve this problem.

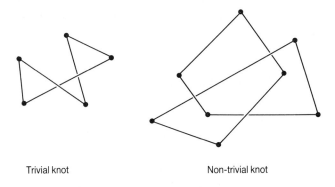

Trivial knot   Non-trivial knot

Figure 4.1 Examples of knots

Example 4.6 An *embedding* of a graph G into three-dimensional space R^3 is a correspondence which associates nodes with points and edges between pairs of nodes with lines connecting the corresponding points. Furthermore, lines must not have points in common (except those corresponding to edges with a common node which have exactly one end point in common).

Consider an embedding of G in R^3; any cycle in G becomes a closed line in R^3. Informally, a closed line represents a *knot* if it cannot be stretched into a circle (also called a trivial knot). Figure 4.1 illustrates two embedded cycles corresponding to a trivial and a non-trivial knot, respectively.

The KNOTLESSNESS decision problem consists of deciding whether an arbitrary graph G can be embedded without knots.

In conclusion, it is fair to say that the class P has a much richer structure than was initially considered and that much work remains to be done to characterize the untractable problems in P from a theoretical point of view.

4.2   The robustness of the class P

An important characteristic of class P is that it is, to some extent, large enough to accomodate not only the basic Turing machines and RAMs described in Sections 2.1 and 2.1.5, respectively, but also several variations of such models. In other words, it is always possible to transform a polynomial-time algorithm obtained for one of these latter models into a polynomial-time algorithm applicable to a basic model.

We already know from Theorem 2.2 how to simulate t steps of a RAM in $\mathbf{O}[t^3]$ steps on a three-tape Turing machine. Conversely, we discussed in Problem 2.13

how to simulate t steps of a Turing machine in $\mathbf{O}[t]$ steps on a RAM. Thus the two basic models of computation considered in Chapter 2 are polynomially related.

Let us consider a first variation relative to the number of tapes used by the Turing machine.

Lemma 4.1 Given any k-tape Turing machine T with $k > 1$, it is always possible to derive from it an equivalent one-tape Turing machine T' which simulates the first t steps of T in $\mathbf{O}[t^2]$ steps.

Proof. We dedicate k consecutive cells of the single tape of T' to storing the set of symbols contained in the ith cells ($i = 0, 1, \ldots$) of the k tapes of T. The k tape heads of T' are simulated by making use of suitable marked symbols. If the hth tape head is scanning the symbol a, then the tape of T' will contain the marked symbol a_h. By convention, after a quintuple of T has been simulated, the (real) tape head of T' is assumed to be positioned on the leftmost marked symbol. The simulation of a quintuple of T proceeds as follows. First, the k marked symbols are scanned sequentially rightward to determine the quintuple of T to be simulated. Next, the tape is scanned k times rightward to replace the old symbols with the new ones and to simulate the k tape moves. Assume that a left (respectively, right) move must be simulated relative to tape h. This is accomplished by shifting the tape head k positions to the left (respectively, right) and by replacing the symbol currently scanned, say a, with the marked symbol a_h. Some caution must be exercised when simulating a left move since the tape is semi-infinite. These situations are easier to deal with by making use of special end-of-tape symbols, say #, so that whenever the symbol to be marked is a #, T' shifts back k positions to the right and marks the new symbol currently scanned in agreement with the convention that a left move from cell 0 is replaced by a still move.

Figure 4.2 illustrates a simple example on a two-tape machine; the tape heads are positioned on symbols c and f, respectively, as shown in (a). The quintuple to be simulated replaces c with x, f with y and then performs a left move on tape 1 and a right one on tape 2. As a result, the tape heads will be positioned as shown in (b). The simulation on a single tape is shown in (c) and (d).

Since the simulation of one step of T requires $\mathbf{O}[t]$ steps of T', the $\mathbf{O}[t^2]$ bound is achieved.   □

Another interesting variation concerns the characteristics of the tape. A tape is said to be *two-way infinite* if it extends arbitrarily both to the left and to the right of the tape head. We assume that the cells of a two-way infinite tape are indexed as $\ldots, -2, -1, 0, 1, 2, \ldots$ and that cell 0 is the cell scanned at the beginning of the computation.

Lemma 4.2 Given a two-way infinite k-tape Turing machine T_{2w}, it is always possible to derive from it an equivalent k-tape Turing machine T that simulates the first t steps of T_{2w} in $\mathbf{O}[t]$ steps.

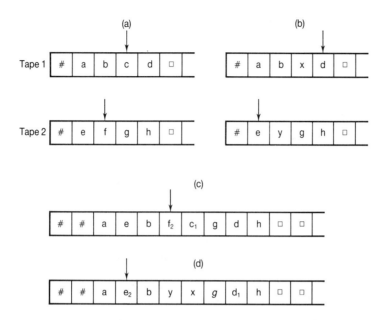

Figure 4.2 Compacting two tapes into one

Proof. For simplicity, we shall consider one-tape machines although the construction can be readily extended to k-tape machines. Let us map the indices i of the two-way infinite tape in the order $0, -1, 1, -2, 2, -3, 3, \ldots$ on the indices j of the one-way infinite tape. For any state q of T_{2w}, T includes two states q_p and q_n which, intuitively, discriminate positive from negative cells. The simulation of a right move is then made according to the following rules. If the state is a 'positive' one, then the head is moved two positions to the right; otherwise it is moved 2 positions to the left. Once again, some caution must be exercised on the boundary between positive and negative cells. When the right move is made from cell -1 (that is, in a negative state), T scans the end-of-tape symbol while attempting to perform two left moves. In this case, it will move one cell rightward and enter a positive state (see Figure 4.3). Similar rules apply to the simulation of a left move. □

Variations of RAMs can also be considered. In fact, it could be observed that the set of instructions listed in Section 2.1.5 is rather too strict to allow an easy formulation of complex algorithms.

The following example introduces a few useful new RAM instructions which transform the basic RAM model into an extended one polynomially related to the first.

Figure 4.3 A right move from cell -1

Example 4.7 The instruction $M_i \leftarrow 1$ can be replaced by the more general one $M_i \leftarrow c$ where c denotes a constant (we did not do this previously in order to simplify the proof of Lemma 2.2).

The division by 2 instruction $M_i \leftarrow \lfloor M_j/2 \rfloor$ can also be replaced by a general division operation of the form $M_i \leftarrow \lfloor M_j/M_k \rfloor$ since this last instruction can be simulated by executing $\mathbf{O}[|m_k|]$ divisions by 2 of M_j where m_k denotes the contents of M_k.

Some caution must be exercised, however, in adding multiplication instructions of the form $M_i \leftarrow M_j * M_k$ because the length of the product may be twice as large as the length of the multiplicands. Clearly, it is possible to derive a number as large as 2^{2^n} by performing only n multiplications. Thus a polynomial number of multiplications may yield, in the general case, a number whose length is exponential with respect to the input length. Only if this does not occur, that is, only if we are certain that the RAM program does not make such an unconventional use of multiplications, are we allowed to claim that the extended model is polynomially related to the basic one.

Many more examples of variations could be added to the basic Turing and RAM models but by now the reader should be convinced of the robustness of class P.

4.3   Polynomial-time reducibility

How can we prove (constructively) that a problem belongs to P? The most natural way is to derive a polynomial-time algorithm solving the problem (this has been done in Examples 4.2–4.4). An alternative way consists of reducing the problem to another one already known to be in P. Clearly, some polynomial-time restrictions to the reducibility introduced in Section 2.3.1 have to be added. We then introduce the following definition.

Given two languages L_1 and L_2, L_1 is *polynomially reducible* to L_2, in symbols, $L_1 \leq L_2$,[2] if a function $f \in$ FP exists such that

$$x \in L_1 \leftrightarrow f(x) \in L_2.$$

---

[2]Although the correct notation should be $L_1 \leq^p_m L_2$, we shall prefer the simpler one $\leq$, omitting both subscript and superscript.

FP is the set of functions computatble in polynomial steps.

The following lemma shows that the $\leq$-reducibility can effectively be applied to prove the P membership of problems.

Lemma 4.3 Let L_1 and L_2 be two languages such that $L_1 \leq L_2$ and $L_2 \in$ P. Then $L_1 \in$ P.

Proof. It suffices to compose the Turing transducer that computes the reduction with the Turing machine that decides L_2. Since a composition of polynomials is still a polynomial, the lemma follows. $\square$

As a first trivial application of the previous lemma, let us consider the following example.

Example 4.8 Given a graph $G = (N, E)$, the 2-COLORABILITY problem consists of deciding whether a total function $f : N \to \{1, 2\}$ exists such that $f(u) \neq f(v)$ whenever $\langle u, v \rangle \in E$. Suppose we do not want to design a polynomial-time algorithm to solve that problem (we do not wish to solve Problem 4.12) but we prefer to rely on the algorithm given in Example 4.4 to solve 2-SATISFIABILITY. We then have to set up a polynomial-time reduction between the two problems. This can be done quite easily by associating a Boolean variable x_i with each node n_i of the graph and by associating the pair of clauses $(x_i \vee x_j)$ and $(\neg x_i \vee \neg x_j)$ with each edge (u_i, u_j). These two clauses express the fact that the two variables cannot be simultaneously **true** or simultaneously **false**.

More interesting applications of Lemma 4.3 have been obtained. One example is the reduction of the maximum matching problem in bipartite graphs to the maximum flow one which yields an efficient algorithm to solve the first problem (see Notes). However, the main applications of polynomial-time reducibilities will be described in the following chapters, which deal with classes of far more difficult problems than those in P. In such cases, the cost of a polynomial-time reduction is found to be negligible with respect to the cost of applying a decision algorithm, and polynomial-time reductions represent a basic tool to study the structures of complexity classes. The next result shows that this last statement does not apply to the class P.

Lemma 4.4 Let B be any language included in P such that $B \neq \emptyset$ and $B \neq \Sigma^*$. Then, for any language A included in P, $A \leq B$.

Proof. Revisit the proof of Lemma 2.4 replacing 'computable' with 'polynomial-time computable' and 'decidable' with 'polynomial-time decidable'. $\square$

The previous result clearly indicates that additional quantitative refinements must be added to reducibilities in order to investigate the inner structure of class P in more detail. This analysis will be carried out in Chapter 8.

4.4   Uniform diagonalization

In Section 1.3.3 we introduced the diagonalization technique as a tool for deriving languages not included in a given class. In this section we extend this technique in order to derive languages not included in the union of two or more classes.

We observe that, according to Lemma 3.7, all time-complexity classes are constructively enumerable. Thus, the diagonalization technique can be readily extended to unions of such classes. However, the next theorem yields a much stronger result since it allows, under suitable assumptions, a diagonal language to be derived which is not 'too difficult', that is, polynomially reducible to the join (see Section 1.5) of two languages known *a priori* not to be in the two classes.

Theorem 4.1 Let C_1 and C_2 be two classes of languages such that

1. C_1 and C_2 are constructively enumerable.
2. C_1 and C_2 are closed with respect to finite variations.
3. Two languages L_1 and L_2 exist with $L_1 \notin C_1$ and $L_2 \notin C_2$.

It is then possible to define a third language L such that $L \notin C_1 \cup C_2$ with $L \leq L_1 \oplus L_2$.

Proof. Intuitively, the language L will be defined as L_1 for some word lengths and as L_2 for the remaining word lengths, so that it will not belong either to C_1 or to C_2. In particular, L is defined as

$$L = (G \cap L_1) \cup (G^c \cap L_2)$$

where G is a language which is alternatively 'full' and 'empty' depending on the word lengths. In the simple example illustrated in Figure 4.4, the words of Σ^* are partitioned according to some sequence of lengths $x_0, x_1 \ldots$. The words of G consist of all words of Σ^* having length included between x_{2i-1} and x_{2i} (the solid lines in the figure).

What properties should G have in order for L to satisfy the theorem?

First, note that, in order to prove that $L \leq L_1 \oplus L_2$, we can define a function f as follows. If $x \in G$ then $f(x) = 1x$, otherwise $f(x) = 0x$. It follows from the definition of the join operation that $x \in L$ if and only if $f(x) \in L_1 \oplus L_2$. To have $f \in \mathrm{FP}$, G *should belong to* P.

Second, we require that $L \notin C_i$ for $i = 1, 2$. Denote by $T_1^i, T_2^i, \ldots$ the enumeration of Turing machines which 'present' C_i and let L_j^i be the language decided by T_j^i. Thus, we are requiring, for any j, a word z to exist such that $z \in L \Delta L_j^i$. In particular, this is satisfied whenever, *for any j, a word z exists such that $z \in L_i \Delta L_j^i$ and $z \in G$.* Indeed, if this is the case it follows from the definition of L that $z \in L \Delta L_j^i$.

The rest of the proof is devoted to defining G so that it satisfies the above two conditions.

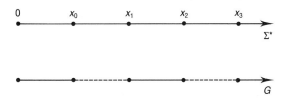

Figure 4.4 The language G

Denote by $z_1^{i,n}$ the smallest word z such that $|z| \geq n$ and $z \in L_1 \triangle L_1^i$. Define $z_2^{i,n}$ in a similar way. Then consider the two following functions:

$$r_1(n) = \max_{i \leq n}\{|z_1^{i,n}|\} + 1$$

and

$$r_2(n) = \max_{i \leq n}\{|z_2^{i,n}|\} + 1.$$

Let us show that the functions r_1 and r_2 are total and computable. If $L_1 \notin \mathcal{C}_1$, then $L_1 \neq L_j^1$ for all j. By assumption, $\mathcal{C}_1$ is closed with respect to finite variations. Given any j and $n \geq j$, a word z of a length at least equal to n included in the symmetric difference of L_1 and L_j^1 must exist. Furthermore, note that the predicate $z \in L_1 \triangle L_j^1$ is decidable since both L_1 and L_j^1 are decidable. In conclusion, r_1 is total and computable. The same reasoning can be applied to show that r_2 is total and computable.

Denote by r a time-constructible function such that $r(n) \geq \max(r_1(n), r_2(n))$ (we know from Lemma 3.4 how to derive such a function). The language G is then defined as

$$G = \{x : r^{2n}(0) \leq |x| < r^{2n+1}(0), n \geq 0\}$$

(in other words, in Figure 4.4 we let x_i be $r^{i+1}(0)$).

First we shall prove that $G \in P$. Let T be a Turing machine witnessing that r is a time-constructible function, that is, a machine that halts in exactly $r(|x|)$ for all x.

A simple algorithm for deciding G consists of computing the pair of values $r^h(0)$ and $r^{h+1}(0)$ until the first pair for which $r^h(0) \leq |x| < r^{h+1}(0)$ is found. However, if r is a rapidly growing function, for instance an exponential one, computing $r^{h+1}(0)$ while $|x|$ is close to $r^h(0)$ may require a hyperpolynomial number of steps. We must therefore use a more complex algorithm that causes T to halt as soon as $|x|$ steps have been executed.

Let us consider the following algorithm where the variable h denotes the number of the iteration considered minus one, while the variable j contains the value $r^h(0)$:

```
begin {input: x}
    if |x| = 0 then accept; {e ∈ G}
    j := 0;
    h := 1;
    while j < |x| do
    begin
        {check if r(j) > |x|}
        simulate |x| steps of T(1ʲ);
        if T(1ʲ) has not terminated then
            {r(j) > |x|, thus rʰ(0) > |x| ≥ rʰ⁻¹(0)}
            if h is odd then accept else reject;
        m := number of steps executed by T(1ʲ);
        {m = r(j) = rʰ(0)}
        if m = |x| then
            if h is even then accept else reject;
        j := m;
        h := h + 1;
    end;
end.
```

It can immediately be verified that the previous algorithm decides G in polynomial time.

It remains to prove that, for any j, a word z exists such that $z \in L_i \Delta L_j^i$ and $z \in G$, for $i = 1, 2$. Let n be a large enough integer such that $r^{2n}(0) \geq j$ and let z be the smallest word for which $|z| \geq r^{2n}(0)$ and $z \in L_i \Delta L_j^i$ (the closure of C_i with respect to finite variations ensures that such a z must exist). Since $r^{2n+1}(0) = r(r^{2n}(0)) \geq r_i(r^{2n}(0))$, it follows from the definition of r_i that $r^{2n+1}(0) > |z|$. Thus $z \in G$.

In conclusion, $L \notin C_1 \cup C_2$ and $L \leq L_1 \oplus L_2$. □

In the next chapter we shall consider an important application of the previous theorem.

Problems

4.1. Show that the class P is closed with respect to union and intersection.

4.2. Given a language L, the language L^* is defined as the set of all words x such that x is the concatenation of words of L. Show that if L belongs to P, then L^* also belongs to P. [Hint: use the dynamic programming technique.]

4.3. Show that P is constructively numerable. More generally, derive an enumeration $T_1, T_2, \ldots$ of oracle Turing machines such that, for any oracle X:

1. $\mathrm{P}^X = \{L : L = L(T_k^X) \text{ for some } k\}$.

2. For any k and for any input x, $T_k^X(x)$ halts after, at most, $n^k + k$ steps.

4.4. Let f be a function in FP and L be a language in P. Define the set $f^{-1}(L) = \{x : f(x) \in L\}$ and show that such a set belongs to P.

4.5. A function is said to be *honest* if, for any y in the codomain of f, an x exists such that $f(x) = y$ and $|x| \leq p(|y|)$ for a given polynomial p. Show that if a function f admits a right inverse function computable in polynomial time, then f is honest (g is a right inverse function of f if, for any y in the codomain of f, $f(g(y)) = y$).

4.6. Let f be an honest function computable in polynomial time. Then a nondeterministic polynomial-time Turing machine NT exists such that $L(NT)$ coincides with the codomain of f.

4.7. Let L be a language decidable in polynomial time by a deterministic Turing machine with oracle L'. Prove that if $L' \in \mathrm{P}$, then $L \in \mathrm{P}$.

4.8. Refer to Example 4.2. Prove that $b = b_0 \geq 2^{k/2} b_k$ for any even $k \geq 2$. Prove the following more refined bound: $b = b_0 \geq Fib(k)$ where k and $Fib(k)$ denote the number of recursive calls of function GCD and the kth Fibonacci number, respectively (remember that $Fib(0) = 0$, $Fib(1) = 1$, and $Fib(i) = Fib(i-1) + Fib(i-2)$ for any $i \geq 2$).

4.9. Show that any Boolean formula f can be transformed in polynomial-time into a Boolean formula g in conjunctive normal form such that f is satisfiable if and only if g is satisfiable. [Hint: any formula $f_1 \vee f_2$ can be transformed into $(f_1 \vee y) \wedge (f_2 \vee \neg y)$ where y is a new variable.]

4.10. A Boolean formula is said to be a *tautology* if it is satisfied by any assignment of values. Give a polynomial-time algorithm to decide whether a Boolean formula is a tautology. [Hint: use the result of the previous problem.]

4.11. A Boolean formula in conjunctive normal form is said to be *Horn* if each clause contains, at most, one non-negated variable. Describe a polynomial-time algorithm to decide whether a Boolean Horn formula is satisfiable. [Hint: start assigning the value **false** to all variables and then proceed ...]

4.12. Describe a polynomial-time algorithm to solve 2-COLORABILITY. [Hint: color the first node white, the adjacent nodes black and proceed.]

4.13. LINEAR EQUATIONS WITH INTEGER COEFFICIENTS: given a linear equation $ax + by + c = 0$ with integer coefficients, does a pair of integers x^* and y^* exist which satisfies it? Show that such a problem belongs to P. [Hint: when $a, b, c \neq 0$ the problem can be reduced to solving the congruence $c \equiv yb \pmod{a}$.]

4.14. k-BOUNDED PARTITION: given a finite set A of n integers whose sum is $2b \leq n^k$, does A admit a subset B of integers whose sum is exactly b? Show that this problem admits an algorithm requiring $O[n^{k+1}]$ steps. [Hint: use the dynamic programming technique.]

4.15. Consider a variation of Turing machine in which the tape is replaced by a two-dimensional tape, that is, an unbounded plane which is subdivided into squares by equidistant sets of vertical and horizontal lines. In addition to left and right moves, the variation will have up and down moves, permitting its head to move vertically in the plane as well as horizontally. Show that a standard multitape Turing machine can simulate such a variation with a quadratic loss of efficiency. [Hint: Use one tape to memorize the entire history of the two-dimensional tape.]

4.16. A multihead Turing machine is a variation of Turing machine in which we allow the possibility of having several heads on each tape with some appropriate rule to prevent two heads from occupying the same cell and giving conflicting instructions. Show that a one-tape two-head machine can be simulated by a multitape one-head machine without loss of efficiency. [Hint: Use three tapes, one containing the left-hand information, one the right-hand information, and one keeping count of the number of tape cells that are stored on both the previous two tapes.]

4.17. Let t be a total function and let T be a two-tape Turing transducer such that, for any natural number n, $T(1^n)$ outputs $1^{t(n)}$ in, at most, $ct(n)$ steps, where c is a constant. Show that any k-tape nondeterministic Turing machine NT working in time $t(n)$ admits an equivalent two-tape nondeterministic Turing machine NT' working in time $O[t(n)]$. [Hint: for any input x, guess an entire sequence of $t(|x|)$ global states of $NT(x)$.]

4.18. Prove that the polynomial m-reducibility is transitive.

4.19. Prove that for any pair of languages L_1 and L_2, $L_1 \leq L_1 \oplus L_2$ and $L_2 \leq L_1 \oplus L_2$.

4.20. Show that an infinite language L exists such that L^c is infinite, $L \not\leq L^c$, and $L \in \text{DTIME}[2^n]$. [Ladner, Lynch, and Selman (1975)]

Notes

The importance of classes P and FP was first realized by Cobham (1964) and Edmonds (1965). In particular, in the latter paper polynomial-time solvable problems were first proposed as a theoretical equivalent to the informal concept of 'tractable' problems.

A wide range of combinatorial problems are known to be either in P or in FP, and researchers are continually attempting to identify new members. The book by Cormen, Leiserson, and Rivest (1990) provides an excellent description and analysis of most significant algorithms, data structures, and programming techniques.

The algorithm for GCD introduced in Example 4.2 is commonly referred to as Euclid's algorithm since it was first described by Euclid about 2300 years ago: it may be considered as one of the oldest non-trivial algorithms.

The algorithm for SHORTEST PATH described in Example 4.3 appeared in Ford and Fulkerson (1962). In fact, this algorithm solves the 'all-pairs' SHORTEST PATH problem since it succeeds in finding the shortest paths between any pair of nodes. For simplicity, we preferred it to the algorithm by Dijkstra (1959) which applies to the 'single-source' version of the problem. For further references on this and many other graph problems, see van Leeuwen (1990).

The algorithm for 2-SATISFIABILITY of Example 4.4 is due to Deming (1979). The best algorithm for the same problem has time-complexity $O[n + m]$ and was presented in Apsvall, Plass, and Tarjan (1979). Many other algorithms were proposed (and this problem is still receiving considerable attention). An experimental comparison of four such algorithms appeared in Petreschi and Simeone (1991).

Non-constructive polynomial-time is discussed in Fellows and Langston (1988) from which the KNOTLESSNESS problem was obtained. Further information on this problem can be found in Conway and Gordon (1983). The basic research, however, has been carried out since 1983 by Robertson and Seymour in a series of papers appearing in the *Journal of Combinatorial Theory (series B)* entitled 'Graph Minors N:...' with N ranging from I to XVI or more. Up to 1993, the two main results needed to establish non-constructive polynomial-time for graph problems, namely a positive solution to Wagner's conjecture and a (constructive) polynomial-time algorithm for a graph problem denoted as H-MINOR CONTAINMENT, were proved for graphs embeddable on surfaces of limited genus and for fixed planar graphs H, respectively. General proofs for arbitrary graphs were merely announced. In Friedman, Robertson, and Seymour (1987), by using a metamathematical proof technique it was shown that no algorithm capable of determining the minimum elements of an arbitrary class of graphs can be formulated in a significant subset of the system of second order arithmetic known as ATR_0 (the original proof refers to trees and a different minor relation). The above results motivated Abrahamson, Fellows, Langston, and Moret (1988) to propose a more restrictive and inherently constructive definition of the class P.

The simulation of a k-tape by a one-tape Turing machine (see Lemma 4.1) was first obtained in Hartmanis and Stearns (1965), while a proof of the simulation of a two-way infinite tape by a one-way infinite tape Turing machine (see Lemma 4.2) can be found in several textbooks. See, for instance, Lewis and Papadimitriou (1981).

Polynomial-time reducibility was first introduced by Karp (1972) as a special kind of m-reducibility. In that paper, several polynomial-time reductions between difficult combinatorial problems were shown, strongly suggesting, but not implying, that these problems, as well as many others, will remain perpetually intractable. Most reducibilities introduced in computability theory have a polynomial-time bounded version. In Ladner, Lynch, and Selman (1975) various forms of such reducibilities were compared and the effect of introducing nondeterminism into reduction procedures was also examined.

The simple reduction from the maximum matching problem to the maximum flow one is described in several textbooks on algorithms such as that by Cormen,

Leiserson, and Rivest (1990).

The theorem on uniform diagonalization was first proved for a specific case in Ladner (1975a). The definition of G_r and its application was introduced in Landweber, Lipton, and Robertson (1981), while the full Theorem 4.1 was proved in Schöning (1982a). Finally, further generalizations of such a theorem are considered in Schmidt (1985).

Chapter 5

The class NP

Here we are concerned with an important complexity class called NP that includes problems that are harder to solve than those considered in the previous chapter. This new class is a natural extension of class P obtained by replacing deterministic algorithms with nondeterministic ones.

Clearly, P ⊆ NP (deterministic algorithms can be considered a restriction of nondeterministic ones). Is it correct to state that P is properly included in NP? This problem, the P ≠ NP *conjecture*, was raised about 20 years ago and is still unsolved. In fact, solving it in the near future seems rather remote.

Intuitively, nondeterministic polynomial-time algorithms appear to be more powerful than deterministic ones since they make use of a machine capable of performing several (deterministic) computations at the same time. It is true that, according to Theorem 2.1, any nondeterministic polynomial-time algorithm can be transformed into a deterministic one. However, the resulting algorithm has an exponential-time complexity.

If P = NP, then, for any nondeterministic polynomial-time algorithm, an equivalent deterministic polynomial-time one exists. This statement, which is much more powerful than Theorem 2.1, is unfortunately contradicted by experimental evidence. In fact, for hundreds of NP problems arising in numerous areas such as graph theory, network design, algebra and number theory, game theory, logic, automata and language theory, no deterministic polynomial-time algorithm capable of solving any of them, without exploring the entire space of possible solutions or an exponentially sized part of it, is known.

In any case, proving or disproving the P ≠ NP conjecture would be of great significance from a practical point of view. On the one hand, a disproof of the conjecture would mean that any exhaustive search algorithm solving an NP problem in exponential time can be systematically replaced by a sophisticated polynomial-time algorithm and we have already observed how substantial is the difference between the two approaches (in other words, proving P = NP implies a 'low' upper bound on the complexity of hundreds of problems). On the other hand, if P ≠ NP, then

69

a superpolynomial lower bound would follow for as many problems, that is, the 'most difficult' ones in NP.

In Section 5.1 the new class NP is defined and a few examples of NP problems are given. In Section 5.2 problems in NP which are complete with respect to polynomial-time reducibility, in short NP-complete problems, are introduced and some of the structural properties of such problems are analysed. In Section 5.3 it is proved that if P is properly included in NP, then NP must include a class of languages which are neither in P nor NP-complete. In Section 5.4 the relative complexities of computing and verifying a function are investigated. Finally, in Section 5.5 extensions of the P $\neq$ NP conjecture to oracle Turing machines are considered which bring some insight into the intrinsic difficulty of solving this conjecture.

5.1   The class NP   *Non-deterministic Turing machines*

Let NTIME$[p_k(n)]$ be the nondeterministic time-complexity class with $p_k(n) = n^k$. The *class NP* is defined as

$$NP = \bigcup_{k \geq 0} NTIME[p_k(n)]$$

Many problems of practical importance, which have been extensively investigated by researchers and for which no deterministic polynomial-time algorithm has been found, belong to NP.

Example 5.1 SATISFIABILITY is a generalization of 2-SATISFIABILITY introduced in Example 4.4 where each clause C_i may include any number of literals rather than exactly two.

A nondeterministic algorithm for SATISFIABILITY can be obtained by guessing any of the 2^n assignments of values to the n variables of f and verifying whether it satisfies f:

begin {input: f}
    guess t **in** set of assignments of values to the n variables of f;
    if t satisfies f **then** accept **else** reject;
end.

Since both the guessing and the checking of the ith assignment can be done in polynomial time, it turns out that such a nondeterministic algorithm is a polynomial-time one.[1]

Example 5.2 3-COLORABILITY is a generalization of 2-COLORABILITY introduced in Example 4.8 where the colours available are three instead of two.

---

[1]A nondeterministic algorithm is said to be polynomial-time if the required number of steps is $O[n^k]$ with k constant.

A polynomial-time nondeterministic algorithm for 3-COLORABILITY can be obtained by guessing any of the 3^n colourings of a graph of n nodes and verifying whether it has the required property.

Example 5.3 TRAVELING SALESMAN: given a complete weighted graph G and a natural number k, does a cycle exist passing through all nodes of G such that the sum of the weights associated with the edges of the cycle is, at most, k?

A polynomial-time nondeterministic algorithm for TRAVELING SALESMAN can be obtained by guessing any of the $n!$ permutations of n nodes and verifying whether it corresponds to a cycle whose cost is, at most, k.

The richness of the class NP is justified by the following theorem. This intuitively states that a problem belongs to this class if and only if the possible solutions are words of a length polynomially related to the length of the instance and it is polynomial-time decidable whether a possible solution is a feasible one. (Note that most of the combinatorial problems we usually encounter share this property.)

Theorem 5.1 A language L belongs to NP if and only if a language $L_{\text{check}} \in \text{P}$ and a polynomial p exist such that

$$L = \{x : \exists y[\langle x, y \rangle \in L_{\text{check}} \wedge |y| \leq p(|x|)]\}.$$

Proof. If $L = \{x : \exists y[\langle x, y \rangle \in L_{\text{check}} \wedge |y| \leq p(|x|)]\}$ where $L_{\text{check}} \in \text{P}$ and p is a polynomial, then the following nondeterministic algorithm decides L in polynomial time:

begin {input: x}
    guess y **in** set of words of length, at most, $p(|x|)$;
    if $\langle x, y \rangle \in L_{\text{check}}$ **then** accept **else** reject;
end.

Conversely, let L be a language in NP. Then a nondeterministic Turing machine NT exists which decides L in polynomial time. It is easy to verify that, for any x, each computation path of $NT(x)$ can be encoded into a word of a length of, at most, $p(|x|)$ where p is a polynomial (see Problem 2.7). The language L_{check} is then defined as follows. $\langle x, y \rangle \in L_{\text{check}}$ if and only if y encodes an accepting computation path of $NT(x)$. It is clear that $L_{\text{check}} \in \text{P}$ and that, for any x,

$$x \in L \leftrightarrow \exists y[|y| \leq p(|x|) \wedge \langle x, y \rangle \in L_{\text{check}}].$$

This concludes the proof.   □

Our aim is to identify within NP problems that are inherently more complex. For this, we need the basic concept of an NP-complete problem.

5.2   NP-complete languages

We have already introduced the polynomial-time reducibility $\leq$ in Section 4.3. We now show that NP includes some languages that are complete with respect to $\leq$, in short, NP-complete languages. As usual, we shall say informally that a problem is NP-complete if the corresponding language is also NP-complete.

By reasoning as in Section 3.2.1, we can identify NPC, the class of NP-complete problems, with the set of problems which are likely members of NP $-$ P. Since P is closed with respect to $\leq$, even if only one of them were solvable in polynomial time by means of a deterministic Turing machine, then all problems in NP would share this property.

How does one show that a problem is NP-complete and, more generally, how does one prove that a complexity class $\mathcal{C}$ admits a complete language L with respect to a given reducibility? Since $\mathcal{C}$ is defined by referring to a model of computation with some resource bound (in the case of NP, the model is the nondeterministic Turing machine and the resource bound is polynomial time), then, for any language $L' \in \mathcal{C}$, we are allowed to refer to a resource-bounded machine M which decides L'. The approach taken is then the following. We derive a reduction f which, given M and an input x, computes a word $f(M, x)$ such that M accepts x if and only if $f(M, x) \in L$. We can then claim that L' is reducible to L and since L' is an arbitrary language in $\mathcal{C}$, L is $\mathcal{C}$-complete.

That is the general aim. Let us now fill in the details by presenting our first completeness proof. The following important theorem obtained by Cook in 1971 shows that NP admits a complete language (with respect to polynomial-time reducibility).

Theorem 5.2 SATISFIABILITY is NP-complete.

Proof. Let L be a language in NP and NT be a nondeterministic Turing machine which decides L in time bounded by a polynomial p. Thus NT accepts a word x of L in, at most, $p(|x|)$ steps.

Denote the symbols of the tape alphabet used by NT by $\sigma_1, \sigma_2, \ldots, \sigma_h$ and the states by $q_1, q_2, \ldots, q_k$. Without loss of generality, we assume that q_1 is the initial state, q_2 is the accepting state and q_3 is the rejecting one. We shall also assume that, initially, the input x is contained in the first $n = |x|$ leftmost cells.

Denote also the maximum number of steps that can be executed by the computation $NT(x)$ with $t^* = p(n)$. Thus, no cell beyond the t^*th will ever be scanned during the computation.

The basic aim is to construct, for any x, a Boolean formula f_x whose assignments of values are, in a certain sense, able to 'simulate' the computation $NT(x)$. In particular, f_x will be satisfiable if and only if NT accepts x.

The formula f_x will make use of the following Boolean variables:

1. $P_{s,t}^i$ is **true** if and only if the sth cell contains the symbol σ_i at time t, that is, when the tth instruction is executed ($1 \leq i \leq h, 1 \leq s \leq t^*, 1 \leq t \leq t^*$).

2. Q_t^i is **true** if and only if NT is in state q_i at time t ($1 \leq i \leq k, 1 \leq t \leq t^*$).
3. $S_{s,t}$ is **true** if and only if the tape head of NT scans the sth cell at time t ($1 \leq s \leq t^*, 1 \leq t \leq t^*$).

Formula f_x is a conjunction of eight main subformulas:

$$f_x = A \wedge B \wedge C \wedge D \wedge E \wedge F \wedge G \wedge H.$$

Subformula A states that, at any time t, the tape head scans exactly one cell. Thus

$$A = A_1 \wedge A_2 \wedge \ldots \wedge A_{t^*}$$

where[2]

$$A_t = (S_{1,t} \vee S_{2,t} \vee \ldots \vee S_{t^*,t}) \wedge (\bigcap_{(i,j)} : 1 \leq i < t^*, i < j \leq t^*)[S_{i,t} \to \neg S_{j,t}].$$

Subformula B states that, at any time t, each cell s contains exactly one symbol. Thus

$$B = B_{1,1} \wedge \ldots \wedge B_{t^*,1} \wedge B_{1,2} \wedge \ldots \wedge B_{t^*,2} \wedge \ldots \wedge B_{1,t^*} \wedge \ldots \wedge B_{t^*,t^*}$$

where

$$B_{s,t} = (P_{s,t}^1 \vee \ldots \vee P_{s,t}^h) \wedge (\bigcap_{(i,j)} : 1 \leq i < h, i < j \leq h)[P_{s,t}^i \to \neg P_{s,t}^j].$$

Subformula C states that, at any time t, the machine NT must be in exactly one internal state. Thus

$$C = C_1 \wedge C_2 \wedge \ldots \wedge C_{t^*}$$

where

$$C_t = (Q_t^1 \vee \ldots \vee Q_t^k) \wedge (\bigcap_{(i,j)} : 1 \leq i < k, i < j \leq k)[Q_t^i \to \neg Q_t^j].$$

Subformula D states that, initially, the input is contained in the first n cells of the tape, the head is positioned on the leftmost cell and the internal state of NT is the initial one. Thus

$$D = Q_1^1 \wedge S_{1,1} \wedge P_{1,1}^{i_1} \wedge \ldots \wedge P_{n,1}^{i_n} \wedge P_{n+1,1}^h \wedge \ldots \wedge P_{t^*,1}^h$$

where $x = \sigma_{i_1} \sigma_{i_2} \ldots \sigma_{i_n}$.
Subformula E states that, at any time t, the values Q_t^i are correctly updated according to the control (the quintuples) of NT.

---

[2]For clarity, we make use of the $\to$ connective defined as $u \to v \equiv \neg u \vee v$.

Subformulas F and G state that, at any time t and for each of the t^* cells, the values $P_{s,t}^i$ and $S_{s,t}$ are updated correctly according to the control of NT.

Subformulas E, F, and G depend on the control of NT and cannot be expressed in a general way. Let us show with an example how they can be derived.

Example 5.4 Assume that the control of NT includes two quintuples $\langle q_i, \sigma_j, \sigma_{j_1}, m_1, q_{i_1} \rangle$ and $\langle q_i, \sigma_j, \sigma_{j_2}, m_2, q_{i_2} \rangle$ which have the first two elements in common. Such quintuples are modeled by the implication

$$(q_i, \sigma_j) \to (\sigma_{j_1}, m_1, q_{i_1}) \vee (\sigma_{j_2}, m_2, q_{i_2}).$$

Since the quintuples of Turing machines are *invariant* with respect to the time and the scanned cell, the previous implication must be instantiated for each t and s with $1 \le s, t \le t^*$, yielding corresponding clauses of subformulas E, F, and G.

With respect to a given time instant t and a given tape cell s, the subclause of E referring to the two above-mentioned quintuples is

$$Q_t^i \wedge P_{s,t}^j \to (Q_t^{i_1} \wedge Q_t^{i_2}).$$

The subclause of F referring to the two above-mentioned quintuples is

$$Q_t^i \wedge P_{s,t}^j \to (P_{s,t+1}^{j_1} \wedge P_{s,t+1}^{j_2}).$$

Similarly, if we assume $m_1 = L$ and $m_2 = R$, the subclause of G is

$$Q_t^i \wedge P_{s,t}^j \to (S_{s-1,t+1} \wedge S_{s+1,t+1}).$$

Finally, subformula H states that NT reaches the accepting state q_2 at the latest at time t^*, that is, within t^* instructions. Thus

$$H = Q_1^2 \vee Q_2^2 \vee \ldots \vee Q_{t^*}^2.$$

If x is accepted by NT within t^* instructions, then it is easy to derive from the computation $NT(x)$ an assignment of values to the sets of variables $P_{s,t}^i, Q_t^i$ and $S_{s,t}$ which satisfies f_x. Such an assignment gives the value **true** to Q_1^1, $S_{1,1}$, $P_{1,1}^{i_1}, \ldots, P_{n,1}^{i_n}, P_{n+1,1}^h, \ldots, P_{t^*,1}^h$. The value **false** is assigned to any other variable whose time index is equal to 1. For any $t > 1$, the values of the variables are then assigned according to the tth step of the computation $NT(x)$. Since NT accepts x within t^* steps, a $t \le t^*$ exists such that the variable Q_t^2 has been assigned the value **true**.

Conversely, from an assignment of values satisfying the formula, it is easy to derive an accepting computation path of $NT(x)$.

The time required to compute f_x from x is clearly polynomial with respect to the length of x; thus, $L \le$ SATISFIABILITY. Since L is an arbitrary language in NP, it follows that SATISFIABILITY is NP-complete. $\qquad\square$

Let us add a few comments to the theorem just proved. Even if SATISFIABILITY was the first NP problem to which it was possible to reduce polynomially all decision problems in NP, several other problems have been discovered for which such a reduction can be carried out in a simple and natural way (see Notes).

Following Cook's result, several other proofs of completeness with respect to different complexity classes have been obtained. In Chapters 7 and 8 we shall encounter other completeness proofs of the same type.

5.2.1 NP-completeness proofs

Now that a first NP-complete problem has been derived, it is possible to prove the NP-completeness of other problems by exploiting the transitive property of polynomial-time reducibility. More precisely, an alternative way to prove the NP-completeness of a problem Π is the following:

1. Show that Π belongs to NP.
2. Find a problem Π' already known to be NP-complete such that $\Pi' \leq \Pi$.

Starting from SATISFIABILITY and using the above approach, hundreds of decision problems, which are significant from both a practical and a theoretical point of view, have been shown to be NP-complete.

Due to lack of space, we will give only a few examples of NP-completeness proofs. The first is a typical example of a 'component design' reduction from SATISFIABILITY. In such reductions, the instance of the new problem is generally formed by three kinds of components: a truth-assignment component, a satisfaction-testing component and a communication component between the two previous ones.

Example 5.5 NODE COVER: given a graph $G = (N, E)$ and a natural number k, does G include a cover of, at most, k nodes, that is, a subset $M \subseteq N$ of, at most, k nodes such that, for each edge $\langle i, j \rangle \in E$, at least, one of the two nodes i and j is included in M?

It is clear that NODE COVER belongs to NP. To prove the NP-completeness of such a problem, we will define a polynomial-time reduction from SATISFIABILITY to NODE COVER. This reduction transforms a conjunctive normal form Boolean formula f into a graph G along with a natural number k so that f is satisfiable if and only if G admits a cover of, at most, k nodes.

Denote by $x_1, x_2, \ldots, x_n$ the variables of f, with m the number of clauses and n_i ($1 \leq i \leq m$) the number of literals of the ith clause. Let us derive a graph $G = (N, E)$ from f as follows:

1. For any variable x_i in f, G contains a pair of nodes x_i^t and x_i^f which are joined by an edge. Thus, to cover such an edge one of the two nodes is necessary and sufficient: intuitively, the chosen node will denote the value assigned to the variable x_i.

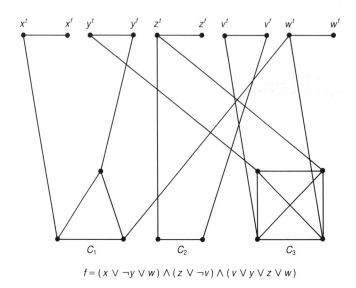

$$f = (\,x \vee \neg y \vee w\,) \wedge (\,z \vee \neg v\,) \wedge (\,v \vee y \vee z \vee w\,)$$

Figure 5.1 An example of reduction from SATISFIABILITY to NODE COVER

2. For any clause C_j, G contains a complete subgraph G_j of n_j nodes, each node corresponding to a literal of the clause. Thus, to cover the edges of such a clique $n_j - 1$ nodes are necessary and sufficient. Intuitively, the remaining node will denote a literal of the clause that has been assigned the value **true**.

3. Finally, some connection edges between pairs and cliques: for any variable x_i and for any clause C_j, if x_i (respectively, $\neg x_i$) is a literal contained in C_j, then G contains the edge between x_i^t (respectively, x_i^f) and the node of G_j corresponding to that literal.

Figure 5.1 shows an application of the above transformation to a simple example.

It is easy to verify that the transformation can be done in polynomial time and that f is satisfiable if and only if G admits a cover of k nodes where

$$k = n + (n_1 - 1) + (n_2 - 1) + \ldots + (n_m - 1).$$

Indeed, if f is satisfiable, then a cover can be derived by an assignment of values satisfying f in the following way:

1. For any variable x_i, select node x_i^t if x_i has been assigned the value **true**, otherwise select node x_i^f.

2. For each clause C_j, select all the n_j nodes of G_j except one among those joined by an edge to a node already selected in the previous step (since the assignment satisfies f, it follows that, at least, one such node must exist).

Conversely, if G admits a cover of k nodes, then an assignment of values satisfying f can be derived by giving, for any variable x_i, the value **true** to x_i if x_i^t belongs to the cover, otherwise the value **false**. To confirm that such an assignment satisfies f, note that, for any clause C_j, only $n_j - 1$ connection edges can be covered by a node in G_j. The remaining one must be covered by a node of some pair. But this implies that the corresponding literal has been assigned the value **true**, hence clause C_j is satisfied.

A simpler kind of reduction is so-called 'local replacement' in which distinct basic components of the original problem are transformed independently of each other. The following example should clarify this point.

Example 5.6 3-SATISFIABILITY: given a Boolean formula in conjunctive normal form such that each clause contains exactly three literals, does an assignment of values exist which satisfies f?

Once again, it is clear that such a problem belongs to NP. To prove that it is NP-complete, we will define a local replacement reduction from SATISFIABILITY to 3-SATISFIABILITY. In this case, the basic components of the original problem are the clauses of the instance of SATISFIABILITY which will be transformed in a set of 'equivalent' clauses containing exactly three literals. More precisely, let C_i be any clause of the instance of SATISFIABILITY. Then C_i is tranformed into the following subformula C_i':

1. If $C_i = l_{i_1}$, then $C_i' = l_{i_1} \vee l_{i_1} \vee l_{i_1}$.

2. If $C_i = l_{i_1} \vee l_{i_2}$, then $C_i' = l_{i_1} \vee l_{i_2} \vee l_{i_1}$.

3. If $C_i = l_{i_1} \vee l_{i_2} \vee l_{i_3}$, then $C_i' = l_{i_1} \vee l_{i_2} \vee l_{i_3}$.

4. If $C_i = l_{i_1} \vee l_{i_2} \vee \ldots \vee l_{i_k}$ with $k > 3$, then $C_i' = (l_{i_1} \vee l_{i_2} \vee y_{i_1}) \wedge (\neg y_{i_1} \vee l_{i_3} \vee y_{i_2}) \wedge \ldots \wedge (\neg y_{i_{k-4}} \vee l_{i_{k-2}} \vee y_{i_{k-3}}) \wedge (\neg y_{i_{k-3}} \vee l_{i_{k-1}} \vee l_{i_k})$, where the y variables are new ones.

Clearly, such a reduction can be done in polynomial time.

First, we will show that any assignment t of values satisfying C_i can be extended to an assignment t' of values to the new variables satisfying C_i' (note how we use the locality of the reduction). This is trivially true whenever C_i contains, at most, three literals. Suppose $C_i = l_{i_1} \vee l_{i_2} \vee \ldots \vee l_{i_k}$ with $k > 3$. Since t satisfies C_i then a literal l_{i_j} exists which has been assigned the value **true**. We then assign values to the additional variables depending on the index j:

1. $j = 1, 2$: l_{i_j} occurs in a clause with the form $(l_{i_1} \vee l_{i_2} \vee y_{i_1})$; in this case, all the ys are assigned the value **false**.

2. $j = k - 1, k$: l_{i_j} occurs in a clause with the form $(\neg y_{i_{k-3}} \vee l_{i_{k-1}} \vee l_{i_k})$; in this case, all the ys are assigned the value **true**.

3. $2 < j < k - 1$: l_{i_j} occurs in a clause with the form $(\neg y_{i_{j-2}} \vee l_{i_j} \vee y_{i_{j-1}})$; in this case, the first $j - 2$ variables ys are assigned the value **true** while the remaining ones are assigned the value **false**.

It is easy to verify that such an extension satisfies all the clauses in C'_i. Conversely, given an assignment of values which satisfies C'_i, it is easy to verify that the same assignment, when restricted to the original variables, satisfies the clause C_i.

In conclusion, the original formula is satisfiable if and only if the transformed formula is satisfiable. That is, 3-SATISFIABILITY is NP-complete.

As has already been stated, hundreds of NP-complete languages have been found. It is not surprising therefore that some of the new problems which arise in practice appear to be very similar to NP-complete problems already known.

Example 5.7 CLIQUE: given a graph $G = (N, E)$ and a natural number k, does G include a clique of, at least, k nodes?

An easy polynomial-time reduction from NODE COVER to CLIQUE is based on the following observations. Given a graph $G = (N, E)$, let $G^c = (N, E^c)$ be the *complement* graph of G with $E^c = \{\langle u, v \rangle : u, v \in N \wedge \langle u, v \rangle \notin E\}$. It is easy to verify that, for any subset N' of N, N' is a node cover for G if and only if $N - N'$ is a clique in G^c. Thus the reduction transforms an instance $\langle G, k \rangle$ of NODE COVER into the instance $\langle G^c, |N| - k \rangle$ of CLIQUE. In conclusion, this latter problem is NP-complete.

Finally, sometimes the new problem is simply a more complicated version of an already known problem. The NP-completeness of the latter is thus a proof of the NP-completeness of the former: this kind of reduction is called reduction by 'restriction'.

Example 5.8 HITTING SET: given a collection C of subsets of a set A and an integer k, does A contain a subset A' with $|A'| \leq k$ such that A' contains, at least, one element from each subset in C?

This problem belongs to NP and it can be restricted to NODE COVER. Indeed, it is sufficient to allow instances where each subset in C contains exactly two elements (intuitively, A corresponds to the set N of nodes of the graph and C to set E of edges).

In conclusion, whenever the NP-completeness of a new problem needs to be proved a tentative strategy could be the following. First, look for an NP-complete problem which is very similar to the one in hand (if not the same!). Second, if one is not found, look for a similar problem and try a reduction by local replacement. Finally, if neither of the two previous steps has been successful, then try a component design reduction (which in most cases considers the SATISFIABILITY problem as the starting one). Obviously, sometimes even this latter step does not succeed. If this is the case, remember that the problem could be polynomial-time solvable, after all!

5.2.2 Isomorphism among NP-complete languages

In spite of a rich variety of NP-complete languages from different areas, an important result of complexity theory states that all these languages are substantially identical, namely, they are identical up to a polynomial-time computable permutation of their elements. In this section we will investigate this in detail.

Two languages A and B are *p-isomorphic* when a function f exists such that

1. $x \in A \leftrightarrow f(x) \in B$.
2. f is bijective.
3. $f, f^{-1} \in \text{FP}$.

Note that if A and B are two NP-complete languages, then $A \leq B$ through f and $B \leq A$ through g where both f and g are polynomial-time computable functions. In general, however, $g \neq f^{-1}$, that is, the existence of f and g does not imply that A and B are p-isomorphic. In which cases does such p-isomorphism exist? Before answering this question, let us introduce a preliminary definition.

A function $f : \Sigma^* \to \Gamma^*$ is *length-increasing* if, for each $x \in \Sigma^*$, $|f(x)| > |x|$. Similarly, f is *length decreasing* if, for each $x \in \Sigma^*$, $|x| > |f(x)|$.

The following theorem gives a set of sufficient conditions for the p-isomorphism between pairs of languages.

Theorem 5.3 Consider two languages $A \subseteq \Sigma^*$ and $B \subseteq \Gamma^*$ with two polynomial-time computable functions $f : \Sigma^* \to \Gamma^*$ and $g : \Gamma^* \to \Sigma^*$ which implement $A \leq B$ and $B \leq A$, respectively. If f and g are length increasing and if they admit polynomial-time computable inverse functions f^{-1} and g^{-1}, then A and B are p-isomorphic.

Proof. Our goal is to derive a polynomial-time reduction $h : \Sigma^* \to \Gamma^*$ from f and g which admits a polynomial-time inverse reduction $h^{-1} : \Gamma^* \to \Sigma^*$. For this purpose, let us partition Σ^* into R_1 and R_2 and Γ^* into S_1 and S_2 in the following way.

Given a word $x \in \Sigma^*$, $x \in R_1$ if an integer $k \geq 0$ exists such that the composition $(f^{-1} \circ g^{-1})^k$ applied to x is defined while, for the same x, $g^{-1} \circ (f^{-1} \circ g^{-1})^k$ is undefined.[3] Conversely, $x \in R_2$ if an integer $k \geq 0$ exists such that the composition $g^{-1} \circ (f^{-1} \circ g^{-1})^k$ applied to x is defined while, for the same x, $(f^{-1} \circ g^{-1})^{k+1}$ is undefined. As shown in Figure 5.2, x belongs to R_1 (respectively, R_2) if the longest feasible composition of g^{-1} and f^{-1} transforms it into a word in Σ^* (respectively, Γ^*). In fact, the figure also suggests one of the basic properties of this procedure. If we leave R_1 (respectively, R_2) we never enter R_2 (respectively, R_1). The reader should try to understand why this is so (we are going to prove it in any case!).

---

[3]Remember that if a function h is undefined for a given input, then the corresponding computation does not terminate. Thus if h is polynomial-time computable, it is possible to decide in polynomial time, for each x, whether $h(x)$ is undefined.

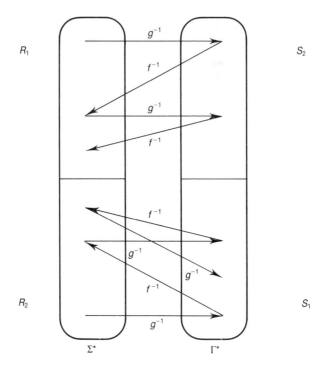

Figure 5.2 Partition of Σ^* and Γ^*

Similarly, given a word $y \in \Gamma^*$, $y \in S_1$ if an integer $k \geq 0$ exists such that the composition $(g^{-1} \circ f^{-1})^k$ applied to x is defined while, for the same x, $f^{-1} \circ (g^{-1} \circ f^{-1})^k$ is undefined. Conversely, $y \in S_2$ if $k \geq 0$ exists such that the composition $f^{-1} \circ (g^{-1} \circ f^{-1})^k$ is defined while $(g^{-1} \circ f^{-1})^{k+1}$ applied to the same x is undefined.

Since f and g are length-increasing f^{-1} and g^{-1} are length-decreasing, thus, for each $x \in \Sigma^*$, we can decide in polynomial time whether x belongs to R_1 or to R_2. Similarly, for each $y \in \Gamma^*$, we can decide in polynomial time whether y belongs to S_1 or to S_2.

We are now ready to define function h as

$$h(x) = \begin{cases} f(x) & \text{if } x \in R_1, \\ g^{-1}(x) & \text{if } x \in R_2, \end{cases}$$

while the inverse function h^{-1} will be defined as

$$h^{-1}(y) = \begin{cases} g(y) & \text{if } y \in S_1, \\ f^{-1}(y) & \text{if } y \in S_2. \end{cases}$$

By assumption, f and g implement $A \leq B$ and $B \leq A$, respectively. Then, for any x, $x \in A \leftrightarrow h(x) \in B$. Furthermore, since f, g, f^{-1} and g^{-1} are polynomial-time computable and since R_1, R_2, S_1 and S_2 are polynomial-time decidable, then h and h^{-1} are polynomial-time computable.

Let us now show that, for each $x \in \Sigma^*$, $h^{-1}(h(x)) = x$ and that, for each $y \in \Gamma^*$, $h(h^{-1}(y)) = y$. Note that if $x \in R_1$, then $f(x) \in S_2$. Indeed, if $f(x) \in S_1$, then an integer $k \geq 0$ exists such that $(g^{-1} \circ f^{-1})^k[f(x)]$ is defined while $f^{-1} \circ (g^{-1} \circ f^{-1})^k[f(x)]$ is undefined. This, in turn, implies that $g^{-1} \circ (f^{-1} \circ g^{-1})^{k-1}$ applied to x is defined while, for the same x, $(f^{-1} \circ g^{-1})^k$ is undefined, that is, $x \in R_2$ contradicting the hypothesis on x. By the same argument, we can show that if $x \in R_2$ then $f(x) \in S_1$, that if $y \in S_1$ then $g(y) \in R_2$ and that if $y \in S_2$ then $g(y) \in R_1$ (that is why the figure has been drawn that way). By the definitions of h and h^{-1}, it thus follows that h^{-1} is the inverse function of h.

Thus, A and B are p-isomorphic. □

The following theorem shows how to derive polynomial-time reductions which admit polynomial-time inverse functions.

Theorem 5.4 Given two languages A, B and a polynomial-time reduction f from A to B, assume that B admits two polynomial-time computable functions p_B and d_B such that

1. $(\forall x, y)[p_B(x, y) \in B \leftrightarrow x \in B]$.
2. $(\forall x, y)[d_B(p_B(x, y)) = y]$.

Then the function $g(x) = p_B(f(x), x)$ is a polynomial-time reduction from A to B which admits a polynomial-time computable inverse function.

Proof. Function p_B is a 'padding' function used to encode any word y along with x in such a way that the compound word belongs to B if and only if x belongs to B; d_B plays the role of a 'decoding' function able to extract y from the composition of x and y through p_B.

We first show that g is actually a polynomial-time reduction from A to B. Indeed, $x \in A$ if and only if $f(x) \in B$ if and only if $p_B(f(x), x) = g(x) \in B$. Furthermore, in accordance with our assumptions on f and p_B, it follows that g is polynomial-time computable.

Next, it is clear that g is injective. Indeed, if $g(x) = g(y)$ then

$$x = d_B(p_B(f(x), x)) = d_B(g(x)) = d_B(g(y)) = d_B(p_B(f(y), y)) = y.$$

Finally, let us define g^{-1} as follows:

$$g^{-1}(x) = \begin{cases} d_B(z) & \text{if } z = p_B(f(d_B(z)), d_B(z)), \\ \text{undefined} & \text{otherwise.} \end{cases}$$

It is easily verifiable that, for each x, $g(x) = p_B(f(d_B(g(x))), d_B(g(x)))$ and thus $g^{-1}(g(x)) = d_B(g(x)) = x$. Conversely, for any $z = g(x)$, $g(g^{-1}(z)) = g(d_B(g(x))) = g(x) = z$. Since both f, p_B and d_B are polynomial-time computable, then g^{-1} is polynomial-time computable. $\square$

By combining Theorems 5.3 and 5.4, we have a powerful tool for proving the p-isomorphism between pairs of NP-complete languages.

Corollary 5.1 Two NP-complete languages A and B are p-isomorphic if both of them admit a polynomial-time computable length-increasing padding function and a corresponding polynomial-time computable decoding function.

Example 5.9 Let us show that SATISFIABILITY and NODE COVER are p-isomorphic. Let $y = b_1 b_2 \ldots b_q$ be the word to encode (without loss of generality, we assume that y consists of q binary symbols b_i).

A padding function for SATISFIABILITY can be obtained by transforming an n-variable Boolean formula f into an $(n + q + 1)$-variable Boolean formula f' in the following way:

$$f' = f \wedge (x_{n+1} \vee \neg x_{n+1}) \wedge l_1 \wedge \ldots \wedge l_q$$

where, for any $i \leq q$, $l_i = x_{n+1+i}$ if $b_i = 1$, otherwise $l_i = \neg x_{n+1+i}$. It is clear that f is satisfiable if and only if f' is satisfiable. Note also that the new clauses are attached to f so that they can be easily distinguished from the original ones and thus decoding y from the padded formula is ensured.

Analogously, a padding function for NODE COVER can be obtained by transforming an n-node graph G into an $(n + 2q + 3)$-node graph G' in the following way:

$$E' = E \cup \{\langle x_{n+1}, x_{n+2}\rangle, \langle x_{n+1}, x_{n+3}\rangle, \langle x_{n+2}, x_{n+3}\rangle\} \cup \{\langle x_{n+2i+2}, x_{n+2i+3}\rangle : b_i = 1\}.$$

It is clear that G admits a cover of, at most, k nodes if and only if G' admits a cover of, at most, $k + n_1 + 2$ nodes where n_1 denotes the number of 1s in y. As in the previous case, decoding y from the padded graph is ensured.

What has been shown for SATISFIABILITY and NODE COVER is true for all known NP-complete languages. Indeed, all such languages admit pairs of padding and decoding functions which are polynomial-time computable. At the same time, no NP-complete language has been found having the property of being not p-isomorphic to other known NP-complete languages. This fact induced Hartmanis and Berman to formulate the so-called *p-isomorphism conjecture*: all NP-complete languages are p-isomorphic.

The next theorem shows, however, that proving such a conjecture is not an easy task.

Theorem 5.5 If all NP-complete languages are pairwise p-isomorphic, then P $\neq$ NP.

Proof. Assume P = NP and, in particular, P = NPC; then every non-empty finite set (which belongs to P) would be NP-complete. But a finite set cannot be isomorphic to an infinite one (such as SATISFIABILITY). □

The p-isomorphism conjecture might also be found to be false and NP-complete languages which are not p-isomorphic to SATISFIABILITY may exist (although they are not likely to be 'natural' languages). In fact, the counter-conjecture has also been formulated along with some convincing arguments (see Notes).

Finally, note that even if we focused our discussion on NP-complete languages, the above considerations can also be applied to simpler languages, namely languages in P. Although some languages in P seem too 'poor' to admit padding and decoding functions (for example, no finite language can admit such functions), languages do exist in P which admit them (see Problem 5.17).

5.2.3 NP-completeness of sparse languages

All known NP-complete languages are 'dense' languages. In fact, the census function of any known NP-complete language grows exponentially with the word length (see Problem 5.18 as an example). On the other hand, the p-isomorphism conjecture holds only if the census functions of all NP-complete languages are polynomially related as clarified by the following lemma.

Lemma 5.1 Let L_1 and L_2 be two p-ismorphic languages. Then two polynomials p_1 and p_2 exist such that, for any n,

$$c_{L_1}(n) \leq c_{L_2}(p_1(n)) \qquad \text{and} \qquad c_{L_2}(n) \leq c_{L_1}(p_2(n)).$$

Proof. Denote by f the p-isomorphism between L_1 and L_2 and let p_1 be the polynomial limiting the computation time of f. Then, for any word x of length n, $|f(x)| \leq p_1(n)$. Since f is injective, it follows that the number of words in L_1 of length, at most, n cannot be greater than the number of words in L_2 of length, at most, $p_1(n)$, that is, $c_{L_1}(n) \leq c_{L_2}(p_1(n))$. The second inequality follows in a similar way. □

The previous lemma suggests a good way to disprove the p-isomorphism conjecture (if that is our goal): just look for a sparse NP-complete language. Furthermore, it would be useful from a practical point of view to have a sparse NP-complete language. Denote it by S and let L be any language in NP. According to the assumption, a polynomial-time reduction f from L to S exists. Then, for any given n, we could build a table containing all words of S of length, at most, $q(n)$ where q is a polynomial limiting the length of f. The size of such a table is, at most, $p(q(n))$ where p denotes a second polynomial witnessing the sparsity of S. We would then have obtained a polynomial size table including the images in S of all words in L of length, at most, n.

Once this table has been derived (the time required to build it is exponential in n since we have to test an exponential number of words), it would then become possible to decide in polynomial time whether any word of length, at most, n belongs to L.

Unfortunately, the result presented in this section shows that the existence of sparse NP-complete languages is very unlikely, and thus also that the existence of polynomial table-lookup algorithms for subsets of languages in NP is doubtful.

Theorem 5.6 If an NP-complete sparse language exists such that its census function is computable in polynomial time, then P = NP. (A census function c_L is said to be computable in polynomial time if a Turing transducer T exists which reads 0^n as input and computes $c_L(n)$ in polynomial time.)

Proof. Let S be an NP-complete sparse language whose census function c_S is computable in polynomial time. Denote by NT the nondeterministic Turing machine which decides S in polynomial time.

The following nondeterministic algorithm shows that the complement language S^c of S also belongs to NP:

begin {input: x}
  $n := |x|$;
  $k := c_S(n)$;
  guess $y_1, \ldots, y_k$ **in** set of k-tuples of distinct words
  each of which has length, at most, n;
  {check whether the guessed k-tuple coincides with $S_{\leq n}$}
  for $i = 1$ **to** k **do**
    if $NT(y_i)$ rejects **then** reject;
  {check if $x \in S_{\leq n}$}
  for $i = 1$ **to** k **do**
    if $y_i = x$ **then** reject;
  accept;
end.

It is easy to verify that the previous algorithm is a polynomial-time one and that it decides S^c. Thus $S^c \in$ NP.

Since S is NP-complete, then SATISFIABILITY$\leq S$ and $S^c \leq S$. According to the properties of polynomial-time reducibility (see Section 2.3.2 and Problem 4.18) it follows that SATISFIABILITY$^c \leq S$. The remaining part of the proof exploits this fact to show that SATISFIABILITY $\in$ P.

Let x be an instance of SATISFIABILITY. Consider the binary tree A_x defined as follows:

1. The root of A_x is labeled with x.
2. If a node is labeled with y, then its children's labels y_0 and y_1 are the two formulas obtained by setting the value of a variable of y, respectively, to **false** and to **true** and by performing all simplifications on y (see Figure 5.3).

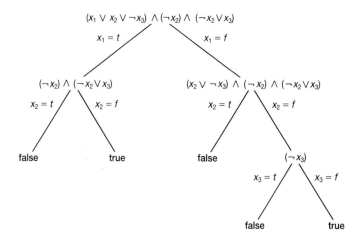

Figure 5.3 An example of a binary tree associated with a Boolean formula

Clearly x is satisfiable if and only if, at least, one leaf of A_x is labeled with **true**. However, A_x can contain up to $2^{n+1} - 1$ nodes where n denotes the number of variables of x. Thus visiting such a tree starting from the root and reaching all leaves would require exponential time in n.

For that reason, we shall use a 'pruning' strategy. Let f be a polynomial-time reduction from SATISFIABILITY^c to S. Whenever we visit a node labeled with y such that $f(y) \in S$, we can infer that y is not satisfiable and it serves no purpose to continue visiting the subtree having that node as root (for this reason, function f is also called a *pruning function*).

However, S is NP-complete and it is not obvious how to decide efficiently whether $f(y) \in S$. Indeed, we shall not decide it directly but we shall progressively build a list of words of S as the visiting of the tree proceeds. Instead of deciding whether $f(y) \in S$, we shall ask whether $f(y)$ belongs to that list.

Initially, the list contains only $f(\textbf{false})$. Successively, for each y such that both $f(y_0)$ and $f(y_1)$ belong to the list (thus neither y_0 nor y_1 are satisfiable), $f(y)$ is added to the list (since y is not satisfiable either). Note that since S is sparse, the list contains, at most, a polynomial number of words with respect to the length of x.

The algorithm to decide SATISFIABILITY is the following:

```
begin {input: x} {main program}
    list := {f(false)};
    if sat(x) then accept else reject;
end.
```

where the recursive function *sat* is defined as

```
function sat(y): Boolean;
begin
  if y = true then sat := true;
  if f(y) ∈ list then sat := false
  else
  begin
    derive y₀ and y₁ from y;
    if ¬sat(y₀) ∧ ¬sat(y₁) then
    begin
    {if both y₀ and y₁ are not satisfiable
    then y is not satisfiable}
      list := list ∪ {f(y)};
      sat := false;
    end
    else sat := true;
  end;
end;
```

Since all nodes of A_x are visited except those belonging to a subtree whose root is labeled with a formula already known to be not satisfiable, it follows that the algorithm correctly decides SATISFIABILITY.

To prove that the algorithm requires a polynomial number of steps, consider two unsatisfiable formulas y and z such that $f(y) = f(z)$ and such that the corresponding nodes are inner ones of the *visited subtree*, that is, they are not leaves of such a subtree. These two nodes must be contained in a common path from the root to one of the leaves. In fact, in the opposite case, one of them, for instance the node labeled y, would have been visited first, $f(y)$ would have been computed and added to the list and the search would have stopped at the node labeled z, contrary to the assumption that such a node is an inner one of the visited subtree.

As a consequence, the number of distinct paths from the root to the inner nodes of the visited subtree is, at most, $p(q(|x|))$ where p is a polynomial witnessing the sparsity of S and q is a polynomial limiting the length of f. Since A_x has height n, the visited subtree has, at most, $np(q(|x|))$ inner nodes labeled with non-satisfiable formulas. An assignment satisfying x may require the visit of $n-1$ additional inner nodes, thus the visited subtree includes, at most, $np(q(|x|)) + n - 1$ inner nodes. If we also consider the leaves, the number of visited nodes is twice as high but still polynomial. □

The proof of the previous theorem can be summarized by the following main points:

1. Given a census function for S *computable in polynomial time*, prove that $S^c \in NP$.

2. Using the previous result, reduce SATISFIABILITY^c to S^c and thus to S.
3. Using a reduction from SATISFIABILITY^c to S as a pruning function, visit the tree A_x of possible assignments for x and show that the pruning is drastic enough to cut the number of visited nodes from an exponential number to a polynomial one.

Notice how important the fact is that c_S, the census function of S, is computable in polynomial time.

Now assume that the first assumption of the previous theorem still holds but that it is no longer possible to compute c_S in polynomial time. Does the theorem still hold? The answer is yes and the approach taken to prove this stronger result consists of 'guessing' the correct value of the census function.

Theorem 5.7 If a sparse NP-complete language exists, then P = NP.

Proof. Let S be a sparse NP-complete language, p a polynomial witnessing the sparsity of S and NT a nondeterministic Turing machine which decides S in polynomial time.

Define the *pseudo-complement* of S as the set $PC(S)$ of triples $\langle x, k, 0^n \rangle$ accepted by the following algorithm:

begin {input: $x, k, 0^n$}
    if $|x| > n \lor k > p(n)$ **then** reject;
    guess $y_1, \ldots, y_k$ in set of k-tuples of distinct words
    each of which is of length, at most, n;
    for $i = 1$ **to** k **do**
        if $NT(y_i)$ rejects **then** reject;
    for $i = 1$ **to** k **do**
        if $y_i = x$ **then** reject;
    accept;
end.

Note that, for each triple $\langle x, k, 0^n \rangle$ such that $|x| \leq n$ and $k \leq p(n)$, the previous nondeterministic algorithm accepts if $k < c_S(n)$ or $k = c_S(n) \land x \in S^c$, otherwise it rejects. Thus, intuitively, if k is the correct value of $c_S(n)$, then the algorithm decides the complement of S. Furthermore, it is easy to verify that it requires polynomial time, that is, $PC(S) \in NP$.

Let us consider next how to select a suitable pruning function. In the proof of Theorem 5.6, the visited tree was pruned by using the polynomial-time reduction from SATISFIABILITY^c to S. Now, we shall use not just one but a polynomially sized set of pruning functions, one of which will be correct.

Let h and g be two reductions to S from SATISFIABILITY and from $PC(S)$, respectively (such reductions must exist since S is NP-complete). Denote by p_h and p_g two polynomials limiting the lengths of h and g, respectively.

Let x be an instance of SATISFIABILITY and let $m = p_h(|x|)$. For each formula y contained in the tree A_x, $|y| \leq |x|$, thus $|h(y)| \leq m$.

Notice that if $k = c_S(n)$, then for each unsatisfiable y of length, at most, n, $g(h(y), k, 0^m)$ must be included in S and we have obtained a reduction from SATISFIABILITY^c to S for words of up to length $|x|$. If, on the other hand, $k \neq c_S(n)$, then we cannot be certain that $g(h(y), k, 0^m)$ belongs to S.

For each n and for each $k \leq p(n)$, let us define $f_{n,k}(y) = g(h(y), k, 0^{p_h(n)})$. Clearly, for each k, function $f_{n,k}$ is computable in polynomial time with respect to the length of y. Furthermore, it follows from the previous considerations that y is not satisfiable if and only if $f_{n,c_S(n)}(y) \in S$.

If $k = c_S(n)$, then a constant c_1 depending on p and an integer n_0 exists such that $|\langle h(y), k, 0^{p_h(n)}\rangle| \leq 2n + c_1 \log n \leq 3n$, for all $n \geq n_0$. The unsatisfiable formulas of length, at most, n are then transformed from $f_{n,k}$ in, at most, $p(p_g(3n))$ distinct words of S, for each $n \geq n_0$.

The tree-visiting algorithm described in the proof of Theorem 5.6 is thus modified so that all possible pruning functions $f_{n,k}$ with $k \leq p(n)$ are considered. If the revised algorithm visits more than $|x|p(p_g(3|x|)) + |x| - 1$ inner nodes, then it infers that $k \neq c_S(n)$ and starts to consider the next value of k.

The new algorithm is thus the following:

begin {input: x}
    for $k = 0$ **to** $p(|x|)$ **do**
    begin
        execute the tree-visiting algorithm described in the
        proof of Theorem 5.6 using $f_{|x|,k}$ as a pruning function
        and visiting, at most, $|x|p(p_g(3|x|)) + |x| - 1$ inner nodes;
        if the algorithm accepts **then** accept;
    end;
    reject;
end.

Clearly the above algorithm requires polynomial time and decides SATISFIABILITY. Thus SATISFIABILITY $\in$ P and P $=$ NP. $\qquad\qquad\qquad\square$

5.3   NP-intermediate languages

In this section we shall make use of Theorem 4.1 to show that if P $\neq$ NP, then the difference set NP $-$ (P $\cup$ NPC) is not empty. Languages in such a set are called NP-intermediate, since they are in neither P or NPC, and the corresponding class is denoted as NPI.

Theorem 5.8 If P $\neq$ NP then a language $L \in$ NP $-$ P exists which is not NP-complete.

Proof. Let us first note that both P and NPC are constructively numerable (see Problems 4.3 and 5.20) and closed with respect to finite variations.

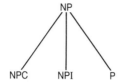

Figure 5.4 The structure of class NP, if P $\neq$ NP

Let $L_2 = \emptyset$, $L_1 =$ SATISFIABILITY, $\mathcal{C}_1 =$P and $\mathcal{C}_2 =$ NPC. If P $\neq$ NP, then the assumptions of Theorem 4.1 are satisfied and the language L defined in the proof of that theorem is in neither P nor NPC.

Since $L \leq L_1 \oplus L_2 =$ SATISFIABILITY and since NP is closed with respect to polynomial-time reducibility (see Problem 5.1), then $L \in$ NP. $\square$

The results obtained so far concerning the structure of NP are shown in Figure 5.4.

Returning to NPI, note that the separator language obtained by means of Theorem 5.8 is, in a certain sense, an artificial language. Does NPI admit languages corresponding to natural problems? To a certain extent the answer is affirmative: problems exist in NP for which neither an NP-completeness proof nor a polynomial-time algorithm has been found so far. It is thus reasonable to conjecture that such problems belong to class NPI.

Typical examples of problems exhibiting the above characteristics are those related to isomorphism between pairs of structures such as graphs, groups, semigroups and latin squares.

5.3.1 Group isomorphism

Let us examine in detail GROUP ISOMORPHISM, the problem of deciding whether two finite groups are isomorphic. We shall prove that this problem can be solved in time strictly less than exponential.

A (finite) *group* G is a pair $\langle S, * \rangle$ where S is a finite set of elements and $*$ is a binary operation such that

1. S is closed with respect to $*$, i.e. $* : S \times S \to S$.
2. The binary operation $*$ is associative, i.e. for any $x, y, z \in S$, $(x * y) * z = x * (y * z)$.
3. There is an element u in S such that $u * x = x * u = x$ for all $x \in S$.
4. Each $x \in S$ admits an element $y \in S$ called the *inverse* of x such that $x * y = y * x = u$.

A group G of n elements is defined by means of a table of n^2 elements whose entries specify the values of all possible operations $x * y$ with $x, y \in S$.

Two groups $G = \langle S, * \rangle$ and $G' = \langle S', *' \rangle$ are *isomorphic* if an isomorphism f exists between them, that is, a bijective function $f : S \to S'$ such that $f(x * y) = f(x) *' f(y)$ for all $x, y \in S$.

The algorithm for GROUP ISOMORPHISM is based on the following well-known property of groups (see Notes). Each n-element group admits a system X of, at most, $m = \lfloor \log(n) \rfloor$ generators ($X \subseteq S$ is a system of generators for G if all elements of S can be obtained by repeatedly composing elements of X). By using this property, it is possible to obtain, in subexponential time, a system of generators for a group $G = \langle S, * \rangle$ by considering all possible m-combinations (subsets of size m) of S until we find a combination that is a system of generators for G.

Since checking whether an m-combination is a system of generators can be done in $O[n^2 m]$ steps (see Problem 5.21), the procedure requires $O[n^2 m n^m]$ steps.

GROUP ISOMORPHISM can then be solved by the following procedure:

1. Derive a system of generators $g_1, g_2, \ldots, g_m$ for G.
2. Associate with each element $x \in S$ its representation $x = g_{i_1} * g_{i_2} * \ldots * g_{i_h}$.
3. For each m-permutation $z_1, z_2, \ldots, z_m$ of S', check whether the following function $f : S \to S'$ is an isomorphism between G and G'.

$$f(x) = \begin{cases} z_i & \text{if } x = g_i, \\ z_{i_1} *' \ldots *' z_{i_h} & \text{if } x = g_{i_1} * \ldots * g_{i_h}. \end{cases}$$

4. If, at least, one m-permutation exists for which f is an isomorphism then accept, otherwise reject.

Checking whether f is an isomorphism requires $O[n^2 m]$ steps while the number of m-permutations is

$$O[n^m m!] \subseteq O[n^m 2^{m \log(m)}] \subseteq O[n^m 2^{m^2}] \subseteq O[n^{2m}].$$

The number of steps required is thus

$$O[n^2 m n^m + n^2 m n^{2m}] \subseteq O[n^2 m n^{2m}] \subseteq O[n^{2\log(n)+3}].$$

We conclude by observing that even if we have proved that GROUP ISOMORPHISM can be solved in time strictly less than exponential (but not polynomial), the problem could still be NP-complete, although this seems quite unlikely (see Notes).

5.3.2   Do sparse languages exist in NPI?

Since sparse languages which are NP-complete do not seem to exist, the next reasonable question is: do sparse languages exist in NPI?

We will not be able to answer this question immediately but we shall content ourselves in this section with showing that the existence of sparse languages in NPI depends on the existence of tally languages in the same class.

Given a binary language L, the *tally language associated with L* is defined as

$$T_L = \{u(x) : x \in L\}$$

where $u : \{0, 1\}^* \to 0^*$ is a function such that, for any x, $u(x) = 0^{n(1x)-1}$ with $n(z)$ denoting the natural number represented by the binary word z.

Lemma 5.2 If a sparse language S belongs to $\mathrm{NP} - \mathrm{P}$, then a tally language exists which belongs to $\mathrm{NP} - \mathrm{P}$.

Proof. Let S be a sparse language in $\mathrm{NP} - \mathrm{P}$ and p a polynomial witnessing the sparsity of S. For each n and for each finite set X of words of length n, let us put the words of X into lexicographic order and let us denote by $y_{n,j}$ the jth word according to such ordering. Consider the binary language

$$L = \{\langle n, k, i, j, b \rangle : \exists X \subseteq S_n[|X| = k \text{ and the } i\text{-th bit of } y_{n,j} \text{ is } b]\}$$

and consider the tally language T_L associated with L.

We will now show that $T_L \in \mathrm{NP}$. Since $S \in \mathrm{NP}$, then a nondeterministic Turing machine NT exists which decides S in polynomial time. The following nondeterministic algorithm decides T_L in polynomial time:

begin {input: x}
  if $x = 0^t \wedge t = \langle n, k, i, j, b \rangle$ **then**
  begin
    {derive a possible subset X of S_n}
    guess $y_1, \ldots, y_k$ **in** set of k-tuples of words of length n
    which are lexicographically ordered;
    {check whether the generated k-tuple is contained in S_n}
    for $h = 1$ **to** k **do**
      if $NT(y_h)$ rejects **then** reject;
    {check whether $\langle n, k, i, j, b \rangle \in L$}
    if ith bit of y_j is b **then** accept **else** reject;
  end
  else reject;
end.

To prove $T_L \notin \mathrm{P}$, we show that S is decidable in polynomial time by a deterministic Turing machine with oracle T_L. Since $S \notin \mathrm{P}$, this clearly implies that $T_L \notin \mathrm{P}$ (see Problem 4.7). The following algorithm describes a deterministic Turing machine with oracle T_L which decides S in polynomial time:

```
begin {input: x}
   n := |x|;
   k := p(n);
   {compute k = |Sₙ|}
   while k > 0 ∧ u(⟨n, k, 1, 1, 0⟩) ∉ T_L ∧ u(⟨n, k, 1, 1, 1⟩) ∉ T_L do k := k − 1;
   {Sₙ is empty }
   if k = 0 then reject;
   {a single X ⊆ Sₙ exists with |X| = |Sₙ| = k}
   for j = 1 to k do
   begin
      {construct the words of Sₙ symbol by symbol }
      z := e;
      for i = 1 to n do
         if u(⟨n, k, i, j, 0⟩) ∈ T_L then z := z0 else z := z1;
      if x = z then accept;
   end;
   reject;
end.
```

We have thus proved $T_L \in \text{NP} - \text{P}$.   □

From Lemma 5.2 and from the fact that each tally language is also sparse we derive the following theorem.

Theorem 5.9 A sparse language exists in $\text{NP} - \text{P}$ if and only if a tally language exists in $\text{NP} - \text{P}$.

Finally, by combining the previous theorem and Theorem 5.7, we get the following result.

Corollary 5.2 If $\text{P} \neq \text{NP}$, then a sparse language exists in NPI if and only if a tally language exists in NPI.

We will apply the above corollary in Chapter 7 to show that the existence of sparse languages in NPI is closely related to the separation of exponential-time complexity classes and it is then considered a likely event.

5.4   Computing and verifying a function

In this section we analyse the difference between computing and verifying a function. *Computing* a function f means defining an algorithm which derives an output $y = f(x)$ from input x, while *verifying* f consists of deciding the predicate $R(x, y)$ which assumes the value **true** if and only if $f(x) = y$.

First, let us note that if a function f is computable within some time bound, then f is verifiable within the same time bound. Indeed, given x and y, if one wants to verify whether $f(x) = y$, it is sufficient to compute $f(x)$ and then to make a comparison of symbols between $f(x)$ and y. Since the comparison can be performed in linear time with respect to y, the time of the overall procedure depends, basically, on that time required to compute $f(x)$. In other words, computing a function is never easier, in terms of computational complexity, than verifying the function itself. In some cases the cost of verifying can be significantly lower than that of computing.

Example 5.10 Consider the function $f(x) = 0^{2^{|x|}}$. The time required to compute f cannot be less than its length and is thus exponential with respect to the input length.

At the same time, it is possible to verify the same f in polynomial time with respect to the combined length of x and y. The verification algorithm simply determines whether y does not contain 1's and whether $\log |y| = |x|$. Both tests can be done in polynomial time.

The existence of functions which are simpler to verify than to compute can also be proved in a much broader framework, such as in the theory of recursive functions (see Notes).

The next result we are going to present is more closely related to complexity theory, even if it can be applied only to a restricted class of functions called multi-valued.

A *multi-valued function* f associates a set of values $I_f(x) = \{y_1, y_2, \ldots\}$ with an input x. A multi-valued function f is *computable* if a Turing transducer exists which can read x and output a value $y \in I_f(x)$ (we can assume that if $I_f(x) = \emptyset$, then the transducer does not halt). It is *verifiable* if a computable predicate $R(x, y)$ exists which assumes the value **true** if and only if $y \in I_f(x)$. Finally, a multi-valued function f is *polynomially limited* if a polynomial p exists such that, for each x and for each $y \in I_f(x)$, $|y| \leq p(|x|)$, that is, the length of the output is not much greater than that of the input (note that the function of Example 5.10 is not polynomially limited).

The problem we shall consider is the following. Given a multi-valued function verifiable in polynomial time, is it true that it is also computable in polynomial time? The next theorem shows that the answer is yes, if and only if P = NP.

To state this result, we first need to introduce two new classes of functions. The *class PC^p* includes all multi-valued polynomially limited functions that are computable in deterministic polynomial time while the *class PV^p* includes all multi-valued polynomially limited functions verifiable in deterministic polynomial time.

Note that all functions included in FP are verifiable in polynomial time while a similar result cannot be extended to multi-valued functions. In general, knowing how to compute a single value of f does not suffice for verifying f. In fact, it is possible to prove that $PC^p \not\subseteq PV^p$ by simply defining a two-valued function whose first output value is 'easy' to compute while the second one is 'hard' to verify (see Problem 5.22). Furthermore, we shall show that the inclusion $PV^p \subseteq PC^p$ is not likely. Therefore it is plausible that PC^p and PV^p are not comparable.

Theorem 5.10 $PV^p \subseteq PC^p$ if and only if P = NP.

Proof. Assume $PV^p \subseteq PC^p$ and consider an arbitrary language $L \in$ NP. From Theorem 5.1, it follows that a language $L_{\text{check}} \in$ P and a polynomial p exist such that

$$L = \{x : \exists y[\langle x, y \rangle \in L_{\text{check}} \wedge |y| = p(|x|)]\}.$$

Let f be a multi-valued function defined as follows. For each x, $I_f(x)$ includes as values all words y of length $p(|x|)$ such that $\langle x, y \rangle \in L_{\text{check}}$; if there are none, then $I_f(x)$ includes a single special value denoted as Ω.

Such a function f is clearly polynomially limited and belongs to PV^p because, for any x and y, it is sufficient to verify whether $\langle x, y \rangle \in L_{\text{check}}$ and $L_{\text{check}} \in$ P. Thus, having assumed $PV^p \subseteq PC^p$, f also belongs to PC^p.

By construction, $x \in L$ if and only if $f(x) \neq \Omega$. For any x, we can then use the polynomial-time deterministic algorithm which computes f and examine the value $f(x)$ to decide in polynomial time whether $x \in L$. Since L is an arbitrary language in NP, it follows that P = NP.

Now assume that P = NP. Let f be a function in PV^p and T the deterministic Turing machine which decides in polynomial time the predicate associated with f (for simplicity, we assume that both x and the words of $I_f(x)$ are binary words).

By assumption, f is polynomially limited, thus an integer h exists such that, for all x and for all $y \in I_f(x)$, $|y| \leq |x|^h$. First, we derive a nondeterministic Turing machine NT_1 which decides in polynomial time, given any x, if $I_f(x) \neq \emptyset$.

begin {input: x}
    guess y **in** set of words of length, at most, $|x|^h$;
    if $T(x, y)$ accepts **then** accept **else** reject;
end.

Since P = NP holds, a deterministic machine T_1 exists which decides in polynomial time, given any x, if $I_f(x) \neq \emptyset$.

Next we derive a nondeterministic Turing machine NT_2 which decides in polynomial time, given any x and z, if z is the prefix of one of the words in $I_f(x)$.

begin {input: x, z}
    guess y **in** set of words of length, at most, $|x|^h - |z|$;
    if $T(x, zy)$ accepts **then** accept **else** reject;
end.

In the same way as for NT_1, denote by T_2 the polynomial-time deterministic machine equivalent to NT_2.

We are now ready to describe a third and last deterministic machine T_3 which, for any x, computes bit by bit a value $z \in I_f(x)$ in polynomial time:

```
begin {input: x; output: z}
   if T₁(x) rejects then cycle {I_f(x) = ∅}
   else
   begin
      z := e;
      i := 1;
      found := false;
      {derive z bit by bit}
      while i ≤ |x|ʰ and not found do
      begin
         if T₂(x, z0) accepts then
            z := z0
         else
            if T₂(x, z1) accepts then
               z := z1
            else found := true;
            i := i + 1;
      end;
   end;
end.
```

We have thus proved $\text{PV}^p \subseteq \text{PC}^p$ and this concludes the proof. $\square$

The proof of the previous theorem relies heavily on the fact that f is a multi-valued function; in fact, no similar result is known for conventional (single-valued) functions.

5.5 Relativization of the P $\neq$ NP conjecture

So far, only two main complexity classes have been defined (but there are more in subsequent chapters!) and yet we are already faced with a difficult open problem: is the P $\neq$ NP conjecture true?

In an effort to solve this conjecture, researchers have also investigated the corresponding *relativized* conjecture, that is, deciding whether $\text{P}^X \neq \text{NP}^X$ or $\text{P}^X = \text{NP}^X$ for some oracle X.

The rationale for such a research effort is that if a result is obtained for a class of oracles, then one might hope to solve the unrelativized conjecture by successively refining the proof until the relativization refers to a trivial oracle language (in fact, the P $\neq$ NP conjecture may be viewed as a special case of $\text{P}^X \neq \text{NP}^X$ with $X = \emptyset$).

Let us turn now to the relativized conjecture $\text{P}^X \neq \text{NP}^X$.

The next two theorems are quite striking. Indeed, they state that

1. An oracle A exists such that $\text{P}^A = \text{NP}^A$.
2. An oracle B exists such that $\text{P}^B \neq \text{NP}^B$.

Before proving them, let us briefly consider their implications. Intuitively, they state that proving or disproving the P $\neq$ NP conjecture requires proof techniques which *do not relativize*, that is, which cannot be readily extended to all oracles. Unfortunately, the main techniques we have used so far, namely diagonalization and simulation, do not seem to be oracle-dependent.

Suppose that we want to prove that P $\subset$ NP using a diagonalization technique, that is, a separator language L included in NP $-$ P. It is found that such a technique seems directly applicable to separate the corresponding relativized classes, for *any* oracle. Thus, if we could separate NP from P by using the diagonalization technique, we could also prove the same separation for any oracle, contradicting the first result.

On the other hand, simulation seems to be the best way to prove that P $=$ NP. In this case, we look for a general method to simulate nondeterministic polynomial-time algorithms by deterministic polynomial-time ones. Once again, the simulation technique seems applicable to relativized classes so that if we could prove P $=$ NP by simulation, then we could also prove the same result for any oracle, contradicting the second result.

The reader should be warned that the previous discussion is rather informal: many concepts have not been precisely defined, such as that of a proof technique which does not relativize, and, indeed, some results (see Notes) seem to weaken the previous interpretation. Nevertheless, we think that the argument was worth mentioning in order to emphasize the subtlety of the P $\neq$ NP question.

We are now ready to prove the first theorem which states that an oracle exists such that P and NP relativized to that oracle are the same. The basic idea is to use as an oracle a language so powerful that nondeterminism is no longer more useful than determinism (essentially, all the work is done by the oracle).

Theorem 5.11 Let A be the language defined as

$$A = \{\langle T, x, 0^k \rangle : T(x) \text{ accepts and uses, at most, } k \text{ tape cells}\}.$$

Then $P^A = NP^A$.

Proof. Obviously, $P^A \subseteq NP^A$ since the same argument used to state that P $\subseteq$ NP holds for oracle machines. We must now prove that $NP^A \subseteq P^A$.

Let $L \in NP^A$. An oracle nondeterministic Turing machine NT exists such that NT with oracle A decides L in, at most, $p(|x|)$ steps where p denotes a polynomial.

Our objective will be to derive a deterministic Turing machine T' using, at most, $q(|x|)$ cells for a polynomial q and equivalent to NT with oracle A. Once this has been done, it becomes easy to derive a deterministic Turing machine with oracle A which decides L. Given any input x, such a machine writes on the query tape the word $\langle T', x, 0^{q(|x|)} \rangle$ and halts according to the answer of the oracle. Thus $L \in P^A$ and since L is an arbitrary language in NP^A, $NP^A \subseteq P^A$ follows.

Let us now show how to derive T' from NT with oracle A. The simulation of each computation path requires, at most, a polynomial number of tape cells and each simulation can be carried on by using the *same* tape cells, that is, by recycling the space. What of the queries? Assume that NT queries the oracle A on the word $\langle T'', y, 0^k \rangle$: T' can answer this query by simulating the k cells space bounded computation $T''(y)$. Clearly, $k \leq p(|x|)$, otherwise NT would not succeed in writing the query onto the oracle tape. In conclusion, T' is able to answer any query of the form $\langle T'', y, 0^k \rangle$ in polynomial space, thus T' decides L using, at most, $q(|x|)$ cells for a polynomial q. $\square$

In Chapter 8 we will show that the oracle A introduced in the previous theorem is a complete language for an important complexity class, namely the class of languages which can be decided in polynomial space.

The next theorem shows instead how to derive an oracle which separates P from NP by diagonalization. As usual, in order to diagonalize a suitable enumeration of oracle Turing machines must be available. In particular, according to Problem 4.3, let $T_1, T_2, \ldots$ be an enumeration of oracle Turing machines such that, for any oracle X,

1. $\mathrm{P}^X = \{L : L = L(T_k^X) \text{ for some } k\}$.
2. For any $k \geq 0$ and for any input x, $T_k^X(x)$ halts after, at most, $n^k + k$ steps (the same integer k is used both as index of the machine and as degree of the bounding polynomial).

Then, for any language X, let us define a new language L_X as

$$L_X = \{0^n : \exists x[x \in X \land |x| = n]\}.$$

Intuitively, L_X captures a property of language X, that is, the non-emptiness property when restricted to words of a given length. It is easy to verify that $L_X \in \mathrm{NP}^X$ for any oracle X. Indeed, in order to check whether 0^n belongs to L_X, it is sufficient to guess in a nondeterministic way all words of length n and verify whether the oracle X includes, at least, one of them. The next theorem shows that an oracle B exists such that no deterministic Turing machine using that oracle is able to decide L_B in polynomial time.

Theorem 5.12 An oracle B exists such that $\mathrm{P}^B \neq \mathrm{NP}^B$.

Proof. The proof consists of deriving by diagonalization an oracle B such that $L_B \notin \mathrm{P}^B$. Since we know that $L_B \in \mathrm{NP}^B$, the theorem will then follow.

The diagonalization process consists of associating with each polynomial-time bounded oracle Turing machine T in the enumeration an integer n such that either $T^B(0^n)$ accepts and $B_n = \emptyset$ or $T^B(0^n)$ rejects and $B_n \neq \emptyset$. This, in turn, implies that no polynomial-time deterministic Turing machine with oracle B exists deciding L_B.

The language B is constructed in stages. Let $B(i)$ denote the finite set of words added to B after the ith stage and let n_i be an upper bound on the length of the words of $B(i)$. Initially we let $B(0)$ be $\emptyset$ and n_0 be 0. The set $B(i)$ is then computed by the following algorithm which assumes that oracle Turing machines are enumerated as previously described:

begin {input: $B(i-1), n_{i-1}$}
    $n_i := \min\{m : m > n_{i-1}^{i-1} + i - 1 \wedge 2^m > m^i + i\}$;
    simulate $T_i^{B(i-1)}(0^{n_i})$;
    if $T_i^{B(i-1)}(0^{n_i})$ accepts **then** $B(i) := B(i-1)$
    else
    begin
        $y :=$ smallest word of length n_i not queried by $T_i^{B(i-1)}(0^{n_i})$;
        $B(i) := B(i-1) \cup \{y\}$;
    end;
end.

The above algorithm is well defined. Indeed, the first step always succeeds in finding the value n_i (after all, it only looks for an integer greater than a finite set of integers). The second step is also meaningful since the computation $T_i^{B(i-1)}(0^{n_i})$ always halts. The only point which remains to be proved is that a word y of length n_i which has not been queried by $T_i^{B(i-1)}(0^{n_i})$ always exists. For that purpose, notice that, at most, $n_i^i + i$ words can be queried by such a computation while the number of distinct words of length n_i is $2^{n_i} > n_i^i + i$.

We may then define the oracle language B as $B = \bigcup_{i>0} B(i)$.

Note that for any i, the behavior of T_i on input 0^{n_i} with oracle $B(i-1)$ is precisely the same as its behavior on the same input with oracle B. In fact, the word eventually added to B at the ith stage is one of those not queried by T_i on input 0^{n_i} while those added in the successive stages have a length greater than $n_i^i + i$.

To conclude the proof we have to show that $L_B \notin P^B$. Conversely, assume that a polynomial-time Turing machine with oracle B exists deciding L_B. Then an integer i exists such that $L_B = L(T_i^B)$. How does $T_i^B(0^{n_i})$ halt? If it accepts, this means that B does not contain any word of length n_i, that is, $0^{n_i} \notin L_B$. On the other hand, if $T_i^B(0^{n_i})$ rejects, then B contains exactly one word of length n_i, that is, $0^{n_i} \in L_B$. In both cases, T_i fails to decide whether 0^{n_i} belongs to L_B and we conclude that no such T_i^B can exist. $\qquad\square$

5.5.1   Strong separation

In the proof of the previous theorem an oracle B was derived such that the corresponding language L_B differs from any language in P^B by, *at least*, one word. However, the language L_B obtained could be 'approximately' included in P^B, that is, an infinite subset of it could belong to that class. A much stronger result consists of obtaining an oracle E such that $L_E \in NP^E$ and such that no infinite subset of L_E belongs to P^E.

Formally, given a class of languages $\mathcal{C}$, an infinite language L is said to be $\mathcal{C}$-*immune* if no infinite subset of L belongs to $\mathcal{C}$.

Theorem 5.13 An oracle E exists such that NP^E contains a P^E-immune language.

Proof. Once again the proof consists of deriving by diagonalization an oracle E such that the corresponding language L_E is P^E-immune. In order to obtain this result a more sophisticated kind of diagonalization is necessary. In fact, saying that L_E is P^E-immune is equivalent to saying that, for any infinite language $L \in \mathrm{P}^E$, $L \cap L_E^c \neq \emptyset$. This, in turn, implies that the diagonalization process has to determine at some stage a word x such that $x \in L - L_E$. The construction in the proof of Theorem 5.12 is not able to determine such words since it looks for words that belong either to L_E or to L but not to both ($x \in L \Delta L_E$ does not imply $x \in L - L_E$).

It then becomes necessary to slow down the diagonalization technique so that an oracle Turing machine in the enumeration is not freed until a word accepted by that machine is found. If such a word is found, then it is not added to L_E! Of course, we cannot continue to analyse the behavior of a single machine because we may never find a word accepted by it (this occurs, for instance, when the set of words produced by the diagonalization has a null intersection with the language decided by that machine). We overcome this problem by simply keeping in a reserve list all machines which have not yet accepted any word and we check every one at each stage. That is why such a process is called a *slow diagonalization*.

As in the proof of Theorem 5.12, the language E will be constructed in stages. Let $E(i)$ denote the finite set of words placed into E after the ith stage and let n_i be an upper bound on the length of all strings in $E(i)$. Furthermore, denote by $R(i)$ the set of indices of oracle Turing machines that are candidates for diagonalization at stage $i + 1$ (this is the reserve list). Initially we let $E(0)$ be $\emptyset$, n_0 be 0 and $R(0)$ be $\{1\}$. The set $E(i)$ is then computed by the following algorithm where, once again, the enumeration of oracle Turing machines defined in Problem 4.3 is assumed:

begin {input: $E(i-1), n_{i-1}, R(i-1)$}

$\quad n_i := \min\{m : m > n_{i-1}^{i-1} + i - 1 \wedge 2^m > \sum_{j \leq i}(m^j + j)\};$

$\quad k := \min\{j : j \in R(i-1) \wedge T_j^{E(i-1)}(0^{n_i})$ accepts (if such a k exists)$\};$

$\quad$**if** such a k exists **then**

$\quad$**begin** {case 1: $T_k^{E(i-1)}$ accepts 0^{n_i}}

$\quad\quad E(i) := E(i-1);$

$\quad\quad R(i) := (R(i-1) - \{k\}) \cup \{i\};$

$\quad$**end**

$\quad$**else**

$\quad$**begin** {case 2: no T_j with oracle $E(i-1)$ accepts 0^{n_i}}

$\quad\quad E(i) := E(i-1) \cup$ least word of length n_i not queried

$\quad\quad\quad$ by any $T_j^{E(i-1)}(0^{n_i})$, for $j \in R(i-1)\};$

$\quad\quad R(i) := R(i-1) \cup \{i\};$

end;
end.

Define E as $E = \bigcup_{i>0} E(i)$. Reasoning as in the proof of Theorem 5.12, it is easy to see that the previous algorithm is well defined and that the behavior of machines T_j with oracle $E(i-1)$ on input 0^{n_i} is precisely the same as their behavior with oracle E on the same input, for any i and for any $j \leq i$.

First we prove that L_E is infinite. Clearly, L_E is infinite if and only if E is infinite. Suppose, on the contrary, that E is finite. Then an integer i_0 exists such that, for any $i > i_0$, case 1 occurs so that, at each stage $i > i_0$, the cardinality of $R(i)$ remains constant, that is, equal to $R(i_0)$. Since there is an infinite number of oracle Turing machines which do not accept any word and the index of each of those machines is never cancelled from the set of candidates, the cardinality of such a set cannot remain constant from a certain stage onwards, contradicting the assumption that E is finite.

To conclude the proof, it remains to show that no infinite subset of L_E belongs to P^E. By way of contradiction, assume that an infinite subset L of L_E exists such that $L \in P^E$. Thus, a polynomial-time deterministic Turing machine with oracle E, say T_i^E, which decides L must exist. Since $L \subseteq L_E$, there are infinitely many n such that $0^n \in L$ and such that T_i^E accepts 0^n. The index i was put into the set of candidates at the end of stage i. Since there is only a finite number of indices less than i, a stage $j > i$ must exist such that $0^{n_j} \in L$ and case 2 with $k = i$ occurs. Hence, no word of length n_j is put into E at that stage and none will be inserted during later stages because of the first step of the algorithm. Thus $0^{n_j} \notin L_E$, contradicting $L \subseteq L_E$.

Hence L_E is P^E-immune. $\square$

5.5.2   Positive relativization

So far, the results obtained for the relativized P $\neq$ NP conjecture do not look very encouraging. The time has come to illustrate some of the 'positive' results associated with relativization.

Intuitively, our goal is to look for results which unequivocally bind the relations between two complexity classes to the relations between the corresponding relativized classes. The results of the previous section tell us that if we want to obtain this type of connection we have to place some restrictions on the oracles to be considered. This can be carried out by bounding either the number of queries to the oracle or the power of the oracle.

Bounding the number of queries
The proof of Theorem 5.12 is based on the fact that, for any oracle X, the language L_X belongs to NP^X. In particular, we recall that L_X is decided by the following polynomial-time nondeterministic algorithm with oracle X:

begin {input: x}
  if $x \notin 0^*$ **then** reject
  else
  begin
    guess y **in** set of words of length equal to $|x|$;
    if $y \in X$ **then** accept **else** reject;
  end;
end.

Note that even though each computation path makes, at most, a polynomial number of queries (actually, at most, one), the whole computation may perform an exponential number of such queries. In other words, the algorithm can analyse a subset of the oracle of exponential size in a nondeterministic way. Intuition suggests that a deterministic oracle Turing machine cannot perform such a search in polynomial time and Theorem 5.12 confirms that intuition.

What if we restrict the global number of queries? Once again, intuition suggests that a nondeterministic oracle Turing machine cannot decide L_X whenever the global number of queries is bounded by a polynomial (and, clearly, P ≠ NP). The next theorem bears this out. In order to prove it, we first have to introduce some notation and preliminary results.

Let NT be a nondeterministic oracle Turing machine. For any oracle X and for any input x, let $Q(NT, X, x)$ denote the set of words y such that in a given computation path of $NT^X(x)$ the oracle is queried about y. Such a set can be further partitioned into two disjoint sets depending on the oracle answers. For any oracle X and for any input x, let $Y(NT, X, x) = Q(NT, X, x) \cap X$, that is, $Y(NT, X, x)$ contains all queries for which the answer relative to X is 'yes'. Analogously, we let $N(NT, X, x)$ be $Q(NT, X, x) \cap X^c$.

Given two finite languages Y and N, an oracle X is said to be *compatible* with Y and N if $Y \subseteq X$ and $N \cap X = \emptyset$. Intuitively, the oracle is compatible with the two sets if those sets can be correctly used to answer a finite subset of queries.

Let NT be any polynomial-time nondeterministic oracle Turing machine and let $\langle x, Y, N, \mathcal{S} \rangle$ be quadruples where x is an input, Y and N are disjoint finite languages, and $\mathcal{S}$ is a global state of $NT(x)$. Consider the language L_{NT} consisting of all quadruples $\langle x, Y, N, \mathcal{S} \rangle$ such that, for any oracle X compatible with Y and N, a computation path of $NT^X(x)$ starting from global state $\mathcal{S}$ exists which queries a word $y \notin Y \cup N$.

Lemma 5.3 Let NT be a polynomial-time nondeterministic oracle Turing machine. Then, $L_{NT} \in$ NP.

Proof. The main characteristics of a polynomial-time nondeterministic Turing machine NT_1 which decides L_{NT} are the following (the details are left to the reader). On input $\langle x, Y, N, \mathcal{S} \rangle$, NT_1 simulates the computation $NT(x)$ starting from global state $\mathcal{S}$. Whenever a computation path queries a word in Y (respectively, N), then the simulation continues in the yes-state (respectively, no-state); whenever a computation path queries a word which does not belong to $Y \cup N$, then the simulation accepts; finally, whenever the simulation reaches a final state, then it rejects. It should be clear that such a machine decides L_{NT} in polynomial time, that is, $L_{NT} \in \text{NP}$.   □

For any oracle X, let NP_b^X be the class of languages which can be decided by a polynomial-time nondeterministic machine NT with oracle X performing a polynomially bounded number of queries to oracle X. More precisely, we require that, for any x, $|Q(NT, X, x)| \leq p(|x|)$ where p denotes a polynomial.

Theorem 5.14 $\text{P} = \text{NP}$ if and only if, for any oracle X, $\text{P}^X = \text{NP}_b^X$.

Proof. Assume that for any oracle X, $\text{P}^X = \text{NP}_b^X$. Choose $X = \emptyset$. In such a case, $\text{P}^\emptyset = \text{P} = \text{NP}_b^\emptyset = \text{NP}$, thus $\text{P} = \text{NP}$ follows immediately.

Conversely, assume that $\text{P} = \text{NP}$ and let X be an arbitrary oracle. Given $L \in \text{NP}_b^X$, let NT be a polynomial-time nondeterministic Turing machine with oracle X which decides L and such that, for any input x, $|Q(NT, X, x)| \leq q(|x|)$ where q denotes a polynomial.

The basic idea is to derive a polynomial-time deterministic Turing machine with oracle X which, for any input x, computes the two disjoint sets $Y(NT, X, x)$ and $N(NT, X, x)$. Once these two subsets are available, the computation $NT^X(x)$ can be simulated without making use of the oracle (indeed, it suffices to look at the two sets), and, since $\text{P} = \text{NP}$, $L \in \text{P}^X$ will follow.

The sets $Y(NT, X, x)$ and $N(NT, X, x)$ will be derived word by word by repeatedly using the fact that, since $\text{P} = \text{NP}$ and because of Lemma 5.3, the language L_{NT} belongs to P. Intuitively, we will perform a binary search through the computation tree of NT with input x by making use of L_{NT} to decide which direction has to be followed.

Without loss of generality, we can assume that the degree of nondeterminism of NT is 2, namely, every global state has, at most, two successors (see Problem 2.8). In fact, we can also assume that every global state $\mathcal{S}$ (except the final ones) has *exactly* two successors: let us denote them as $\mathcal{S}_l$ and $\mathcal{S}_r$. Furthermore, if $\mathcal{S}$ is a global state in which a query is performed, we denote by $\mathcal{S}_y$ and $\mathcal{S}_n$ the global states reached if the queried word, respectively, belongs and does not belong to the oracle. The following polynomial-time algorithm with oracle X computes the two finite sets $Y(NT, X, x)$ and $N(NT, X, x)$ associated with the computation $NT^X(x)$:

```
begin {input: x; output: Y,N}
   Y := ∅;
   N := ∅;
   while ⟨x, Y, N, S₀⟩ ∈ L_NT do
   begin {there are still some unknown queries}
      S := S₀;
      while S is not querying a word not in Y ∪ N do
      {decide which path has to be followed}
```

    if S is querying a word $y \in Y \cup N$ **then**
        if $y \in Y$ **then** $S := S_y$
        else $S := S_n$
    else
        if $\langle x, Y, N, S_l \rangle \in L_{NT}$ **then** $S := S_l$
        else $S := S_r$;
   {a new query has been found}
   $y :=$ content of query tape of NT when in global state S;
   if $y \in X$ **then** $Y := Y \cup \{y\}$
   else $N := N \cup \{y\}$;
  end;
end.

First, let us prove the correctness of the algorithm. Since Y and N are both initialized to $\emptyset$ and successively modified according to X, it is clear that at each step of the algorithm X is compatible with Y and N. By the definition of L_{NT}, it follows that the test of membership in L_{NT} performed at the beginning of the outer **while** loop will correctly tell us whether a query in $Q(NT, X, x)$ exists which is not yet in $Y \cup N$. Furthermore, the other tests in the inner **while** loop will correctly guide our search of that query. Thus, at the end of the algorithm Y and N will coincide with, respectively, $Y(NT, X, x)$ and $N(NT, X, x)$.

Now consider the running time of the procedure. First, observe that, according to the hypothesis $P = NP$ and because of Lemma 5.3, every test of membership relative to L_{NT} can be performed in polynomial time. Then, each execution of the inner **while** loop takes, at most, polynomial time, since it essentially follows one computation path and NT is a polynomial-time oracle Turing machine. Finally, the outer **while** loop iterates, at most, $q(|x|)$ times, since at the end of each iteration one new word is added to the set $Y \cup N$ and we know that $|Q(NT, X, x)| \leq q(|x|)$. Thus, the entire procedure can be implemented to run in polynomial time relative to the oracle X.

Let us now consider the language L_1 defined as follows. $\langle x, Y, N \rangle \in L_1$ if and only if NT^Y accepts x and if all words y queried by that computation belong to $Y \cup N$. Clearly, such a language is in NP and, since we are assuming $P = NP$, it is also in P. Furthermore, note that $x \in L$ if and only if $\langle x, Y(NT, X, x), N(NT, X, x) \rangle \in L_1$. We have just seen that both $Y(NT, X, x)$ and $N(NT, X, x)$ can be computed in polynomial time with oracle X, thus $L \in P^X$ follows.

Since L is an arbitrary language in NP_b^X, $NP_b^X \subseteq P^X$. The converse is clearly true and we have thus proved that, for any oracle X, $P^X = NP_b^X$.   □

Bounding the oracle

Once again, let us consider the proof of Theorem 5.12. If we look at the definition of oracle B, we immediately realize that such an oracle is sparse: indeed, for any length n, at most, one word of such a length belongs to B. What if we demand that B is tally? Intuitively, this does not seem an easy task since in the algorithm deriving B we would no longer be sure that a word $y \in 0^*$ exists which has not been queried. Once more, the next theorem confirms that intuition.

Theorem 5.15 P = NP if and only if, for any tally oracle T, $P^T = NP^T$.

Proof. Clearly, if, for any tally oracle T, $P^T = NP^T$ then P = NP. In fact, it suffices to observe that, by taking $T = \emptyset$, it holds that $P = P^\emptyset = NP^\emptyset = NP$.

Conversely, let T be a tally oracle and let $L \in NP^T$. In this case, a polynomial-time oracle Turing machine NT exists which, with oracle T, decides L. Let q be a polynomial bounding the computation time of NT.

As in the proof of Theorem 5.14, the basic idea is to derive, for any input x, two finite sets $Y(T, x)$ and $N(T, x)$ of T which can simulate the computation $NT^T(x)$ without making use of the oracle. In particular, any query made in $NT^T(x)$ which has been answered 'yes' (respectively, 'no') must be in $Y(T, x)$ (respectively, $N(T, x)$).

Note that, since computation $NT^T(x)$ takes, at most, $q(|x|)$ steps, no word of length greater than $q(|x|)$ is queried. Thus, the following deterministic algorithm with oracle T computes the two sets $Y(T, x)$ and $N(T, x)$ in polynomial time:

```
begin {input: x; output: Y,N}
   Y  :=  ∅;
   N  :=  ∅;
   for k = 1 to q(|x|) do
      if 0ᵏ ∈ T then Y  :=  Y ∪ {0ᵏ}
      else N  :=  N ∪ {0ᵏ};
end.
```

Clearly, the above algorithm computes $Y(T, x)$ and $N(T, x)$ in polynomial time.

Let us now consider the language L_1 defined as follows. $\langle x, Y, N \rangle \in L_1$ if and only if NT^Y on input x accepts x and if y is a string that is queried in the computation, then $y \in Y \cup N$. Such a language is in NP and, since we are assuming P = NP, it is also in P. Note that $x \in L$ if and only if $\langle x, Y(T, x), N(T, x) \rangle \in L_1$. We have just seen that both $Y(T, x)$ and $N(T, x)$ can be computed in polynomial time with oracle T, thus $L \in P^T$.

Since L is an arbitrary language in NP^T, $NP^T \subseteq P^T$. The converse is clearly true.

We have thus proved that, for any tally oracle T, $P^T = NP^T$. □

As a consequence of Theorems 5.14 and 5.15, two approaches in proving P $\neq$ NP consist of constructing an oracle D such that $P^D \neq NP_b^D$ or a tally oracle T such that $P^T \neq NP^T$. If diagonalization is used to define these oracles, the relativized version of NP should be as large as possible so as to make the separation from the relativized version of P easier. Unfortunately, these considerations, though interesting *per se*, have not been fruitful so far.

Problems

5.1. Show that class NP is closed with respect to intersection and union and to polynomial-time reducibility.

5.2. Remember that, given a language L, the language L^* is defined as the set of all words x such that x is the concatenation of words of L. Show that if L belongs to NP, then L^* also belongs to NP.

5.3. Fix an alphabet Σ with, at least, three symbols. An encoding is a mapping from Σ to Σ (not necessarily onto). It can be extended to words (map each symbol) and to languages (map each word). Show that P is closed with respect to encodings if and only if P = NP. [Hint: for the 'if' part, show that NP is closed with respect to encodings. For the 'only if' part, prove that if P is closed with respect to encodings, then SATISFIABILITY belongs to P.]

5.4. An honest function (see Problem 4.5) is said to be *one-way* if it is computable in polynomial time but no polynomial-time right inverse function exists for it. Prove that if P $\neq$ NP, then one-way functions exist. [Balcazar, Diaz, and Gabarro (1988)]

5.5. A nondeterministic Turing machine is said to be *unambiguous* if no input has more than one accepting computation path. The *class* UP is the set of languages decided by unambiguous machines in polynomial time. Show that if one-way functions exist, then P $\neq$ UP [Selman (1989)]. Combine this result with the previous one showing that one-way functions exist if and only if P $\neq$ UP if and only if P $\neq$ NP.

5.6. We have already observed in Chapter 2 that nondeterministic could be defined by requiring that, for any input x, all halting computation paths compute the same value. Let FNP be the set of functions computed in polynomial time by such nondeterministic transducers. Prove that P = NP if and only if FP = FNP. [Hint: for the 'if' part, derive the output value in a bit-by-bit mode.]

5.7. Define the language L as

$$L = \{\langle NT, x, 0^t \rangle : NT \text{ accepts } x \text{ in, at most, } t \text{ steps}\}.$$

Show that L is NP-complete. [Hint: reduce languages in NP to L.]

5.8. Prove that 3-COLORABILITY is NP-complete. [Hint: show that 3-SATISFIABILITY is polynomially reducible to 3-COLORABILITY.]

5.9. 3-DIMENSIONAL MATCHING: given three finite sets X, Y and W having the same cardinality q and a subset M of $X \times Y \times W$, does a set $M' \subseteq M$ exist such that all $3q$ elements of X, Y and W appear in exactly one triple of M'? Prove that this problem is NP-complete. [Hint: show that 3-SATISFIABILITY is polynomially reducible to 3-DIMENSIONAL MATCHING.]

5.10. HAMILTONIAN CIRCUIT: given a graph $G = (N, E)$, does G admit a Hamiltonian circuit, that is, a circuit of $|N|$ nodes? Prove that this new problem is NP-complete. [Hint: show that NODE COVER is polynomially reducible to HAMILTONIAN CIRCUIT.]

5.11. Prove that TRAVELING SALESMAN is NP-complete. [Hint: show that HAMILTONIAN CIRCUIT is polynomially reducible to TRAVELING SALESMAN.]

5.12. PARTITION: given a finite set A of positive integers whose sum is equal to $2b$, can A be partitioned into two subsets so that the sum of the integers in each subset is exactly b? Prove that this problem is NP-complete. [Hint: show that 3-DIMENSIONAL MATCHING is polynomially reducible to PARTITION.]

5.13. COVER: given a finite set A, a collection C of subsets of A, and a constant k, does C admit a cover of size, at most, k, that is, a subset C' such that every element of A belongs to, at least, one member of C'? Prove that this problem is NP-complete. [Hint: show that 3-DIMENSIONAL MATCHING is polynomially reducible to COVER.]

5.14. Prove that KNAPSACK is NP-complete. [Hint: show that PARTITION is polynomially reducible to KNAPSACK.]

5.15. A language L is *self-reducible* if a deterministic polynomial-time oracle Turing T exists such that $L = L(T^L)$ and, for any input x of length n, $T^L(x)$ queries the oracle for words of length, at most, $n - 1$. Show that SATISFIABILITY is self-reducible. Is this result sufficient to state that any NP-complete language is self-reducible?

5.16. Let L be a self-reducible language via the oracle machine T. Prove that, for any language L' and for any integer n, if $L'_{\leq n} = L(T^{L'})_{\leq n}$, then $L_{\leq n} = L'_{\leq n}$. [Hint: by induction on n.]

5.17. Find a problem in P which admits a pair of polynomial-time computable padding and decoding functions satisfying the conditions of Lemma 5.4.

5.18. Show that the census function of SATISFIABILITY grows exponentially with the input size.

5.19. Prove that if SATISFIABILITY^c is decidable in polynomial time by a deterministic Turing machine T with a tally oracle such that T makes a constant number of queries, then P = NP.

5.20. Show that NPC is constructively enumerable. [Hint: starting from the standard enumeration of polynomial-time deterministic transducer Turing machines and from that of NP, derive a constructive enumeration $T_1, \ldots, T_n, \ldots$ of deterministic Turing machines such that, for any i, either $L(T_i)$ is NP-complete or it coincides with SATISFIABILITY almost everywhere.]

5.21. SYSTEM OF GENERATORS: given a group $G = \langle S, * \rangle$ of n elements and a $\log(n)$-combination of S, is such combination a system of generators for G? Describe an algorithm which solves this problem in time $O[n^2 \log(n)]$. [Hint: distinguish the elements of S as: not yet generated, generated but not used, and generated and already used.]

5.22. Prove that PC$^p \not\subseteq$ PV^p. [Hint: define a function f such that, for any x, $I_f(x)$ *always* includes one element which is easy to compute, and *eventually* includes one element which is hard to verify.]

5.23. Define the *class* PC_t as the set of multi-valued total functions which are computable in polynomial time and the *class* PV_t as the set of multi-valued total functions which are verifiable in polynomial time. Prove that, if P = NP, then $PV_t \subseteq PC_t$.

5.24. Prove that an oracle E exists such that $NP^E \neq coNP^E$.

5.25. Prove that NP = coNP if and only if, for any oracle D, $NP_b^D = coNP_b^D$.

5.26. Prove that NP = coNP if and only if, for any tally oracle T, $NP^T = coNP^T$.

Notes

The definition of the class NP has certainly been a breakthrough in the theory of computational complexity. Although this class and the related P $\neq$ NP conjecture were first formulated in Karp (1972), it is surprising to observe that Gödel was probably the first to consider the computational complexity of what is now known as an NP-complete problem. Indeed, as referred to by Hartmanis (1989), in a 1956 letter, Gödel asked von Neumann how many Turing machine steps are required to decide if there is a proof of length n for a formula F in predicate calculus. It is also interesting to note Gödel's optimism that this NP-complete problem could be solved in linear or quadratic time!

The proof of Theorem 5.2, which appeared in Cook (1971), placed a powerful tool at the disposal of researchers who wished to prove the 'intractability' of combinatorial problems. Since then, attempts to prove NP-completeness results have been the natural counterpart of developing algorithmic techniques to solve problems. These two activities interact in such a way that we can hardly imagine them isolated.

An exhaustive overview of class NP, NP-complete problems, and reduction techniques is contained in Garey and Johnson (1979). In addition to that text, many new interesting results concerning proofs of NP-completeness and new NP-complete problems can be found in the review 'The on-going NP-completeness column' by Johnson which appears periodically in the *Journal of Algorithms*.

An alternative proof of the existence of NP-complete languages can be found in Lewis and Papadimitriou (1981). Such a proof consists of showing the polynomial-time reduction of nondeterministic computations to instances of a problem called TILING which is a rectangle-packing problem with additional constraints on the orientation and on the affinity between edges of distinct rectangles.

All NP-completeness proofs contained in this chapter are due to Karp (1972), except those of SATISFIABILITY and of 3-SATISFIABILITY which appeared in Cook (1971).

The p-isomorphism among NP-complete problems was studied in Berman and Hartmanis (1977): in that paper, the results of Section 5.2.2 were first derived. In Joseph and Young (1985), the p-isomorphism conjecture was related to the existence of 'hard to invert' functions. In particular, it was conjectured that if such functions exist, then there is a special class of NP-complete languages, called k-creative, whose members are not p-isomorphic to SATISFIABILITY. Perhaps partly as a result of this counter-conjecture, there has been intense interest in the p-isomorphism conjecture in the past few year. We refer the interested reader to the surveys of Kurtz, Mahaney, and Royer (1990) and Young (1990).

In Berman and Hartmanis (1977), the authors conjectured that no sparse NP-complete languages exist. The path to solving this conjecture can be summarized as follows. The pruning technique appearing in the proof of Theorem 5.6 was first introduced in Berman (1978) and successfully applied in Hartmanis and Mahaney (1980) in order to obtain the theorem itself. Finally, Theorem 5.7 was obtained in Mahaney (1982).

As already observed, Theorem 5.8 appeared for the first time in Ladner (1975a) while our formulation, as an application of Theorem 4.1, is taken from Schöning (1982a).

A proof that each finite group G of n elements admits a system of generators of at most $\log(n)$ elements can be found in several books on group theory such as that by Hoffmann (1982), while the algorithm to test group isomorphism was introduced in Miller (1978). Some evidence that problems related to isomorphism between structures such as graphs are not NP-complete is given in Schöning (1986).

The study of the relationships between complexity classes using the properties of tally and sparse sets was initiated in Book (1974); in particular, Lemma 5.2 appeared in Hartmanis (1983).

The existing relationships between computing and verifying a function were considered in Valiant (1976). In addition to Theorem 5.10, that paper contains other interesting results along this line of research. The comment about the theory of recursive functions refers to the following property of general recursive functions. Given any such function which is not a primitive recursive function (for instance, Ackermann's function) the corresponding decision problem is primitive recursive. For additional information on this topic, we suggest Rogers (1967).

The study of the relativized version of the $P \neq NP$ conjecture started with the paper by Baker, Gill, and Solovay (1975) where Theorem 5.11 and 5.12 appeared for the first time. Since then research on relativization of complexity classes has gone beyond expectation. Even though this chapter considered relativizations only of the classes P and NP, essentially all complexity classes defined in the literature were relativized and many other oracle-separation results were obtained. For a list of such results, we refer to the Notes of the following chapters. Moreover, in Chapter 10 we shall consider two important complexity classes which coincide although an oracle exists separating the corresponding relativized classes!

The concept of strong separation was initially studied in Bennett and Gill (1981) where the existence of an oracle A such that NP^A contains a P^A-immune language was proved. In Homer and Maass (1983) and, independently, in Schöning (1982b) it was shown that such a set A can be taken to be recursive. The proof of Theorem 5.13 is inspired by Schöning and Book (1984) where further generalizations were also presented.

The concept of 'positive relativization' was introduced in Book, Long, and Selman (1985). This paper contains many results based on restricting the number of oracle queries (one of them is Theorem 5.14). Long and Selman (1986) studied the bound on the density of the oracle: Theorem 5.15 is inspired by that paper. In Book (1989) the reader can find an interesting survey on such restricted relativizations.

Chapter 6

The complexity of optimization problems

An important characteristic of decision problems is that all feasible solutions are considered equally acceptable. In many practical applications, however, this assumption does not hold and it becomes necessary to rank the solutions according to some criterion. This is usually done by associating a measure to each solution. Depending on the application, the best solution is then the one having the maximum measure or, conversely, the minimum measure.

Problems of this kind are called optimization problems. Some of them, such as scheduling, routing, and flow control, have been thoroughly investigated in the past few decades and in many cases heuristic techniques leading to good but suboptimal solutions have been developed.

In addition to these empirical developments, two main questions have arisen concerning optimization problems, namely, whether a polynomial-time algorithm yielding an optimal solution exists, and, in the negative case, whether there is a polynomial-time algorithm yielding a suboptimal solution with some degree of accuracy. Complexity theory has provided a set of tools to answer both questions and we shall present them in this chapter.

First, let us informally introduce the concept of an underlying decision problem. Instead of requesting the best solution, we content ourselves with determining whether a solution having a measure, at least, k (or, at most, k) exists. It should be clear that the computational complexity of an optimization problem cannot be smaller than that of its underlying decision problem. Assume we have an algorithm which computes a solution having maximum measure. We can then easily test[1] whether its measure is, at least, k and thus solve the underlying decision problem (if the algorithm computes a solution having minimum measure, we then test whether its measure is, at most, k).

This chapter is concerned with optimization problems whose underlying decision problems belong to NP. In Section 6.1 we formally define the concept of an opti-

---

[1]Here we are implicitly assuming that computing the measure of a solution is almost without cost.

mization problem and introduce two important classes of such problems, called PO and NPO. In Section 6.2 we analyse the relation between an optimization problem and its underlying decision problem while in Section 6.3 we compare the complexity of evaluating the optimum measure, i.e. the measure of an optimum solution, and that of computing an optimum solution.

In Section 6.4 we introduce the concept of an approximable optimization problem. The widespread belief that some optimization problems cannot be solved in polynomial time made researchers look for strategies leading to suboptimal solutions, that is, strategies whose objective is to find a polynomial-time algorithm which always finds solutions *close* to the optimum. In this section we define three classes of problems that admit different kinds of approximation algorithms and analyse their relations.

Finally, in Section 6.5 we introduce a natural reducibility between optimization problems and show the existence of NPO-complete problems, that is, problems which do not admit approximation algorithms unless P = NP.

6.1 Optimization problems

The basic ingredients of an optimization problem are the same as those of a decision problem along with a function which measures the 'goodness' of feasible solutions. The problem consists of finding a solution with either maximum measure (in the case of a maximization problem) or minimum measure (in the case of a minimization problem). If the measure can only assume two values, e.g. 0 and 1, then the optimization problem essentially becomes a decision one. In general, however, this is not true and the measure can assume an arbitrary range of values. In this chapter, we shall consider only optimization problems whose measure assumes positive integer values.

Thus, an *optimization problem* is a tuple $\langle I, S, \pi, m, \text{GOAL} \rangle$ such that

1. I is a set of words that encode instances of the problem.
2. S is a function that maps an instance $x \in I$ into a non-empty finite set of words that encode possible solutions of x.
3. π is a predicate such that, for any instance x and for any possible solution $y \in S(x)$, $\pi(x, y) = \textbf{true}$ if and only if y is a feasible solution. Furthermore, we assume that, for any instance x, a feasible solution of x exists.
4. m is a function that associates with any instance $x \in I$ and with any feasible solution y a positive integer $m(x, y)$ that denotes the *measure* of solution y.
5. $\text{GOAL} = \max$ or $\text{GOAL} = \min$.

Solving an optimization problem $\langle I, S, \pi, m, \text{GOAL} \rangle$ consists of finding an *optimum solution* for a given instance $x \in I$, that is, a feasible solution y such that

$$m(x, y) = \text{GOAL}\{m(x, z) : z \in S(x) \wedge \pi(x, z) = \textbf{true}\}.$$

In particular, we say that a Turing transducer T *solves* an optimization problem $\langle I, S, \pi, m, \text{GOAL} \rangle$ if, for any $x \in I$, $T(x)$ outputs a word encoding an optimum solution.

From now on, OPT will denote the function that associates the measure of an optimum solution with any instance $x \in I$.

Example 6.1 MINIMUM COVER: given a finite set A and a collection C of subsets of A, find a minimum size subset $C' \subseteq C$ such that every element of A belongs to, at least, one member of C'. Thus MINIMUM COVER $= \langle I, S, \pi, m, \min \rangle$ where

1. I is the set of pairs $\langle A, C \rangle$ where A is a finite set and C is a collection of subsets of A.

2. S associates with any instance $\langle A, C \rangle \in I$ the set of all subsets $C' \subseteq C$.

3. For any instance $\langle A, C \rangle \in I$ and for any subset $C' \in S(A, C)$, $\pi(\langle A, C \rangle, C') = \textbf{true}$ if and only if the union of the members of C' is equal to A.

4. For any instance $\langle A, C \rangle \in I$ and for any $C' \in S(A, C)$ such that $\pi(\langle A, C \rangle, C') = \textbf{true}$, $m(\langle A, C \rangle, C') = |C'|$.

Example 6.2 MAXIMUM CLIQUE: given a graph G, find a maximum size clique contained in G. Thus, MAXIMUM CLIQUE $= \langle I, S, \pi, m, \max \rangle$ where

1. I is the set of graphs G.

2. S associates with any instance $G \in I$ the set of all subgraphs contained in G.

3. For any instance $G \in I$ and for any $G' \in S(G)$, $\pi(G, G') = \textbf{true}$ if and only if G' is a clique.

4. for any instance $G \in I$ and for any clique $G' \in S(G)$, $m(G, G') = |G'|$, that is, $m(G, G')$ denotes the number of nodes of G'.

We now introduce two classes of optimization problems, called NPO and PO, which correspond in some way to the classes of decision problems NP and P.

6.1.1 The class NPO

An optimization problem $\langle I, S, \pi, m, \text{GOAL} \rangle$ belongs to the *class NPO* if the following conditions hold.

1. The set I belongs to P.
2. A polynomial p exists such that, for any $x \in I$ and for any $y \in S(x)$, $|y| \leq p(|x|)$.

3. For any $x \in I$ and for any y such that $|y| \leq p(|x|)$, it is decidable in polynomial time whether $y \in S(x)$.

4. The predicate π is decidable in polynomial time.

5. The function m belongs to FP.

Example 6.3 Let us show that the problem MINIMUM COVER introduced in Example 6.1 satisfies conditions 1-5 and, thus, belongs to NPO.

1. $I \in \mathrm{P}$ since, given any x, it suffices to check whether $x = \langle A, C \rangle$ where A is a finite set and C is a collection of subsets of A.

2. For any $C' \subseteq C$, it is clear that $|C'| \leq |C| \leq |\langle A, C \rangle|$.

3. For any $\langle A, C \rangle$ and for any y with $|y| \leq |\langle A, C \rangle|$, we can decide whether y is a possible solution simply checking whether $y = C'$ with $C' \subseteq C$.

4. For any $\langle A, C \rangle$ and for any $C' \subseteq C$, we can easily check in polynomial time whether the union of the members of C' is equal to A.

5. For any C', the cardinality of C' can obviously be computed in polynomial time.

Example 6.4 The problem MAXIMUM CLIQUE introduced in Example 6.2 belongs to NPO. By choosing $S(G)$ as the set of all subsets of nodes of G, it can be immediately verified that conditions 2-5 hold.

Example 6.5 MINIMUM NODE COVER: given a graph $G = (N, E)$, find a minimum size subset $N' \subseteq N$ such that, for each edge $\langle u, v \rangle \in E$, at least, one of u and v belongs to N'. This problem belongs to NPO: by choosing $S(G)$ as in the previous example, it can be immediately verified that conditions 2-5 hold.

Example 6.6 MINIMUM TRAVELING SALESMAN: given a complete weighted graph G, find a cycle passing through all nodes of G which minimizes the sum of the weights associated with the edges of the cycle. This problem belongs to NPO: by choosing $S(G)$ as the set of all permutations of the node indices of G, it can be immediately verified that conditions 2-5 hold.

6.1.2 The class PO

An optimization problem in NPO belongs to the *class PO* if it is solvable in polynomial time by a deterministic Turing transducer.

Example 6.7 BIPARTITE MATCHING: given a bipartite[2] graph $G = (N, E)$, find a maximum matching in G, that is, a maximum cardinality set of edges $E' \subseteq E$ such that no two edges of E' are incident.

---

[2] A graph $G = (N, E)$ is said to be *bipartite* if the set of nodes can be partitioned into two sets N_1 and N_2 such that each edge in E has one node in N_1 and one node in N_2.

This is a well-known optimization problem which is solvable in polynomial time by making use of the augmenting path technique. Given a matching M, an edge belonging to M is called matched, while the other edges are called free. A node incident to a matched edge is also called matched, while the other nodes are free. An *augmenting path* for M is a path whose edges are alternatively free and matched and whose first and last nodes are free. We first observe that a matching is of maximum cardinality if and only if it admits no augmenting path. Indeed, if M has an augmenting path, then reversing the roles of the matched and free edges in the path results in a new matching of size $|M|+1$, that is, M is not maximum. Conversely, let M be a matching which is not maximum, that is, there is a matching M' such that $|M'| > |M|$. Consider the edges in $M \triangle M'$. These edges form a subgraph whose nodes have degree 2 or less and if a node has degree 2 then it is incident to one edge in M and to one edge in M'. Thus, that subgraph is formed by either paths or cycles of even length. In all cycles we have the same number of edges of M as that of M'. Since $|M'| > |M|$, then a path exists with more edges from M' than from M. This path is thus an augmenting path for M.

The algorithm which solves BIPARTITE MATCHING is therefore based on repeatedly searching augmenting paths (starting from an initial matching M) and is the following:

begin {input $G = (N_1, N_2, E)$; output: M}
   for any node x **do** set x unlabeled;
   $M := \emptyset$;
   while an unlabeled free node $x \in N_1$ exists **do**
     if an augmenting path starting from x exists **then**
      augment M by such a path
     else set x labeled;
end.

Note that if no augmenting path starts from a free node x (at any step), then there never will be an augmenting path from x and that node can be ignored in later steps (that is, it becomes labeled). From the above discussion it follows that the previous algorithm correctly computes a matching of maximum cardinality.

Clearly there can be, at most, $|N|/2$ augmentations (since the number of matched edges increases by 1 at each augmentation). Furthermore, looking for an augmenting path starting from a free node in N_1 takes $\mathbf{O}[|E|]$ time. Indeed, such a process can be performed by a breadth-first search starting from the free node. Hence, the algorithm runs in polynomial time and BIPARTITE MATCHING belongs to PO.

Example 6.8 SCHEDULING FIXED JOBS: given n jobs J_j, each with a starting time s_j and a completion time t_j ($j = 1 \ldots, n$) which can be executed by any machine M_i from a set of identical machines, determine an optimum schedule that minimizes the number of machines required. A *schedule* assigns to each J_j a machine M_i from s_j to t_j; a schedule is *feasible* if the processing intervals (s_j, t_j) on M_i are non-overlapping for all i; a schedule is *optimal* if it is feasible and if it minimizes the maximum completion time of the jobs. A simple example of optimum schedule is represented in Figure 6.1.

An easy scheme to derive an optimal schedule consists of ordering, first, jobs according to non-decreasing starting times and of next scheduling each successive job on a machine, giving priority to a machine that has previously completed another job. It is not hard to

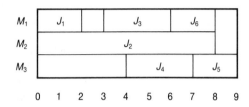

j:	1	2	3	4	5	6
s_j:	0	0	3	4	7	6
t_j:	2	8	6	7	9	8

Figure 6.1 A simple example of an optimum schedule

realize that, at the end, the number of machines to which jobs have been assigned is equal to the maximum number of jobs that require simultaneous processing. The optimality of the resulting schedule follows.

Denote by u an array of length $2n$ containing all starting and completion times in non-decreasing order. The informal notation $u_k \sim s_j$ (respectively, $u_k \sim t_j$) will serve to indicate that the kth element of u corresponds to the starting (respectively, completion) time of J_j. The algorithm also uses a stack S of idle machines such that the machine that has most recently completed a job, if any, is always placed on top of the stack:

```
begin {input: s₁,t₁,…,sₙ,tₙ};
    sort the sⱼ,tⱼ in non-decreasing order in (u₁,…,u₂ₙ),
    if tⱼ = sₖ for some j,k then insert tⱼ before sₖ in u;
    S := stack of n machines;
    for k = 1 to 2n do
    begin
        if uₖ ~ sⱼ then pop machine from S and assign it to Jⱼ;
        if uₖ ~ tⱼ then push machine assigned to Jⱼ on top of S;
    end;
end.
```

Clearly, the number of steps required by the above algorithm is $\mathbf{O}[n \log(n)]$.

6.2 Underlying languages

We have already observed in the introduction to this chapter how optimization problems may be considered as an extension of decision problems. Conversely, given an optimization problem we can always derive from it an *underlying language* (or *underlying decision problem*) in the following way. Instead of looking for the best solution of instance x, we ask whether x admits a solution having measure, at least, k (or, at most, k) and, in the affirmative case we include the pair $\langle x, k \rangle$ in the underlying language. Thus, that language consists of all pairs $\langle x, k \rangle$, with $x \in I$ and $k > 0$, such that a feasible solution y exists with $m(x, y) \geq k$ if GOAL = max and $m(x, y) \leq k$ otherwise.

Example 6.9 The underlying language of MINIMUM COVER, introduced in Example 6.1, is the set of triples $\langle A, C, k \rangle$ such that a cover exists for A of size k or less, that is, it coincides with NODE COVER which was introduced in Example 5.5.

Example 6.10 The underlying language of MAXIMUM CLIQUE, introduced in Example 6.2, is the set of pairs $\langle G, k \rangle$ such that G contains a clique of size k or more, that is, it coincides with CLIQUE which was introduced in Example 5.7.

The next lemma justifies our interest in the class NPO.

Lemma 6.1 If an optimization problem belongs to NPO, then the underlying language belongs to NP.

Proof. Let $\langle I, S, \pi, m, \text{GOAL} \rangle$ be an optimization problem in NPO and let p be the polynomial limiting the length of the feasible solutions. The following nondeterministic algorithm decides the underlying language:

```
begin {input: x, k}
    if x ∉ I then reject;
    guess y in set of words of length, at most, p(|x|);
    if not y ∈ S(x) then reject;
    if not π(x, y) then reject;
    if GOAL = max then
        if m(x, y) ≥ k then accept else reject
    else if m(x, y) ≤ k then accept else reject;
end.
```

From conditions 1-5 it follows that the above algorithm works in polynomial time. □

We have already observed that the complexity of an optimization problem in NPO cannot be smaller than that of the underlying language: if an optimum solution can be computed in polynomial time, then the underlying language also is polynomial-time decidable. The next lemma formalizes this observation.

Lemma 6.2 If an optimization problem belongs to PO, then the underlying language belongs to P.

Proof. Let $\langle I, S, \pi, m, \text{GOAL} \rangle$ be an optimization problem in PO. By hypothesis, for any instance x, the optimum measure $\text{OPT}(x)$ for that problem can be computed in polynomial time. Since, for any instance $\langle x, k \rangle$, it is possible to compare $\text{OPT}(x)$ with k in polynomial time, then the underlying language belongs to P. $\quad\square$

An immediate consequence of Lemma 6.2 is the next lemma, which says that if $P \neq NP$, many optimization problems of practical interest are computationally intractable.

Lemma 6.3 If $P \neq NP$, then any problem $\langle I, S, \pi, m, \text{GOAL} \rangle$ in NPO whose underlying language is NP-complete does not belong to PO.

Proof. Given an optimization problem $\langle I, S, \pi, m, \text{GOAL} \rangle$ in NPO, let L be the underlying language. Since L is NP-complete and $P \neq NP$, then L does not belong to P. From Lemma 6.2, it follows that $\langle I, S, \pi, m, \text{GOAL} \rangle$ does not belong to PO. $\quad\square$

We have already encountered NPO problems whose underlying languages are NP-complete. Therefore, the following corollary results from the application of Lemma 6.3.

Corollary 6.1 If $P \neq NP$, then PO $\neq$ NPO.

6.3 Optimum measure versus optimum solution

Solving an optimization problem means deriving an effective optimal solution for it. We may also consider a slightly less ambitious objective, namely, that of computing the optimal measure without producing an optimum solution. For example, instead of determining the nodes of a maximum clique of a given graph, we may content ourselves with computing the size of a maximum clique.

In the case of optimization problems in NPO, the measure function is computable in polynomial time. Hence, a polynomial-time algorithm which computes the optimum measure can immediately be derived from a polynomial-time algorithm yielding an optimum solution. What of the reverse case? In general, it does not seem possible to obtain an optimum solution, even if we know its measure. Even if we could evaluate the optimum measure of arbitrary instances in polynomial time, the problem of obtaining an optimum solution is not likely to be solvable in polynomial time. In other words, it seems that optimum solutions are harder to obtain, since they yield additional information.

In some cases, however, optimum solutions can be derived from optimum measures as we shall see in the remaining part of this section.

Given a problem $\langle I, S, \pi, m, \text{GOAL} \rangle$ in NPO, the *prefix version* is a new optimization problem $\langle I_p, S_p, \pi_p, m_p, \text{GOAL} \rangle$ where

1. $I_p = I \times \Sigma^*$.

2. For any instance $\langle x, a \rangle \in I_p'$, $S_p(x, a) = S(x)$.
3. For any instance $\langle x, a \rangle \in I_p$ and for any possible solution y, $\pi_p(\langle x, a \rangle, y) = $ **true** if and only if $\pi(x, y) = $ **true** and a is a prefix of y.[3]
4. For any instance $\langle x, a \rangle \in I_p$ and for any feasible solution y, $m_p(\langle x, a \rangle, y) = m(x, y)$.

Let OPT_p denote the function that computes the optimum measure of the prefix version.

Theorem 6.1 If $\langle I, S, \pi, m, \text{GOAL} \rangle$ is an optimization problem in NPO such that $\text{OPT}_p \in \text{FP}$, then $\langle I, S, \pi, m, \text{GOAL} \rangle$ belongs to PO.

Proof. The following polynomial-time algorithm computes an optimum solution a for $\langle I, S, \pi, m, \text{GOAL} \rangle$ symbol by symbol:

begin {input: x; output: a}
  $a := e$;
  {$\text{OPT}_p(x, e)$ coincides with $\text{OPT}(x)$}
  while $a \notin S(x) \vee \neg\pi(x, a) \vee \text{OPT}_p(x, e) \neq m(x, a)$ **do**
  begin
    look for a $\sigma \in \Sigma$ such that $\text{OPT}_p(x, a\sigma) = \text{OPT}_p(x, e)$;
    {since, at least, one optimum solution exists then such a σ must exist}
    $a := a\sigma$;
  end;
end.

It is easy to verify that, since $|a| \leq r(|x|)$, for some polynomial r, and OPT_p is computable in polynomial time with respect to $|\langle x, a \rangle|$, the algorithm has polynomial-time complexity with respect to the length of x. $\qquad\square$

An interesting consequence of Theorem 6.1 is the next corollary, which provides a sufficient condition for computing an optimum solution in polynomial time, assuming that the optimum measure can be evaluated in polynomial time.

Corollary 6.2 Let $\langle I, S, \pi, m, \text{GOAL} \rangle$ be an optimization problem in NPO. If $\text{OPT} \in \text{FP}$ implies $\text{OPT}_p \in \text{FP}$, then $\text{OPT} \in \text{FP}$ implies that $\langle I, S, \pi, m, \text{GOAL} \rangle$ belongs to PO.

Example 6.11 Let us consider the prefix version of MINIMUM COVER introduced in Example 6.1 where prefix a denotes subsets D of C. If $\text{OPT} \in \text{FP}$, then, given an instance

---

[3]If the problem does not admit feasible solutions having prefix a, we can always appropriately modify S_p, π_p and m_p obtaining a new prefix version which, for any instance $\langle x, a \rangle$, admits, at least, one feasible solution (see Problem 6.4).

$\langle\langle A, C\rangle, D\rangle$, we can compute $\text{OPT}_p(\langle\langle A, C\rangle, D\rangle)$ in the following way. If $A' = A - \bigcup_{d\in D} d$ and, for any $c \in C$, $c' = c - \bigcup_{d\in D} d$, then $\text{OPT}_p(\langle\langle A, C\rangle, D\rangle) = \text{OPT}(\langle A', C'\rangle) + |D|$.

The previous procedure can easily be extended to prefixes which do not correspond to subsets of C but rather to partial encodings of such subsets (see Problem 6.5). Thus, if we can evaluate in polynomial time the optimum measure of MINIMUM COVER, then we can compute in polynomial time an optimum solution for it. Since the underlying language of MINIMUM COVER is NP-complete (see Problem 5.13), this seems unlikely.

In fact, the next theorem shows that not only MINIMUM COVER but all problems whose underlying languages are NP-complete do not seem to admit an optimum measure computable in polynomial time.

Theorem 6.2 The following statements are equivalent:

1. P = NP.
2. For any optimization problem in NPO, OPT $\in$ FP.
3. PO = NPO.

Proof. $2 \rightarrow 1$. This follows from Example 6.11, Corollary 6.2 and Lemma 6.3.

$3 \rightarrow 2$. This follows from the discussion at the beginning of this section.

$1 \rightarrow 3$. Given an optimization problem in NPO, the underlying language belongs to NP and, according to the hypothesis, to P. Given any instance of the optimization problem, we can then evaluate its optimum measure through a binary search (see Problem 6.7) and, then, use this value to compute an optimum solution (see Problem 6.8). □

6.4   Approximability

Lemma 6.3 shows that it is unlikely that an optimization problem whose underlying language is NP-complete admits a polynomial-time algorithm yielding an optimum solution. In these cases we sacrifice optimality and start looking for approximate solutions computable in polynomial time.

Example 6.12 Recall that MINIMUM NODE COVER is an NPO problem whose underlying language is NP-complete (see Example 5.5).

Let us consider the following polynomial-time algorithm:

```
begin {input: G = (N, E); output: N'}
   {N' denotes the cover and E' the candidate edges}
   N' := ∅;
   E' := E;
   while E' ≠ ∅ do
   begin
      pick any edge ⟨u, v⟩ ∈ E';
```

$E' := E' - \{\langle u, v \rangle\};$
$\{\langle u, v \rangle$ is still uncovered $\}$
if $u \notin N' \wedge v \notin N'$ **then** $N' := N' \cup \{u, v\};$
end;
end.

Clearly, the subset $N' \subseteq N$ computed by the algorithm is a vertex cover corresponding to a set of disjoint edges whose cardinality is $|N'|/2$ (since for any edge both its endpoints have been added to N'). Since, by definition, any cover must 'touch' all the edges of such set, then it must contain, at least, $|N'|/2$ nodes. Thus, the cardinality of N' is, at most, twice the cardinality of an optimum cover.

6.4.1   The class APX

The previous example shows that optimization problems exist in NPO for which it is possible to get 'close enough' to an optimum solution. To characterize such problems, let us introduce some definitions.

Let $\langle I, S, \pi, m, \text{GOAL} \rangle$ be an optimization problem. For any instance $x \in I$ and for any feasible solution y, the *relative error* of y (with respect to x) is defined as

$$|\text{OPT}(x) - m(x, y)|/\text{OPT}(x).$$

Given an optimization problem $\langle I, S, \pi, m, \text{GOAL} \rangle$ and a positive rational ϵ, a Turing transducer T is an *ϵ-approximating algorithm* for $\langle I, S, \pi, m, \text{GOAL} \rangle$ if, for any instance $x \in I$, $T(x)$ computes in polynomial time a feasible solution whose relative error is less than or equal to ϵ.

An optimization problem is *approximable* if it admits an ϵ-approximating algorithm, for a given ϵ. Note that, for most of the 'natural' maximization problems in NPO, it is always possible to derive a Turing transducer computing a feasible solution y in polynomial time, for any instance $x \in I$. In this case the definition of approximability only makes sense if $\epsilon < 1$ (since the measure of a feasible solution is greater than 0, all 'natural' maximization problems admit a 1-approximating algorithm).

The *class APX* is defined as the set of all approximable optimization problems in NPO.

Example 6.13 The algorithm presented in Example 6.12 is a 1-approximating algorithm for the problem MINIMUM VERTEX COVER. In fact, we have already observed that such an algorithm computes a feasible solution whose measure is, at most, twice the optimum measure. If $y = T(x)$, then

$$\frac{|\text{OPT}(x) - m(x, y)|}{\text{OPT}(x)} = \frac{m(x, y) - \text{OPT}(x)}{\text{OPT}(x)} \leq \frac{2\text{OPT}(x)}{\text{OPT}(x)} - 1 = 1.$$

The next theorem shows that if $P \neq NP$, then not all optimization problems in NPO are approximable.

Theorem 6.3 If P $\neq$ NP, then an optimization problem that is not approximable exists in NPO.

Proof. Let $L \in$ NP $-$ P and let NT be a polynomial-time nondeterministic Turing machine that decides L. We have already discussed how to encode the computation paths of $NT(x)$ as words whose length is bounded by $p(|x|)$, for a polynomial p.

Let us define the maximization problem $\langle I, S, \pi, m, \max \rangle$ where

1. $I = \Sigma^* - \{e, 0, 1\}$.
2. For any instance x, $S(x) = \{y : y \in \Sigma^* \land |y| \leq p(|x|)\}$.
3. For any instance x and for any possible solution y, $\pi(x, y) = $ **true** if and only if y encodes a computation path of $NT(x)$.
4. For any instance x and for any feasible solution y,

$$m(x, y) = \begin{cases} |x| & \text{if } y \text{ encodes an accepting computation} \\ & \text{path,} \\ 1 & \text{otherwise.} \end{cases}$$

Note that, for any $x \in I$, $\text{OPT}(x) = |x|$ if and only if $x \in L$.

Assume that the previous problem admits an ϵ-approximating algorithm T for some $\epsilon < 1$. Let n_0 be a natural number such that $(n_0 - 1)/n_0 > \epsilon$. We shall prove that, for any x whose length is, at least, n_0, $m(x, T(x)) = \text{OPT}(x)$. This, in turn, implies that a polynomial-time Turing machine exists that decides L. Indeed, such a machine with input x simulates $T(x)$ and accepts if and only if the output encodes an accepting computation path of $NT(x)$. Since $L \notin$ P, the theorem follows.

Let x be an instance of length, at least, n_0. If $x \notin L$, then $\text{OPT}(x) = 1$ and, of course, $m(x, T(x)) = \text{OPT}(x)$. Conversely, if $x \in L$, then $\text{OPT}(x) = |x|$. The measure of $T(x)$ must then be equal to $\text{OPT}(x)$, otherwise the relative error would be

$$\frac{\text{OPT}(x) - m(x, T(x))}{\text{OPT}(x)} = \frac{|x| - 1}{|x|} \geq \frac{n_0 - 1}{n_0} > \epsilon,$$

contradicting the assumption.

$\square$

An immediate consequence is the following corollary.

Corollary 6.3 If P $\neq$ NP, then APX $\neq$ NPO.

6.4.2   The class PAS

Finding an approximating algorithm for an optimization problem whose underlying language is NP-complete could be considered a good result. An even better one would consist of approximating such a problem *for any* ϵ. In this case, the inputs of the algorithm computing approximate solutions should include both the instance x and the required accuracy, that is, the value ϵ.

Given an optimization problem $\langle I, S, \pi, m, \text{GOAL} \rangle$, a *polynomial approximation scheme* for $\langle I, S, \pi, m, \text{GOAL} \rangle$ is a Turing transducer T such that, for any instance $x \in I$ and for any positive rational ϵ, $T(x, \epsilon)$ computes a feasible solution whose relative error is, at most, ϵ in polynomial time with respect to $|x|$.

The *class PAS* is defined as the set of all the optimization problems in NPO that admit a polynomial approximation scheme.

Example 6.14 MINIMUM PARTITION: given a set of n integer numbers $A = \{a_1, \ldots, a_n\}$, find a partition of A into two disjoint subsets A_1 and A_2 which minimizes the value $\max\{\sum_{a_i \in A_1} a_i, \sum_{a_i \in A_2} a_i\}$. The underlying language of MINIMUM PARTITION is NP-complete (see Problem 5.12).

Without loss of generality, we can assume that the n numbers are ordered in a non-increasing way. For any fixed h, let us consider the following algorithm T_h that partitions the first h elements of A optimally and then adds each remaining element to the smaller set:

begin {input: A; output: A_1, A_2}
   if $h > n$ **then** $h := n$;
   find an optimum partition $\langle A_1, A_2 \rangle$ for the first h elements;
   for $i = h + 1$ **to** n **do**
      if $\sum_{a_j \in A_1} a_j \leq \sum_{a_j \in A_2} a_j$ **then** $A_1 := A_1 \cup \{a_i\}$
      else $A_2 := A_2 \cup \{a_i\}$;
end.

The time complexity of the first step of the algorithm is exponential in h (but remember that h is fixed), while the remaining steps can be performed in polynomial time with respect to n. We shall now show that the relative error is always less than or equal to $1/(h+1)$.

Note that $\text{OPT}(A) \geq L$ where $L = \frac{1}{2} \sum_{i=1}^{n} a_i$. Let $\langle A_1, A_2 \rangle$ be the partition computed by the algorithm and assume that $\sum_{a_j \in A_1} a_j \geq \sum_{a_j \in A_2} a_j$. Let $\bar{a}$ be the last element added to A_1. If $\bar{a}$ is added during the first step of the algorithm, then $\langle A_1, A_2 \rangle$ is an optimum solution. Otherwise, $\sum_{a_j \in A_1} a_j - \bar{a} \leq \sum_{a_j \in A_2} a_j$ and, thus, $\sum_{a_j \in A_1} a_j - L \leq \bar{a}/2$ (see Figure 6.2).

Since the numbers are ordered in a non-decreasing way and $\bar{a}$ is added after the first step of the algorithm, then $\sum_{i=1}^{n} a_i \geq (h+1)\bar{a}$. This in turn implies that $L \geq (h+1)\bar{a}/2$ and, hence, the following inequalities hold:

$$\frac{\sum_{a_j \in A_1} a_j - \text{OPT}(A)}{\text{OPT}(A)} \leq \frac{\sum_{a_j \in A_1} a_j - L}{L} \leq \frac{\bar{a}}{2L} \leq \frac{1}{h+1}.$$

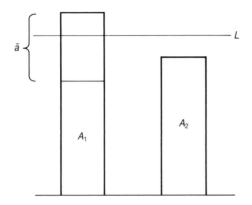

Figure 6.2 An approximation scheme for PARTITION

Thus, for any ϵ, the algorithm T_h with $h = \frac{1}{\epsilon} - 1$ outputs a solution whose relative error is, at most, ϵ. Furthermore, the time required is $\mathbf{O}[n2^{1/\epsilon}]$. It follows that MINIMUM PARTITION belongs to PAS.

6.4.3 The class FPAS

We have already observed that the algorithm presented in Example 6.14 computes a solution whose relative error is, at most, ϵ in exponential time with respect to $1/\epsilon$. In fact, the definition of an approximation scheme does not limit the time complexity to being polynomial with respect to $1/\epsilon$. Thus, computations with small ϵ values may be found to be practically unfeasible.

An approximation scheme is *fully polynomial* if it runs in polynomial time with respect to both the length of the instance *and* $1/\epsilon$.

The *class FPAS* is defined as the set of all of the optimization problems in NPO that admit a fully polynomial approximation scheme.

We will now describe a useful technique to develop fully polynomial approximation schemes.

Pseudo-polynomiality and full approximability

Let us consider the MINIMUM PARTITION problem again (see Example 6.14). The following algorithm computes a matrix T with $n \times \sum_{i=1}^{n} a_i$ Boolean entries such that $T(i, j) = \mathbf{true}$ if and only if the set $\{a_1, \ldots, a_i\}$ can be partitioned into two disjoint sets A_1 and A_2 with $\sum_{a \in A_1} a = j$:

begin {input: A; output: T}

$b := \sum_{i=1}^{n} a_i;$
{initialize the matrix T}
for $i = 1$ **to** n **do**
  for $j = 0$ **to** b **do**
    $T(i, j) :=$ **false**;
$T(1, 0) :=$ **true**;
$T(1, a_1) :=$ **true**;
for $i = 2$ **to** n **do**
  {compute the values of the ith row by using the values of the $(i-1)$th one}
  for $j = 0$ **to** b **do**
    $T(i, j) := T(i-1, j) \vee (j \geq a_i \wedge T(i-1, j-a_i));$
end.

It is easy to see that the above algorithm runs in time $\mathbf{O}[n \sum_{i=1}^{n} a_i]$. Once we have computed the matrix T we can derive the measure of an optimum solution by simply looking in the last row of the matrix for the integer h such that $T(n, h) =$ **true** and $\max\{h, \sum_{i=1}^{n} a_i - h\}$ is as small as possible. This additional step requires time $\mathbf{O}[\sum_{i=1}^{n} a_i]$. As a result, if $a_{\max}$ denotes the maximum number in A, then we can compute the optimum measure in time $\mathbf{O}[n^2 a_{\max}]$. Note also that the above algorithm can be slightly modified in order to derive not only the optimum measure but also an optimum solution.

We have already observed that the underlying language of MINIMUM PARTITION is NP-complete. Have we thus proved that P = NP? Of course not, and the reader should justify this answer before reading it in the following paragraph.

Note that, in general, the value $a_{\max}$ is not polynomial with respect to the length of the instance. In fact, $\log a_{\max}$ digits are sufficient to encode $a_{\max}$, and, thus, the length of an instance of MINIMUM PARTITION is $\mathbf{O}[n \log a_{\max}]$, while $n^2 a_{\max}$, in general, is not polynomial with respect to such a length. For this reason, algorithms such as the one presented above are called 'pseudo-polynomial'. Besides deceiving us (it looked as though we had proved P = NP!), such algorithms also suggest a way in which fully polynomial approximation schemes can be obtained.

In fact, if all the values a_i of an instance of MINIMUM PARTITION are 'small', then the above algorithm becomes very efficient. More precisely, if they are bounded by a polynomial n^k, then $a_{\max}$ is also bounded by n^k too, and the time complexity of the algorithm is $\mathbf{O}[n^{k+2}]$, that is polynomial (see Problem 4.14). Obviously this is not always the case, but we can still make use of that observation. Let us try to make the numbers small!

The most natural way to carry out such a plan is *ignoring the least significant (decimal) digits* of the numbers a_i. For instance, assume that we ignore the last digit of each, namely, for any a_i, we set $a_i' = \lfloor a_i/10 \rfloor$, and we then solve the new instance. Obviously the solution we obtain will be different in general from the optimum solution of the original instance, but let us see to what extent it is.

Let $\langle A_1, A_2 \rangle$ denote an optimum solution of the original instance, and $\langle A_1', A_2' \rangle$ an optimum solution of the truncated instance. The measure of the latter solution is always less than:

$$\max\{\textstyle\sum_{a_i \in A'_1}(10a'_i + 10), \sum_{a_i \in A'_2}(10a'_i + 10)\} \quad \text{since } 10a'_i \geq a_i - 10$$
$$\leq \max\{\textstyle\sum_{a_i \in A'_1} 10a'_i, \sum_{a_i \in A'_2} 10a'_i\} + 10n \quad \text{since } |A'_1|, |A'_2| \leq n$$
$$\leq \max\{\textstyle\sum_{a_i \in A_1} 10a'_i, \sum_{a_i \in A_2} 10a'_i\} + 10n \quad \text{since } \langle A'_1, A'_2 \rangle \text{ is optimum}$$
$$\leq \max\{\textstyle\sum_{a_i \in A_1} a_i, \sum_{a_i \in A_2} a_i\} + 10n \quad \text{since } 10a'_i \leq a_i$$

Thus,

$$\max\{\sum_{a_i \in A'_1} a_i, \sum_{a_i \in A'_2} a_i\} - \max\{\sum_{a_i \in A_1} a_i, \sum_{a_i \in A_2} a_i\} < 10n.$$

Since

$$a_{\max} \leq \max\{\sum_{a_i \in A_1} a_i, \sum_{a_i \in A_2} a_i\} \leq n a_{\max}$$

where $a_{\max}$ is the maximum of the numbers in A, then the relative error is less than $10\frac{n}{a_{\max}}$.

More generally, if we ignore the last t decimal digits of the numbers in A, then the relative error will be less than $10^t \frac{n}{a_{\max}}$. Thus, for any ϵ and $t = \lfloor \log_{10}(\epsilon \frac{a_{\max}}{n}) \rfloor$, the algorithm computes a solution whose relative error is, at most, ϵ.

Let us now evaluate the complexity of the algorithm. We have already seen that the time complexity is $\mathbf{O}[n^2 a'_{\max}]$, that is, $\mathbf{O}[n^2 a_{\max} 10^{-t}]$. Since $a_{\max} 10^{-t} \leq \frac{n}{\epsilon}$, then the time complexity is $\mathbf{O}[n^3 \frac{1}{\epsilon}]$.

We conclude that MINIMUM PARTITION admits a fully polynomial approximation scheme.

6.5 Reducibility and optimization problems

To summarize the results of the previous section, five classes of optimization problems have been identified:

1. NPO: optimization problems whose underlying languages are in NP.
2. APX: NPO-problems which are approximable within a fixed relative error ϵ.
3. PAS: NPO-problems which can be approximated within *any* ϵ by algorithms having an instance x and ϵ as input and whose time-complexity is polynomial in $|x|$ for each fixed ϵ.
4. FPAS: NPO-problems which can be approximated within *any* ϵ by algorithms having an instance x and ϵ as input and whose time-complexity is polynomial both in $|x|$ *and* in $1/\epsilon$.
5. PO: NPO-problems which are solvable in polynomial time.

Clearly, PO $\subseteq$ FPAS $\subseteq$ PAS $\subseteq$ APX $\subseteq$ NPO and, by means of techniques similar to that of Theorem 6.3, we can show that all those inclusions are strict unless P $=$ NP (see Problem 6.17). It is therefore worth looking for problems which are likely to separate such classes. Once again, using the complete problem concept seems to be the best way to proceed.

In the following we shall consider only minimization problems, even though similar results can be obtained for those of maximization. Furthermore, we shall focus our attention on the APX $\subseteq$ NPO inclusion. Similar interesting results are known for subsets of APX but, due to lack of space, we will not present them here (see Notes).

Our goal is to introduce an 'approximation preserving' reducibility, that is, a reducibility such that if problem A reduces to problem B and $B \in$ APX, then $A \in$ APX. First, note that, in order to define a suitable reducibility among minimization problems, it is not sufficient to map instances of one problem into those of another one. We also need an efficient way of reconstructing a feasible solution of the former problem from a feasible solution of the latter. Furthermore, if we want to preserve approximability properties, then we also have to guarantee that the quality of the reconstructed solution is comparable to that of the original one. These considerations lead us to the following definition.

A minimization problem $A = \langle I_A, S_A, \pi_A, m_A, \min \rangle$ is *APX-reducible* to a second minimization problem $B = \langle I_B, S_B, \pi_B, m_B, \min \rangle$, in symbols $A \leq_{\text{APX}} B$, if two functions $f : \Sigma^* \to \Sigma^*$ and $g : \Sigma^* \times \Sigma^* \to \Sigma^*$ exist such that (see Figure 6.3)

1. f and g are polynomial-time computable.
2. For any $x \in I_A$, $f(x) \in I_B$, that is, f maps instances of A into instances of B.
3. For any $x \in I_A$ and for any $y \in S_B(f(x))$, $g(x, y) \in S_A(x)$, that is, g maps feasible solutions of B into feasible solutions of A.
4. For any positive rational ϵ, a positive rational ϵ' exists such that, for any $x \in I_A$ and for any $y \in S_B(f(x))$,

$$\frac{m_B(f(x), y) - \text{OPT}_B(f(x))}{\text{OPT}_B(f(x))} \leq \epsilon \Rightarrow \frac{m_A(x, g(x, y)) - \text{OPT}_A(x)}{\text{OPT}_A(x)} \leq \epsilon'.$$

It is clear that if $A \leq_{\text{APX}} B$ and B admits an ϵ-approximating algorithm, then A admits a ϵ'-approximating algorithm which is, basically, a composition of the reduction and the approximation algorithm for B.

A minimization problem A is *NPO-complete* if $A \in$ NPO and, for any other minimization problem $B \in$ NPO, $B \leq_{\text{APX}} A$. It thus follows that no NPO-complete minimization problem belongs to APX, unless P $=$ NP (note that the proof of Theorem 6.3 can be easily modified in order to obtain a minimization 'separator' problem).

We are now faced with the following question. Do NPO-complete minimization problems exist? As in the case of our first NP-complete problem, we shall see that a positive answer is based on the simulation of machines by formulas.

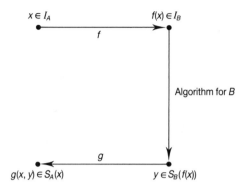

Figure 6.3 The APX-reducibility

Example 6.15 The MINIMUM SATISFIABILITY problem is defined similarly to the SATIS-FIABILITY problem, but a non-negative integer weight is associated to each variable. We are asked to find a satisfying truth-assignment which minimizes the sum of the weights of the true variables. In order to avoid an empty set of feasible solutions (this can happen whenever the formula is not satisfiable), we assume that the truth-assignment that makes all variables true is always a feasible solution, even though it may not satisfy the formula.

Theorem 6.4 MINIMUM SATISFIABILITY is NPO-complete.

Proof. It is easy to see that such a problem belongs to NPO.

To prove its NPO-completeness, first note that, for any minimization problem $A = \langle I, S, \pi, m, \min \rangle$ in NPO and for any $x \in I$, the set of feasible solutions is defined as

$$F(x) = \{y : |y| \leq p(|x|) \wedge \pi(x, y)\}$$

where p is a polynomial limiting the length of the possible solutions. Furthermore, for any $x \in I$, $\text{OPT}(x) = \min\{m(x, y) : y \in F(x)\}$.

Let us define a machine T which on input x and y first checks whether $x \in I$, then checks whether $y \in F(x)$ and finally computes $m(x, y)$. We can assume that if one of the two tests fails then T rejects, otherwise it accepts after having written $m(x, y)$ on a special tape. Since $I \in$ P, and both π and m are polynomial-time computable, it follows that T runs in polynomial time. From Theorem 5.2, we already know how to derive, for any x, a Boolean formula f_x which is satisfiable if and only a word y exists such that $T(x, y)$ accepts (in fact, since we assumed that a feasible solution always exists, f_x is always satisfiable). Let $y_1, \ldots, y_r$ be the Boolean variables describing the word y and let $m_1, \ldots, m_s$ the Boolean variables which correspond to the tape cells on which T prints the value $m(x, y)$. We then assign a zero weight to all variables excluding the m_is, which instead receive the weight 2^{s-i}.

For any truth-assignment which satisfies f_x, we then recover a feasible solution y for A by simply looking at the values of y_i's variables. It is clear that $m(x, y)$ is exactly equal to the sum of the weights of the true variables. Hence we have proved that $A \leq_{\text{APX}}$ MINIMUM SATISFIABILITY.

Since A is an arbitrary minimization problem in NPO, it follows that MINIMUM SATISFIABILITY is NPO-complete.   □

Starting from MINIMUM SATISFIABILITY it is possible to prove the NPO-completeness of other minimization problems. This is due to the fact that $\leq_{\text{APX}}$-reducibility, like polynomial-time reducibility, is transitive (see Problem 6.18). The following is a simple example.

Example 6.16 MINIMUM 0-1 PROGRAMMING: given a $m \times n$ matrix A of integers, m integers $b_1, \ldots, b_m$ and n integers $c_1, \ldots, c_n$, find n numbers $x_1, \ldots, x_n$ with $x_i \in \{0, 1\}$ such that, for any $i \leq m$,

$$\sum_{j=1}^{n} a_{ij} x_j \geq b_i$$

and the value

$$\sum_{i=1}^{n} c_i x_i$$

is as small as possible.

Once again, in order to avoid an empty set of feasible solutions, we assume that the solution with all x_i's equal to 1 is always a feasible one. Under this assumption, it is clear that MINIMUM 0-1 PROGRAMMING belongs to NPO.

We will now define an APX-reduction from MINIMUM SATISFIABILITY to MINIMUM 0-1 PROGRAMMING.

Let f be a Boolean formula in conjunctive normal form and denote by $u_1, \ldots, u_n$ the variables and by $c_1, \ldots, c_m$ the clauses of such a formula. First, the matrix A is defined as follows: $a_{ij} = 1$ if u_j occurs in c_i while $a_{ij} = -1$ if $\neg u_j$ occurs in c_i. In all other cases, $a_{ij} = 0$. Then, for any $i \leq m$, b_i is defined as 1 minus the number of negated variables in c_i. Finally, for any $i \leq m$, c_i is defined as the weight of u_i.

For example, consider the formula f with $c_1 = (u_1 \vee \neg u_2 \vee u_3)$, $c_2 = (u_4 \vee \neg u_5)$, and $c_3 = (u_2 \vee u_3 \vee u_4 \vee u_5)$ and with the weights of u_1, u_2, u_3, u_4 and u_5 defined as 2, 3, 0, 1 and 2, respectively. In the corresponding instance of MINIMUM 0-1 PROGRAMMING we are asked to minimize the value

$$2x_1 + 3x_2 + x_4 + 2x_5$$

subject to the following constraints:

$$
\begin{aligned}
x_1 - x_2 + x_3 &\geq 0 \\
x_4 - x_5 &\geq 0 \\
x_2 + x_3 + x_4 + x_5 &\geq 1
\end{aligned}
$$

and $x_i \in \{0, 1\}$.

It is easy to prove that any feasible solution of the instance of MINIMUM 0-1 PROGRAMMING corresponds to a truth-assignment for f having the same measure. Indeed, it is sufficient to interpret a 1 as **true** and a 0 as **false**. This proves that MINIMUM 0-1 PROGRAMMING $\leq_{\text{APX}}$ MINIMUM SATISFIABILITY and hence that it is NPO-complete.

The number of known NPO-complete problems is much smaller than that of NP-complete ones. On the one hand, proving NPO-completeness seems harder than proving NP-completeness because of the more constrained reducibility and, on the other, many NP-complete problems admit approximation algorithms and cannot be NPO-complete unless P = NP. Nevertheless, the concept of completeness seems to be the right way to obtain general results and, in fact, several interesting completeness proofs relative to subclasses of NPO have been obtained (see Notes).

Problems

6.1. MAXIMUM CUT: given a graph $G = (N, E)$, find a partition of N into two disjoint sets N_1 and N_2 such that the number of edges that have one endpoint in N_1 and one endpoint in N_2 is maximum. Prove that the underlying language is NP-complete. [Karp (1972)] A graph is said to be *planar* if it can be embedded into two-dimensional space R^2 (see Example 4.6). Prove that MAXIMUM CUT belongs to PO when restricted to planar graphs. [Hint: consider the dual graph of G whose nodes correspond to regions in the embedding of G and whose edges denote the fact that two regions share an edge in G.]

6.2. A graph is said to be *chordal* if, for any cycle of length greater than three, at least, one edge exists between two non-consecutive nodes of the cycle. Show that MAXIMUM CLIQUE belongs to PO when restricted to chordal graphs. [Gavril (1972)]

6.3. A *subset system* is a pair $\langle X, C \rangle$ where X is a finite set and C is a subset of 2^X closed under inclusion. A subset system is said to be a *matroid* if, for any c and c' in C such that $|c'| = |c| + 1$, an element $x \in c' - c$ exists such that $c \cup \{x\} \in C$. Given a subset system $\langle X, C \rangle$ along with a weight function $w : X \to N$, consider the following greedy algorithm:

```
begin {input: X, C, w; output: c}
  c := ∅;
  while X ≠ ∅ do
  begin
    choose an element x of X with maximum weight;
```

$X := X - \{x\};$
  if $c \cup \{x\} \in C$ **then** $c := c \cup \{x\};$
  end;
end.

Show that $\langle X, C \rangle$ is a matroid if and only if the above algorithm computes a subset of C with maximum weight. Observe that if we require the algorithm to run in polynomial time with respect to $|X|$, we cannot represent the set C by listing all its elements. However, if the predicate $c \in C$ can be decided in polynomial time, then we can represent C by an algorithm computing this predicate. Can you think of an application of the above result to prove that an optimization problem belongs to PO? [Papadimitriou and Steiglitz (1982)]

6.4. Show how to modify the definition of the prefix version of an optimization problem so that it always admits a feasible solution. [Hint: add a 'dummy' solution which is always feasible and whose measure is very small (respectively, large) if the problem is a maximization (respectively, minimization) one.]

6.5. Generalize Example 6.11 to the case where the prefixes do not exactly encode a subcollection.

6.6. Prove that, for MINIMUM VERTEX COVER, if it is possible to evaluate the optimum measure in polynomial time, then it is also possible to compute an optimum solution in polynomial time. [Hint: use the same technique as in Example 6.11.]

6.7. Prove that, for any optimization problem in NPO, if the underlying language belongs to P, then OPT is in FP. [Hint: use binary search.]

6.8. Prove that if P = NP, then, for any optimization problem in NPO, it is possible to compute an optimum solution by using the optimum measure. [Hint: use the technique of Theorem 5.10.]

6.9. Can the algorithm presented in the Example 6.12 be used to obtain an approximating algorithm for MAXIMUM CLIQUE? Justify your answer.

6.10. MINIMUM BIN PACKING: given a finite set S of numbers and an integer b, find a minimum size set of subsets of S such that the sum of the elements of each subset is, at most, b. Prove that the underlying language, called BIN PACKING, is NP-complete. [Hint: prove that PARTITION is polynomial-time reducible to BIN PACKING.] Furthermore, prove that MINIMUM BIN PACKING is approximable. [Hint: consider an algorithm that assigns a number to the first subset that can contain it or to a new subset if the number is too large.]

6.11. MAXIMUM 2-SATISFIABILITY: given a Boolean formula f in conjunctive normal form such that each clause contains exactly two literals, find an assignment of values which maximizes the number of satisfied clauses. Show that the underlying language is NP-complete. [Hint: use 3-SATISFIABILITY.] Prove that MAXIMUM 2-SATISFIABILITY admits a 1/2-approximating algorithm. [Hint: for each variable, decide its value based on the number of clauses in which it appears positive.] Generalize this result to MAXIMUM SATISFIABILITY in which clauses are allowed to contain any number of literals.

6.12. Prove that MINIMUM NODE COVER is approximable when restricted to planar graphs. [Baker (1983)]

6.13. Show that MAXIMUM KNAPSACK (the optimization version of KNAPSACK) belongs to FPAS. [Hint: first show that MAXIMUM KNAPSACK has a pseudo-polynomial algorithm, then apply the 'scaling' technique of Section 6.4.3.]

6.14. Prove that, for any graph G, it is possible to compute in polynomial time a graph G' such that G contains a clique of size k if and only if G' contains a clique of size k^2. [Hint: G' contains a copy of G for any node of G itself. Given a copy corresponding to a node u, connect any node of such a copy to each node of the copies corresponding to nodes adjacent to u.]

6.15. Prove that if, for *some* $\epsilon < 1$, an ϵ-approximating algorithm for MAXIMUM CLIQUE exists, then such a problem admits a δ-approximating algorithm, for *any* $\delta < 1$. [Hint: use the result of the previous problem.]

6.16. Show that if an optimization problem is such that

1. It admits no pseudo-polynomial algorithm.

2. For any instance x, $\text{OPT}(x) \leq p(maxint(x))$ where p and $maxint(x)$ denote a polynomial and the largest integer in x, respectively,

then it does not belong to FPAS. Use this result and the previous one to show that either MAXIMUM CLIQUE is in NPO − APX or it is in PAS − FPAS (unless P = NP).

6.17. Prove that if P $\neq$ NP, then PAS $\neq$ APX and FPAS $\neq$ PAS. [Hint: use a technique similar to that presented in the proof of Theorem 6.3.]

6.18. Show that the APX-reducibility is transitive.

6.19. Show that if MAXIMUM CLIQUE is approximable, then MAXIMUM 2-SATISFIABILITY belongs to PAS. [Hint: 'reduce' the latter problem to the former one.]

6.20. Prove that MINIMUM TRAVELING SALESMAN is NPO-complete. [Hint: show that MINIMUM SATISFIABILITY is APX-reducible to MINIMUM TRAVELING SALESMAN.]

Notes

Optimization has provided much of the motivation for the development of NP-completeness theory. However, although all known NP-complete problems are reducible to each other (in fact, they are p-isomorphic), their corresponding optimization versions can have dramatically different properties with respect to approximability (e.g. MINIMUM PARTITION and MINIMUM 0-1 PROGRAMMING). It thus seems that more sophisticated techniques are needed to study the 'structure' of classes of optimization problems.

After initial success in deriving approximation algorithms for several problems, over the last fifteeen years a great research effort has been devoted to a more complexity-theoretic attempt at finding a unified framework for treating approximability of optimization problems. A few examples of such efforts are Ausiello, D'Atri, and Protasi (1980), Ausiello, Marchetti Spaccamela, and Protasi (1980), Paz and Moran (1981), Orponen and Mannila (1987), Krentel (1988), Papadimitriou and Yannakakis (1991), and Crescenzi and Panconesi (1991). Most of these results are surveyed in Bruschi, Joseph, and Young (1991).

The papers of Ausiello, D'Atri, and Protasi (1980) and of Paz and Moran (1981) contain most of the definitions and results presented in Section 6.1, 6.2, and 6.3: in particular, Theorems 6.1 and 6.2 appeared in the latter paper. The algorithm discussed in Example 6.7 is hinted at in Berge (1957) and, independently, in Norman and Rabin (1959) (for additional references, see Galil, 1986), while the algorithm of Example 6.8 appeared in Gupta, Lee, and Leung (1979).

One of the first studies on the approximability of optimization problems was contained in Johnson (1974) where the definitions used in Section 6.4 were presented and some approximation algorithms were derived. Papadimitriou and Steiglitz (1982) contains a good chapter on approximability: some of the examples and problems presented here are taken from there.

Pseudo-polynomiality was first analysed in Garey and Johnson (1978). In that paper the pseudo-polynomial algorithm for MINIMUM PARTITION and the concept of *strong* NP-completeness were introduced, and it was proved that the latter is closely tied to the existence of fully polynomial approximation schemes.

Several kinds of reducibilities between optimization problems were proposed. The one presented in this text was first defined in Orponen and Mannila (1987), which also contains Theorem 6.4 and the reduction of Example 6.16. This reducibility was further refined in Crescenzi and Panconesi (1991). In this paper some other natural reducibilities were introduced in order to study the relations between classes of approximable problems, but no examples of interesting complete problems were obtained. The most successful effort in this direction was the work of Papadimitriou and Yannakakis (1991) where a complexity class of approximable optimization problems, denoted as MAXSNP, was defined and several interesting complete problems were formulated. It is also worth mentioning that in Arora, Lund, Motwani, Sudan, and Szegedy (1992) it was proved that such a class is not contained in PAS, unless P = NP. This is essentially the first very general and practically significant result in the study of the approximability properties of optimization problems.

Chapter 7

Beyond NP

In Chapters 4 and 5 we introduced the complexity classes P and NP which allowed us to make a first rough distinction between computationally 'tractable' and 'intractable' decision problems. As its title suggests, in this chapter we shall study new classes of decision problems that do not seem to belong to NP. Indeed, even though we have already observed that most of the combinatorial problems occurring in practice fall within NP, a variety of interesting types of problems exist which do not seem to be included in NP, thus justifying the definition of additional complexity classes.

As an initial example, consider the 'asymmetry' inherent in the definition of NP. For a word to be accepted it suffices to have an accepting computation path while for one to be rejected none of the computation paths can be an accepting one. This one-sidedness of the class NP will be emphasized in Section 7.1 where the complement class *co*NP of NP is defined and some of its properties are analysed.

The new class *co*NP can be used with the class NP to classify problems related to the search for *exact* answers. For instance, in the exact answer version of CLIQUE, given a graph and a natural number k, we are asked whether the maximum clique size is exactly k. These considerations will lead us in Section 7.2 to the definition of a hierarchy of complexity classes based on the classes NP and *co*NP.

Both classes NP and *co*NP are defined by referring to nondeterministic Turing machines operating in polynomial time. Our next step in defining richer complexity classes will consist of making use of more powerful Turing machines, namely oracle Turing machines. In Section 7.3 we introduce a second hierarchy of complexity classes called the polynomial hierarchy which may be viewed as a computational analog to the Kleene arithmetic hierarchy of recursion theory.

It is only fair to state that none of these new complexity classes contains a problem which has been proved to be intractable. Even though this seems quite unlikely, we cannot entirely rule out the possibility that all of them collapse to the class P. In contrast, in Section 7.4 we introduce richer complexity classes (in fact, the richest ones to be considered in this text), namely the exponential-time complexity classes, that are *known* to include intractable problems (no need for conjecture!).

7.1   The class coNP

The complement class $co\mathcal{C}$ of a class of languages $\mathcal{C}$ was introduced in Section 3.2 and we know from Lemma 3.5 that for any deterministic time-complexity class $\mathcal{C}$, $\mathcal{C} = co\mathcal{C}$ holds. The same lemma, however, does not seem to hold for nondeterministic time-complexity classes. Let us try to understand why this happens by using a simple example.

Example 7.1 Denote by SATISFIABILITY^c the complement problem of SATISFIABILITY, that is, the problem of deciding whether a Boolean formula in conjunctive normal form does not admit *any* assignment of values which satisfies it.

Let NT be a nondeterministic machine which decides SATISFIABILITY in polynomial time and let NT' be the machine obtained from NT by exchanging the accepting and the rejecting states as in the proof of Lemma 3.5. It can immediately be verified that the language accepted by NT' is not SATISFIABILITY^c but rather the language consisting of all formulas which admit at least one assignment which does not satisfy them.

All attempts to design a nondeterministic polynomial-time Turing machine deciding SATISFIABILITY^c have failed up to now.

Apart from the negative result of the previous example, it may be found that some other NP-complete problems do admit nondeterministic polynomial-time algorithms for their complement problems. The next lemma states that if this were true even for a single language, then NP would coincide with its complement class coNP.

Lemma 7.1 If an NP-complete language L exists such that $L^c \in$ NP, then coNP = NP.

Proof. Since L is NP-complete and $L^c \in$ NP, $L^c \leq L$, that is, $L \leq L^c$. For any $L_1 \in$ NP, it follows that $L_1 \leq L \leq L^c$. Since coNP is closed with respect to $\leq$, then $L_1 \in co$NP and NP $\subseteq co$NP. Similarly, we can prove that coNP $\subseteq$ NP (remember that according to the properties of reducibilities discussed in Section 2.3.2, the complement language L^c of an NP-complete language L is coNP-complete).   □

Despite many attempts, no NP-complete problem satisfying the conditions of the previous lemma has been found. For this reason, the NP $\neq co$NP conjecture has been proposed. The following lemma shows that this new conjecture is stronger than the well-known P $\neq$ NP conjecture.

Lemma 7.2 If coNP $\neq$ NP, then P $\neq$ NP.

Proof. According to Lemma 3.5 P $=$ coP. Assume coNP $\neq$ NP and P $=$ NP; in that case, both coNP $=$ NP and coNP $\neq$ NP would hold. $\square$

Notice that both P $\neq$ NP and coNP $=$ NP could hold at the same time although this seems rather unlikely.

7.1.1 Testing primality

An interesting application of Lemma 7.1 is the following. Assume that we have a language L such that both L and L^c belong to NP. Then the lemma allows us to state that unless NP $=$ coNP, L cannot be NP-complete.

Example 7.2 PRIME NUMBER: given an integer n, is n prime?

Since the introduction of number theory, mathematicians have been fascinated by this problem. In particular, the problems of generating primes, primality testing, and looking for prime divisors have received considerable attention. While primes are still found by sieves, not by formulas, and factoring is still considered very difficult, primality testing has advanced to a stage where the primality of 100-digit numbers can now be checked in a few seconds. That is why current research efforts are directed towards proving that this problem belongs to P (see Notes).

We show in this section that PRIME NUMBER is unlikely to be NP-complete since the next theorem states that it belongs to NP $\cap$ coNP. In order to prove this result we need to introduce some number-theoretic notations and to prove a few preliminary lemmas.

The basic idea consists of giving an alternative (and efficient) definition of primality based on the following result due to Fermat.

Lemma 7.3 If a number $n > 2$ is prime, then, for any integer a with $1 \leq a < n$, $a^{n-1} \equiv 1 \pmod{n}$.

Proof. Given an integer a with $1 \leq a < n$, let $m_i = ia$, for any $i \leq n - 1$. Note that, for any i and j, $m_i \not\equiv m_j \pmod{n}$ since otherwise n would divide $(i - j)a$ while both $i - j$ and a are numbers smaller than n. Similarly, for any i, $m_i \not\equiv 0 \pmod{n}$. Thus the numbers $m_1, m_2, \ldots, m_{n-1}$ must be equivalent modulo n to the numbers $1, 2, \ldots, n - 1$ considered in a suitable order. It follows that

$$a^{n-1} \prod_{i=1}^{n-1} i = \prod_{i=1}^{n-1} m_i \equiv \prod_{i=1}^{n-1} i \pmod{n},$$

that is,

$$(a^{n-1} - 1) \prod_{i=1}^{n-1} i \equiv 0 \pmod{n}.$$

Clearly, n cannot divide the product $\prod_{i=1}^{n-1} i$. This implies that n divides $a^{n-1}-1$, that is, $a^{n-1} \equiv 1 \pmod{n}$. $\qquad\square$

The above necessary condition, which we shall call *Fermat's test*, is also sufficient. In order to prove this, we need the following lemmas.

Lemma 7.4 Given two integers a and n, $GCD(a,n) = 1$ if and only if an integer b exists such that $ab \equiv 1 \pmod{n}$.

Proof. By Euclid's algorithm (see Example 4.2) it follows that $GCD(a,n) = 1$ if and only if two integers b and c exist such that $ab + nc = 1$. This in turn is true if and only if an integer b exists so that n divides $1 - ab$ which holds true if and only if an integer b exists such that $ab \equiv 1 \pmod{n}$. $\qquad\square$

Lemma 7.5 If a number $n > 2$ is composite, then an integer a with $1 \le a < n$ exists such that $a^{n-1} \not\equiv 1 \pmod{n}$.

Proof. If n is composite, then an integer a with $1 \le a < n$ exists such that $GCD(a,n) \ne 1$: indeed, it suffices to choose a as any of the prime divisors of n. Assume $a^{n-1} \equiv 1 \pmod{n}$. Then a admits an inverse modulo n, that is, a^{n-2}, contradicting Lemma 7.4. Thus $a^{n-1} \not\equiv 1 \pmod{n}$. $\qquad\square$

Note that Fermat's test is a 'universal' condition which does not seem to be verifiable in nondeterministic polynomial time. However, its negation can.

Lemma 7.6 PRIME NUMBER belongs to *co*NP.

Proof. Consider the following nondeterministic algorithm:

begin {input: n}
   guess a **in** $\{1, 2, \ldots, n-1\}$;
   if $a^{n-1} \equiv 1 \pmod{n}$ **then** reject **else** accept;
end.

Since $a^{n-1} \bmod n$ can be computed in $O[\log^2 n]$ steps (see Problem 7.2), the above algorithm requires a polynomial number of steps. From Lemmas 7.3 and 7.5 it follows that it correctly decides the complement of PRIME NUMBER. $\qquad\square$

In order to prove that PRIME NUMBER belongs to NP, we need to add more constraints to Fermat's test to make it 'existential'. In particular, the condition we will provide states that n is prime if and only if an integer a exists with $1 \le a < n$ such that not only a passes Fermat's test but also the $(n-1)$th power of a is the only power of a which is equivalent to 1 modulo n.

For any integer n, the *set $\Phi(n)$ of invertible elements modulo n* is defined as the set of all natural numbers less than n which are 'relatively prime' to n. That is,

$$\Phi(n) = \{a : 1 \le a < n \wedge GCD(a,n) = 1\}.$$

Clearly, if n is prime, $\Phi(n)$ includes the first $n-1$ integers and the complement set $\Phi^c(n) = \{1, \ldots, n-1\} - \Phi(n)$ is empty. The cardinality of $\Phi(n)$ (respectively, $\Phi^c(n)$) is denoted as $\phi(n)$ (respectively, $\phi^c(n)$).

Example 7.3 Let $n = 18$. Then $\Phi(18) = \{1, 5, 7, 11, 13, 17\}$, $\phi(18) = 6$, $\Phi^c(18) = \{2, 3, 4, 6, 8, 9, 10, 12, 14, 15, 16\}$, and $\phi^c(18) = 11$.

Lemma 7.7 For any integer n whose divisors are $d_1, \ldots, d_h$,

$$n = \sum_{i=1}^{h} \phi(d_i).$$

Proof. Let us consider the n ratios $r_j = j/n$, for $0 \leq j \leq n-1$. By reducing such ratios, we can partition them into h groups of ratios such that the ith group contains $\phi(d_i)$ ratios with denominator d_i, one for each element in $\Phi(d_i)$. Thus the lemma follows. □

Example 7.4 For $n = 18$, the 18 ratios are

$$\frac{0}{18}, \frac{1}{18}, \frac{2}{18}, \frac{3}{18}, \frac{4}{18}, \frac{5}{18}, \frac{6}{18}, \frac{7}{18}, \frac{8}{18}, \frac{9}{18}, \frac{10}{18}, \frac{11}{18}, \frac{12}{18}, \frac{13}{18}, \frac{14}{18}, \frac{15}{18}, \frac{16}{18}, \frac{17}{18}$$

while the reduced ratios are

$$\frac{0}{1}, \frac{1}{18}, \frac{1}{9}, \frac{1}{6}, \frac{2}{9}, \frac{5}{18}, \frac{1}{3}, \frac{7}{18}, \frac{4}{9}, \frac{1}{2}, \frac{5}{9}, \frac{11}{18}, \frac{2}{3}, \frac{13}{18}, \frac{7}{9}, \frac{5}{6}, \frac{8}{9}, \frac{17}{18}.$$

The above ratios can be grouped as shown in Table 7.1.

Table 7.1 The reduced basic fractions with denominator 18

d	$\phi(d)$	Ratios
1	1	$0/1$
2	1	$1/2$
3	2	$1/3, 2/3$
6	2	$1/6, 5/6$
9	6	$1/9, 2/9, 4/9, 5/9, 7/9, 8/9$
18	6	$1/18, 5/18, 7/18, 11/18, 13/18, 17/18$

We are now ready to prove the alternative characterization of primality.

Lemma 7.8 A number $n > 2$ is prime if and only if an integer a exists such that

1. $1 < a < n$.
2. $a^{n-1} \equiv 1 \pmod{n}$.
3. For all q such that q is a prime divisor of $n-1$, $a^{(n-1)/q} \not\equiv 1 \pmod{n}$.

Proof. Let n be a prime number and a be any element of $\Phi(n)$. First note that an integer k exists such that $a^k \equiv 1 \pmod{n}$. Indeed, if this not the case, then two integers k_1 and k_2 with $k_1 > k_2$ exist such that $a^{k_1} \equiv a^{k_2} \pmod{n}$ which in turn implies that $a^{k_1 - k_2} \equiv 1 \pmod{n}$, contradicting the assumption.

Let k_a denote the smallest integer such that $a^{k_a} \equiv 1 \pmod{n}$. In order to prove the necessity, it then suffices to show that an a in $\Phi(n)$ exists such that $k_a = n-1$.

Clearly the only powers of a which are equivalent to 1 modulo n are those that are multiples of k_a and, from Lemma 7.3, it follows that k_a divides $n-1$.

For any k, let R_k denote the set of elements a of $\Phi(n)$ such that $k_a = k$ and let $r_k = |R_k|$. Clearly, each $a \in R_k$ is a root of $x^k \equiv 1 \pmod{n}$. A well-known result in number theory states that if n is prime, then any polynomial of degree k that is not identically zero has, at most, k distinct roots modulo n (see Problem 7.3). Thus $r_k \leq k$. Let a be any element of R_k. For any $i < k_a$, we have that a^i is also a root of $x^k \equiv 1 \pmod{n}$: indeed, $(a^i)^k = (a^k)^i \equiv 1 \pmod{n}$. It also holds true that, for any i and j with $j < i < k_a$, $a^i \not\equiv a^j \pmod{n}$ since otherwise $a^{i-j} \equiv 1 \pmod{n}$, contradicting the assumption that k_a is the smallest power of a equivalent to 1 modulo n. Thus $R_k \subseteq \{a^i : 0 \leq i < k\}$. But we can do better. Note in fact that if $i < k$ and $GCD(i, k) = d \neq 1$, then $(a^i)^{k/d} \equiv 1 \pmod{n}$, that is, $k_{a^i} \leq k/d < k$. Thus $R_k \subseteq \{a^i : 0 \leq i < k \wedge GCD(i, k) = 1\}$. This in turn implies that $r_k \leq \phi(k)$.

Finally, let $d_1, \ldots, d_r$ be the divisors of $n-1$. Since $r_k = 0$ when k does not divide $n-1$ and $\sum_{k=1}^{n-1} r_k = n-1$ (any element $a \in \Phi(n)$ admits a k_a), it follows that

$$n - 1 = \sum_{i=1}^{r} r_{d_i} \leq \sum_{i=1}^{r} \phi(d_i) = n - 1$$

where the last equality is due to Lemma 7.7. Thus, for any k, $r_k = \phi(k)$. In particular, $r_{n-1} = \phi(n-1) > 0$ and an element of $\Phi(n)$ satisfying the conditions of the lemma exists.

Conversely, suppose that an integer a exists such that $1 < a < n$, $a^{n-1} \equiv 1 \pmod{n}$, and, for all q such that q is a prime divisor of $n-1$, $a^{(n-1)/q} \not\equiv 1 \pmod{n}$. We will show that the numbers $a^1 \bmod n, \ldots, a^{n-1} \bmod n$ are distinct and relatively prime to n. This in turn implies that the numbers $1, \ldots, n-1$ are relatively prime to n, that is, n is prime.

If $a^i \equiv a^j \pmod{n}$ for some $j < i < n$, then $a^{i-j} \equiv 1 \pmod{n}$, that is, an integer k exists such that the kth power of a is equivalent to 1 modulo n. Once again, let k_a be the minimum of such powers. Then the only powers of a which are equivalent to 1 are those that are multiples of k_a and, since $a^{n-1} \equiv 1 \pmod{n}$, it follows that k_a divides $n-1$, that is, $k_a m = (n-1)/q$ for some integer m

and for some prime divisor q of $n - 1$. We then have that $a^{(n-1)/q} = a^{k_a m} = (a^{k_a})^m \equiv 1 \pmod{n}$, contradicting the assumptions on a. Thus the numbers $a^1 \bmod n, \ldots, a^{n-1} \bmod n$ are distinct.

In order to prove that they are relatively prime to n, note that, since $a^{n-1} \equiv 1 \pmod{n}$, for any i with $1 \leq i < n$, a^i admits an inverse modulo n, that is, $a^{n-(i+1)}$. From Lemma 7.4, it then follows that $GCD(a^i, n) = 1$. $\quad\square$

Finally, we can state the main result of this section.

Lemma 7.9 PRIME NUMBER belongs to NP.

Proof. The nondeterministic algorithm which decides PRIME NUMBER in polynomial time can be derived in a straightforward way from the above lemma and is the following:

begin {input: n}
  if $prime(n)$ **then** accept **else** reject;
end.

where the recursive function *prime* is defined as

function $prime(n)$: **boolean**;
begin
  guess x **in** set of numbers between 2 and $n - 1$;
  if $x^{(n-1)} \not\equiv 1 \pmod{n}$ **then** $prime := $ **false**
  else
  begin
    guess $n_1, \ldots, n_k$ **in** set of possible factorizations of $n - 1$
    if $n_1 \times n_2 \times \ldots \times n_k \neq n - 1$ **then** $prime := $ **false**
    else
    begin
      if $prime(n_1) \wedge \ldots \wedge prime(n_k)$ **then**
        if $x^{(n-1)/n_1} \not\equiv 1 \pmod{n} \wedge \ldots \wedge x^{(n-1)/n_k} \not\equiv 1 \pmod{n}$ **then**
          $prime := $ **true**
        else $prime := $ **false**
      else $prime := $ **false**;
    end;
  end;
end;

Since any possible factorization of a number r consists of, at most, $\log r$ numbers ranging from 2 to $(r - 1)/2$, the above algorithm requires a polynomial number of steps. Thus, PRIME NUMBER belongs to NP. $\quad\square$

From Lemmas 7.6 and 7.9 we have the following result.

Theorem 7.1 PRIME NUMBER belongs to NP $\cap$ coNP.

7.2 The Boolean hierarchy

Before introducing complexity classes which refer to more powerful machines, let us try to derive additional classes by combining NP and *co*NP. This section is based on the assumption that NP $\neq$ *co*NP.

We are encouraged to proceed in this direction by the existence of a few 'natural' problems which do not seem to belong either to NP or to *co*NP, but which can easily be defined as the intersection of languages in these two classes.

Example 7.5 EXACT NODE COVER: given a graph G and a positive integer k, is k the size of the minimum node cover included in G? The same problem can be expressed as the conjunction of the following two subproblems:

1. G admits a node cover of size k.

2. G does not admit a node cover of size $k - 1$.

The first subproblem corresponds to NODE COVER which is known to be in NP while the second corresponds to the complement of NODE COVER and belongs to *co*NP. Thus the language corresponding to EXACT NODE COVER can be defined as

$$L_{\text{EXACT NODE COVER}} = \{\langle\langle G, k\rangle, \langle G, k - 1\rangle\rangle : \langle G, k\rangle \in L_{\text{NODE COVER}}$$
$$\wedge \langle G, k - 1\rangle \in L^c_{\text{NODE COVER}}\}.$$

Let us extend the technique used in the previous example by considering all three Boolean set operators, namely, union, intersection and complement.

The *Boolean hierarchy* is a collection $\{\text{BH}_i : i \geq 1\}$ of classes of languages such that

BH$_1$ = NP;
BH$_2 = \{L_A \cap L^c_B : L_A, L_B \in \text{NP}\}$;
BH$_{2i+1} = \{L_A \cup L_B : L_A \in \text{BH}_{2i} \wedge L_B \in \text{NP}\}$ with $i \geq 1$;
BH$_{2i+2} = \{L_A \cap L^c_B : L_A \in \text{BH}_{2i+1} \wedge L_B \in \text{NP}\}$ with $i \geq 1$.

The infinite union of all BH$_i$s is denoted as BH and it is possible to prove (see Problem 7.5) that BH coincides with the *Boolean closure* of NP, that is, with the smallest class which includes NP and which is closed with respect to the union, intersection, and complement of languages, hence the name Boolean hierarchy.

The second level of the Boolean hierarchy, namely BH$_2$, is of special interest since it is able to capture the complexity of several interesting problems related to the search for an exact answer (see Example 7.5). Another interesting property of BH$_2$ is that it admits a complete language with respect to polynomial-time reducibility.

We already know that SATISFIABILITY is BH$_1$-complete. Let us consider an extension of SATISFIABILITY denoted as SATISFIABILITY(2). Given two Boolean formulas f and g in conjunctive normal form, is it true that f is satisfiable and g is not?

Theorem 7.2 SATISFIABILITY(2) is BH_2-complete.

Proof. Define the language L_1 (respectively, L_2) consisting of pairs of Boolean formulas in conjunctive normal form $\langle f, g \rangle$ such that f (respectively, g) is satisfiable. Clearly, both L_1 and L_2 belong to NP (in fact, they are NP-complete). According to the definition, SATISFIABILITY(2) $= L_1 \cap L_2^c$ and thus belongs to BH_2. From Cook's theorem, it follows that SATISFIABILITY(2) is BH_2-complete. $\square$

As shown in the next example, other interesting BH_2-completeness results can be obtained via a polynomial reduction from SATISFIABILITY(2).

Example 7.6 Let us consider the EXACT NODE COVER problem introduced in Example 7.5. Clearly, such a problem belongs to BH_2. Let us then prove its BH_2-completeness by showing that SATISFIABILITY(2) $\leq$ EXACT NODE COVER.

Observe first that, given a Boolean formula $f = C_1 \wedge C_2 \wedge \ldots \wedge C_m$, f is satisfiable if and only if

$$f' = (C_1 \vee y) \wedge (C_2 \vee y) \wedge \ldots \wedge (C_m \vee y) \wedge \neg y$$

is satisfiable, where y is a new variable. In addition, we also have that either f' is satisfiable or all but one clause of f' can be satisfied by simply assigning the value **true** to variable y. Now, as in Example 5.5, starting from f' we can construct a graph G and an integer k such that if f' is satisfiable then G admits a node cover of size k, otherwise it admits a node cover of size $k + 1$ (intuitively, only one extra node is needed for the unsatisfied clause $\neg y$).

Let $\langle f, g \rangle$ be an instance of SATISFIABILITY(2) and let G_f and k_f (respectively, G_g and k_g) be the graph and the integer obtained starting from f (respectively, g) and applying the above reduction. The instance of EXACT NODE COVER is then formed by the graph G given by two copies of G_f and one copy of G_g (each not connected with the other) and the integer $k = 2k_f + k_g + 1$. From the previous discussion it easily follows that f is satisfiable and g is not satisfiable if and only if k is the size of the minimum node cover included in G. We have thus proved that SATISFIABILITY(2) is polynomial-time reducible to EXACT NODE COVER.

Starting from SATISFIABILITY(2), it is also easy to derive a BH_i-complete language SATISFIABILITY(i) for any class BH_i.

Does each class BH_i properly contain BH_{i-1} and BH_{i-2} for all $i \geq 3$? If this were not the case, a *collapsing* of the Boolean hierarchy would occur at some level k, that is, for all $j > k$ $BH_j = BH_k$ would hold. This event is considered unlikely although a formal proof that BH includes an infinite number of levels has not yet appeared. Figure 7.1 represents in a schematic way the infinite levels of BH (it is assumed that no collapsing occccurs).

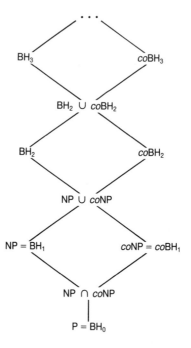

Figure 7.1 Inclusions between classes of BH

7.3   The polynomial hierarchy

Our next step in defining richer complexity classes will require referring to more powerful Turing machines, namely oracle Turing machines.

It is easy to convince ourselves that the number of oracles available does not play a significant role in the sense that, in many cases, a single carefully chosen oracle can replace any finite set of two or more oracles.

Example 7.7 Assume machine T makes use of two oracles L_1 and L_2 belonging to NP. The language decided by T can also be decided by another machine T' which makes use of a single language L' included in NPC. Denote by f and g two polynomial-time reductions from L_1 to L' and from L_2 to L', respectively. Whenever T queries oracle L_1 (respectively, L_2) about some y, T' simulates T by querying the oracle L' about $f(y)$ (respectively, $g(y)$).

The approach used in the previous example can easily be generalized to include machines querying a finite number of oracles belonging to complexity class $\mathcal{C}$ and it can be shown that such machines can be simulated by other machines which make use of a single oracle, provided that class $\mathcal{C}$ admits a complete language. The basic idea will then consist of increasing their *complexity* instead of their *number*.

7.3.1 A first definition

The polynomial hierarchy is an infinite union of time-complexity classes whose interest derives from the fact that it captures the inherent complexity of some interesting and 'natural' decision problems as shown in the following example.

Example 7.8 Denote by U a set of n Boolean variables. Let E be a Boolean formula consisting of variables in U, Boolean constants **true** and **false**, left and right parentheses, and logical operators $\neg$, $\wedge$ and $\vee$, and let k denote a natural number.

Given an instance $\langle E, k \rangle$, EQUIVALENT FORMULAS consists of deciding whether E admits an equivalent formula E' including, at most, k occurrences of literals (two Boolean formulas E and E' are *equivalent* if for any assignment of values E is satisfied if and only if E' is satisfied).

It is easy to verify that SATISFIABILITY can be solved in polynomial time by a deterministic Turing machine with oracle EQUIVALENT FORMULAS. For this, we note that only two types of formulas exist equivalent to a formula including 0 occurrences of literals, that is, a formula consisting only of Boolean constants: those equivalent to **true**, also called *tautologies*, which are satisfied by all possible assignments of values, and those equivalent to **false** which cannot be satisfied by any assignment of values.

Let E be a formula in conjunctive normal form. To decide whether E is satisfiable it is sufficient to check first whether E is a tautology. If so, E is satisfiable; otherwise, we only have to check whether E is equivalent to a formula containing 0 occurrences of literals. If this is the case, E is not satisfiable, otherwise it is satisfiable.

The first check can be done in polynomial time (see Problem 4.10); the second can also be done in polynomial time by querying the oracle EQUIVALENT FORMULAS with the word $\langle E, 0 \rangle$. If the oracle answers positively, E is not satisfiable, otherwise it is satisfiable.

It is far less obvious how to proceed in the opposite direction. Thus far no deterministic Turing machine having an NP-complete language as oracle and deciding EQUIVALENT FORMULAS in polynomial time has been found.

It is, however, possible to define a *nondeterministic* Turing machine having the above characteristics. Indeed, the nondeterminism can be exploited to generate all possible formulas E' including, at most, k occurrences of literals and to query the oracle to determine whether E' is not equivalent to E, that is, if $\neg((\neg E' \vee E) \wedge (\neg E \vee E'))$ is satisfiable. If this last formula is not satisfiable, then E' is the required k-literal formula. Conversely, if all k-literal formula E' are not equivalent to E, then the instance $\langle E, k \rangle$ does not belong to EQUIVALENT FORMULAS.

Let us generalize the previous example by introducing two classes of languages whose definition is based on oracle Turing machines which make use of oracle languages belonging to a given class $\mathcal{C}$.

Given a class of languages $\mathcal{C}$, the class $\mathrm{P}^{\mathcal{C}}$ is defined as

$$\mathrm{P}^{\mathcal{C}} = \bigcup_{L \in \mathcal{C}} \mathrm{P}^L$$

while the class $\mathrm{NP}^{\mathcal{C}}$ is defined as

$$\mathrm{NP}^{\mathcal{C}} = \bigcup_{L \in \mathcal{C}} \mathrm{NP}^L$$

where P^L and NP^L denote the classes P and NP relativized with respect to oracle L, respectively.

Example 7.9 According to Example 7.8, the problem SATISFIABILITY belongs to the class $\mathrm{P}^{\text{EQUIVALENT FORMULAS}}$ while EQUIVALENT FORMULAS belongs to $\mathrm{NP}^{\mathrm{NP}}$.

The technique introduced to define new classes of languages by referring to existing ones can obviously be iterated. The new class of languages we are going to present is based on this observation.

The *polynomial hierarchy* is an infinite set $\{\Sigma_k^{\mathrm{p}}, \Pi_k^{\mathrm{p}}, \Delta_k^{\mathrm{p}} : k \geq 0\}$ of classes of languages such that

1. $\Sigma_0^{\mathrm{p}} = \Pi_0^{\mathrm{p}} = \Delta_0^{\mathrm{p}} = \mathrm{P}$.
2. $\Sigma_{k+1}^{\mathrm{p}} = \mathrm{NP}^{\Sigma_k^{\mathrm{p}}}$, $\Pi_{k+1}^{\mathrm{p}} = co\Sigma_{k+1}^{\mathrm{p}}$ and $\Delta_{k+1}^{\mathrm{p}} = \mathrm{P}^{\Sigma_k^{\mathrm{p}}}$ with $k \geq 0$.

The infinite union of all Σ_k^{p}s (or of all Π_k^{p}s or of all Δ_k^{p}s) is denoted as PH.

7.3.2 Some properties

From the definition of polynomial hierarchy, it follows that $\Sigma_1^{\mathrm{p}} = \mathrm{NP}$, $\Pi_1^{\mathrm{p}} = co\mathrm{NP}$, $\Delta_1^{\mathrm{p}} = \mathrm{P}$, $\Sigma_2^{\mathrm{p}} = \mathrm{NP}^{\mathrm{NP}}$ and $\Delta_2^{\mathrm{p}} = \mathrm{P}^{\mathrm{NP}}$.

The next lemma illustrates some relationships among classes in the polynomial hierarchy. Those relationships are represented schematically in Figure 7.2.

Lemma 7.10 For each $k \geq 0$, the following inclusion relationships hold:

$$\Sigma_k^{\mathrm{p}} \cup \Pi_k^{\mathrm{p}} \subseteq \Delta_{k+1}^{\mathrm{p}} \subseteq \Sigma_{k+1}^{\mathrm{p}} \cap \Pi_{k+1}^{\mathrm{p}}.$$

Proof. First note that $L \in \mathrm{P}^L$ and $\mathrm{P}^L \subseteq \mathrm{NP}^L \cap co\mathrm{NP}^L$ for all languages L.

If $L \in \Sigma_k^{\mathrm{p}}$, then $\mathrm{P}^L \subseteq \Delta_{k+1}^{\mathrm{p}}$ and $L \in \Delta_{k+1}^{\mathrm{p}}$. Thus, $\Sigma_k^{\mathrm{p}} \subseteq \Delta_{k+1}^{\mathrm{p}}$. It can be shown in a similar way that $\Pi_k^{\mathrm{p}} \subseteq \Delta_{k+1}^{\mathrm{p}}$.

If $L \in \Delta_{k+1}^{\mathrm{p}}$, then a language $L' \in \Sigma_k^{\mathrm{p}}$ exists such that $L \in \mathrm{P}^{L'}$. Since $\mathrm{P}^{L'} \subseteq \mathrm{NP}^{L'} \cap co\mathrm{NP}^{L'}$, then $L \in \mathrm{NP}^{L'} \cap co\mathrm{NP}^{L'}$ and thus $L \in \Sigma_{k+1}^{\mathrm{p}} \cap \Pi_{k+1}^{\mathrm{p}}$. We have therefore shown that $\Delta_{k+1}^{\mathrm{p}} \subseteq \Sigma_{k+1}^{\mathrm{p}} \cap \Pi_{k+1}^{\mathrm{p}}$. $\square$

It has not yet been settled whether the inclusion relationships of Lemma 7.10 are proper. In fact, the following questions remain unanswered:

1. Is $\Sigma_k^{\mathrm{p}} \neq \Sigma_{k+1}^{\mathrm{p}}$ for each $k \geq 0$?
2. Is $\Sigma_k^{\mathrm{p}} \neq \Pi_k^{\mathrm{p}}$ for each $k \geq 1$?
3. Is $\Delta_k^{\mathrm{p}} \neq \Sigma_k^{\mathrm{p}} \cap \Pi_k^{\mathrm{p}}$ for each $k \geq 1$?

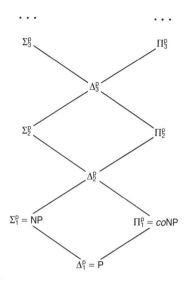

Figure 7.2 Inclusions between classes of PH

7.3.3   An alternative definition

The following theorem yields an alternative characterization of the polynomial hierarchy.

Theorem 7.3 For each $k \geq 0$, a language L belongs to Σ_k^p if and only if a language $A \in \mathrm{P}$ and a polynomial p exist such that

$$x \in L \leftrightarrow (\exists y_1)(\forall y_2) \ldots (Q y_k)[\langle x, y_1, \ldots, y_k \rangle \in A]$$

where $|y_i| \leq p(|x|)$ with $1 \leq i \leq k$ and where the sequence of quantifiers consists of an alternation of existential and universal quantifiers. As a consequence, Q must be read as $\exists$ or as $\forall$ depending on whether k is odd or even.

Similarly, for each $k \geq 0$, a language L belongs to Π_k^p if and only if a language $A \in \mathrm{P}$ and a polynomial p exist such that

$$x \in L \leftrightarrow (\forall y_1)(\exists y_2) \ldots (Q y_k)[\langle x, y_1, \ldots, y_k \rangle \in A]$$

where the y_is are again polynomially bounded in $|x|$ and the sequence of quantifiers is alternated.

Proof. The proof is by induction on k. The case $k = 0$ immediately follows from the definitions. Let us assume that the theorem holds both for Σ_h^P and for Π_h^P for all $0 \le h < k$.

Assume $L \in \Sigma_k^P$ (a similar reasoning holds when $L \in \Pi_k^P$ is assumed, see Problem 7.8). According to the definition, a language $L_1 \in \Sigma_{k-1}^P$ and a nondeterministic Turing machine NT with oracle L_1 exist such that NT^{L_1} decides L in polynomial time. Denote by q the polynomial limiting the number of steps of NT. We already know that for any input x any computation path of $NT(x)$ can be encoded into a word of length, at most, $q(|x|)$. Then define the following languages:

1. $\langle x, w \rangle \in A_1$ if and only if w encodes a computation path of $NT^{L_1}(x)$ which halts in the accepting state.
2. $\langle u, v \rangle \in A_2$ if and only if $u = \langle u_1, \ldots, u_{h_u} \rangle$, $v = \langle v_1, \ldots, v_{h_v} \rangle$ and, for each i and j, $u_i \ne v_j$ (u and v encode two pairwise disjoint finite sets of words).
3. $\langle x, w, u \rangle \in A_3$ if and only if $u = \langle u_1, \ldots, u_{h_u} \rangle$ coincides with the set of words queried by the computation path w of $NT^{L_1}(x)$ obtaining a yes answer (by assumption, $|u_i| \le q(|x|)$).
4. $\langle x, w, v \rangle \in A_4$ if and only if $v = \langle v_1, \ldots, v_{h_v} \rangle$ coincides with the set of words queried by the computation path w of $NT^{L_1}(x)$ obtaining a no answer (by assumption, $|v_i| \le q(|x|)$).
5. $u \in A_5$ if and only if $u = \langle u_1, \ldots, u_{h_u} \rangle$ and $u_i \in L_1$ for each i.
6. $v \in A_6$ if and only if $v = \langle v_1, \ldots, v_{h_v} \rangle$ and $v_i \notin L_1$ for each i.

The six languages A_i allow us to state that a polynomial r exists such that $x \in L$ if and only if three words w, u and v with $|w|, |u|, |v| \le r(|x|)$ exist such that

$$\langle x, w \rangle \in A_1 \wedge \langle u, v \rangle \in A_2 \wedge \langle x, w, u \rangle \in A_3 \wedge \langle x, w, v \rangle \in A_4 \wedge u \in A_5 \wedge v \in A_6.$$

It is easy to verify that the languages A_i ($1 \le i \le 4$) are polynomial-time decidable.

Denote by A the language such that

$$\langle x, w, u, v \rangle \in A \leftrightarrow \langle x, w \rangle \in A_1 \wedge \langle u, v \rangle \in A_2 \wedge \langle x, w, u \rangle \in A_3 \wedge \langle x, w, v \rangle \in A_4.$$

It follows that

$$x \in L \leftrightarrow (\exists \langle w, u, v \rangle)[\langle x, w, u, v \rangle \in A \wedge u \in A_5 \wedge v \in A_6].$$

It is also easy to verify that since $L_1 \in \Sigma_{k-1}^P$ (respectively, $L_1^c \in \Pi_{k-1}^P$), then $A_5 \in \Sigma_{k-1}^P$ (respectively, $A_6 \in \Pi_{k-1}^P$) (see Problem 7.7). According to the induction hypothesis, a language $B_1 \in P$ and a polynomial r_1 exist such that

$$u \in A_5 \leftrightarrow (\exists z_1)(\forall z_2) \ldots (Q z_{k-1})[\langle u, z_1, z_2, \ldots, z_{k-1} \rangle \in B_1]$$

where $|z_i| \le r_1(|u|)$, for $1 \le i \le k - 1$, and the sequence of quantifiers is alternated.

Similarly, a language $B_2 \in P$ and a polynomial r_2 exist such that

$$v \in A_6 \leftrightarrow (\forall w_2)(\exists w_3) \ldots (Q w_k)[\langle v, w_2, w_3, \ldots, w_k \rangle \in B_2]$$

where $|w_i| \leq r_2(|n|)$, for $2 \leq i \leq k$, and the sequence of quantifiers is alternated.

We can now merge adjacent quantifiers of the same type by using standard rules of classical logic and obtaining

$$x \in L \quad \leftrightarrow \quad (\exists \langle w, u, v, z_1 \rangle)(\forall \langle z_2, w_2 \rangle) \ldots (Q w_k)[\langle x, w, u, v \rangle \in A \wedge$$
$$\langle u, z_1, z_2, \ldots, z_{k-1} \rangle \in B_1 \wedge \langle v, w_2, w_3, \ldots, w_k \rangle \in B_2].$$

Since the lengths of the quantified tuples can be bounded by a suitable polynomial p, the first part of the theorem has been proved.

Let us now consider the second part. Assume a language $A \in P$ and a polynomial p exist such that

$$x \in L \leftrightarrow (\exists y_1)(\forall y_2) \ldots (Q y_k)[\langle x, y_1 \ldots, y_k \rangle \in A]$$

where $|y_i| \leq p(|x|)$, for $1 \leq i \leq k$, and the sequence of quantifiers is alternated.

Define C as $C = \{\langle x, y_1 \rangle : (\forall y_2) \ldots (Q y_k)[\langle x, y_1 \ldots, y_k \rangle \in A]\}$. Then, $x \in L$ if and only if $(\exists y_1)[\langle x, y_1 \rangle \in C]$.

By induction hypothesis, $C \in \Pi_{k-1}^p$ (because the first quantifier is a universal one) and thus $C^c \in \Sigma_{k-1}^p$. Let us derive a nondeterministic Turing machine with oracle C^c which decides L. On input x such a machine generates all possible words y_1 such that $|y_1| \leq p(|x|)$ and then uses oracle C^c to check whether $\langle x, y_1 \rangle \in C$. These tasks can be performed in polynomial time, thus $L \in \Sigma_k^p$. $\square$

An immediate application of Theorem 7.3 confirming a result already obtained in Example 7.8 is the following.

Example 7.10 Define the language $A \in P$ as $\langle \langle x, k \rangle, y_1, y_2 \rangle \in A$ if and only if y_2 is an assignment of values which satisfies the formula $(\neg x \vee y_1) \wedge (\neg y_1 \vee x)$ where y_1 denotes a formula which includes, at most, k occurrences of literals.

Clearly, a word $\langle x, k \rangle$ belongs to the language associated with EQUIVALENT FORMULAS if and only if a formula y_1 exists such that, for all possible assignments of values y_2, $\langle \langle x, k \rangle, y_1, y_2 \rangle \in A$ holds. We conclude that EQUIVALENT FORMULAS belongs to Σ_2^p.

Another interesting application of Theorem 7.3 is given in the following corollary whose proof is left as a problem (see Problem 7.18).

Corollary 7.1 For all $k \geq 0$, a language L belongs to $\Sigma_k^p + 1$ (respectively, to $\Pi_k^p + 1$) if and only if a k-alternating deterministic Turing machine with an existential (respectively, universal) initial state exists which decides L in polynomial time.

7.3.4   Complete languages in the polynomial hierarchy

As usual, we are interested in determining whether the classes Σ_k^p and Π_k^p admit complete languages with respect to the polynomial reducibility. Indeed, if we consider the fact that the polynomial hierarchy does not collapse as plausible, then proving that a language is complete with respect to a given Σ_k^p (or Π_k^p) is equivalent to identifying the correct kth level in the hierarchy where that language is to be placed.

Example 7.11 Let E be a Boolean formula built on a set of Boolean variables $\bigcup_{i=1}^k X_i$ where $X_i = \{x_{ij} : 1 \leq j \leq m_i\}$ with m_i positive integer. Let us shorten as $\exists X_i$ (respectively, $\forall X_i$) the sentence 'there exists an (respectively, for all) assignment(s) of values to the variables $x_{i1}, \ldots, x_{im_i}$'. The problem k-QBF consists of deciding whether the formula

$$(\exists X_1)(\forall X_2)\ldots(QX_k)[E(X_1, \ldots, X_k)]$$

is true (as usual, the sequence of quantifiers consists of an alternation of existential and universal quantifiers and Q must be read as $\exists$ or as $\forall$ depending on whether k is odd or even).

The next theorem shows that k-QBF is one of the 'hardest' problems in Σ_k^p.

Theorem 7.4 For all $k \geq 1$, k-QBF is Σ_k^p-complete (and thus k-QBF^c is Π_k^p-complete).

Proof. Theorem 7.3 ensures that k-QBF belongs to Σ_k^p for all $k \geq 0$. Indeed the same formula $(\exists X_1)(\forall X_2)\ldots(QX_k)[E(X_1, \ldots, X_k)]$ of k-QBF can replace both x and the right-hand formula in the 'if and only if' formulation of the theorem when the language A is chosen as the set of k-variable assignments for which E is **true**. Furthermore, the construction used in the proof of Theorem 7.3 shows that any language L decided in polynomial-time by some NT^{L_1} with $L_1 \in \Sigma_{k-1}^p$ is polynomial-time reducible to k-QBF since it transforms the computations $NT^{L_1}(x)$ into formulas of k-QBF. Thus k-QBF is Σ_k^p-complete. $\square$

Despite the previous result, very few interesting problems have been shown to be complete with respect to a given level of the polynomial hierarchy. For example, it is not known whether EQUIVALENT FORMULAS is Σ_2^p-complete.

7.3.5   The collapse of the polynomial hierarchy

Although we are unable to prove that each level of PH properly includes the previous one, we may link this new conjecture with the ever-present $P \neq NP$ conjecture. This result derives from the following theorem which is preceded, in turn, by a technical lemma.

Lemma 7.11 For all $k \geq 1$, given a language $A \in \Sigma_k^p$ and a polynomial q, the language $B = \{x : (\exists y)[\langle x, y \rangle \in A \wedge |y| \leq q(|x|)]\}$ belongs to Σ_k^p. In other words, Σ_k^p is closed with respect to polynomially limited existential quantifiers.

Similarly, Π_k^p is closed with respect to polynomially limited universal quantifiers.

Proof. Let $A \in \Sigma_k^p$. Denote by L a language $L \in \Sigma_{k-1}^p$ and with NT a nondeterministic Turing machine with oracle L deciding A in polynomial time. The following nondeterministic algorithm uses such a machine NT to decide B in polynomial time:

begin {input: x}
    guess a word y **in** set of words y with $|y| \leq q(|x|)$;
    if $NT^L(x, y)$ accepts **then** accept **else** reject;
end.

Thus, $B \in \Sigma_k^p$. The closure of Π_k^p with respect to polynomially limited universal quantifiers can be proved in a similar way. $\qquad\square$

Theorem 7.5 If $\Sigma_k^p = \Pi_k^p$ for some $k \geq 1$, then $\Sigma_m^p = \Pi_m^p = \Sigma_k^p$ for all $m \geq k$.

Proof. The proof is by induction on m. The base $m = k$ is obvious. Assume then that for some $m > k$, $\Sigma_{m-1}^p = \Pi_{m-1}^p = \Sigma_k^p$ holds. We shall prove that $\Sigma_m^p \subseteq \Sigma_k^p$ ($\Sigma_m^p = \Sigma_k^p$ follows immediately). Let $A \in \Sigma_m^p$. Theorem 7.3 ensures that a language $B \in \Pi_{m-1}^p$ and a polynomial p exist such that $x \in A \leftrightarrow (\exists y)[\langle x, y \rangle \in B]$ with $|y| \leq p(|x|)$.

Since $\Pi_{m-1}^p = \Sigma_k^p$ has been assumed, $B \in \Sigma_k^p$. According to Lemma 7.11, $A \in \Sigma_k^p$. Thus $\Sigma_m^p \subseteq \Sigma_k^p$. $\qquad\square$

An interesting application of the previous theorem is illustrated in the following corollary.

Corollary 7.2 P$\neq$NP if and only if P$\neq$PH.

Proof. The necessity is obvious since P $= \Sigma_0^p$ and NP $= \Sigma_1^p$. Conversely, assume that P $\neq \Sigma_k^p$ for some $k \geq 1$. If P $=$ NP, then $\Sigma_1^p = \Pi_1^p$ (see Lemma 7.2) and, according to Theorem 7.5, P $= \Sigma_k^p$ should hold for all $k \geq 1$, which is a contradiction. $\qquad\square$

Even assuming P $\neq$ NP, a collapse of the polynomial hierarchy might occur. The following question which we are unable to answer is therefore meaningful. If the polynomial hierarchy collapses, what is the smallest k for which $\Sigma_k^p = \Sigma_{k+1}^p$?

7.4   Exponential-time complexity classes

All time-complexity classes considered so far have been defined according to the following schema. $\mathcal{C}$ is the class of languages decided by Turing machine X (deterministic, nondeterministic, with oracle) in polynomial time with respect to the input length. Clearly, additional complexity classes defined in terms of hyperpolynomial time-constructible functions may also be considered and in this section we shall introduce a few time-complexity classes based on some exponential functions. In fact, these new classes are the largest in our classification of problem complexity since most natural problems have subexponential time complexity and very few interesting problems have been shown to be complete with respect to these new classes (see Notes).

From a slightly different perspective, it may be said that exponential-time complexity classes are the richest classes of languages investigated by complexity theory while hyperexponential classes of functions are mainly investigated in computability theory.

Let $l_k(n) = 2^{kn}$ and $h_k(n) = 2^{n^k}$ and let DTIME$[l_k(n)]$ and DTIME$[h_k(n)]$ be the corresponding deterministic time-complexity classes. The *classes LEXP* and *PEXP* are defined as

$$\text{LEXP} = \bigcup_{k \geq 0} \text{DTIME}[l_k(n)]$$

and

$$\text{PEXP} = \bigcup_{k \geq 0} \text{DTIME}[h_k(n)],$$

respectively. The nondeterministic complexity classes *NLEXP* and *NPEXP* are defined in a similar way.

An algorithm (deterministic or nondeterministic) is said to be *exponential* if it requires a number of steps bounded by $\mathbf{O}[2^{n^k}]$ with k constant.

It is easy to prove by diagonalization that $P \subset \text{LEXP}$ and that $\text{LEXP} \subset \text{PEXP}$ (see Problem 7.19) and that both results can be extended to the nondeterministic case. It is also easy to show that $\Sigma_k^p \subseteq \text{LEXP}$ for all $k \geq 0$ (see Problem 7.20) although it is not known whether such inclusions are strict.

7.4.1   The LEXP $\neq$ NLEXP conjecture

According to the definitions of LEXP and NLEXP, LEXP is included in NLEXP. Is the inclusion strict? Although we cannot provide a definite answer, we can reduce this conjecture to a second one which refers to the existence of tally languages in NPI.

Theorem 7.6 LEXP $\neq$ NLEXP if and only if NP $-$ P includes a tally language.

Proof. Let L be a binary language in NLEXP $-$ LEXP. Let $u : \{0,1\}^* \rightarrow \{0\}^*$ be the function introduced in Section 5.3.2 which maps binary numbers onto unary ones and denote by $b : \{0\}^* \rightarrow \{0,1\}^*$ the inverse function of u. The pair of functions b and u establish a bijection between a unary and a binary alphabet. Note that $|x| \leq \lceil \log(|u(x)|) \rceil$ and that $|z| < 2^{|b(z)|+1}$.

According to the definition, the tally language U_L associated with L is

$$U_L = \{u(x) : x \in L\}.$$

Let us prove that $U_L \in$ NP $-$ P.

Denote by NT the nondeterministic Turing machine which decides L in exponential time. Consider the machine NT' which checks, for any input z, whether z consists only of 0s and, in the affirmative case, simulates NT with input $b(z)$. Clearly, NT' decides U_L in polynomial time. Thus, $U_L \in$ NP.

Assume $U_L \in$ P. A deterministic Turing machine T would then exist deciding U_L in polynomial time. Consider the machine T' which, on input x, computes in exponential time $u(x)$ and then simulates T with input $u(x)$. Such a T' would be able to decide L in exponential time, contradicting the assumption that $L \notin$ LEXP. Thus, $U_L \in$ NP $-$ P.

Conversely, let U be a tally language in NP $-$ P. The binary langage L_U associated with U is defined as

$$L_U = \{b(z) : z \in U\}.$$

Let us prove that $L_U \in$ NLEXP $-$ LEXP. $L_U \in$ NLEXP since a machine NT which first computes $u(x)$ in exponential time and then simulates NT' (the machine which decides U in polynomial time) with input $u(x)$ can immediately be derived.

Suppose L_U belongs to LEXP. A machine T which decides L_U in exponential time could then be used to decide U in polynomial time. Indeed, a new machine T' which derives $b(z)$ from z and then simulates T with input $b(z)$ can be obtained. Thus U would belong to P, which is a contradiction. $\square$

An immediate consequence of the previous theorem is expressed in the following corollary.

Corollary 7.3 If LEXP $\neq$ NLEXP, then P $\neq$ NP.

According to Theorem 7.6 and Lemma 5.2 we obtain one more corollary which makes the existence of sparse languages in NPI plausible.

Corollary 7.4 LEXP $\neq$ NLEXP if and only if NP $-$ P includes a sparse language.

Problems

7.1. Show that NP $=$ *co*NP if and only if, for any maximization problem A in NPO, a minimization problem B in NPO exists such that $I_A = I_B$ and, for every $x \in I_A$, $\text{OPT}_A(x) = \text{OPT}_B(x)$. [Kolaitis and Thakur (1991)]

7.2. Describe a deterministic algorithm which computes x^r in, at most, $\mathbf{O}[\log^2 r]$ steps. [Hint: square x repeatedly for $\lfloor \log(r) \rfloor$ times; if r is not a power of 2, then repeat the procedure on $x^{r'}$ with $r' < r$.]

7.3. Show that, if n is prime, then any polynomial of degree k that is not identically zero has, at most, k distinct roots modulo n. [Hint: By induction on k, consider a polynomial $p(x) = a_k x^k + \ldots a_1 x + a_0$ with at least $k+1$ roots $x_1, \ldots, x_{k+1}$ and define the polynomial $p'(x) = p(x) - a_k \prod_{i=1}^{k}(x - x_i)$.]

7.4. A language L is said to be *expressible by hardware over* NP if it belongs to the Boolean closure of NP. Prove that if L is expressible by hardware over NP, then it is a finite union of languages in BH_2 and a finite intersection of languages in $co\text{BH}_2$. [Hint: if a language is expressible by hardware over NP, then it is accepted by a 'hardware tree' connecting NP languages.]

7.5. Prove that BH is the Boolean closure of NP, that is, it coincides with the smallest class containing NP which is closed with respect to union, intersection and complement. [Hint: show that, for any $k \geq 0$, $L \in \text{BH}_{2k}$ if and only if $L = (L_1 - L_2) \cup \ldots \cup (L_{2k-1} - L_{2k})$ with $L_i \in$ NP.]

7.6. EXACT CLIQUE: given a graph G and a positive integer k, is k the size of the maximum clique included in G? Prove that EXACT CLIQUE is BH_2-complete.

7.7. Let $\mathcal{C}$ denote a class of the polynomial hierarchy. Given a language L define the language L' as $L' = \{\langle x_1, \ldots, x_n \rangle : n \geq 0 \wedge \forall i \leq n[x_i \in L]\}$. Prove that $L \in \mathcal{C}$ if and only if $L' \in \mathcal{C}$.

7.8. Complete the proof of Theorem 7.3 in the case $k > 0$ and $L \in \Pi_k^p$.

7.9. Show that if $\Sigma_k^p \subseteq \Pi_k^p$, then $\Sigma_k^p = \Pi_k^p$.

7.10. Define the language $L(2)$ as

$$L(2) = \{\langle NT, x, 0^t \rangle : NT^L \text{ accepts } x \text{ in, at most, } t \text{ steps}\}.$$

where L is a NP-complete language. Show that $L(2)$ is Σ_2^p-complete. Generalize this result to any level of the polynomial hierarchy.

7.11. An *integer expression* f and the set X_f it represents are defined inductively as follows:

1. The binary representation of an integer n is an integer expression representing the single set $\{n\}$.

2. Given two integer expressions f and g, $(e \cup f)$ is an integer expression representing the set $X_f \cup X_g$.

3. Given two integer expressions f and g, $(e + f)$ is an integer expression representing the set $\{m + n : m \in X_f \wedge n \in X_g\}$.

INTEGER EXPRESSION INEQUIVALENCE: given two integer expressions f and g, is X_f different from X_g? Prove that this problem is Σ_2^p-complete. [Stockmeyer and Meyer (1973)]

7.12. Prove that Δ_2^p admits complete languages. Generalize this result to Δ_k^p for any $k \geq 0$.

7.13. Show that all classes of the polynomial hierarchy are constructively numerable. Show also that, for any $k \geq 0$, the set of Σ_k^p-complete languages is constructively enumerable.

7.14. Show that if $\Sigma_k^p - \Sigma_{k-1}^p \neq \emptyset$, then languages in $\Sigma_k^p - \Sigma_{k-1}^p$ exist which are not Σ_k^p-complete. [Hint: use the uniform diagonalization technique.]

7.15. Let L be a self-reducible language (see Problem 5.15) such that $L \in \Sigma_k^{p,L}$ for some $k \geq 0$ and some sparse language S. Prove that $\Sigma_2^{p,L} \subseteq \Sigma_{k+2}^p$. [Hint: based on Theorem 7.3, define a language corresponding to L but assuming that the oracle answers are given as a part of the input. You will probably need the result of Problem 5.16.]

7.16. A language L is said to be NP-*equivalent* if $\Delta_2^p = P^L$. Show that a language is NP-equivalent if and only if for any language $L' \in \Delta_2^p$, a polynomial-time deterministic Turing machine with oracle L exists deciding L'.

7.17. Prove that if NP $\neq$ *co*NP, then a language in Δ_2^p exists which is neither NP-equivalent, nor in NP, nor in *co*NP. [Schöning (1983)]

7.18. Prove the Corollary 7.1.

7.19. Use diagonalization to prove that P $\subset$ LEXP and that LEXP $\subset$ PEXP.

7.20. Use simulation to prove that $\Sigma_k^p \subseteq$ PEXP.

7.21. Use diagonalization to prove that NP $\subset$ NPEXP.

7.22. Show how to derive a PEXP-complete language from a LEXP-complete one. [Hint: use padding arguments increasing artificially the length of the inputs so that the 'padded' language is easier to decide than the initial one.]

Notes

Lemma 7.3 was obtained by Fermat in 1640: more modern proofs can be found in any text on number theory, such as Schroeder (1984), or in discrete mathematics, such as Graham, Knuth, and Patashnik (1989). The proof that every prime number has a 'succinct' certificate (Lemma 7.8) and thus that PRIME NUMBER belongs to NP is due to Pratt (1975). A polynomial-time deterministic algorithm for the same problem was devised in Miller (1976). However, the proof of its correctness relies on the still-open 'extended Riemann's hypothesis' and therefore does not constitute a proof of P membership. For a survey of subexponential algorithms for primality testing see Kranakis (1986).

A problem similar to that discussed in Example 7.5 appeared in Papadimitriou and Yannanakakis (1984). The motivation was to obtain negative results concerning the facets of the polytopes associated to many important combinatorial optimization problems. For that purpose, the class BH_2, denoted as D^p, was introduced and several interesting completeness results were obtained, including Theorem 7.2. In addition to problems related to the search for exact answers, the class BH_2 also contains the *critical* version of some decision problems. As an example, the critical version of SATISFIABILITY consists of deciding whether a formula is not satisfiable but deleting any single clause is enough to make it satisfiable (see Papadimitriou and Wolfe (1988)). The same class also includes *uniqueness* problems, that is, problems related to the existence of a unique solution (see Blass and Gurevich (1982)). The full Boolean hierarchy appears in passing in many papers and was defined explicitly in Wechsung (1985). Most results regarding structural properties and applications of this hierarchy were discussed in Cai *et al.* (1988, 1989).

The polynomial hierarchy was introduced in Stockmeyer (1977) as a time-bounded version of the arithmetic hierarchy of functions introduced by Kleene (see Rogers (1967)). In that paper, some properties of the hierarchy proved in Section 7.3 were presented. Theorems 7.3 and 7.4 were proved in Wrathall (1977) although the latter theorem was first noted in Meyer and Stockmeyer (1972). As in the case of the Boolean hierarchy, the practical significance of PH is restricted to the first few levels. In particular, the classes at these levels were found to be a useful tool to investigate the complexity of several problems arising in the field of artificial intelligence.

The LEXP $\neq$ NLEXP conjecture and the related Theorem 7.6 appeared in Hartmanis, Immerman, and Sewelson (1985). An interesting example of LEXP-complete problem related to game theory is discussed in Robson (1984) while Stockmeyer and Meyer (1973) show the NPEXP-completeness of a few word problems.

Finally, relativized separation results were obtained for all classes presented in this chapter (remember that according to Theorem 5.11 an oracle exists such that all classes up to PH collapse to P). In particular, Baker, Gill, and Solovay (1975) showed an oracle separating NP from *co*NP, Cai and Hemachandra (1986) proved the existence of an oracle with respect to which the Boolean hierarchy is infinite, and Yao (1985) obtained a similar result for the polynomial hierarchy. In addition to proper inclusion relationships between complexity classes, structural properties of such classes have also been studied via relativization. For instance, Sipser (1982) showed that an oracle exists such that the class NP $\cap$ *co*NP has no complete languages. More recently, Bovet, Crescenzi, and Silvestri (1992) introduced a uniform approach to obtaining such relativized results. In particular, they gave a sufficient and necessary condition for proving separation of relativized complexity classes, a characterization of complexity classes with complete languages and a sufficient condition for deriving strong separations from simple ones. In Bovet, Crescenzi, and Silvestri (1991) such an approach is also applied to problems related to positive relativizations.

Chapter 8

Space-complexity classes

The previous five chapters have dealt mainly with time-complexity classes and, although the dynamic measure $SPACE$ was introduced in Chapter 3, little attention, if any, has been paid to space-complexity classes. Such classes will be defined in Section 8.1 and the following issues will be discussed.

First, do relations between time-complexity and space-complexity classes exist? Clearly, the time is generally not bounded by the same function bounding the space since memory cells can repeatedly be used by the computation. We do, however, know that any deterministic Turing machine working in space $\mathbf{O}[s(n)]$ runs in time $\mathbf{O}[2^{ks(n)}]$ with k constant (see Lemma 3.1). This result also holds true in the nondeterministic case and no better one is known. On the other hand, since each new tape cell used by a computation requires at least one step to move the tape head onto that cell, we may state that a bound on the time implies an equal bound on the space. Can we do better? In Section 8.2 we shall see that for one-tape Turing machines tighter bounds do exist.

Second, the role of nondeterminism in space-complexity classes will be analysed. We have already seen how a nondeterministic Turing machine can be simulated by a deterministic one whose running time is exponential with respect to the running time of the former machine (see Theorem 2.1). In Section 8.3 such a simulation will be performed in a more efficient way from a space-complexity point of view.

Third, we already know from the previous chapters that nondeterministic time-complexity classes are not likely to coincide with their complement classes (we have conjectured NP $\neq$ coNP, $\Sigma_k^p \neq \Pi_k^p$, etc.). Surprisingly, we shall see in Section 8.4 that the opposite is true for nondeterministic space-complexity classes.

Finally, in Sections 8.5 and 8.6 we shall consider two popular complexity classes, that is, LOGSPACE and PSPACE, which contain languages decidable in logarithmic and polynomial space, respectively.

8.1   Space-complexity classes

As for the definition of time-complexity classes, some constraints have to be placed on the functions used to define space-complexity classes.

Formally, a *space-constructible function* s is a function mapping natural numbers onto natural numbers such that a multitape Turing machine exists which uses exactly $s(|x|)$ tape cells before halting for any input x.

Given a space-constructible function s, the *deterministic space-complexity class* $DSPACE[s(n)]$ is defined as

$$\text{DSPACE}[s(n)] = \{L : \exists T_i[L = L(T_i) \wedge SPACE_i(x) \in \mathbf{O}[s(|x|)]]\}.$$

Similarly, we define the *nondeterministic space-complexity class* $\text{NSPACE}[s(n)]$ by replacing deterministic machines T_i with nondeterministic ones NT_i in the previous formula.

8.2   Relations between time and space

Let us consider the following problem. Given a language $L \in \text{DTIME}[t(n)]$, what is the smallest space-complexity class including L? As stated above, we know that $L \in \text{DSPACE}[t(n)]$: the next theorem shows that this bound can be considerably lowered at least for one-tape machines. In order to prove this, we shall first introduce some preliminary definitions and facts.

Let T be a one-tape Turing machine and x be an input. Let us focus our attention on the boundary between the ith and the $(i+1)$th tape cell. During the computation $T(x)$, this boundary is likely to be crossed several times and, each time the tape head crosses the boundary, T must be in a given state. The sequence of T states as its tape head crosses the boundary is called the *crossing sequence at boundary i with input x*, in symbols $S_i(x)$.

Example 8.1 The crossing sequence at boundary i of the computation represented in Figure 8.1 is given by q_2, q_4, q_2, q_5, q_4.

More generally, a *crossing sequence* is a list of states. Denote two crossing sequences by $S = q_1, \ldots, q_r$ and $S' = q'_1, \ldots, q'_s$. The basic idea underlying the next result is a relation of 'compatibility' between S, S', and a portion y of the tape, that is, a range of tape cells together with their contents. Intuitively, S, S' and y are *compatible* if, starting T at the leftmost tape cell of y in state q_1, S and S' are generated at the left and right boundaries of y whenever the following two rules are applied (see Figure 8.2):

1. If T crosses the left boundary of y moving left in state q_i with i even, then its tape head is placed on the leftmost tape cell of y and its state is set to q_{i+1}.

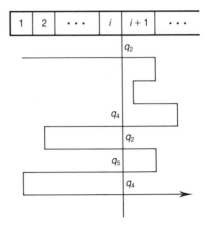

Figure 8.1 An example of a crossing sequence at boundary i

2. If T crosses the right boundary of y moving right in state q_i' with i odd, then its tape head is placed on the rightmost tape cell of y and its state is set to q_{i+1}'.

In other words, the odd subsequence of S, that is, $q_1, q_3, q_5, \ldots$, denotes the sequence of states of T when entering into y from the left, while the even subsequence, that is, $q_2, q_4, q_6, \ldots$, denotes the sequence of states of T when leaving y to the left. A similar interpretation holds for odd and even subsequences of S' (we hope that such an intuitive definition is clear enough: for more formality see Notes).

Note now that if T runs in time $\mathbf{O}[t(n)]$, then, for any input x, at most, $ct(|x|)$ tape cells will be used by the computation $T(x)$, where c is a constant. The basic idea is to partition these $ct(|x|)$ tape cells into blocks of equal size and to consider the crossing sequences at the boundaries of such blocks. In particular, for any i and d, let $l = \lceil (ct(|x|) - i)/d \rceil$. The first $ct(|x|)$ cells are partitioned into $l + 1$ blocks with the first block y_0 containing the first i cells and block y_j, with $1 \le j \le l$, containing cells $i + d(j-1)$ through $i + dj - 1$ (see Figure 8.3).

The *ith crossing sequence sample of distance d and length l with input x* is the list of crossing sequences $S_0(x), S_i(x), S_{i+d}(x), S_{i+2d}(x), \ldots, S_{i+ld}(x)$, that is, the list of crossing sequences at the boundaries of the blocks y_j. More generally, a *crossing sequence sample of length l* is a list of $l + 2$ crossing sequences.

Lemma 8.1 Given two integers i and d, let $l = \lceil (ct(|x|) - i)/d \rceil$. A crossing sequence sample $S_0, S_1, S_2, \ldots, S_{l+1}$ of length l is the ith crossing sequence sample of distance d and length l with input x if and only if for any j with $0 \le j \le l$, S_j, S_{j+1} and y_j are compatible.

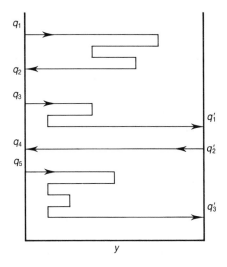

Figure 8.2 Compatibility between crossing sequences and a tape

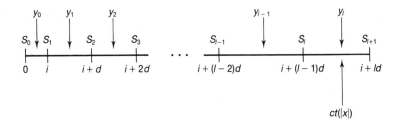

Figure 8.3 Partition of the tape into blocks

Proof. The proof is straightforward and is left as a problem (see Problem 8.3). □

The above lemma guarantees that the acceptance of a given input can be checked by testing iteratively for the compatibility of crossing sequences and portions of the tape. This will be exploited in the following theorem.

Theorem 8.1 Let t be any time-constructible function such that $t(n) \geq n^2$ and $\sqrt{t}$ is space-constructible. If a language L is decided by a one-tape deterministic Turing machine T in time $\mathbf{O}[t(n)]$, then L can be decided by a one-tape deterministic Turing machine using space $\mathbf{O}[\sqrt{t(n)}]$.

Proof. First, note that an integer $1 \leq i \leq \sqrt{ct(|x|)}$ exists such that the sum of the lengths of the crossing sequences included in the ith crossing sequence sample of distance $d = \sqrt{ct(|x|)}$ and length l as in the above lemma is, at most, $\sqrt{ct(|x|)}$. In fact, the sum of the lengths of *all* the ith crossing sequence samples, for $1 \leq i \leq \sqrt{ct(|x|)}$, gives the total number of times the tape head crosses the boundary between two tape cells. This number cannot be greater than $ct(|x|)$. Hence there must be a crossing sequence sample whose length is, at most, $\sqrt{ct(|x|)}$.

The new machine systematically generates crossing sequence samples of length, at most, $\sqrt{ct(|x|)}$. For each, it tests adjacent crossing sequences and the corresponding portion of the tape for compatibility (according to the definition of compatibility, this test can be performed using, at most, $k\sqrt{t(|x|)}$ tape cells with k constant), and accepts if all the previous tests have been successful and an accepting global state has been encountered during one of them. The details of the machine are left to the reader. □

In addition to the previous result, other important relationships between time and space have been found. Due to lack of space, we cannot present them here but refer the interested reader to the Notes.

Finally, a more ambitious goal would be to look for tradeoffs between time and space. For example, is it possible to save time by consuming more space? Unfortunately, at present, no general technique is known for deriving from a machine T working in time t and space s an equivalent machine T' operating in time $t' < t$ but space $s' > s$.

8.3 Nondeterminism, determinism and space

The following theorem is analogous to Theorem 2.1 which, surprisingly, yields a more efficient space bound.

Theorem 8.2 For any space-constructible function s such that $s(n) \geq n$,

$$\mathrm{NSPACE}[s(n)] \subseteq \mathrm{DSPACE}[s^2(n)].$$

Proof. Let L be an arbitrary language in $\mathrm{NSPACE}[s(n)]$ and NT be a nondeterministic Turing machine which decides L in space $\mathbf{O}[s(n)]$. Thus, for any input x of length n, if NT accepts x, then a computation path of $NT(x)$ requiring, at most, $ks(n)$ cells must exist, where k is a constant. According to Lemma 3.1, the length of such a computation path is, at most, $2^{cs(n)}$ with c constant.

Let us make a few simplifying assumptions. First, NT is a one-tape machine (see Lemma 4.1); second, each global state is encoded by exactly $ks(n)$ symbols (see Problem 2.7); finally, before reaching the accepting final state q_A, NT cleans the tape and positions the tape head on cell 0 so that both a single initial global state $\mathcal{S}_0$ and a single accepting global state $\mathcal{S}_\Omega$ exist (see Problem 2.5).

Consider the predicate $reachable(\mathcal{S}, \mathcal{S}', j)$ which is true if and only if the global state $\mathcal{S}'$ is reachable from the global state $\mathcal{S}$ in at most 2^j steps, that is, the computation tree $NT(x)$ contains a path from $\mathcal{S}$ to $\mathcal{S}'$ of length, at most, 2^j. Then, according to previous observations, $x \in L$ if and only if $reachable(\mathcal{S}_0, \mathcal{S}_\Omega, cs(n)) =$ **true**.

Now comes the difficult part, namely, the algorithm for the predicate $reachable$. Note that instead of asking whether it is possible to go from $\mathcal{S}$ to $\mathcal{S}'$ in, at most, 2^j steps, we can divide the problem into two somewhat easier ones and ask whether a global state $\mathcal{S}''$ exists such that it is possible to go from $\mathcal{S}$ to $\mathcal{S}''$ in, at most, 2^{j-1} steps and from $\mathcal{S}''$ to $\mathcal{S}'$ in, at most, 2^{j-1} steps. This breaking-down process can then be iterated for increasingly smaller values of j until transforming a call to $reachable$ with $j = 1$ (that is, two steps) into two calls to $reachable$ with $j = 0$ (that is, one step). These latter calls can easily be computed by simply investigating the quintuples of NT.

The following algorithm formalizes the above discussion:

function $reachable(\mathcal{S}, \mathcal{S}', j)$: **Boolean**;
begin
    if $j = 0$ **then**
        if $(\mathcal{S} = \mathcal{S}')$ **or** (a quintuple exists causing the transition from $\mathcal{S}$ to $\mathcal{S}'$)
        then $reachable$:= **true**
        else $reachable$:= **false**
    else
    begin
        $reachable$:= **false**;
        for each global state $\mathcal{S}''$ **do**
            if $(reachable(\mathcal{S}, \mathcal{S}'', j - 1))$ **and** $(reachable(\mathcal{S}'', \mathcal{S}', j - 1))$ **then**
                $reachable$:= **true**;
    end;
end;

Let us now check the space requirements of the above algorithm. By construction, the nesting level of recursive calls is $\mathbf{O}[s(n)]$ and, at each level, $\mathbf{O}[s(n)]$ space must be used to save the two parameter values $\mathcal{S}$ and $\mathcal{S}'$. In conclusion, the algorithm requires $\mathbf{O}[s(n)^2]$ space. $\qquad\square$

8.4 Nondeterminism, complement and space

Theorem 8.2 suggests that nondeterminism is less powerful with respect to space than it is with respect to time. The following theorem provides some further evidence of this.

Theorem 8.3 For any space-constructible function s such that $s(n) \geq n$,

$$\text{NSPACE}[s(n)] = co\text{NSPACE}[s(n)].$$

Proof. Given any language $L \in \text{NSPACE}[s(n)]$, denote by NT the nondeterministic machine which decides L in space $\mathbf{O}[s(n)]$. Then, for any input x of length n, $NT(x)$ uses, at most, $cs(n)$ tape cells where c is a constant. In order to prove the result, we will derive a second machine denoted as NT' which decides L^c in space $\mathbf{O}[s(n)]$.

As in the proof of Theorem 8.2, we assume that NT is a one-tape machine, that global states are encoded in exactly $cs(n)$ symbols of an alphabet Γ, and that a single initial global state $\mathcal{S}_0$ associated with input x and a single accepting global state $\mathcal{S}_\Omega$ exist.

Denote by $I_m(x)$ the set of global states reachable from $\mathcal{S}_0$ in, at most, m steps. Since the number of steps in any accepting computation path of $NT(x)$ is bounded by $|\Gamma|^{cs(n)}$, it follows that

$$NT \text{ accepts } x \leftrightarrow \mathcal{S}_\Omega \in I_{|\Gamma|^{cs(n)}}(x).$$

Note that it is easy to derive a nondeterministic machine NT_1 deciding whether a global state $\mathcal{S}$ belongs to $I_m(x)$ for some m. Such a machine simply guesses a computation path starting from $\mathcal{S}_0$ and consisting of, at most, m global states and checks whether $\mathcal{S}$ is in the path. Formally, NT_1 can be defined as follows:

begin {input: $x, \mathcal{S}, m$}
  {$\mathcal{S}_0 \in I_m$ for all m}
  if $\mathcal{S} = \mathcal{S}_0$ **then** accept;
  $\mathcal{S}_1 := \mathcal{S}_0$;
  {check whether $\mathcal{S}$ is reachable from $\mathcal{S}_0$ in m steps}
  for $i = 1$ **to** m **do**
  begin
    guess a global state $\mathcal{S}_2$;
    if a quintuple exists causing a transition from $\mathcal{S}_1$ to $\mathcal{S}_2$ **then**
      if $\mathcal{S} = \mathcal{S}_2$ **then** accept
      else $\mathcal{S}_1 := \mathcal{S}_2$
    else reject;
  end;
  reject;
end.

However, in order to decide whether $x \in L^c$ the nondeterministic Turing machine NT' has to be capable of deciding whether $\mathcal{S}_\Omega$ *does not belong* to $I_{|\Gamma|^{cs(n)}}(x)$ (remember, we cannot simply invert the roles of accepting and rejecting final states in the definition of NT_1). The basic idea is as follows.

First NT' inductively computes the cardinalities $|I_0(x)|, |I_1(x)|, \ldots, |I_{|\Gamma|^{cs(n)}}(x)|$. Once the cardinality of $I_{|\Gamma|^{cs(n)}}(x)$ is known, it successively considers all global states until it finds all those included in $I_{|\Gamma|^{cs(n)}}(x)$ and if $\mathcal{S}_\Omega$ is not one of those states then it accepts, otherwise it rejects.

Let us first show how the cardinalities of the sets $I_m(x)$ can be computed in an inductive way. By construction, $I_0(x) = \{\mathcal{S}_0\}$ and thus $|I_0(x)| = 1$. Assume now that $|I_m(x)|$ has been computed. In order to compute $|I_{m+1}(x)|$, each global state $\mathcal{S}$ is considered to check whether another global state $\mathcal{S}'$ exists belonging to $I_m(x)$ such that $\mathcal{S}$ is reachable from $\mathcal{S}'$ in, at most, one step. If so, the value of a counter is increased by one. The final value of the counter will be equal to $|I_{m+1}(x)|$.

The nondeterministic algorithm computing $|I_{|\Gamma|^{cs(n)}}(x)|$ is then the following:

```
function cardinality(x, cs(n)): integer;
begin
  {card1 and card2 denote |Im| and |Im+1|, respectively}
  card1 := 1;
  for k = 1 to |Γ|^cs(n) do
  begin
    card2 := 0;
    for each global state S do
    begin
      counter := card1;
      answer := false;
      for each global state S' do
      begin
        {check whether S' ∈ Im}
        simulate NT1(x, S', m);
        if NT1(x, S', m) accepts then
        begin
          counter := counter − 1;
          if S is reachable from S' in one step then
            answer := true;
        end;
      end;
      {check whether all global states of Im have been considered}
      if counter = 0 then
        if answer then card2 := card2 + 1;
      {by inducing an infinite loop at this point
       NT1 eliminates all computation paths which
       have not considered all global states of Im}
      else cycle for ever;
    end;
```

```
    card1  :=  card2;
  end;
  cardinality  :=  card1;
end;
```

Notice that the above algorithm is described by means of a nondeterministic transducer. Did not we promise in Section 2.1.2 to consider nondeterministic acceptor machines only? Well, there is an exception to every rule; in any case, the above algorithm does not lead to any ambiguity since, for any input, all the halting computation paths compute the same value.

Finally, the second part of machine NT' is as follows:

function $find\_S_\Omega(x, |I_{|\Gamma|^{cs(n)}}(x)|)$: **boolean**;
begin
  $i := 0$;
  $isin := $ **false**;
  {derive $I_{|\Gamma|^{cs(n)}}(x)$ and check whether S_Ω belongs to it}
  for each global state S **do**
  begin
    simulate $NT_1(x, S, |\Gamma|^{cs(n)})$;
    if $NT_1(x, S, |\Gamma|^{cs(n)})$ accepts **then**
    begin
      $i := i + 1$;
      if $S = S_\Omega$ **then** $isin := $ **true**;
    end;
  end;
  if $i = |I_{|\Gamma|^{cs(n)}}(x)|$ **then**
    if $isin$ **then** $find_S_\Omega := $ **false** **else** $find_S_\Omega := $ **true**
  else $find_S_\Omega := $ **false**;
end;

It is easy to verify that the space requirement of all the above algorithms is the same as that of machine NT. Thus $L^c \in \text{NSPACE}[s(n)]$. Since L can be any language in $\text{NSPACE}[s(n)]$, it follows that $\text{NSPACE}[s(n)] = co\text{NSPACE}[s(n)]$. $\square$

8.5   Logarithmic space

We have already observed that, whenever the input encoding is reasonable, all input symbols have to be read and thus the linear space is a lower bound for any computation. We can refine the above analysis by examining more closely the storage requirements of a computation. On the one hand, tape cells are needed to contain the input value and, in the case of transducers, the output value. On the other, the computation may require additional cells to store the internal data structures (variables, counters, lists, etc.) used by the algorithm. Let us concentrate on storage requirements of this second kind.

For this purpose, we shall impose some minor constraints on the use of the tapes of a k-tape Turing machine. Tape 1 which contains the input x must be used as a read-only tape. If the machine is a transducer, then the output must be written on tape 2, called the *output tape* which must be used as a write-move tape, that is, a write-only tape on which only right moves are allowed. The remaining tapes, called *working tapes*, are unrestricted read/write tapes.

We then define a new dynamic measure of complexity denoted as $WSPACE$. Given a computation $T_i(x)$, $WSPACE_i(x)$ is defined as the number of working tape cells needed by the computation.

This new definition allows us to define subclasses of the classes P and FP introduced in Section 4.1. The first of such classes is the *class LOGSPACE* defined as the set of languages L which can be decided by a deterministic Turing machine T_i requiring $WSPACE_i(x) \in \mathbf{O}[\log(|x|)]$.

Many problems in P can be shown to belong to LOGSPACE. The intuitive reason for this is that many deterministic polynomial-time algorithms are based on tests for local properties of a problem instance.

Example 8.2 The problem of deciding whether a given word is a palindrome can be solved in logarithmic working space by making use of the algorithm described in Example 3.18. Indeed, it suffices to maintain a counter of how many symbols have already been checked.

Example 8.3 DEGREE ONE: given a graph $G = (N, E)$, does G include a node of degree 1? This problem can be solved by checking the number of adjacent nodes of each of the $|N|$ nodes of G. Only the index of the node currently examined must be kept in the working tapes. Thus this problem belongs to LOGSPACE.

Similarly, we shall define a subset of the class of functions FP. This class denoted as the *class FLOGSPACE* is the class of all functions computable in logarithmic WSPACE by a deterministic transducer Turing machine. The class FLOGSPACE comprises a large set of functions. For example, the sum and product functions are computable in logarithmic space. Similarly it can be shown (see Problems 8.8 and 8.10) that matrix multiplication and sorting a list of numbers can be done in logarithmic space. More surprisingly, it turns out that all known polynomial-time functions used to prove the NP-completeness of problems also belong to FLOGSPACE (see Problem 8.12).

Finally, let us consider the nondeterministic version of LOGSPACE. Formally, the *class NLOGSPACE* is defined as the set of languages L which can be decided by a nondeterministic Turing machine NT_i requiring $WSPACE_i(x) \in \mathbf{O}[\log(|x|)]$.

The following is an example of problem in NLOGSPACE which highlights the role of nondeterminism.

Example 8.4 DIRECTED GRAPH ACCESSIBILITY: given a *directed* graph $G(N, E)$ with $N = \{1, \ldots, n\}$, does G admit a directed path from node 1 to node n? The following nondeterministic algorithm solves DIRECTED GRAPH ACCESSIBILITY:

```
begin {input: G(N, E)}
  r := n;
  i := 1;
  while r > 0 do
    if (i, n) ∈ E then accept
    else
    begin
      guess j in N;
      r := r - 1;
      if (i, j) ∈ E then i := j else reject;
    end;
  reject;
end.
```

Since the working tape of the above algorithm only needs to contain the values of r, i, and j, a logarithmic number of tape cells is sufficient, and thus the problem belongs to NLOGSPACE. It is not known whether it also belongs to LOGSPACE. If the graph is not directed, however, the corresponding GRAPH ACCESSIBILITY problem can easily be shown to belong to LOGSPACE (see Problem 8.9).

Clearly, NLOGSPACE includes LOGSPACE; the next theorem shows that, somewhat surprisingly, this class is not larger than P.

Theorem 8.4 NLOGSPACE ⊆ P.

Proof. First note that any global state of a nondeterministic Turing machine NT working in logarithmic space can be encoded as a word of a logarithmic length (see Problem 8.11). Thus, for any x, we can derive a directed graph of polynomial size whose nodes denote global states of $NT(x)$ and whose edges denote one-step transitions between pairs of global states. Clearly, NT accepts x if and only if a path exists from the initial global state to the accepting one. This latter problem can easily be solved in polynomial time. □

8.5.1 P-complete problems

From the previous theorem and since LOGSPACE ⊆ NLOGSPACE, it follows that LOGSPACE is included in P. We are unable, however, to specify whether the inclusion is a proper one. Even if it seems likely that languages in P - LOGSPACE do exist, this conjecture has not yet been proved. We must then content ourselves with inserting it into the list of hard-to-prove conjectures which have been challenging computer scientists for the past two decades.

Since we are unable to prove such a conjecture, once again we shall look for the hardest problems in P unlikely to be in LOGSPACE. Before doing that, however, we need to introduce a restricted form of polynomial-time reducibility.

A language L is said to be *logspace-reducible* to a second language L', in symbols $L \leq_{log} L'$, if a function $f \in$ FLOGSPACE exists providing an m-reduction between L and L'.

The next lemma shows that logspace reducibility is reflexive and transitive, therefore the class LOGSPACE is closed with respect to it.

Lemma 8.2 The logspace reducibility $\leq_{log}$ is reflexive and transitive.

Proof. Clearly, $\leq_{log}$ is reflexive since the identity function is computable in zero space.

It remains to prove that $\leq_{log}$ is also transitive. For this, let L, L_1 and L_2 be arbitrary languages such that $L \leq_{log} L_1 \leq_{log} L_2$. Denote by T_1 and T_2 the two deterministic transducers which compute the reductions from L to L_1 and from L_1 to L_2, respectively, in logarithmic space. It suffices to prove that a machine T can be defined which reduces L to L_2 in logarithmic space. We first observe that the straightforward approach consisting of cascading together T_1 with T_2 will not work, in general, since the working tape of the resulting T should be large enough to contain the output of T_1 whose length may be more than logarithmic with respect to the input length (remember that the output tape is not considered when evaluating the space complexity of T_1).

For that reason, machine T will make use of the following technique. Whenever T_2 needs to read the ith symbol of the output of T_1, T initializes a counter to 0, starts simulating T_1 and increases the counter by 1 every time T_1 wants to write a new symbol in its output tape (remember that this tape is a write-move one) without really performing that writing. When the counter reaches the value $i - 1$, T knows that the new symbol to be written by T_1 is the symbol needed by T_2.

Since both T_1 and T_2 work in logarithmic space and since the length of the counter is clearly logarithmic with respect to the input length, then machine T works in logarithmic space.   □

A language L is P-*complete with respect to* $\leq_{log}$, in short P-*complete*, if it belongs to P and if all languages in P are logspace-reducible to it.

Thus if LOGSPACE $\neq$ P, then Lemma 3.2 ensures that any P-complete language belongs to P $-$ LOGSPACE.

Do P-complete languages exist? As in the case of NP-complete languages, if we can prove the existence of at least one, then it becomes relatively easy to prove the completeness of other languages via a chain of reductions.

Example 8.5 SOLVABLE PATH SYSTEMS: given a finite set X and three sets $R \subseteq X \times X \times X$, $X_s \subset X$ and $X_t \subset X$, does X_t include at least one element of the least subset A of X such that (i) $X_s \subseteq A$ and (ii) if $y, z \in A$ and $\langle x, y, z \rangle \in R$ then $x \in A$?

Intuitively, X_s and X_t correspond to 'source' and 'terminal' nodes of a graph, respectively, and the objective is to decide whether a set of paths (or, equivalently, a set of derivations) based on triples of R and connecting a terminal node with some source nodes exists.

The following result shows that SOLVABLE PATH SYSTEMS plays the same role for P-complete problems as SATISFIABILITY does for NP-complete problems.

Theorem 8.5 SOLVABLE PATH SYSTEMS is P-complete.

Proof. The problem belongs to P. Indeed, it can be solved by the following simple polynomial-time algorithm. A list L of nodes which initially contains the nodes of X_s is derived; in the successive steps, all nodes $x \notin L$ such that $\langle x, y, z \rangle \in R$ and $y, z \in L$ are added to L. When no new nodes can be added to L, the algorithm halts and accepts the input if and only if L includes at least one element of X_t.

In order to prove completeness, let T_i and x be a deterministic polynomial-time Turing machine and an input value, respectively. The proof will consist of producing a logspace-reduction f which transforms the pair $\langle T_i, x \rangle$ into an instance $f(T_i, x)$ of SOLVABLE PATH SYSTEMS such that T_i accepts x if and only if $f(T_i, x)$ is a yes-instance.

The reduction makes use of a clever trick which deserves a few words of explanation. If we observe the moves of a tape head along a tape during a computation, in general, we will not be able to determine any correlation between the tape head positions and the steps of the computation. We may consider, for instance, a computation which in some phases focuses on a limited portion of the tape while in others it sweeps back and forth between the two extremities of the used tape.

It turns out, however, that a neat correlation between the tape head position and the number of steps executed can be established, albeit sacrificing some efficiency. This is accomplished by a special kind of Turing machine which we shall denote as *pendulum machine*.

For simplicity and without loss of generality, we shall limit our attention to one-tape machines. The tape head moves of a pendulum machine are best described in terms of *oscillations*. Assume that the tape head is positioned on cell 0 at time 0. Then the first oscillation scans cells 1 and 0 at times 1 and 2, respectively. The second oscillation scans cells 1, 2, 1, and 0 at times 3, 4, 5 and 6, respectively. In general, each new oscilation scans one new cell to the right with respect to the previous oscillation and then returns to cell 0 as shown in Figure 8.4.

It is easy to verify (see Problem 8.14) that, given any polynomial-time machine, it is always possible to derive from it an equivalent polynomial-time pendulum machine. We may thus limit our attention to polynomial-time pendulum machines.

Let us start by introducing a few simple functions which make explicit the correlation between tape head position and step number. Denote by *cell* the function yielding the index of the cell scanned at step t, by *tprev* the function yielding the last step before step t at which the cell $cell(t)$ has been scanned (if that cell is scanned for the first time at step t, then assume $tprev(t) = -1$), and, finally, with *initialvalue* the function yielding the contents of $cell(t)$ at step 0.

Let us now compute the three previous functions (remember that according to the definition, the ith oscillation is performed in $2i$ steps and consists of i right tape head moves followed by i left ones, for $i = 1, 2, \ldots$):

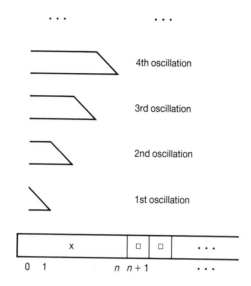

Figure 8.4 Tape head motion of a pendulum machine

1. If $0 \le t \le 2$, then

$$cell(t) = \begin{cases} 0 & \text{if } t = 0, 2, \\ 1 & \text{if } t = 1; \end{cases}$$

if $t > 2$, then derive the index i^* of the last oscillation which terminated before step t, that is,

$$i^* = \max\{i : i \ge 1 \wedge \sum_{j=1}^{i} 2j < t\}.$$

Let $i = i^* + 1$. According to the previous definitions, the cell c scanned at step t is included among those scanned during the ith oscillation. Subtract from t the number of steps required to perform the i^* oscillations preceding the ith and denote the resulting value as t'. Thus,

$$t' = t - \sum_{j=1}^{i^*} 2j = t - i^*(i^* + 1).$$

The value $cell(t)$ for $t > 2$ can then be computed from i and t' as

$$cell(t) = \begin{cases} t' & \text{if } t' \le i, \\ 2i - t' & \text{otherwise.} \end{cases}$$

2. Similarly, $tprev(t)$ can be computed by first deriving the index i of the oscillation including t and then the corresponding t'. The value $tprev(t)$ is then computed as

$$tprev(t) = \begin{cases} -1 & \text{if } (0 \leq t \leq 1) \vee (t' = i), \\ t - 2t' & \text{if } 1 \leq t' < i, \\ t - 2(t' - i) & \text{if } i < t' \leq 2i. \end{cases}$$

3. Finally, for any input $x = x_0 x_1 \ldots x_{n-1}$ of length n, the third function *initialvalue* is defined as

$$initialvalue(t) = \begin{cases} x_{cell(t)} & \text{if } 0 \leq cell(t) \leq n - 1, \\ \square & \text{otherwise.} \end{cases}$$

We may now proceed with the reduction. Let T_i be a pendulum machine, x an input of length n and denote by $t^* = p(n)$ the upper bound to the number of steps executed by the computation $T_i(x)$ where p is a polynomial. The set X of nodes of the SOLVABLE PATH SYSTEMS instance is defined as $X = \{0, \ldots, t^*\} \times Q \times \Sigma$ where Q and Σ denote the set of states and the tape alphabet of T_i, respectively.

The set X_s consists of a single-source node, namely, $\langle 0, q_0, x_0 \rangle$, while the set of terminal nodes X_t consists of all nodes $\langle t, q_A, \sigma \rangle$ with $0 \leq t \leq t^*$ and $\sigma \in \Sigma$ (q_0 and q_A denote the initial state and the accepting state of T_i, respectively).

The triples of R are derived form the quintuples of T_i in two possible ways (we use the notation $y, z \rightarrow x$ instead of $\langle x, y, z \rangle$ to emphasize the derivation implied by a triple):

1. Associate to each quintuple $\langle q, \sigma, \sigma', m, q' \rangle$ of T_i the triples

$$\langle t, q, \sigma \rangle, \langle t, q, \sigma \rangle \rightarrow \langle t + 1, q', \sigma'' \rangle$$

for all values t with $0 \leq t < t^*$ such that $initialvalue(t + 1) = \sigma''$ and $tprev(t + 1) = -1$.

2. Associate to each pair of quintuples $\langle q_1, \sigma_1, \sigma_1', m_1, q_1' \rangle$ and $\langle q_2, \sigma_2, \sigma_2', m_2, q_2' \rangle$ of T_i the triples

$$\langle t, q_1, \sigma_1 \rangle, \langle t_1, q_2, \sigma_2 \rangle \rightarrow \langle t + 1, q_1', \sigma_2' \rangle$$

for all values t with $0 \leq t < t^*$ such that $tprev(t + 1) = t_1$.

The first rule deduces the value at step $t+1$ of the state and that of the observed symbol assuming that cell $cell(t+1)$ has not been scanned previously. In that case, the observed symbol is the initial symbol, that is, the symbol contained at step 0, while the state depends on the pair state-symbol at step t.

The second rule deduces the value at step $t + 1$ of the state and that of the observed symbol assuming that cell $cell(t+1)$ has previously been scanned at step

t_1. In that case, the observed symbol depends on the pair state-symbol at step t_1, while the state depends on the pair state-symbol at step t.

It immediately follows from the above construction that T_i accepts x if and only if the corresponding instance $\langle X, X_s, X_t, R \rangle$ of SOLVABLE PATH SYSTEMS is a yes-instance.

Since the number of quintuples of T_i is constant, the total number of triples derived according to rules 1 and 2 is bounded by kt^* where k is a constant. Furthermore, it is easy to verify that functions *cell*, *tprec*, and *initialvalue* belong to FLOGSPACE (see Problem 8.13) and that the triples of R can be derived one at a time using, at most, $h \log(t^*)$ cells with h constant. The reduction described requires logarithmic space. Since T_i was a generic pendulum machine, it follows that SOLVABLE PATH SYSTEMS is P-complete. $\qquad\square$

Many other interesting P-complete problems have been defined. We shall discuss a few in the last part of the book.

8.6 Polynomial space

Let $p_k(n) = n^k$ and denote by DSPACE$[p_k(n)]$ the corresponding deterministic space-complexity class. The *class PSPACE* is then defined as

$$\text{PSPACE} = \bigcup_{k \geq 0} \text{DSPACE}[p_k(n)]$$

The same reasoning applied in Section 4.2 to show the robustness of class P with respect to variations in the model of computation can be applied to class PSPACE. In other words, it is always possible to transform a polynomial-space algorithm obtained for a modified model into a polynomial-space algorithm applicable to the basic one.

Let us further explore the similarities between P and PSPACE. What is the role of nondeterminism? Does it make sense to define NPSPACE as an infinite union of nondeterministic polynomial space-complexity classes and examine the relations between PSPACE and NPSPACE? The answer is negative since it suffices to apply Theorem 8.2 to polynomial functions to obtain the following result.

Corollary 8.1 PSPACE = NPSPACE.

8.6.1 An alternative characterization

In this section we present an alternative characterization of PSPACE based on alternating Turing machines. Define the *class AP* as the class of languages which can be decided in polynomial time by an alternating Turing machine.

Theorem 8.6 PSPACE = AP.

Proof. By using a technique similar to that used in the proof of Theorem 8.2, it is relatively easy to show that PSPACE $\subseteq$ AP (see Problem 8.18).

Conversely, let $L \in$ AP and let AT be an alternating Turing machine which decides L in polynomial time. The following construction shows how to derive from AT a corresponding deterministic Turing machine T which decides L in polynomial space.

Given an input x, T executes a depth-first visit of the computation tree associated with $AT(x)$ to check whether an alternating tree which accepts x exists. The detailed procedure is illustrated below (the notation used is similar to the one used in the proof of Theorem 8.2):

```
begin {input: x}
    S₀ := initial global state;
    if visit(S₀) then accept else reject;
end.
```

where the function *visit* is defined as

```
function visit(S): Boolean;
begin
    if S is the accepting state then visit := true;
    if S is the rejecting state then visit := false;
    if S is an existential state then
    begin
        b := false;
        {check whether an accepting subtree exists}
        while (not b) and unvisited successors of S exist do
        begin
            select a successor S' not yet visited;
            b := visit(S');
        end;
        if b then visit := true else visit := false;
    end;
    if S is a universal state then
    begin
        b := true;
        {check if all subtrees accept}
        while b and unvisited successors of S exist do
        begin
            select a successor S' not yet visited;
            b := visit(S');
        end;
        if b then visit := true else visit := false;
    end;
end;
```

It is easy to verify that the above algorithm decides L in polynomial space. $\square$

8.6.2   PSPACE-complete problems

Once again we are interested in characterizing the 'most difficult' problems of a given complexity class, namely of PSPACE. Our approach will consist of looking for PSPACE-complete problems with respect to polynomial-time reducibility. The next example, which is a slight modification of the problem $k-\text{QBF}$ introduced in Example 7.11, describes a first problem for which it is relatively easy to prove PSPACE-completeness.

Example 8.6 QBF: given a Boolean formula E on n variables $x_1, \ldots, x_n$ and a sequence of n quantifiers $Q_1, \ldots, Q_n$, is the prenex formula

$$F = (Q_1 x_1)(Q_2 x_2) \ldots (Q_n x_n) E(x_1, \ldots, x_n)$$

true? Note how in this new problem the number of alternations between quantifiers is no longer required to be constant.

Theorem 8.7 QBF is PSPACE-complete.

Proof. It is easy to see that QBF belongs to PSPACE. We will now outline the completeness proof leaving the details to the reader.

Let T be any machine deciding a language in polynomial space and let x be any input. The objective is to derive a polynomial-time reduction f which transforms the pair $\langle T, x \rangle$ into a quantified Boolean formula F_x such that F_x is true if and only if T accepts x.

Denote by n the length of x and with $s(n)$ the polynomial limiting the space requirements of T. Thus $T(x)$ uses, at most, $s^* = s(n)$ tape cells and executes, at most, $t^* = 2^{cs(n)}$ steps, for a constant c.

Assume that global states are encoded as binary words of a fixed length L. These words, in turn, can be viewed as assignments of values to L-tuples of Boolean variables. Thus, in the following, the notation $\exists X$ (respectively, $\forall X$) with $X = \langle x_1, \ldots, x_L \rangle$ will stand both for 'an assignment of values to variables $x_1, \ldots, x_L$ exists' (respectively, 'for all assignments of values to variables $x_1, \ldots, x_L$') and for 'a global state X exists' (respectively, 'for all global state X').

Using the same assumptions as in the proof of Theorem 8.2, we can transform the predicate $reachable(\mathcal{S}, \mathcal{S}', j)$ into a quantified Boolean formula F_j such that global state $\mathcal{S}'$ can be reached from global state $\mathcal{S}$ in, at most, 2^j steps if and only if the corresponding F_j is true. Clearly T accepts x if and only if the formula corresponding to $reachable(\mathcal{S}_0, \mathcal{S}_\Omega, cs^*)$ is true.

In order to derive formula F_j we need the following Boolean formulas whose formal definitions are left to the reader:

1. $gs(X)$ is true if and only if X encodes a global state.

2. $yield(X, Y)$ is true if and only if global state Y can be reached from global state X in, at most, one step.
3. $init(X)$ is true if and only if X encodes the initial global state.
4. $accept(X)$ is true if and only if X encodes the accepting global state.

Formula F_j is then constructed inductively as follows. For $j = 0$, the corresponding formula $F_0(X, Y)$ is expressed as

$$F_0(X, Y) = gs(X) \wedge gs(Y) \wedge yield(X, Y).$$

In the inductive step, we might define $F_{j+1}(X, Y)$ as

$$F_{j+1}(X, Y) = (\exists Z)(F_j(X, Z) \wedge (F_j(Z, Y))).$$

However, this approach already used in the pseudo-Pascal algorithm *reachable* does not suit our purpose since the length of the resulting formula F_{j+1} grows exponentially with j. We can resolve this problem by reformulating F_{j+1} as

$$F_{j+1}(X, Y) = \begin{aligned}&(\exists Z)(\forall X')(\forall Y') \\ &[((X' = X \wedge Y' = Z) \vee (X' = Z \wedge Y' = Y)) \to F_j(X', Y')].\end{aligned}$$

It is not difficult to convince ourselves that the two definitions of F_{j+1} are equivalent and that the length of F_{j+1} defined in this alternative way grows polynomially with j.

Finally, formula F_x is defined as

$$F_x = (\exists X)(\exists Y)[init(X) \wedge accept(Y) \wedge F_{cs^*}(X, Y)].$$

This concludes the proof.   □

In addition to QBF, the set of PSPACE-complete problems includes many interesting problems in widely different areas such as automata theory, computational linguistics and game theory. In the last area, a rich source of PSPACE-complete problems comes from the class of two-player games, that is, games which can be described by specifying the 'initial' and 'final' configurations and the rules according to which each of the two players can alternatively make a move.

Denote by WHITE and BLACK the two players, with $\mathcal{S}_0$ the initial configuration and assume that WHITE moves first. In such a case, asking whether WHITE will win in exactly n moves is equivalent to asking whether

a move of WHITE from $\mathcal{S}_0$ to $\mathcal{S}_1$ exists such that,
for all moves of BLACK from $\mathcal{S}_1$ to $\mathcal{S}_2$,
a move of WHITE from $\mathcal{S}_2$ to $\mathcal{S}_3$ exists such that,
:

a move of WHITE from $\mathcal{S}_{n-2}$ to $\mathcal{S}_{n-1}$ exists such that,

for all moves of BLACK from $\mathcal{S}_{n-1}$ to $\mathcal{S}_n$,
$\mathcal{S}_n$ is a winning configuration for WHITE.

The reader will notice the similarity of the above formulation of a two-player game with QBF and it is thus not surprising that many decisional problems consisting of deciding whether WHITE wins in n moves are PSPACE-complete (see Problem 8.20).

Problems

8.1. Prove an analog of Problem 3.13 for space complexity classes.

8.2. Show that P $\neq$ DSPACE[n]. [Hint: use padding arguments to prove that if DSPACE[n] $\subseteq$ P, then DSPACE[n^k] $\subseteq$ P for any $k \geq 1$.]

8.3. Prove Lemma 8.1.

8.4. Show that a weaker form of Theorem 8.2 holds when function s is not space-constructible. Prove that in this case it is possible to derive a deterministic machine T which *accepts* (instead of *decides*) the same language as NT.

8.5. Assume that a graph is encoded through its adjacency matrix with rows separated by suitable delimiters and consider the following algorithm for DEGREE ONE (see Example 8.3). Check whether a row of the matrix exists containing a single 1. Clearly this test can be done in constant space. Can we infer from this fact that DEGREE ONE is solvable in constant space?

8.6. For any integer i, let $b(i)$ denote the binary representation of i (without leading 0s). Show that the language $L = \{b(1)\#b(2)\#\ldots\#b(n) : n \geq 1\}$ belongs to DSPACE[$\log(\log(n))$].

8.7. Prove that k-CLIQUE (see Example 4.5) belongs to LOGSPACE.

8.8. Show that the product of two matrices can be computed in logarithmic space.

8.9. Show that GRAPH ACCESSIBILITY belongs to LOGSPACE. [Hint: use the result obtained in Problem 8.8.]

8.10. Show that sorting belongs to FLOGSPACE.

8.11. Prove that Theorems 8.2 and 8.3 still hold by replacing $s(n) \geq n$ with $s(n) \geq \log n$ and by replacing SPACE with WSPACE. [Hint: show that any global state of a Turing machine working in logarithmic space can be encoded as words of logarithmic length.]

8.12. In Garey and Johnson (1979) it is stated that all known polynomial reductions used to prove NP-completeness results require logarithmic space. Show that this is true at least for all reductions described in the examples of Section 5.2.

8.13. Prove that the functions *cell*, *tprev* and *initialvalue* introduced in the proof of Theorem 8.5 belong to FLOGSPACE.

8.14. Show how it is possible to derive from machine T_i which decides L in polynomial time a pendulum machine TP_i equivalent to T_i which also runs in polynomial time (see Theorem 8.5).

8.15. Prove that DIRECTED GRAPH ACCESSIBILITY is NLOGSPACE-complete. [Hint: given a nondeterministic machine NT operating in logarithmic space and an input x, compute the global state graph whose nodes correspond to global states of $NT(x)$ and whose edges correspond to possible transitions.]

8.16. Show that NLOGSPACE is strictly included in PSPACE.

8.17. Show that if P is equal to PSPACE, then any function computable in polynomial space belongs to FP. [Hint: use a bit-by-bit construction technique.]

8.18. Prove that PSPACE $\subseteq$ AP. [Hint: refer to the function *reachable* introduced in the proof of Theorem 8.2.]

8.19. Prove that the language A defined in Theorem 5.11 is PSPACE-complete.

8.20. The generalized hexagon game is played on a board whose topology is described by a graph $G = (N, E)$. The nodes correspond to squares of the board and the edges represent the existing links betweens squares.

The two players alternatively place white and black tokens on the squares of the board. The objective of WHITE, who starts with a token in a fixed node s, is to create a path consisting of contiguous white tokens between s and a second fixed node t of G. The objective of BLACK is to block WHITE from reaching his or her objective (clearly, BLACK is not allowed to place a token into node t).

GENERALIZED HEXAGON: given an initial configuration and an integer n, is WHITE able to win in exactly n moves? Show that this problem is PSPACE-complete. [Even and Tarjan (1976)]

Notes

In addition to Theorem 8.1, contained in the pioneering paper of Hopcroft and Ullman (1968), other important relationships between time and space have been found. Denote by T (respectively, NT) a deterministic (respectively, nondeterministic) Turing machine running in time $\mathbf{O}[f(n)]$ with $f(n) \geq n^2$ and by T' (respectively, NT') a space-bounded machine which simulates it. Then:

- If T is a k-tape machine, then T' is a k-tape machine requiring space bounded by $\mathbf{O}[f(n)/\log(n)]$ (see Hopcroft, Paul, and Valiant (1977)).
- If T is a one-tape deterministic machine, then T' is a one-tape deterministic machine running in time $\mathbf{O}[f(n)^{3/2}]$ but requiring space bounded by $\mathbf{O}[f(n)^{1/2}]$ (see Liskiewicz and Lorys (1989)).
- If NT is a one-tape machine, then NT' is a one-tape machine running in the same time but requiring space $\mathbf{O}[f(n)^{1/2}]$ (see Lorys and Liskiewicz (1988)).

Theorem 8.2 appeared in Savitch (1970) while Theorem 8.3 was proved in Immerman (1988). An interesting application of this latter theorem is the following. It was conjectured in Kuroda (1964) that the class of languages derivable from type 1 grammars[1] is closed with respect to the complement. In the same paper, it was shown that this class coincides with the linear nondeterministic space complexity class NSPACE[n]. According to Theorem 8.3, NSPACE[n] = coNSPACE[n] and the conjecture is proved in a positive sense.

In Jones (1975) it was proved that the problem DIRECTED GRAPH ACCESSIBILITY is NLOGSPACE-complete with respect to logspace-reducibility: this result implies that if this problem belongs to LOGSPACE, then NLOGSPACE = LOGSPACE. As usual, starting from this first result several other problems were shown to be NLOGSPACE-complete. Besides allowing a deeper insight into the structure of P, the classes LOGSPACE (also called L) and NLOGSPACE (also called NL) are closely related to the field of parallel algorithms (see Chapter 12).

Other interesting classes such as POLYLOGSPACE (the class of problems solvable in polylogarithmic space) or SC (the class of problems solvable in polylogarithmic space and polynomial time) was also studied and we refer the reader to Johnson (1990) for an exhaustive survey.

Theorem 8.5 was proved in Cook (1974) although the term P-completeness is due to Goldschlager (1977). Exhaustive lists of P-complete problems can be found in Miyano, Shiraishi, and Shoudai (1989) and in Greenlaw, Hoover, and Ruzzo (1991). P-complete problems were also defined in Cook (1985) by making use of another reducibility denoted as NC-reducibility. We shall deal with this in the last part of this book.

The equivalence between classes PSPACE and AP was established in Chandra, Kozen, and Stockmeyer (1981). In the same paper, a few other significant complexity classes were defined by referring to alternating Turing machines. The PSPACE-completeness of QBF was shown in Stockmeyer and Meyer (1973).

Finally, a few words on relativizations. An oracle separating PH from PSPACE was shown in Yao (1985) via a result due to Furst, Saxe, and Sipser (1984) while it is not clear whether any reasonable way to construct relativizations of classes with sublinear space bounds exists.

---

[1]Type i grammars ($0 \leq i \leq 3$) were studied in Chomsky (1959). Type 0 grammars are unrestricted models of computation while the remaining grammars correspond to models with additional restrictions.

Chapter 9

Probabilistic algorithms and complexity classes

Probability theory has several applications in the analysis of algorithms. For instance, instead of considering the 'worst case' complexity of an algorithm (which has been the approach followed so far) probabilistic techniques can be used to evaluate the 'average case' complexity of the algorithm itself with respect to a given probability distribution. In fact, many algorithms have been developed over the past years for NP-complete problems whose average case complexity has been found to be computationally tractable.

In this chapter, however, we will focus our attention on a different application of probability theory, namely, the development of probabilistic algorithms. Intuitively, such algorithms are deterministic ones that make random choices in the course of their execution. Even for a fixed input, different runs of a probabilistic algorithm algorithm may thus give different results and it is inevitable that the analysis of a probabilistic algorithm involves probabilistic statements. However, instead of fixing the probability distribution over the inputs (as in the case of average complexity evaluation), the probabilistic analysis will assume a probability distribution over the outputs of the algorithm.

To acquaint the reader with this kind of algorithm and its analysis, in Section 9.1 we will present a few examples of probabilistic algorithms in the field of number theory, polynomial identities, and graph theory and we will show how probabilistic algorithms with bounded error probability can be used to obtain a correct answer with probability as high as desired by simply iterating the algorithm a limited number of times.

The above considerations justify the definition of classes of problems which are solvable by probabilistic algorithms. Just as Turing machines have been introduced to formalize the concept of algorithm, in order to study probabilistic algorithms formally in Section 9.2 we define our probabilistic model of computation which is essentially a nondeterministic Turing machine with a different interpretation of its branchings in the computation tree. In Section 9.3 by making use of such machines we define several important complexity classes and we show some properties of such classes and relations between them.

9.1 Some probabilistic algorithms

In order to describe probabilistic algorithms we add to our pseudo-Pascal language the function **random**(n, m) whose value is uniformly distributed between n and m. Note that in practice such a random number generator does not exist. A possible solution could be to use a physical phenomenon considered random, even though there could be disagreement regarding the real nature of randomness. Furthermore, such physical sources of randomness generate correlated sequences of numbers, rather than the independent random numbers that one would ideally want. Another possibility is to use so-called 'cryptographically secure pseudorandom number generators', that is, generators designed so that distinguishing them from truly random ones is computationally equivalent to solving a presumably difficult problem. Due to lack of space, we will not cover these topics and we shall focus on more theoretical aspects of probabilistic algorithms.

9.1.1 Compositeness testing

Several polynomial-time probabilistic algorithms are available for testing compositeness (see Notes). All are based on a very simple technique, called the 'abundance of witnesses'. The input of a problem often satisfies a certain property whenever a certain object, called a witness, exists. While it may be difficult to find such a witness deterministically, it is sometimes possible to prove that enough witnesses exist to allow one of them to be efficiently searched for by simple random generation.

In the case of compositeness testing, the input is an integer n and the property is whether or not n is composite. From Lemma 7.5 we would be tempted to let the role of witness be played by any integer a with $1 \leq a < n$ for which Fermat's test is not verified, that is, $a^{n-1} \not\equiv 1 \pmod{n}$. Clearly, if a witness a exists then n is composite. But the question is: if n is composite, how many witnesses of its compositeness exist?

First, remember that, for any integer n, the set $\Phi(n)$ of invertible elements modulo n is defined as

$$\Phi(n) = \{a : 1 \leq a < n \wedge GCD(a, n) = 1\},$$

and that its cardinality is denoted as $\phi(n)$.

As we have already seen in Section 7.1.1, if $\Phi^c(n)$ is not empty then $a \in \Phi^c(n)$ implies $a^{n-1} \not\equiv 1 \pmod{n}$ (otherwise a would be invertible modulo n contradicting Lemma 7.4). In other words, each element of $\Phi^c(n)$ is a witness of n's compositeness.

One might then hope that, for any composite number n, either $\Phi^c(n)$ is sufficiently large or $\Phi^c(n)$ is small but $\Phi(n)$ is rich in witnesses. Unfortunately, some strange composite numbers n exist for which neither of the two above cases holds, that is, $\Phi^c(n)$ is relatively small and no element of $\Phi(n)$ is a witness. Such numbers are defined as follows. For any integer n, let K_n be the set of integers a such that $1 \leq a < n$ and $a^{n-1} \equiv 1 \pmod{n}$. A composite number n is said to be a *Carmichael number* if $K_n = \Phi(n)$.

Example 9.1 The first column of Table 9.1 shows the first five Carmichael numbers, while the last column shows the frequency of witnesses.

Table 9.1 The first five Carmichael
numbers

n	Factorization	$\phi(n)$	Percentage
561	$3 \cdot 11 \cdot 17$	320	0.43
1105	$5 \cdot 13 \cdot 17$	768	0.3
1729	$7 \cdot 13 \cdot 19$	1296	0.25
2465	$5 \cdot 17 \cdot 29$	1792	0.27
2821	$7 \cdot 13 \cdot 31$	2160	0.23

The next theorem shows that the above concept of compositeness witness is 'good' for numbers which are not Carmichael numbers. In order to prove this, we first need the following group-theoretic fact.

Lemma 9.1 For any finite group G and for any proper subgroup S of G, the cardinality of S is a divisor of the cardinality of G.

Proof. Let R_S be the binary relation in G such that $\langle x, y \rangle \in R_S$ if and only if $x^{-1}y \in S$ where x^{-1} denotes the inverse of x in G. It is easy to see that R_S is an equivalence relation. Let $[x]_S$ denote the *equivalence class* determined by x, that is, the set of elements of G such that $R_S(x, y) = \textbf{true}$. Clearly, if $R_S(x, y) = \textbf{false}$ then $[x]_S \cap [y]_S = \emptyset$. Thus G is found to be partitioned into n_S equivalence classes for a given integer n_S.

Given $x \in G$, let f_x be the function defined as $f_x(s) = xs$, for any $s \in S$. It can immediately be verified that f_x is a bijection from S onto $[x]_S$. Thus $|[x]_S| = |S|$ for any $x \in G$. This in turn implies that $|G| = n_S|S|$, that is, $|S|$ divides $|G|$. $\square$

Theorem 9.1 If a composite number n is not a Carmichael number, then the number of witnesses of n's compositeness is at least $\phi(n)/2$.

Proof. Note that, for any n, according to Lemma 7.4 $\Phi(n)$ is a group under multiplication modulo n. Note also that K_n is a proper subgroup of $\Phi(n)$ (see Problem 9.1). It thus follows from Lemma 9.1 that $|K_n|$ is a divisor of $\phi(n)$. Hence $|K_n| \leq \phi(n)/2$, that is, the number of witnesses of n's compositeness is at least $\phi(n)/2$. $\square$

It then remains to treat the case in which n is a Carmichael number. In order to do this, we first need to modify the definition of witness as follows. Given an integer n, an integer a is a *compositeness witness* for n if the following two conditions hold true:

1. $1 \leq a < n$.
2. Either $a^{n-1} \not\equiv 1 \pmod{n}$ or an integer i exists such that 2^i divides $n-1$ and $1 < GCD(a^{(n-1)/2^i} - 1, n) < n$.

Once again, it is clear that if a witness a exists then n is composite. Furthermore, since the new definition encompasses the previous one, Theorem 9.1 still applies. In order to prove a similar result for Carmichael numbers we first need the following lemmas.

Lemma 9.2 For any prime number p and for any integer $k \geq 1$, $\phi(p^k) = p^{k-1}(p-1)$.

Proof. First note that, for any integer a with $1 < a < p^k$, $GCD(a, p^k) = 1$ if and only if p does not divide a. Since the multiples of p which are less than p^k are $\{p, 2p, \ldots, p^k - p\}$, there are $p^{k-1} - 1$ of them. Including the number 1 yields $\phi(p^k) = p^k - p^{k-1} = p^{k-1}(p-1)$. $\square$

Lemma 9.3 If n is an odd[1] Carmichael number, then n is the product of r different odd prime factors $p_1, \ldots, p_r$ with $r \geq 3$.

Proof. For any odd integer number $n = p_1^{k_1} \ldots p_r^{k_r}$, let

$$\lambda(n) = LCM(\phi(p_1^{k_1}), \ldots, \phi(p_r^{k_r}))$$

where LCM denotes the least common multiple function. Then, for any $a \in \Phi(n)$, $a^{\lambda(n)} \equiv 1 \pmod{n}$. Indeed, if $r = 1$ then $a^{\lambda(n)} = a^{\phi(n)}$ and from a simple generalization of Lemma 7.3 it follows that $a^{\phi(n)} \equiv 1 \pmod{n}$ (see Problem 9.2). Otherwise, since $\lambda(n)$ is a multiple of every $\phi(p_i^{k_i})$ with $1 \leq i \leq r$, we have that $a^{\lambda(n)} \equiv 1 \pmod{p_i^{k_i}}$ which in turn implies that $a^{\lambda(n)} \equiv 1 \pmod{n}$.

Furthermore, as in the proof of Lemma 7.8, we can show that $\lambda(n)$ is the least exponent such that, for any $a \in \Phi(n)$, $a^{\lambda(n)} \equiv 1 \pmod{n}$. Hence, n is a Carmichael number if and only if $\lambda(n)$ is a factor of $n-1$. This in turn implies that $GCD(n, \lambda(n)) = 1$. Hence, n does not contain a repeated prime factor since such

---

[1]It can be shown that all Carmichael numbers are odd, but we do not need this result since even numbers are composite.

a prime would be a factor of both n and $\lambda(n)$. Moreover, n cannot be a product of two prime numbers. Indeed, let $n = pq$ with $p < q$ and p, q primes. Then $\lambda(n)$ is a factor of $n-1$, that is, of $pq-1$. Also, $\lambda(n) = LCM(\phi(p), \phi(q)) = LCM(p-1, q-1)$, therefore $\lambda(n)$ is a multiple of $q-1$ which should divide $pq-1$. But

$$\frac{pq-1}{q-1} = p + \frac{p-1}{q-1},$$

and since $(p-1)/(q-1)$ is not an integer this is not possible.

Thus n must be the product of three or more different prime factors.   □

Theorem 9.2 If n is an odd Carmichael number, then the number of witnesses of n's compositeness is at least three fourths of $\phi(n)$.

Proof. Let p_1, p_2 and p_3 be three different odd prime factors of n. From the proof of Lemma 9.3 it follows that, for any $i = 1, 2, 3$, $\phi(p_i) = p_i - 1$ divides $n - 1$.

Denote by e_i the largest j such that 2^j divides $p_i - 1$ and assume $e_1 = e_2 = e_3 = e$ (similar analysis of cases $e_1 = e_2 < e_3$ and $e_1 < e_2 \leq e_3$ is left to the reader). Since $p_i - 1 = 2^e m_i$ where m_i is an odd integer and since $p_i - 1$ divides $n - 1$, it follows that $n - 1 = 2^e 2^k m$ where m is an odd integer divisible by m_i and $k \geq 0$. Let $d = (n-1)/2^{k+1} = 2^e m/2$. Clearly $p_i - 1$ does not divide d: indeed, $d/(p_i - 1) = \frac{2^e m}{2} \frac{1}{2^e m_i} = m/2m_i$ which is not an integer. Furthermore $(p_i - 1)/2$ divides d: indeed, $\frac{d}{(p_i-1)/2} = \frac{2^e m}{2} \frac{2}{2^e m_i} = m/m_i$ which is an integer.

Let b_i be a 'primitive root' modulo p_i, that is, for any integer t, $b_i^t \equiv 1 \pmod{p_i}$ if and only if $p_i - 1$ divides t (the existence of this b_i follows from the proof of Lemma 7.8). Reasoning as in the proof of Lemma 7.3, it is easy to verify that the powers $b_i, b_i^2, \ldots, b_i^{p_i-1}$ are equivalent modulo p_i to the numbers $1, 2, \ldots, p_i - 1$ taken in a suitable order. Thus, for each $a \in \Phi(n)$, a corresponding r_i with $1 \leq r_i < p_i$ must exist such that $a \equiv b_i^{r_i} \pmod{p_i}$.

Note now that if r_i is even (respectively, odd) then p_i divides (respectively, does not divide) $a^d - 1$. Indeed, since $r_i = 2r_i'$, then $a^d \equiv b_i^{2r_i'd} \equiv 1 \pmod{p_i}$ because $p_i - 1$ divides $2d$ (we can treat similarly the case in which r_i is odd).

Thus, for any $a \in \Phi(n)$ such that the corresponding triple $\langle r_1, r_2, r_3 \rangle$ contains at least one even number and at least one odd number, we have that a is a witness, that is, $1 < GCD(a^d - 1, n) < n$. If, for instance, r_1 is even and r_2 is odd, then p_1 divides both $a^d - 1$ and n and p_2 does not divide $a^d - 1$, therefore $1 < GCD(a^d - 1, n) < n$. It can be shown that there are eight equally frequent possibilities for the parities of $r_1, r_2,$ and r_3 (see Problem 9.3). Thus, at least three fourths of the elements of $\Phi(n)$ are witnesses.   □

By combining Theorems 9.1 and 9.2 we have the following result.

Corollary 9.1 If n is an odd composite number, then it admits at least $(n-1)/2$ witnesses.

Let us then consider the following simple probabilistic algorithm:

```
begin {input: n > 2}
  if n is even then accept
  else
  begin
    a := random(1, n − 1);
    if a witnesses the compositeness of n then accept
    else reject;
  end;
end.
```

It is easy to see that it can be checked whether a is a witness in polynomial time (see Problem 9.4). Furthermore, from the above corollary it follows that the error probability of the algorithm is less than $1/2$, that is, if the algorithm accepts, then we are certain that n is composite, while if it rejects, then we can state that n is prime with probability at least $1/2$.

9.1.2 Testing polynomial identities

Another important use of randomization was discovered for testing polynomial identities (in the next section we will see how this technique can be applied to graph theory). In particular, let us consider the following problem.

ZERO POLYNOMIAL: given a multivariate polynomial $p(x_1, \ldots, x_n)$ of degree d (the degree of a multivariate polynomial is defined as the largest among the degrees of its variables), is p identically zero? Note that if p is given in standard simplified polynomial form, then it is easy to test whether p is identically zero: we simply determine whether all the coefficients of p are zero. However, if p is given as an arbitrary arithmetic expression, then no polynomial-time algorithm is known for solving the above problem.

The following result will allow us to derive a simple polynomial-time probabilistic algorithm which is still based on the 'abundance of witnesses' principle.

Theorem 9.3 Let $p(x_1, \ldots, x_n)$ be a multivariate polynomial of degree d. If p is not identically zero, then the number of n-tuples $\langle a_1, \ldots, a_n \rangle$ of integers between $-nd$ and nd such that $p(a_1, \ldots, a_n) = 0$ is, at most, $nd(2nd + 1)^{n-1}$.

Proof. The proof is by induction on n. The case $n = 1$ is obvious, since a polynomial of degree d can have, at most, d roots. Assume the asserted result to be true for any polynomial in $n − 1$ variables and let $p(x_1, \ldots, x_n)$ be a polynomial of degree d in n variables. Note that p can be written as a polynomial in x_1 whose coefficients are, in turn, polynomials in the remaining $n-1$ variables $x_2, \ldots, x_n$. In particular, consider the highest degree coefficient p' of x_1 which is not identically zero (such a coefficient must exist since p is not identically zero). For any $(n − 1)$-tuple $\langle a_2, \ldots, a_n \rangle$ of integers between $-nd$ and nd two cases can occur: either $p'(a_2, \ldots, a_n)$ is zero or it is not. In the first case, $p(x_1, a_2, \ldots, a_n)$ might be zero for all possible values of x_1 between $-nd$ and nd, while in the second case $p(x_1, a_2, \ldots, a_n)$ can be zero for, at most, d of such values (since $p(x_1, a_2, \ldots, a_n)$ is a non-zero polynomial of degree, at most, d). By the induction hypothesis, p' has, at most, $(n-1)d(2nd+1)^{n-2}$ roots between $-nd$ and nd. Thus, the number of zeros of p between $-nd$ and nd is, at most,

$$(2nd+1)(n-1)d(2nd+1)^{n-2} + d(2nd+1)^{n-1} = nd(2nd+1)^{n-1},$$

which is the required bound. □

Since the number of n-tuples of integers between $-nd$ and nd is equal to $(2nd+1)^n$, it follows from the above theorem that if the polynomial is not identically zero then if we randomly choose such a tuple the probability that the polynomial will take on the value zero is, at most,

$$\frac{nd(2nd+1)^{n-1}}{(2nd+1)^n} = \frac{1}{2 + 1/nd} < 1/2.$$

This guides us to the following probabilistic algorithm:

begin {input: $p(x_1, \ldots, x_n)$}
  d := degree of p;
  for $i = 1$ **to** n **do** a_i := **random**$(-nd, nd)$;
  if $p(a_1, \ldots, a_n) \neq 0$ **then** reject **else** accept;
end.

Note that it is trivial to compute the degree of a polynomial. Thus the previous algorithm is a polynomial-time one.

9.1.3 Testing for matchings in graphs

The last example of a probabilistic algorithm refers to a graph-theoretic problem.

PERFECT MATCHING: given a graph $G = (N, E)$, does G contain a *perfect matching*, that is, a subset $E' \subseteq E$ such that, for any node u, one and only one edge in E' exists with u as one of its endpoints? Although this problem admits polynomial-time deterministic algorithms, they are not as simple as the probabilistic algorithm we are going to present (see Notes).

The basic idea is to reduce PERFECT MATCHING to ZERO POLYNOMIAL. The following theorem gives a necessary and sufficient 'algebraic' condition for a graph to have a perfect matching.

Theorem 9.4 Let G be a graph with vertex set $\{1, \ldots, n\}$ and let A be a matrix of $|n|^2$ elements defined as follows:

$$a_{ij} = \begin{cases} x_{ij} & \text{if } i \text{ is adjacent to } j \text{ and } i < j, \\ -x_{ji} & \text{if } i \text{ is adjacent to } j \text{ and } i > j, \\ 0 & \text{otherwise.} \end{cases}$$

Then G has a perfect matching if and only if the determinant of A is not identically zero.

Proof. By definition, the determinant of A is equal to

$$\sum_{\pi} \sigma_{\pi} \prod_{i=1}^{n} a_{i\pi(i)}$$

where π denotes a permutation of $\{1, \ldots, n\}$ and σ_{π} is 1 (respectively, -1) if π is the product of an even (respectively, odd) number of transpositions.[2] Note that, for any permutation π, $\prod_{i=1}^{n} a_{i\pi(i)} \neq 0$ if and only if i is adjacent to $\pi(i)$ for $1 \le i \le n$, that is, any non-vanishing permutation π corresponds to a subgraph G_{π} of G consisting of the edges $\langle i, \pi(i) \rangle$ for $1 \le i \le n$.

By definition, each of such subgraphs consists of disjoint cycles that cover the entire set of nodes of G.

First, observe that all permutations π such that G_{π} contains at least one odd cycle do not contribute at all to the determinant of A. Indeed, such permutations can be grouped into pairs that cancel each other's contribution in the following way. We associate a permutation π with a permutation π' that is identical to π except that an odd cycle is reversed. Since $\prod_{i=1}^{n} a_{i\pi(i)} = -\prod_{i=1}^{n} a_{i\pi'(i)}$ and $\sigma_{\pi} = \sigma_{\pi'}$, the total contribution to the determinant for π and π' is zero.

As a consequence, we have to consider permutations whose corresponding subgraphs consists only of even cycles. With each of such permutations we can associate another permutation π^r in which all cycles are reversed (observe that $\sigma_{\pi} = \sigma_{\pi^r}$).

Let us then distinguish the following two cases (given a perfect matching E', $t_{E'}$ will denote the product of the xs corresponding to the edges of E'):

1. $\pi = \pi^r$. In this case, G_{π} consists of cycles of length 2 only and π corresponds to a perfect matching E' such that $\prod_{i=1}^{n} a_{i\pi(i)} = (t_{E'})^2$.

2. $\pi \neq \pi^r$. In this case both π and π^r correspond to the union of two perfect matchings E' and E'' obtained by alternatively selecting edges within the cycles so that

$$\prod_{i=1}^{n} a_{i\pi(i)} + \prod_{i=1}^{n} a_{i\pi^r(i)} = 2t_{E'}t_{E''}.$$

---

[2] A *transposition* is an exchange of two elements which transforms a permutation into a new one.

Figure 9.1 An example of graph G with two perfect matchings

In conclusion, the determinant of A is found to be equal to

$$(t_{E'_1} + t_{E'_2} + \ldots + t_{E'_h})^2$$

where E'_i denotes the ith perfect matching, and thus it is identically zero if and only if G has no perfect matching.   □

Example 9.2 Consider the graph shown in Figure 9.1.
The corresponding matrix A is the following:

$$\begin{pmatrix} 0 & x_{12} & 0 & x_{14} \\ -x_{12} & 0 & x_{23} & x_{24} \\ 0 & -x_{23} & 0 & x_{34} \\ -x_{14} & -x_{24} & -x_{34} & 0 \end{pmatrix}$$

whose determinant is given by $(x_{12}x_{34} + x_{14}x_{23})^2$. Note how the two terms correspond to the two perfect matchings contained in G.

In conclusion, the problem of deciding whether a graph G has a perfect matching has been reduced to whether a polynomial is identically zero. From the previous section, we know how to solve the latter problem probabilistically in polynomial time.

9.1.4   Iteration of probabilistic algorithms

How can we deal with the failure of probabilistic algorithms to deliver a correct answer? A simple solution consists of designing algorithms with a *bounded error probability*, that is, algorithms whose error probability is, at most, $1 - \epsilon$ for some constant $0 < \epsilon \leq 1$ independent of the input size. For instance, both the probabilistic algorithms for COMPOSITE NUMBER and for ZERO POLYNOMIAL have a bounded error probability of $1/2$.

For such algorithms, the error probability can be made arbitrarily small by simply iterating the algorithm on the same input a certain number of times with independent random choices. For instance, if we run the algorithm deciding whether a number is composite k times (assuming that at each iteration the probability of choosing a number a between 1 and $n-1$ remains uniform), then the probability of rejecting a composite number becomes less than $1/2^k$. If $k = 50$ and the algorithm accepts at each iteration, then it is more likely that n is composite than that a failure in our hardware has interfered with the computation!

Clearly, the greater the initial error probability, the greater the number of iterations, but this number will still be independent of the instance size.

Thus probabilistic algorithms with bounded error probability (that is, whose error probability can be made arbitrarily small) seem to be extremely useful in efficiently solving decision problems. There is little hope, however, that polynomial-time probabilistic algorithms with bounded error probability solving some NP-complete problem can be found since this would imply that any problem in NP would admit such an algorithm (see Problem 9.16). The latter event appears unlikely since a problem solvable with arbitrarily small error probability in polynomial time should be considered tractable rather than untractable (think of an error probability less than 2^{-100}).

In conclusion, two possible applications of probabilistic algorithms seem to be the most promising. On the one hand, one could look for probabilistic algorithms solving problems in P which are more efficient (or even simpler) than previously known deterministic algorithms (the algorithm solving the matching problem falls into this category). On the other, one could look for polynomial-time probabilistic algorithms for NP-intermediate problems for which no deterministic polynomial-time algorithm is known (the two algorithms solving the compositeness problem and the polynomial identity problem, respectively, fall into this second category).

9.1.5   Monte Carlo versus Las Vegas

All the above algorithms are called 'Monte Carlo' algorithms: such algorithms are efficient but they may give incorrect answers (even though the probability is small). For example, the algorithm testing whether a number is composite may sometimes declare a number to be prime even if it is composite.

In contrast, the 'Las Vegas' algorithms are not only efficient but are also reliable because instead of giving an incorrect answer, they give a 'don't know' one whenever they are uncertain. Thus a Las Vegas algorithm deciding a language L neither accepts a word which does not belong to L nor rejects one which belongs to L but, when applied to certain words, it may halt in a 'don't-know' state (the formal definition of such algorithms will be given in the next section).

Very few Las Vegas algorithms are known. One of them solves the primality testing problem. Due to lack of space we will not present it here in detail, but will outline the basic idea. As we have seen, the compositeness testing algorithm is based on the abundance of compositeness witnesses (if n is indeed composite). Assume that a type of primality witness is available which is easily checkable and abundant. Then we can provide the following Las Vegas algorithm for testing primality. Given n, randomly choose a candidate a as being a witness of n's primality and test whether a is indeed a witness. If the test succeeds then accept; otherwise randomly choose a candidate b as being a witness of n's compositeness and test whether b is indeed a witness. If the test succeeds then reject; otherwise halt in the 'don't-know' state. According to our assumptions, the algorithm never lies. Furthermore, since n is either prime or composite and because of the abundance of witnesses, the probability that the algorithm halts in the 'don't-know' state is very small. A witness of primality with the above properties has recently been found (see Notes).

9.2   Probabilistic Turing machines

In order to define our probabilistic model of computation in a simple way we will make the following assumptions.[3]

First we shall only consider nondeterministic Turing machines working in polynomial time and we will no longer specify the time bound. Then, for any nondeterministic Turing machine NT, we shall assume that

1. The degree of nondeterminism of NT is 2.
2. Every step of NT is nondeterministic (thus any global state has exactly two possible successors).
3. For any input x, any computation path of $NT(x)$ executes the same number of steps.

From the above hypothesis it follows that, for any input x, the computation tree $NT(x)$ is a perfect binary tree. For clarity, we will denote with a white circle the leaves corresponding to accepting global states and with a black circle those corresponding to rejecting global states (see Figure 9.2 where four computation paths accept and four reject).

Probabilistic Turing machines PT will then be defined as nondeterministic Turing machines with different acceptance criteria and, in a specific case, with a suitable final state, that is, the 'don't-know' state, added to the more familar accepting and rejecting ones. Before continuing, however, let us briefly consider the interpretation of the branchings in a computation tree. Such branchings no longer denote guessing steps but 'coin-flipping' steps: the next global state depends on the outcome of such a random choice. It should then be clear that while nondeterministic Turing machines accept if an accepting computation path exists, the acceptance

---

[3]It is easy to see that such assumptions are not restrictive (see Problem 9.6).

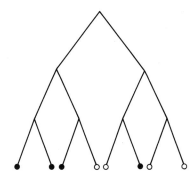

Figure 9.2 A computation perfect tree

of probabilistic Turing machines will depend on the *number* of accepting computation paths, that is, the probability of obtaining an accepting computation path (provided that we are using a fair coin).

Given a probabilistic Turing machine PT and an input x, let $\alpha(PT, x)$ (respectively, $\beta(PT, x)$) denote the ratio of the number of accepting (respectively, rejecting) computation paths of $PT(x)$ to the total number of computation paths of $PT(x)$. The *error probability* is then defined as $\beta(PT, x)$ (respectively, $\alpha(PT, x)$) if $PT(x)$ accepts (respectively, rejects) where the acceptance criterion will be specified in the following sections.

Finally, a probabilistic Turing machine PT *decides* a language L if, for any x, $PT(x)$ accepts if and only if $x \in L$.

9.2.1 PP-machines

A probabilistic Turing machine PT is said to be of *PP type* if

1. For any x, $PT(x)$ accepts if $\alpha(PT, x) > 1/2$.
2. For any x, $PT(x)$ rejects if $\beta(PT, x) \geq 1/2$ (see Figure 9.3).

Example 9.3 1/2-SATISFIABILITY: given a Boolean formula f, is f satisfied by more than half the possible assignments of values? It can immediately be verified that such a problem can be decided by a PP-machine (see Problem 9.8).

From a practical point of view, the PP-machines correspond to the least useful probabilistic algorithms. Indeed, the error probability of such a machine can be of the form $1/2 - 1/2^{p(n)}$ where p is the polynomial bounding the running time and

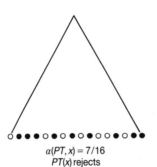 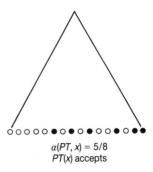

$\alpha(PT, x) = 7/16$ $\alpha(PT, x) = 5/8$
PT(x) rejects   *PT*(x) accepts

Figure 9.3 A PP-machine

n is the input length. This unfortunate case can occur when the number of 'right' computation paths is only one greater than the number of 'wrong' ones. Note that in order to make the error probability arbitrarily small, an exponential number of iterations is needed.

9.2.2   BPP-machines

A probabilistic Turing machine PT is said to be of *BPP type* if a constant $\epsilon \in (0, 1/2)$ exists such that

1. For any x, either $\alpha(PT, x) > 1/2 + \epsilon$ or $\beta(PT, x) > 1/2 + \epsilon$.
2. For any x, $PT(x)$ accepts if $\alpha(PT, x) > 1/2 + \epsilon$.
3. For any x, $PT(x)$ rejects if $\beta(PT, x) > 1/2 + \epsilon$ (see Figure 9.4).

Clearly, BPP-machines are not more powerful than PP-machines. Indeed, if a language L is decided by a BPP-machine PT, then the very same machine PT interpreted as a PP-machine decides L (see Problem 9.9).

In contrast to the PP-machines, the BPP-machines can be iterated a polynomial number of times in order to make the error probability arbitrarily small.

Theorem 9.5 Let PT be a BPP-machine and let q be a polynomial. Then a probabilistic Turing machine PT' exists such that, for any x with $|x| = n$, if $PT(x)$ accepts then $\alpha(PT', x) > 1 - 2^{-q(n)}$ and if $PT(x)$ rejects then $\beta(PT', x) > 1 - 2^{-q(n)}$.

Proof. From the hypothesis it follows that a constant $\epsilon \in (0, 1/2)$ exists such that, for any x, $PT(x)$ accepts if $\alpha(PT, x) > 1/2 + \epsilon$ and $PT(x)$ rejects if $\beta(PT, x) > 1/2 + \epsilon$.

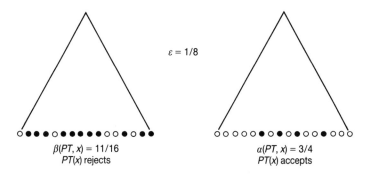

$\varepsilon = 1/8$

$\beta(PT, x) = 11/16$
$PT(x)$ rejects

$\alpha(PT, x) = 3/4$
$PT(x)$ accepts

Figure 9.4 A BPP-machine

Let t be an odd number to be specified later. The probabilistic Turing machine PT' is thus the following:

begin {input: x}
    $acc := 0$;
    for $i = 1$ **to** t **do**
    begin
       simulate $PT(x)$;
       if $PT(x)$ accepts **then** $acc := acc + 1$;
    end;
    if $acc > t/2$ **then** accept **else** reject;
end.

If $PT(x)$ accepts, the ratio of the number of computation paths of $PT'(x)$ such that the value of acc is exactly i, with $i \leq t/2$, to the total number of computation paths is given by[4]

$$\binom{t}{i} \left(\frac{1}{2} + \epsilon\right)^i \left(\frac{1}{2} - \epsilon\right)^{t-i}$$

$$\leq \binom{t}{i} \left(\frac{1}{2} + \epsilon\right)^i \left(\frac{1}{2} - \epsilon\right)^{t-i} \left(\frac{\frac{1}{2} + \epsilon}{\frac{1}{2} - \epsilon}\right)^{t/2-i}$$

$$= \binom{t}{i} \left(\frac{1}{4} - \epsilon^2\right)^{t/2}.$$

---

[4]Remember that the probability of an event of probability at least p occurring exactly i times in t independent trials is, at most, $\binom{t}{i} p^i (1-p)^{t-i}$.

The ratio of the number of rejecting computation paths of $PT'(x)$ to the total number of computation paths is then given by

$$
\sum_{i=0}^{(t-1)/2} \binom{t}{i} \left(\frac{1}{2}+\epsilon\right)^i \left(\frac{1}{2}-\epsilon\right)^{t-i} \leq \sum_{i=0}^{(t-1)/2} \binom{t}{i} \left(\frac{1}{4}-\epsilon^2\right)^{t/2}
$$

$$
= 2^{t-1} \left(\frac{1}{4}-\epsilon^2\right)^{t/2}
$$

$$
= \frac{1}{2}\left(1-4\epsilon^2\right)^{t/2}.
$$

In order to prove the theorem, it suffices to select t so that

$$
1-\frac{1}{2}\left(1-4\epsilon^2\right)^{t/2} \geq 1-2^{-q(n)},
$$

that is,

$$
2\left(\frac{1}{1-4\epsilon^2}\right)^{t/2} \geq 2^{q(n)}
$$

which is satisfied whenever

$$
t \geq \frac{2(q(n)-1)}{\log(1/(1-4\epsilon^2))}.
$$

We can deal similarly with the case in which $PT(x)$ rejects. Thus the 't-iterated' machine PT' is capable of simulating PT in polynomial time. $\qquad\square$

BPP-machines can thus have exponentially small error probabilities. However, no such machine is known to solve an interesting decision problem (not solvable by more constrained machines).

9.2.3 R-machines

Clearly, the compositeness test presented in the previous section is a BPP-machine whose error probability is, at most, $1/2$. However, that algorithm has another important characteristic: if the input is prime, then the error probability is zero. This leads us to the definition of a 'one-sided' version of BPP-machines.

A probabilistic Turing machine PT is said to be of *R type* if

1. For any x, either $\alpha(PT,x) > 1/2$ or $\beta(PT,x) = 1$.
2. For any x, $PT(x)$ accepts if $\alpha(PT,x) > 1/2$.
3. For any x, $PT(x)$ rejects if $\beta(PT,x) = 1$ (see Figure 9.5).

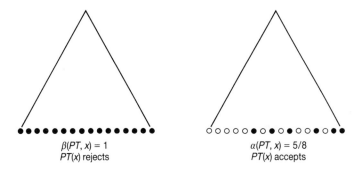

Figure 9.5 An R-machine

In the case of R-machines, the error probability is zero for rejected inputs. The most popular probabilistic algorithms developed so far, among which are those described in Section 9.1, are based on such machines.

The next theorem states that R-machines are not more powerful than BPP-machines.

Theorem 9.6 Given a language L decided by an R-machine PT, a BPP-machine PT' exists deciding L.

Proof. For any x, if $PT(x)$ accepts, then $\beta(PT, x) < 1/2$. Let PT' be the BPP-machine which simulates PT twice similarly as in the proof of Theorem 9.5 and such that any computation path accepts if *at least* one computation path of $PT(x)$ has accepted. It is easy to see that if $PT(x)$ accepts, then $\alpha(PT', x) > 1 - 1/4$ and that if $PT(x)$ rejects, then $\beta(PT', x) = 1$. Thus taking $\epsilon = 1/4$ yields $\alpha(PT', x) > 1/2 + \epsilon$ and $PT(x)$ accepts if and only if $PT'(x)$ accepts. $\qquad\square$

The previous theorem also shows the usefulness of R-machines: as for BPP-machines, the error probability can efficiently be made arbitrarily small.

9.2.4   ZPP-machines

All the previous kinds of probabilistic machines implement Monte Carlo algorithms, that is, they are allowed to lie. It is now time to present the last kind of machine, implementing Las Vegas algorithms.

A probabilistic Turing machine PT is said to be of *ZPP type* if

1. PT has an extra final state, called a *don't-know state*.

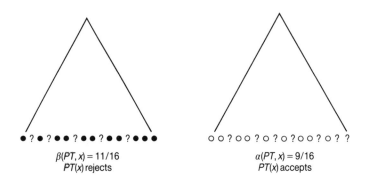

$\beta(PT, x) = 11/16$
$PT(x)$ rejects

$\alpha(PT, x) = 9/16$
$PT(x)$ accepts

Figure 9.6 A ZPP-machine

2. For any x, either $\alpha(PT, x) > 1/2 \wedge \beta(PT, x) = 0$ or $\beta(PT, x) > 1/2 \wedge \alpha(PT, x) = 0$.
3. For any x, $PT(x)$ accepts if $\alpha(PT, x) > 1/2$.
4. For any x, $PT(x)$ rejects if $\beta(PT, x) > 1/2$ (see Figure 9.6 where the don't-know states are represented as question marks).

Thus the computation of a ZPP-machine does not contain contradicting computation paths, that is, no computation path can lie. The primality problem is an example of a problem decided by a ZPP-machine (see Notes).

Once again, the next theorem shows that ZPP-machines are not more powerful than R-machines.

Theorem 9.7 Given a language L decided by a ZPP-machine PT, an R-machine PT' exists deciding L.

Proof. Machine PT' is obtained from PT simply by identifying the reject and the don't-know states. $\square$

9.3 Probabilistic complexity classes

Let us associate with each type of probabilistic Turing machine defined previously the corresponding class of languages decided by such a machine. For instance, the *class PP* is the set of languages L such that a PP-machine exists deciding L. We can similarly define the *classes BPP, R* and *ZPP*.

The next theorem shows some algebraic properties of probabilistic complexity classes.

Theorem 9.8 Classes PP, BPP, and ZPP are closed under complementation. Furthermore, classes BPP, R, and ZPP are closed under union and intersection.

Proof. In order to prove the first statement, it suffices to observe that, for any PP-machine (respectively, BPP- or ZPP-machine) which decides a language L, a probabilistic Turing machine of the same type deciding L^c can be obtained by simply reversing the roles of the accepting and rejecting states.

In order to prove that BPP is closed under union, let L_1 and L_2 be two languages in BPP. From Theorem 9.5 it follows that, for any constant $\epsilon \in (0, 1/2)$, two BPP-machines PT_1 and PT_2 exist such that, for $i = 1, 2$, $x \in L_i \rightarrow \alpha(PT_i, x) > 1 - \epsilon$ and $x \notin L_i \rightarrow \beta(PT_i, x) > 1 - \epsilon$.

Let PT be the BPP-machine which, on input x, successively simulates $PT_1(x)$ and $PT_2(x)$ and accepts if and only if at least one of the two simulations accepts. It is easy to verify that if $x \in L_1 \cup L_2$, then $\alpha(PT, x) > 1 - \epsilon$ and that if $x \notin L_1 \cup L_2$, then $\beta(PT, x) > (1 - \epsilon)^2$. By choosing ϵ so that $(1 - \epsilon)^2 > 1/2$, it follows that PT decides $L_1 \cup L_2$ (with constant $\epsilon_1 = (1 - \epsilon)^2 - 1/2$). Thus $L_1 \cup L_2 \in$ BPP. Similarly, we can prove that R and ZPP are closed under union.

Since BPP and ZPP are closed under both complementation and union, they are also closed under intersection. In order to prove that R is closed under intersection we can proceed as in the above paragraph and modify PT so that it accepts if and only if both the computations $PT_1(x)$ and $PT_2(x)$ accept (see Problem 9.11). □

9.3.1 Some inclusion relations

Figure 9.7 summarizes all known inclusions, which we will prove in this section, between the previously defined probabilistic complexity classes, P, NP, and PSPACE. The dotted rectangle in the figure contains those classes which may be considered as computationally tractable: indeed, for these classes the error probability can be made arbitrarily small by a polynomial number of iterations (note that in the case of P the initial error probability is zero).

Theorem 9.9 The following hold true:

1. P $\subseteq$ ZPP.
2. ZPP $=$ R $\cap$ *co*R.
3. R $\cup$ *co*R $\subseteq$ BPP.
4. R $\subseteq$ NP and *co*R $\subseteq$ *co*NP.
5. BPP $\subseteq$ PP.
6. NP $\cup$ *co*NP $\subseteq$ PP.
7. PP $\subseteq$ PSPACE.

Proof. The seven inclusion relationships are proved as follows:

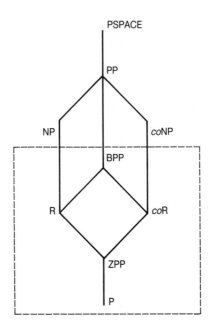

Figure 9.7 The probabilistic world

1. For any $L \in$ P, a deterministic Turing machine T exists deciding L in polynomial time. Let PT be the ZPP-machine such that, for any x, the computation paths of $PT(x)$ are all equal to the computation $T(x)$. Clearly, if $x \in L$, then $\alpha(PT, x) = 1$ and if $x \notin L$, then $\beta(PT, x) = 1$. Thus PT decides L.
2. From Theorems 9.7 and 9.8 it follows that ZPP $\subseteq$ R $\cap$ coR. Conversely, for any $L \in$ R $\cap$ coR, two R-machines PT_1 and PT_2 exist deciding L and L^c, respectively. Let us define the following ZPP-algorithm PT:

begin {input: x}
   simulate $PT_1(x)$;
   if $PT_1(x)$ accepts **then** accept;
   simulate $PT_2(x)$;
   if $PT_2(x)$ accepts **then** reject
   else don't-know;
end.

Since PT_1 and PT_2 are R-machines, it is easy to verify that if $x \in L$, then $\alpha(PT, x) > 1/2$ and $\beta(PT, x) = 0$ and, conversely, if $x \notin L$, then $\alpha(PT, x) = 0$ and $\beta(PT, x) > 1/2$. Thus PT decides L. Since L is an arbitrary language in R $\cap$ coR, it follows that R $\cap$ coR $\subseteq$ ZPP.

3. It follows from Theorems 9.6 and 9.8.

4. For any $L \in$ R, an R-machine PT exists deciding L. By modifying the acceptance criterion of PT so that it becomes a standard nondeterministic Turing machine NT, it follows that NT decides L. Indeed, if $x \in L$, then $\alpha(PT, x) > 1/2$ and an accepting computation path of $NT(x)$ exists. Conversely, if $x \notin L$, then $\alpha(PT, x) = 0$ and no computation path of $NT(x)$ accepts.

5. It follows from the comment made immediately after the definition of BPP-machines.

6. For any $L \in$ NP, a nondeterministic Turing machine NT exists deciding L in polynomial time. Let PT be the PP-machine which, on input x, nondeterministically chooses to perform one of the following two steps: (1) simulates $NT(x)$; (2) for any step of $NT(x)$, performs a branching and at the end accepts without further computation. If $x \in L$, then at least one computation path which has chosen step 1 accepts and, thus, $\alpha(PT, x) > 1/2$, otherwise $\alpha(PT, x) = 1/2$. It then follows that PT decides L.

7. For any $L \in$ PP, a PP-machine PT exists deciding L in time $p(n)$ where p is a polynomial. Thus L can be decided by the following deterministic algorithm:

begin {input: x}
   $n := |x|$;
   $acc := 0$;
   {acc is the number of accepting computation paths}
   for $i = 1$ **to** $2^{p(n)}$ **do**
      if the ith computation path of $PT(x)$ accepts **then** $acc := acc + 1$;
   {check whether $\alpha(PT, x) > 1/2$}
   if $acc > 2^{p(n)-1}$ **then** accept **else** reject;
end.

Since the simulation of a computation path of $PT(x)$ requires, at most, a polynomial number of tape cells and since the $(i+1)$th computation path can be simulated using the same tape cells as used during the ith computation, the previous algorithm requires a polynomial number of tape cells. Thus $L \in$ PSPACE.

□

None of the above inclusions is known to be strict (even though all of them are conjectured to be so).

9.3.2 PP-complete languages

Once again, we are faced by 'difficult-to-prove' conjectures and searching for complete problems appears to be the best way to find candidates for separating the classes at hand. Since it can immediately be verified that all probabilistic complexity classes are closed with respect to polynomial-time reducibility (see Problem 9.16), we will make use of this reducibility.

Unfortunately, it is not known whether complete languages exist for the classes BPP, R, and ZPP and, indeed, there is some evidence that they do not (see Notes). In this section, instead, we prove that PP-complete languages do exist.

Example 9.4 MAXIMUM SATISFIABILITY: given a Boolean formula f and an integer i, is f satisfied by more than i assignments of values?

Since PP is closed with respect to the polynomial-time reducibility and since 1/2-SATISFIABILITY belongs to PP, the next lemma shows that MAXIMUM SATISFIABILITY also belongs to PP.

Lemma 9.4 MAXIMUM SATISFIABILITY $\leq$ 1/2-SATISFIABILITY.

Proof. Let $\langle f, i \rangle$ be an instance of MAXIMUM SATISFIABILITY where f is a Boolean formula on variables $x_1, \ldots, x_n$ and i is an integer smaller than 2^n. Let $i = 2^{n-r_1} + 2^{n-r_2} + \ldots + 2^{n-r_k}$ with $1 \leq r_1 < r_2 < \ldots < r_k \leq n$. We then define

$$
\begin{aligned}
g_i = \ & (x_1 \wedge \ldots \wedge x_{r_1}) \\
& \vee (\neg x_1 \wedge \ldots \wedge \neg x_{r_1} \wedge x_{r_1+1} \wedge \ldots \wedge x_{r_2}) \\
& \vee (\neg x_1 \wedge \ldots \wedge \neg x_{r_2} \wedge x_{r_2+1} \wedge \ldots \wedge x_{r_3}) \\
& \ldots \\
& \ldots \\
& \vee (\neg x_1 \wedge \ldots \wedge \neg x_{r_{k-1}} \wedge x_{r_{k-1}+1} \wedge \ldots \wedge x_{r_k}).
\end{aligned}
$$

Clearly the hth clause of g_i, with $1 \leq h \leq k$, is satisfied by precisely 2^{n-r_h} assignments of values. Furthermore, the negated variables ensure that all assignments of values satisfying one clause cannot satisfy any of the other clauses. Thus the total number of assignments of values which satisfy g_i is precisely $2^{n-r_1} + 2^{n-r_2} + \ldots + 2^{n-r_k} = i$ while the total number of assignments of values which satisfy $\neg g_i$ is precisely $2^n - i$.

Let

$$ g = (y \wedge f) \vee (\neg y \wedge \neg g_i) $$

where y is a new variable not included in $\{x_1, \ldots, x_n\}$. It thus follows that f is satisfied by at least i assignments of values if and only if g is satisfied by more than half of the possible assignments of values. It is also easy to see that g can be derived in polynomial time. Thus MAXIMUM SATISFIABILITY is polynomial-time reducible to 1/2-SATISFIABILITY. $\square$

Theorem 9.10 MAXIMUM SATISFIABILITY is PP-complete.

Proof. Because of the previous lemma, it suffices to show that, for any $L \in$ PP, $L \le$ MAXIMUM SATISFIABILITY. Let PT be a PP-machine deciding L. For any x, f_x denotes the Boolean formula 'encoding' the computation $PT(x)$ (see Theorem 5.2). It is easy to verify that a one-to-one correspondence exists between accepting computation paths of $PT(x)$ and assignment of values satisfying f_x. Thus $PT(x)$ accepts if and only if f_x is satisfied by more than $2^{p(|x|)}/2$ assignments of values where p is the polynomial bounding the running time of PT.

Finally, the reduction f is defined as $h(x) = \langle f_x, 2^{p(|x|)-1} \rangle$, for any x. Clearly h is computable in polynomial time and $x \in L$ if and only if $h(x) \in$ MAXIMUM SATISFIABILITY.

Thus $L \le$ MAXIMUM SATISFIABILITY. Since L was an arbitrary language in PP, MAXIMUM SATISFIABILITY is PP-complete. $\square$

The following corollary is an immediate consequence of Lemma 9.4 and of the above theorem.

Corollary 9.2 1/2-SATISFIABILITY is PP-complete.

Problems

9.1. For any integer n, let K_n be the set of integers a such that $1 \le a < n$ and $a^{n-1} \equiv 1$ (mod n). Show that K_n is a subgroup of $\Phi(n)$.

9.2. Prove that, for any integer n and for any $a \in \Phi(n)$, $a^{\phi(n)} \equiv 1 \pmod{n}$.

9.3. Refer to the proof of Theorem 9.2. Show that there are eight equally frequent possibilities for the parities of r_1, r_2, and r_3. [Hint: make use of the Chinese remainder theorem to show that the correspondence between elements of $\Phi(n)$ and triples $\langle r_1, r_2, r_3 \rangle$ satisfies the following two conditions: it is surjective and the cardinality of the inverse image of a triple is the same for all triples.]

9.4. Provide a polynomial-time algorithm deciding whether, given an integer n and an integer $a \in \{1, 2, \ldots, n-1\}$, a is a witness of n's compositeness.

9.5. MATRIX PRODUCT: given three $n \times n$ matrices A, B and C, is $AB = C$? Clearly such a problem belongs to P: however, no deterministic algorithm whose running time is $\mathbf{O}[n^2]$ is known (the best-known algorithm runs in time $\mathbf{O}[n^{2,5}]$). Consider instead the following probabilistic algorithm:

```
begin {input: A, B and C}
   for i = 1 to n do
   begin
      {generate an array of n elements in {-1,1}}
      x[i] := random(0,1);
      if x[i] = 0 then x[i] := -1;
```

end;
    if $A(Bx) \neq Cx$ **then** reject **else** accept;
end.

Prove that the error probability of the above algorithm is, at most, $1/2$ and that the running time is $\mathbf{O}[n^2]$. [Hint: show that if $AB \neq C$, then, for any x such that $A(Bx) = Cx$, an x' exists so that $A(Bx') \neq Cx'$.]

9.6. Show that the assumptions on nondeterministic Turing machines presented at the beginning of Section 9.2 are not restrictive, that is, the class of languages decided by such machines is equal to NP.

9.7. Prove that the constant $1/2$ in the definition of PP-machines can be replaced by any constant greater than 0 without changing the power of such machines. [Simon (1975)]

9.8. Describe a PP-machine which decides $1/2$-SATISFIABILITY.

9.9. Show that if a language L is decided by a BPP-machine PT, then L is also decided by PT interpreted as a PP-machine.

9.10. Prove that if $L \in \text{NSPACE}[s(n)]$, then L can be decided by an R-machine using space $\mathbf{O}[s(n)]$. [Gill (1977)]

9.11. Prove that R is closed under intersection.

9.12. Show that if L_1 and L_2 belong to PP, then $L_1 \triangle L_2$ also belongs to PP. [Hint: simulates the two machines one after the other and accepts if and only if exactly one of the two simulations accepts.]

9.13. Prove that if $\text{NP} \subseteq \text{BPP}$, then $\text{NP} = \text{R}$. [Ko (1982)]

9.14. Prove that $\text{BH}_2 \subseteq \text{PP}$. [Hint: use the result of the previous problem.] Generalize this fact to the entire Boolean hierarchy.

9.15. Give an analog of Theorem 5.1 for classes PP and BPP.

9.16. Show that PP, BPP, R, and ZPP are closed with respect to the polynomial-time reducibility. Note that if L is an NP-complete language admitting a probabilistic algorithm with bounded error probability, then any language in NP admits such an algorithm.

9.17. Let BPP(NP) denote the class of languages L for which a language $L_{\text{check}} \in \text{NP}$ and a polynomial p exist such that

    1. If $x \in L$, then $|\{y : |y| \leq p(|x|) \wedge \langle x, y \rangle \in L_{\text{check}}\}| \geq 2/3$.

    2. If $x \notin L$, then $|\{y : |y| \leq p(|x|) \wedge \langle x, y \rangle \in L_{\text{check}}\}| \leq 1/3$.

Prove that if $co\text{NP} \subseteq \text{BPP(NP)}$, then $co\text{BPP(NP)} \subseteq \text{BPP(NP)}$. [Hint: first prove an analog of Theorem 9.5 for BPP(NP) and successively define a suitable check language for any member of $co\text{BPP(NP)}$.]

9.18. Show that if *co*NP is contained in BPP(NP), then PH $\subseteq$ BPP(NP). [Hint: by induction on k, prove $\Sigma_k^p \subseteq$ BPP(NP).] Since BPP(NP) $\subseteq \Pi_2^p$, this result implies that if *co*NP is contained in BPP(NP), then the polynomial hierarchy collapses to the second level.

9.19. Prove that MAXIMUM SATISFIABILITY is self-reducible (see Problem 5.15).

Notes

The compositeness testing algorithm described in Section 9.1 was derived in Rabin (1976); it is perhaps the most famous probabilistic algorithm along with that described in Solovay and Strassen (1977) which solved the same problem. Although the technical details of the two approaches differ, they both rely on the concept of compositeness witness and on the abundance of such witnesses. It is also worth noting that Rabin's algorithm has a running time of $\mathbf{O}[\log^3 n]$ while, even assuming the extended Riemann hypothesis, the best running time currently known for a deterministic primality testing algorithm is $\mathbf{O}[\log^5 n]$. Our presentation of the algorithm differs slightly from the original one and is inspired partly by that of Kozen (1992) and partly by that of Rabin (1980). In particular, Theorem 9.1 is taken from Kozen's book while Theorem 9.2 is due to Rabin. The Carmichael numbers were introduced in Carmichael (1912) in order to find a necessary and sufficient condition for a composite number n satisfying $a^{n-1} \equiv 1 \pmod{n}$ when a is any number relatively prime to n. In that paper, Lemma 9.3 was proved.

Schwartz (1980) presented probabilistic algorithms for testing asserted multivariate polynomial identities, as well as other asserted or conjectured relationships between sets of polynomials. Theorem 9.3 and the related probabilistic algorithm for ZERO POLYNOMIAL are taken from that paper. Moreover, in dealing with polynomials with integer coefficients the author adopted the technique of carrying out all calculations in modular arithmetic in order to avoid having to deal with very large integers.

Theorem 9.4 is attributed to Tutte (1952) while the corresponding probabilistic algorithm for PERFECT MATCHING was suggested in Lovasz (1979). It is fair to observe that this algorithm does not give us a method of actually finding a perfect matching when one exists; in fact, this can be done probabilistically but it is a little more complicated (see Chapter 12). The deterministic algorithm of Edmonds (1965) has a running time of $\mathbf{O}[n^3]$, however, it is a very complicated algorithm. For many programmers its implementation would take exponential time!

The survey by Karp (1990) presents a wide variety of examples intended to illustrate the range of applications of probabilistic algorithms and the general principles and approaches that are of the greatest use in their construction. The examples are drawn from many areas, including number theory, algebra, graph theory, pattern matching, selection, sorting, searching, computational geometry, combinatorial enumeration, and parallel and distributed computation.

The distinction between Monte Carlo and Las Vegas algorithms was introduced by Babai (1979) in conjunction with his research into probabilistic algorithms for the graph isomorphism problem. In particular, a Las Vegas algorithm was described solving a variant of that problem. This result, however, was shortly afterwards updated by the deterministic polynomial-time algorithm of Furst, Hopcroft, and Luks (1980). The Las Vegas algorithm for testing primality appeared in Adleman and Huang (1988).

Formal models for probabilistic algorithms were first studied in de Leeuw *et al.* (1956), Santos (1969), and Gill (1977). In this latter paper the problem of whether probabilistic machines can be proven to require less time or space than deterministic ones was analysed. In order to provide an answer to this question, probabilistic Turing machines were introduced, classes PP, BPP, R (called VPP), and ZPP were defined, and many properties of these classes were demonstrated (among them Theorems 9.8 and 9.9). Although the model presented in this text slightly differs from that of Gill, it can be easily shown that the two models are equivalent.

It is interesting to note that in his paper, Gill left as an open question whether PP is closed under intersection; this problem remained open for almost twenty years until Beigel, Reingold, and Spielman (1990) provided a positive answer.

The proof of Theorem 9.5 follows that of Schöning (1985) which also contains several other interesting results on probabilistic classes and, in general, on structural complexity theory.

Theorem 9.10 appeared in Simon (1975) while Lemma 9.4 is due to Gill (1977). In Sipser (1982) it is shown that a relativization of class R exists which does not admit complete languages; such a result can also be extended to classes BPP and ZPP.

The most important question about probabilistic classes is their relationships with classes P and NP. From a relativized point of view, in Hunt (1978) and in Balcazar and Russo (1988), an oracle was derived such that P is different from ZPP and ZPP is different from NP, respectively. Moreover, in Stockmeyer (1985) the existence of an oracle such that BPP is not contained in NP was proved, thus suggesting that the two classes are incomparable. One of the most important results obtained in this area is certainly that contained in Toda (1989) which states that if PP is included in the polynomial hierarchy then this hierarchy collapses.

Finally, an alternative application of probabilistic algorithms consists of deriving algorithms that always find correct answers, but whose running time obeys some probability distribution. For example, in Rabin (1976) a probabilistic algorithm was proposed finding the nearest pair in a collection of points in a unit square. The expected running time is $\mathbf{O}[n]$ for every instance, as opposed to the $\mathbf{O}[n \log n]$ worst-case running time of the best deterministic algorithm.

Chapter 10

Interactive proof systems

The concept of a proof is an intuitive one. However, theorem-proving procedures may differ in the underlying definition of a proof. The most natural one consists of writing down the proof in a book, but a more general way of communicating a proof is based on the concept of interaction, and consists of explaining the proof to some recipients, as in the case of a teacher–student environment. In this way, the prover (that is, the teacher) can take full advantage of the possibility of interacting with the verifiers (the students). These latter may ask questions at crucial points of the explanation and receive answers. This make the prover's life much easier. Indeed, writing down a proof that can be understood and checked by every verifier without interaction is a much harder task because, in some sense, the prover has to answer all possible questions in advance.

In this chapter, we consider proving procedures, called interactive proof systems, in which a prover wants to convince a verifier of the correctness of a proof. Although these systems have been fruitfully applied in other areas such as cryptology (see Notes), we shall limit ourselves to discussing a few fundamental results related to complexity theory.

In typical complexity-theoretic fashion we shall view an interactive proof system simply as a new method for recognizing languages. To that end, the characteristics of the new model will be gradually introduced in Section 10.1 and a new complexity class based on interactive proof systems and denoted as IP will be introduced. Next, it is shown in Section 10.2 that, surprisingly, IP coincides with PSPACE. On the one hand, this result seems to weaken the importance of IP; on the other, the equivalence proof is inherently different from those encountered so far since it *does not relativize*. In fact, we shall succeed in constructing an oracle A such that $IP^A \neq PSPACE^A$, thus obtaining (for the first time!) a result which 'is contrary' to the unrelativized one.

In the last section of the chapter, we shall consider theorem-proving procedures from a different point of view. Having assumed that the proof is available somewhere, how much of it does the verifier have to know in order to be convinced that

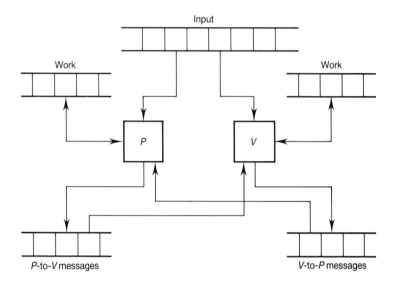

Figure 10.1 A deterministic interactive proof system

the proof is correct? Clearly, if the verifier is deterministic, the proof has to be read in its entirety. However, if it is probabilistic, then a sublinear number of random bits and message bits is sufficient to characterize interesting complexity classes. Furthermore, this kind of proof-checking procedure has surprising applications in the field of approximation algorithms.

10.1   Interactive proof systems

The interactive system we shall consider is a very simple one which consists of two Turing machines denoted as P (the *prover*) and V (the *verifier*). The two machines, as represented in Figure 10.1, can exchange messages although suitable limitations will be placed on both the number and the length of the messages.

The exchange of messages takes place in the two communication tapes labeled P-to-V tape and V-to-P tape. The first tape is a write-only tape for P and a read-only one for V while the second is a write-only tape for V and a read-only one for P. Both P and V have their own working tape and both are able to read the same input from a read-only tape.

Let us make the following assumptions on the power of P and V and on the allowed interactions:

1. The verifier V is a polynomial-time deterministic Turing machine.
2. The prover P is a computationally unlimited (in both time and space) deterministic Turing machine.
3. P and V take turns in being active and V starts the computation. When a machine is active, it can perform internal computation, read and write on the correct tapes and send a message to the other machine by writing on the appropriate communication tape.
4. Both the length and the number of messages exchanged between P and V are bounded by suitable polynomials in the input length.
5. V can, during its turn, terminate the interactive computation by entering either the accepting or the rejecting state.

The acceptance criterion is straightforward. (P, V) accepts input x if V halts in an accepting state while it rejects x if V halts in a rejecting state.

A language L *admits a deterministic interactive proof* if a verifier V exists such that

1. A prover P^* can be derived such that (P^*, V) accepts all $x \in L$.
2. For all provers P, (P, V) rejects all $x \notin L$.

Condition 1 says that if x belongs to L, then a way exists to easily prove this fact to V; in other words, it is possible to prove a true theorem with an easily verifiable proof. Condition 2 states that if x does not belong to L, then no strategy for convincing V of the contrary exists; in other words, it is not possible to prove a false theorem. This latter condition is motivated by the fact that, in general, we do not want V to trust the prover with which it is interacting. If $x \notin L$, then even if a prover is providing incorrect answers, V must be able to detect it. In the opposite case, trusted provers would behave exactly as unbounded oracles.

Denote by DIP the class of languages which admit a deterministic interactive proof. The following lemma shows that this first class is of little interest.

Lemma 10.1 DIP $=$ NP.

Proof. Let us first show that NP $\subseteq$ DIP. We have already seen in Theorem 5.1 that NP can be viewed as the set of languages which have short polynomial-time verifiable membership proofs (for instance, a proof that a formula is satisfiable simply consists of a satisfying assignment of values). Thus, if $x \in L$, then the prover which is computationally unlimited computes a membership proof y and sends it to the verifier. The verifier, whose running time is bounded by a polynomial in the length of x, checks that y is a membership proof. Conversely, if $x \notin L$, then it is clear that no prover can persuade V that x is in L.

Let us now show that DIP $\subseteq$ NP. Let $L \in$ DIP and let V be a verifier for L. Given an input x, the number of messages exchanged between P and V is polynomial with respect to the input length. Thus a nondeterministic polynomial-time machine NT can be derived which alternatively simulates V and guesses all

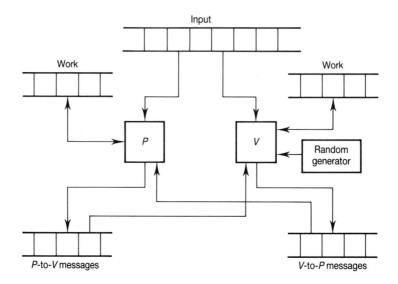

Figure 10.2 An interactive proof system

possible messages from P. Clearly, if $x \in L$, then at least the computation path corresponding to prover P^* accepts; otherwise all computation paths reject, since no prover can induce V to accept x.   □

We can extend the above model of 'efficient interactive proof systems' by allowing V to be a probabilistic Turing machine (see Figure 10.2) and by requiring that, for all $x \in L$, the prover can convince the verifier with high probability, and, for all $x \notin L$, no prover can convince the verifier that x is in L with better than negligible probability.

Formally, the acceptance criterion is similar to that of the BPP-machines. Indeed, the computation paths of (P, V) with input x can be arranged in a binary tree similar to that of a probabilistic Turing machine's computation. The leaves of such a tree correspond to the final states reached by the verifier. Let $\alpha(P, V, x)$ (respectively, $\beta(P, V, x)$) denote the ratio of the number of accepting (respectively, rejecting) computation paths of the tree to the total number of computation paths.

For all x, we then say that (P, V) *accepts* (respectively, *rejects*) x if $\alpha(P, V, x) > 2/3$ (respectively, $\beta(P, V, x) > 2/3$). It is easy to verify (see Problem 10.1) that the constant $2/3$ can be replaced by any other constant greater than $1/2$.

The resulting model of computation is called an *interactive proof system* and, as in the case of DIP languages, we say that a language L *admits an interactive proof* if a verifier V exists such that the above conditions 1 and 2 hold.

An implicit assumption of interactive proof systems is that the verifier's random generator is *private*: the prover only receives information computed by the verifier based on the previous history and the coin tosses. In this way, we ensure that the verifier cannot be fooled by the prover even when the latter knows V's algorithm.

10.1.1   The class IP

Denote by IP the class of languages which admit an interactive proof. We know from Lemma 10.1 that IP includes NP.

The following example suggests that the inclusion is strict. The algorithms for P and V will be described, as usual, in pseudo-Pascal and two new constructs denoted as **transmit** and **receive** will be introduced to denote the transmission and the reception of a message, respectively.

Example 10.1 GRAPH ISOMORPHISM: given two graphs $G_1 = (N_1, E_1)$ and $G_2 = (N_2, E_2)$, are they isomorphic, that is, does a bijection $f : N_1 \rightarrow N_2$ exist such that, for all $x, y \in N_1$, $\langle x, y \rangle \in E_1$ if and only if $\langle f(x), f(y) \rangle \in E_2$?

We now show that the complement of this problem admits an interactive proof: note that no polynomial-time nondeterministic algorithm is known for this problem. The verifier's algorithm is the following:

```
begin {input: G₁, G₂}
    succ := true;
    repeat twice
    begin
        i := random(1, 2);
        randomly create a graph H isomorphic to Gᵢ;
        transmit H;
        receive j;
        if i ≠ j then succ := false;
    end;
    if succ then accept else reject;
end.
```

Note that the above algorithm is polynomial: indeed, the random generation of a graph isomorphic to G_i can be realized by randomly selecting a permutation of the nodes of G_i. Note also that, according to the algorithm, the verifier and the prover will interact twice.

First, we show that a prover P^* exists such that, for any pair $\langle G_1, G_2 \rangle$ of nonisomorphic graphs, the interactive proof system (P^*, V) accepts $\langle G_1, G_2 \rangle$. P^*'s algorithm is the following:

```
begin {input: G₁,G₂ }
    receive H;
    if H is isomorphic to G₁ then transmit 1 else transmit 2;
end.
```

Clearly, if G_1 and G_2 are not isomorphic, then the verifier accepts $\langle G_1, G_2 \rangle$ with probability 1 since P^* always returns the correct value.

Conversely, given an input $\langle G_1, G_2 \rangle$ with G_1 isomorphic to G_2, a prover P which has no way of knowing whether the graph received has been generated from G_1 or G_2 can only answer randomly. In such a case, the probability that P correctly answers a message j is $1/2$ and thus the combined probability that P correctly answers two consecutive messages inducing V to accept the input is, at most, $1/4$.

10.2   The power of IP

We have already noticed that IP is likely to strictly include NP. Indeed, we have seen in Example 10.1 that GRAPH ISOMORPHISM^c belongs to IP, while the same problem does not seem to belong to NP (even though it clearly belongs to coNP). For some years the relations existing between IP and other complexity classes such as coNP were not clear. Indeed, researchers generally believed IP to be slightly larger than NP and it was conjectured that coNP-complete problems did not belong to IP.

Furthermore, the following result which refers to the relativized version of IP suggests that proving the contrary would be a hard task (in the relativized version of IP, only the verifiers need to make use of oracles since the computational power of the prover is assumed to be unlimited).

Theorem 10.1 An oracle A exists such that coNP^A − IP^A is not empty.

Proof. As in the case of Theorem 5.12, the separator language will capture a suitable property of the oracle, that is, the fullness property when restricted to words of a given length. In particular, for any language X, let us define a new language L_X^* as

$$L_X^* = \{0^n : X_n = \Sigma_n^*\}.$$

It is easy to verify that $L_X^* \in co$NP^X for any oracle X. In fact, in order to check whether 0^n does not belong to L_X^*, it is sufficient to guess in a nondeterministic way all words of length n and to verify whether the oracle X does not include at least one of them. We now derive an oracle A such that no interactive proof using that oracle exists for L_A^*.

The proof proceeds similarly to that of Theorem 5.12. In particular, let $V_1, V_2, \ldots$ be an enumeration of all possible polynomial-time oracle verifiers such that, for any i (and for any oracle), the running time of V_i is bounded by the polynomial $p_i(n) = n^i$.

The diagonalization process used to derive the oracle A associates with each polynomial-time oracle verifier V in the enumeration an integer n such that either

$A_n = \Sigma_n^*$ and no prover can convince V to accept 0^n or $A_n \neq \Sigma_n^*$ and a prover exists that causes V to accept 0^n.

Formally, the language A is constructed in stages. Let $A(i)$ denote the finite set of words added to A after the ith stage and let n_i be an upper bound on the length of the words of $A(i)$. Moreover, let $Q(i)$ be the set of queries to the oracle which have been posed in any of the first i stages. At the beginning we let $A(0)$ be $\emptyset$, n_0 be 0, and $Q(0)$ be $\emptyset$. Successively, we let

$$n_i = \min\{m : m > n_{i-1}^{i-1} \wedge 2^m > 3m^i\}$$

and define the set $A(i)$ distinguishing the following two cases:

1. No prover P exists such that $(P, V_i^{A(i-1) \cup (\Sigma^* - Q(i-1))})$ accepts 0^{n_i}. In this case, we denote by $R(i)$ the set of words distinct from those in $Q(i-1)$ which have been queried by at least one (P, V_i) with input 0^{n_i} and we let $A(i) = A(i-1) \cup \Sigma_{n_i}^* \cup R(i)$.

2. A prover P^* exists such that $(P^*, V_i^{A(i-1) \cup (\Sigma^* - Q(i-1))})$ accepts 0^{n_i}. In this case, we denote by $S(i)$ the set of words distinct from those in $Q(i-1)$ which have been queried by (P^*, V_i) with input 0^{n_i} and we let $A(i) = A(i-1) \cup (\Sigma_{n_i}^* - \{y_i\}) \cup S(i)$ where y_i denotes any word of length n_i that has been queried in, at most, $p_i(n_i)/2^{n_i}$ of all computation paths. Clearly, at least one such word y_i must exist since, in the opposite case, the total number of queries of length n_i in the computation tree would be greater than $p_i(n_i)$ times the number of computation paths.

We may then define the oracle language A as $A = \bigcup_{i>0} A(i)$.

Note that in case 1, for any i, the behavior of V_i on input 0^{n_i} with oracle $A(i-1) \cup (\Sigma^* - Q(i-1))$ is precisely the same as its behavior on the same input with oracle A.

This is no longer true in case 2, since A does not include the word y_i which might have been essential for accepting 0^{n_i}. In such a case, we know that y_i has been queried in, at most, $p_i(n_i)/2^{n_i}$ of all computation paths, that is, in less than one third of all the computation paths. According to the definition of acceptance, this means that the prover P^* will convince V_i with oracle A to accept with probability greater than one third but less than two thirds. Thus V_i^A cannot be a verifier for a relativized interactive proof system and we may discard V_i from the enumeration.

To conclude the proof we have to show that $L_A^* \notin \mathrm{IP}^A$. In contrast, assume that a verifier V_i with oracle A exists witnessing $L_A^* \in \mathrm{IP}^A$. If no prover P exists such that the interactive proof system (P, V_i^A) accepts 0^{n_i}, then from case 1 it follows that $A_{n_i} = \Sigma_{n_i}^*$, that is, $0^{n_i} \in L_A^*$. On the other hand, if a prover P exists such that the interactive proof system (P, V_i^A) accepts 0^{n_i}, then from the above paragraph it follows that $(P, V_i^{A(i-1) \cup (\Sigma^* - Q(i-1))})$ accepts 0^{n_i}. From case 2, we then have that $A_{n_i} \neq \Sigma_{n_i}^*$, that is, $0^{n_i} \notin L_A^*$. In both cases, V_i fails to correctly decide whether 0^{n_i} belongs to L_A^* and we conclude that no such V_i can exist. $\qquad\square$

As noted in Chapter 5, the above result shows that, in order to settle the question whether IP contains coNP, we need techniques that do not relativize. Surprisingly, one example of these techniques has been recently found!

10.2.1   Arithmetization of Boolean formulas

The basic idea of this proof technique is to 'arithmetize' a Boolean formula, obtaining a low-degree polynomial, so that the problem of deciding whether the formula is satisfiable reduces to that of verifying whether the corresponding polynomial admits a value different from zero.

Given an n-variable Boolean formula f in conjunctive normal form with three literals per clause, an arithmetic formula A_f is derived from it in the following inductive way:

1. Arithmetization of a literal: $A_{x_i} = 1 - z_i$ where x_i is a Boolean variable and z_i is an integer variable; similarly, $A_{\neg x_i} = z_i$.
2. Arithmetization of a clause: $A_{l_1 \lor l_2 \lor l_3} = 1 - A_{l_1} A_{l_2} A_{l_3}$ where l_1, l_2, l_3 are literals.
3. Arithmetization of f: $A_f = A_{c_1 \land \ldots \land c_m} = A_{c_1} \ldots A_{c_m}$ where $c_1, \ldots, c_m$ are the clauses of f.

(note that such A_f is a polynomial of degree, at most, $3m$ where m denotes the number of clauses).

Clearly, a formula f is not satisfiable if and only if the corresponding A_f is equal to 0 for all $(0,1)$-assignments to the variables of A_f. The fact that each member of this exponentially large collection of quantities vanishes can be expressed concisely as follows:

$$\sum_{z_1=0}^{1} \sum_{z_2=0}^{1} \cdots \sum_{z_n=0}^{1} A_f(z_1, \ldots, z_n) = 0$$

(it can immediately be verified that the above sum cannot exceed the value 2^n).

Let us now define for each i with $0 \leq i \leq n$, the set of polynomials $A_f^i(z_1, \ldots, z_i)$ as

$$A_f^i(z_1, \ldots, z_i) = \sum_{z_{i+1}=0}^{1} \cdots \sum_{z_n=0}^{1} A_f(z_1, \ldots, z_n).$$

Clearly, $A_f^n = A_f$; furthermore, $A_f^0 = 0$ if and only if f is not satisfiable and, for each i, $A_f^{i-1} = A_f^i(z_i = 0) + A_f^i(z_i = 1)$ (using self-explanatory notation for substitution).

Let us now show a first application of arithmetization of Boolean formulas.

Theorem 10.2 coNP $\subseteq$ IP.

Proof. The proof consists of deriving an interactive proof for the complement of the 3-SATISFIABILITY problem which is *co*NP-complete. Since IP is closed with respect to polynomial-time reducibility (see Problem 10.6), it follows that *co*NP $\subseteq$ IP.

Let f be a Boolean formula of m clauses on n variables and denote by A_f the corresponding arithmetic formula.

The protocol is the following. First, the prover chooses a sufficiently large prime number p and the verifier probabilistically checks that p is indeed prime (see Section 9.1). Successively, the protocol proceeds in n rounds. At the end of the ith round, the verifier picks a random number $r_i \in \{0, 1, \ldots, p-1\}$ and computes a value b_i (with $b_0 = 0$) which is transmitted to the prover. The prover, on the other hand, will be asked to send the coefficients of a suitable polynomial.

In particular, by the beginning of round $i \geq 1$, the numbers $r_1, \ldots, r_{i-1}$ have been selected and the values $b_0, b_1, \ldots, b_{i-1}$ computed. Now the prover is requested to state the coefficients of the univariate polynomial

$$g_i(x) = A_f^i(r_1, \ldots, r_{i-1}, x).$$

Let g_i' denote the polynomial stated by the prover. The verifier first performs a 'consistency test' by checking the condition $b_{i-1} = g_i'(0) + g_i'(1)$. If this test fails, the verifier rejects, or else generates the random number r_i and computes the value $b_i = g_i'(r_i)$.

At the end of round n, the verifier performs a 'final test' by checking that $b_n = A_f(r_1, \ldots, r_n)$. The verifier accepts if all the n consistency tests as well as the final test have been passed.

Formally, the algorithm for V is the following:

```
begin {input: f};
    construct A_f from f;
    send ask_prime;
    receive p;
    if p is not prime or p < 2^|f| then reject;
    b_0 := 0;
    for i = 1 to n do
    begin
        send b_{i-1};
        receive coefficients of univariate polynomial g_i';
        if b_{i-1} ≠ g_i'(0) + g_i'(1) then reject;
        r_i := random(0, p-1);
        b_i := g_i'(r_i);
    end;
    if b_n = A_f(r_1, ..., r_n) then accept else reject;
end.
```

First, note that according to Bertrand's postulate, for any $i > 0$, a prime p with $2^i < p < 2^{i+1}$ always exists (see Notes). Moreover, a polynomial-time probabilistic primality testing has been already described in Section 9.1. Thus the above algorithm operates in polynomial time.

Let us now prove the correctness of the algorithm itself. Clearly, if f is not satisfiable, then it is easy to derive a prover which can always answer correctly (that is, $g'_i = g_i$ for each i). In order to prove the correctness of the protocol in the case where f is satisfiable, we will exploit the fact that if the prover wants to cheat, he or she is likely to be forced to cheat on polynomials with increasingly fewer variables, eventually reaching a constant, the correctness of which the verifier can check by a single substitution into the explicit polynomial behind the summations.

In particular, we shall prove that if f is satisfiable, then, for any i, the probability that g'_i is different from g_i assuming that the first i consistency tests have succeeded is at least $(1 - 3m/p)^i$. In particular, the probability that the final test fails is at least $(1 - 3m/p)^n$. Since p is greater than $2^{|f|}$, it follows that such probability is greater than $2/3$.

The proof is by induction on i. The case $i = 1$ follows from the fact that if g'_1 is equal to g_1, then the consistency test at the first round always fails. Assume now that the first $i - 1$ tests have succeeded and that g'_{i-1} is distinct from g_{i-1}. According to the induction hypothesis, this will occur with a probability of at least $(1 - 3m/p)^{i-1}$. Since both g'_{i-1} and g_{i-1} are distinct univariate polynomials of degree, at most, $3m$, then they can agree on, at most, $3m$ points. Thus, for at least $p - 3m$ points r, $g'_{i-1}(r) \neq g_{i-1}(r)$. For each of such r, since the consistency test at the ith round succeeds, it follows that g'_i must be different from g_i. In conclusion, the probability that g'_i is different from g_i assuming that the first i consistency tests have succeeded is at least $(1 - 3m/p)^{i-1}(1 - 3m/p) = (1 - 3m/p)^i$.   □

The above theorem thus shows that IP is more 'powerful' than originally believed. However, it cannot be more powerful than PSPACE as shown by the following result.

Theorem 10.3 IP $\subseteq$ PSPACE.

Proof. Given an interactive proof system (P, V) and an input x, let us define the text of a computation as the sequence of messages exchanged between the prover and the verifier. Since the total number of messages is polynomial in $|x|$ and each message has a length polynomial in $|x|$, the length of the text is polynomial in the length of the input.

Let $L \in$ IP and let V be a verifier for L. For any x, we can then derive the tree of all possible texts. A node of the tree corresponding to a verifier's turn can be any of the possible messages from V to the prover (these messages depend on the random choices of V) and will be called random, while a node of the tree corresponding to a prover's turn can be any of the possible messages from the prover to V (these messages depend on the prover) and will be called existential. An admissibile subtree is obtained by deleting all but one of the subtrees rooted at each interior existential node (yes, all this is very similar to alternating Turing machines). It is then clear that $x \in L$ if the corresponding tree contains an admissible subtree in which more than two-thirds of the leaves are accepting.

By simply merging the proof techniques of Theorems 8.6 and 9.9 we can then visit the entire tree of all possible texts and decide whether x belongs to L. We leave the details of such a visit to the reader (see Problem 10.8). □

As usual, the question as to whether the above inclusion is strict arises. Until 1990, the answer would certainly have been 'Presumably, yes...'. But the technique introduced in the proof of Theorem 10.2 can be once again applied to state that the answer is 'NO!' In order to prove such a result, we first need a few notations and a preliminary lemma.

Let p be a multivariate polynomial. For any variable x, we then define

1. $AND_x(p) = p(x = 0)p(x = 1)$.
2. $OR_x(p) = p(x = 0) + p(x = 1) - p(x = 0)p(x = 1)$.
3. $RED_x(p) = p(x = 0) + (p(x = 1) - p(x = 0))x$; note that p and $RED_x(p)$ coincide on all $(0, 1)$-substitutions.

Example 10.2 Since the three above operations will be applied to arithmetizations of Boolean formulas, let us consider the formula $f = (x_1 \vee x_2 \vee x_3) \wedge (\neg x_1 \vee \neg x_2 \vee x_4)$. The corresponding polynomial is

$$A_f(z_1, z_2, z_3, z_4) = (1 - (1 - z_1)(1 - z_2)(1 - z_3))(1 - z_1 z_2 (1 - z_4)).$$

By selecting z_1 as x, we obtain

1. $AND_x(A_f) = (1 - (1 - z_2)(1 - z_3))(1 - z_3(1 - z_4))$.

2. $OR_x(A_f) = (1 - (1 - z_2)(1 - z_3)) + (1 - z_3(1 - z_4)) - (1 - (1 - z_2)(1 - z_3))(1 - z_3(1 - z_4))$.

3. $RED_x(A_f) = (1 - (1 - z_2)(1 - z_3)) + ((1 - z_3(1 - z_4)) - (1 - (1 - z_2)(1 - z_3)))z_1$.

The following lemma states that IP is, in some sense, 'closed' with respect to the above three operations.

Lemma 10.2 Let $p(x_1, \ldots, x_n)$ be a polynomial and let p-CHECK be the problem of deciding whether, given $a_1, \ldots, a_n$, and b, $p(a_1, \ldots, a_n) = b$. If p-CHECK belongs to IP, then both $AND_x(p)$-CHECK, $OR_x(p)$-CHECK and $RED_x(p)$-CHECK belong to IP.

Proof. We shall limit ourselves to succinctly describing the protocols, leaving to the reader the tasks of formally defining them and of proving their correctness.

In order to prove that $AND_x(p)$-CHECK is in IP, consider the following protocol. Given $a_2, \ldots, a_n$, and b as input, the prover sends to the verifier the coefficients of an univariate polynomial $s'(x)$ claimed to be equal to $s(x) = p(x, a_2, \ldots, a_n)$. The verifier first performs a consistency test checking whether $s'(0)s'(1) = b$: if this is not the case, then the verifier rejects. Otherwise, it generates a random number

r and creates the instance $r, a_2, \ldots, a_n$, and $s'(r)$ for the p-CHECK problem. Note that the prover can fool the verifier either during the protocol for the instance of the p-CHECK problem (but since this problem is assumed to be in IP, the probability of this event is negligible) or if s and s' differ but they coincide on the random point r (but once again this probability can be made arbitrarily small by choosing a sufficiently large domain for the variables). Thus, $AND_x(p)$-CHECK belongs to IP.

Similarly, we can prove the other two assertions. In the case of the $OR_x(p)$-CHECK problem the consistency test consists of checking that $s'(0) + s'(1) - s'(0)s'(1) = b$, while in the $RED_x(p)$-CHECK problem it consists of checking that $s'(0) + (s'(1) - s'(0))a_1 = b$. $\qquad\square$

Theorem 10.4 IP = PSPACE.

Proof. In order to prove that PSPACE $\subseteq$ IP, it suffices to derive an interactive proof for the QBF problem which is PSPACE-complete. In order to do this, we would like to arithmetize quantified Boolean formulas in a way similar to that used in the proof of Theorem 10.2. This can easily be done by replacing each existential quantifier with a summation and each universal quantifier with a product. However, the resulting intermediate polynomials may have exponential degrees. To circumvent this problem we can make use of a degree-reduction technique. Intuitively, any arithmetization of a quantifier will be followed by a sequence of degree reductions on all the other variables.

Let $F = (Q_1 x_1)(Q_2 x_2) \ldots (Q_n x_n) f(x_1, \ldots, x_n)$ be a quantified Boolean formula where f is a Boolean formula in conjunctive normal form on n variables $x_1, \ldots, x_n$ and the Q_is are quantifiers. Consider the polynomial A_f corresponding to f and defined in the proof of Theorem 10.2. We then modify A_f in the following way:

Step 0 sequentially apply $RED_{x_1}, \ldots, RED_{x_n}$.
Step k if $Q_{n-k+1} = \forall$ then apply $AND_{x_{n-k+1}}$, otherwise apply $OR_{x_{n-k+1}}$; then sequentially apply $RED_{x_1}, \ldots, RED_{x_{n-k}}$ (if $k < n$).

Note that after these $n + 1$ steps, we get a constant which is equal to 0 or 1 depending on the Boolean value of F. Note also that the degree of the intermediate polynomials cannot be greater than the degree of A_f. Indeed, the RED operations at step 0 reduce it to 1 and later all degrees are no greater than 2. By repeatedly applying Lemma 10.2, we can then reduce the problem of deciding whether F is true to that of checking whether $A_f(a_1, \ldots, a_n) = b$ for given values $a_1, \ldots, a_n$, and b. This last task can clearly be performed in polynomial time by the verifier. $\qquad\square$

10.3 Probabilistic checking of proofs

A related model of interactive proofs is one where the prover is assumed to be a non-adaptive entity, that is, an oracle. Intuitively, in this model the proof is written in a book and the verifier has random access to any part of it. In this section, we examine such proofs from two points of view. On the one hand, we ask how robust oracle proofs are with respect to local perturbations, that is, how many parts of the proof we can change still maintaining the proof recognizable as a correct one. On the other, we can ask how much randomness we need to check the correctness of a proof.

Formally, we say that L admits a *probabilistically checkable proof* if an oracle BPP-machine PT exists such that

1. PT is allowed only to generate random bits, that is, the **random** function of PT can only assume binary values.
2. For every $x \in L$, an oracle X_x exists such that PT^{X_x} accepts x.
3. For every $x \notin L$ and for every oracle X, PT^X rejects x.

Note that the oracle X_x can be viewed as a language depending on the input x (each true theorem has its own proof). Moreover, it can be assumed to be finite since, for a given x, the number of possible queries made by PT is bounded by an exponential function with respect to the length of x.

The *class* $PCP(f, g)$ is the set of languages which admit a probabilistically checkable proof such that the corresponding machines PT generate, at most, $\mathbf{O}[f(n)]$ random bits and, at most, $\mathbf{O}[g(n)]$ queries.

10.3.1 PCP classes and approximation algorithms

We observed at the end of Chapter 6 that the concept of completeness in the field of optimization problems has not been as fruitful as in the area of decision problems (even though we still believe it has yet to be explored in depth).

Besides proving completeness results, however, the non-approximability of an optimization problem can be proved by making use of the so-called *gap technique* which is intuitively summarized as follows. Suppose that an NP-complete language L can be 'reduced' to an NPO-maximization problem A so that, for any x, if $x \in L$ then $\text{OPT}_A[f(x)] \geq c(x)$, otherwise $\text{OPT}_A[f(x)] < c(x)(1 - g)$ where f and c are two polynomial-time computable functions and g is a constant (namely, the gap). Then it is clear that, for any $\epsilon \leq g$, A does not admit an ϵ-approximating algorithm unless P = NP. Similarly, this technique can be applied to minimization problems. Unfortunately, the creation of the above gap in the measure function is usually a difficult task.

In this last section, we emphasize an interesting (and perhaps surprising) connection between probabilistically checkable proofs and approximation algorithms. This connection can be intuitively described as follows. A probabilistically checkable proof for an NP-complete language requires a large gap in the probability of acceptance of correct and incorrect inputs (e.g. two-thirds versus one-third). Such proofs can then be used to construct a family of instances of an optimization problem with a large gap in the measure function, thus proving its non-approximability unless P = NP.

Theorem 10.5 If NP $\subseteq$ PCP(log, log), then the MAXIMUM CLIQUE problem does not belong to APX, unless P = NP.

Proof. First note that from Problem 6.15, it follows that if MAXIMUM CLIQUE is approximable, then it admits a 1/2-approximating algorithm T.

Assume now that SATISFIABILITY $\in$ PCP(f, g). For any Boolean formula f of size n, we will construct a graph G_f with, at most, $2^{f(n)+g(n)}$ nodes such that if f is satisfiable then the maximum clique in G_f has size $\frac{2}{3}2^{f(n)}$, otherwise it has size less than $\frac{1}{3}2^{f(n)}$. Let us run T on input G_f and distinguish the following two cases:

1. T outputs a clique of size greater than or equal to $\frac{1}{3}2^{f(n)}$. In this case the maximum clique must have size $\frac{2}{3}2^{f(n)}$ and thus f is satisfiable.
2. T outputs a clique of size less than $\frac{1}{3}2^{f(n)}$. In this case the maximum clique must have size $\frac{1}{3}2^{f(n)}$ since otherwise the relative error is greater than 1/2. Thus f is not satisfiable.

In both cases, by simply checking the size of the clique yielded by T we are able to decide whether f is satisfiable. In particular, whenever $f(n) = g(n) = \log(n)$ the above procedure runs in polynomial time (assuming that the construction of G_f requires a polynomial time). In conclusion, assuming the approximability of MAXIMUM CLIQUE implies that P = NP.

It thus remains to show how G_f is constructed. Let PT be a BPP-machine witnessing that SATISFIABILITY belongs to PCP(f, g). In the following q_i will denote a generic query and a_i the corresponding answer. Furthermore, a sequence of random bit generations will be denoted as a binary word r.

A *transcript* of PT on input x is a tuple $\langle r, q_1, a_1, q_2, a_2, \ldots, q_l, a_l \rangle$ with $|r| \leq c_1 f(|x|)$ and $l \leq c_2 g(|x|)$ for some constants c_1 and c_2 such that, for any i with $1 \leq i \leq l$, q_i is the ith query made by $PT(x)$ assuming that the answer to q_j is a_j for $1 \leq j < i$ and the random bit generations made so far are 'consistent' with r. A transcript t is an *accepting transcript* if PT with input x, random bit generations r and query-answer sequence $\langle q_1, a_1, \ldots, q_l, a_l \rangle$ accepts x. Finally, we say that two transcripts $t = \langle r, q_1, a_1, \ldots, q_l, a_l \rangle$ and $t' = \langle r', q_1', a_1', \ldots, q_{l'}', a_{l'}' \rangle$ are *consistent* if, for every i and j, if $q_i = q_j'$ then $a_i = a_j'$.

The nodes of G_f are all the accepting transcripts. In order to construct the set of nodes of G_f we enumerate all transcripts (this takes exponential time with respect to the length of the longest transcript, that is, $2^{f(n)+g(n)}$), and then run PT on each transcript to check that it is accepting. Two nodes are adjacent if and only if they are consistent.

Assume that f is satisfiable. Then an oracle X_f exists such that the ratio of the number of accepting computation paths of $PT^{X_f}(f)$ to the total number of computation paths of $PT^{X_f}(f)$ is at least 2/3. The number of transcripts which are consistent with oracle X_f is thus $2^{f(n)}$ and 2/3 of them are accepting. That is, G_f contains a clique of size $\frac{2}{3}2^{f(n)}$.

Conversely, if f is not satisfiable, then for any oracle X the ratio of the number of accepting computation paths of $PT^X(f)$ to the total number of computation paths of $PT^X(f)$ is less than 1/3, that is, G_f does not contain a clique of size greater than or equal to $\frac{1}{3}2^{f(n)}$.

This concludes the proof.   □

The above theorem thus yields a new approach to proving negative results in the field of approximation algorithms. Indeed, this approach has been found to be very useful (see Notes). In particular, it has been proved that NP is equal to PCP(log, 1) (a constant number of queries!) and, as a consequence, that the MAXIMUM CLIQUE problem is not approximable (if P ≠ NP). Whoever at the beginning of this chapter thought 'interactive proofs are just another strange model of computation' should now be convinced that, as usual, science is full of surprises!

Problems

10.1. Show that the constant 2/3 in the acceptance criterion of an interactive proof system can be substituted by any other constant greater than 1/2 without changing the definition.

10.2. Prove that any interactive proof systems can be simulated by another interactive proof system such that the messages between V and P are one bit long.

10.3. QUADRATIC RESIDUE: given two integers $n < m$ and $GCD(n, m) = 1$, does an integer x exist such that $x^2 \equiv n \pmod{m}$? Consider the following algorithm V:

```
begin {input: n,m}
   k := |m|;
   randomly choose z₁,...,zₖ such that zᵢ < m and GCD(zᵢ,m) = 1;
   randomly choose b₁,...,bₖ with bᵢ ∈ {0,1};
   for i = 1 to k do
      if bᵢ = 1 then wᵢ := zᵢ² mod m
      else wᵢ := nzᵢ² mod m;
   transmit w₁,...,wₖ;
   receive c₁,...,cₖ;
   for i = 1 to k do
      if cᵢ ≠ bᵢ then reject;
   accept;
end.
```

Prove that V witnesses that the complement of QUADRATIC RESIDUE belongs to IP.

10.4. Show that if GRAPH ISOMORPHISM is NP-complete, then the polynomial hierarchy collapses to the second level. [Hint: use Problem 9.18 and the fact that the complement of GRAPH ISOMORPHISM belongs to IP.]

10.5. An *Arthur–Merlin interactive proof system* is an interactive proof system such that the verifier's messages consist only of the outcome of its coin tosses. Let AM denote the class of languages which admit an Arthur–Merlin interactive proof. Prove that AM coincides with IP. [Goldwasser (1989)]

10.6. Prove that IP is closed with respect to polynomial-time reducibility.

10.7. ARITHMETIC EXPRESSION EQUALITY: given an integer a and a multivariate polynomial p of degree, at most, d in each variable, is it true that

$$\sum_{z_1=0}^{1} \sum_{z_2=0}^{1} \cdots \sum_{z_n=0}^{1} p(z_1, z_2, \ldots, z_n) = a?$$

Show that this problem admits an interactive proof. [Hint: use the technique of Theorem 10.2.]

10.8. Conclude the proof of Theorem 10.3.

10.9. A quantified Boolean formula is said to be *simple* if every occurrence of each variable is separated from its point of quantification by, at most, one universal quantifier. Prove that every quantified Boolean formula of size n can be transformed into an equivalent simple quantified Boolean formula whose size is polynomial in n. [Hint: add dummy variables in the following way: after each $\forall$, add $\exists x'(x' = x)\wedge$ for each c created between that $\forall$ and the previous one.]

10.10. Given a quantified Boolean formula $F = (Q_1 x_1)(Q_2 x_2)\ldots(Q_n x_n)f(x_1, \ldots, x_n)$, let A_F denote the arithmetization of F obtained by replacing each universal quantification $\forall x_i$ with the product $\prod_{z_i \in \{0,1\}}$, each existential quantification $\exists x_i$ with the sum $\sum_{z_i \in \{0,1\}}$, and the Boolean formula $f(x_1, \ldots, x_n)$ with the corresponding polynomial $A_f(z_1, \ldots, z_n)$. Prove that, for any quantified Boolean formula F of size n, a prime p exists of length polynomial in n such that $A_F \not\equiv 0 \pmod{p}$ if and only if F is true. [Hint: use the Chinese remainder theorem.]

10.11. Given a quantified Boolean formula F and the corresponding arithmetization A_F, let $A_F(z_1)$ denote the univariate polynomial obtained by A_F by eliminating the leftmost product or sum. Show that if F is simple, then the degree of $A_F(z_1)$ grows, at most, linearly with the size of F.

10.12. Give an alternative proof of Theorem 10.4 based on the previous three problems. Note that this proof is the first that appeared in the literature.

10.13. A natural extension of the notion of interactive proof systems is that of allowing the verifier to interact with more than one prover. In particular, assume that the verifier can communicate with each of the provers but different provers cannot communicate with each other. Clearly, the number of provers must be as large as a polynomial in the size of the input; otherwise the verifier does not have enough time to access all the provers (note that if the number of provers is 1, then we obtain the concept of interactive proof system).

The *class MIP* is then defined as the set of all languages which admit a multi-prover interactive proof. Prove that a language belongs to MIP if and only if it admits a probabilistically checkable proof. [Hint: for the 'if' part, define a verifier that asks each oracle query to a different prover, while for the 'only if' part define an oracle whose words suitably encode the history of the communication between the verifier and each of the provers.]

10.14. Show that if a language admits a probabilistically checkable proof, then it admits a two-prover interactive proof. [Hint: repeat a sufficient number of times the following step. Ask all the oracle queries to the first prover, then select one query at random and verify the answer with the second prover. Repeat the above a sufficient number of times.] As a consequence of this result and of that of the previous problem, the multi-prover model is not more powerful than the two-prover one.

10.15. Prove that if NP $\subseteq$ PCP(log, 1), then the MAXIMUM SATISFIABILITY problem (see Problem 6.11) does not belong to PAS, unless P $=$ NP.

Notes

The concept of efficiently verifiable proof can be thought as originating with Cook (1971). Indeed, Theorem 5.2 can be reinterpreted as showing that NP coincides with the class of languages which have short and easy-to-verify proofs of membership (see also Lemmas 5.1 and 10.1). The interactive and probabilistic proof systems, however, were defined later in Goldwasser, Micali, and Rackoff (1989) and, independently, in Babai (1985). The main motivation for the former paper was that of measuring the amount of knowledge required to communicate a proof in order to develop a mathematical theory of cryptographic protocols, while in the latter paper the focus was on problems of membership in and on the order of a matrix group given by a list of generators. Besides having different motivations, the two papers followed two slightly different approaches: on the one hand, the interactive proof-systems as described in this text, and, on the other, the Arthur–Merlin games where, obviously, Arthur plays as a verifier and Merlin plays as a prover.

The main difference between interactive proof-systems and Arthur–Merlin protocols is that Arthur's messages consist only of the outcome of his coin tosses. In Goldwasser and Sipser (1986), however, it was shown that the two approaches are equivalent, that is, the corresponding two classes IP and AM coincide (see Problem 10.5).

Before continuing, the reader should be advised that the material covered in this chapter constitutes only a small part of a subject which is still being actively developed. Indeed, we preferred to focus on two very important applications of interactive proofs which seem to be particularly promising: proof techniques which do not relativize and approximation algorithms. However, several other aspects of this theory have been studied in depth such as the number of rounds in a computation and the amount of communicated knowledge. We refer the interested reader to the survey by Goldwasser (1989), to Chapter 11 of Balcazar, Diaz, and Gabarro (1990), and, particularly for the zero-knowledge area of research, to the surveys by Blum (1986), Goldwasser (1989), and to the last section of Goldreich (1988). In these, many other references can be found.

The interactive proof-system for the complement of GRAPH ISOMORPHISM is due to Goldreich, Micali, and Wigderson (1986) while the proof of Theorem 10.1 appeared in Fortnow and Sipser (1988).

The application of algebraic methods in interactive proofs started with Lund *et al.* (1992) in order to obtain Theorem 10.2: our presentation of the proof of that theorem is partly inspired by Babai, Fortnow, and Lund (1991). Immediately after that result, Theorem 10.4 was proved in Shamir (1992) by making use of the arithmetization of quantified Boolean formulas (see Problem 10.12); however, our proof is a simplified version of the original one due to Shen (1992). The proof of Theorem 10.3 first appeared in Papadimitriou (1983).

Bertrand's postulate states that, for any positive integer n, a prime p exists such that $n < p < 2n$. This postulate was proved by Chebyshev in 1852.

The probabilistic checking of proofs started with Babai *et al.* (1991) where the notion of transparent proof was introduced. Informally, a transparent proof that a word belongs to a given language either proves a correct statement or alternatively mistakes will appear in the proof almost everywhere, thus enabling a probabilistic verifier to check it by a cursory examination. The probabilistically checkable proof is a refinement of this notion and was defined in Arora and Safra (1992) where the class PCP was also introduced. Theorem 10.5 appeared in a slightly different formulation in Feige *et al.* (1991). This paper led to an interesting series of results which can be summarized as follows:

- NP $\subseteq$ PCP$(\log(n) \log(\log(n)), \log(n) \log(\log(n)))$ in Feige *et al.* (1991);
- NP $\subseteq$ PCP$(\log(n), \log^k(\log(n)))$ in Arora and Safra (1992);
- NP $\subseteq$ PCP$(\log(n), 1)$ in Arora *et al.* (1992).

By using similar techniques, other optimization problems such as node coloring and set covering have been shown to be non-approximable (see Lund and Yannakakis (1993)).

Chapter 11

Models of parallel computers

As a result of the achievements attained in the area of microprocessor design it has become possible in the last decade to build massively parallel computers, that is, computers consisting of a very large number (up to a few tens of thousands) of processors capable of operating in parallel. At the same time, a theory of parallel computations whose main objective is to characterize the problems most suitable for being solved by such new machines has begun to take shape. This branch of complexity theory is closely related to practical applications. We are no longer dealing with decidable languages but only about a subset of computationally tractable problems, namely, those problems in P which can be most effectively solved by parallel computers. Similarly, the proof that a given problem can be efficiently solved by a parallel computer will generally consist of a time-complexity analysis of a parallel algorithm solving that problem.

Unfortunately, even if the concept of parallel computation is rather intuitive, research activity in this new field has not concentrated on a single model of parallel computer, but rather on several classes (see Notes), paying differing levels of attention to physical constraints such as the placements of components on a chip or the interconnection pattern between processors. In agreement with the objectives of asymptotic complexity, we shall ignore real-life constraints and we shall concentrate on a class of models that ignore the communication costs between processors and on the computational costs of parallel computations. Although the level of performance predicted by such models is unreachable with real-life parallel computers, the results we shall obtain must be considered quite significant since they represent useful lower bounds on the execution times one can hope to obtain while solving specific problems with parallel computers.

We shall start in Section 11.1 by describing a model whose processing units have limited power since they are only able to compute Boolean functions. We shall then introduce in Section 11.2 a model of parallel computer known as PRAM which views parallel computers as sets of powerful processors connected to a global memory whose cells can be accessed in unit time by any processor. The relations

221

between circuits and PRAMs are considered in Section 11.5. Finally, in Section 11.6, we shall prove that sequential space and parallel time are polynomially related to each other, at least for the models of parallel computers considered in this chapter.

11.1   Circuits

A *circuit c* consists of $n + q$ *gates* g_i connected by *lines*. The first n gates are called *input gates* while the remaining q are called *circuit gates*; in particular, gate g_{n+q} is called the *output gate*. Each circuit gate g_h computes a Boolean function o_h. It is common to restrict oneself to circuits based on unary and binary functions only. It is well known that a single binary function exists (for instance, the NAND function) which forms a complete basis[1] by itself. We shall refer, however, to the most common circuit basis according to which $o_h \in \{\lor, \land, \neg\}$ (note that either the $\lor$ or the $\land$ could be avoided but, for clarity, we prefer to make use of both). The $\lor$ and the $\land$ circuit gates have two inputs and one output while the $\neg$ circuit gates have only one input and one output. The input gates have one output and no input. A single circuit line connects the output of a gate with the input of another gate. Altogether, the set of circuit lines must satisfy the following properties:

1. *Exactly* one line is connected to each input of each gate (with the exception of the input gates which have no input line).
2. *At least* one line is connected to the output of each gate (with the exception of the output gate whose output line is not connected to other gates).
3. If a line connects the output of a gate, say g_i, with an input of another gate, say g_j, then $i < j$, that is, we are assuming that the enumeration of the gates corresponds to a topological ordering of the gates themselves.

Alternatively, a circuit may be defined as a directed acyclic graph where the nodes correspond to gates and the edges to lines. The n input gates correspond to nodes with no incoming edge, the output gate to a node with no outgoing edge, and the number of incoming edges of the circuit gates depends on their operation type (one for $\neg$ gates, two for $\lor$ and $\land$ gates).

An example of circuit is illustrated in Figure 11.1 where, according to a standard notation, whenever a gate has several output lines, those lines are drawn as a single line connected to several inputs.

Let c be a circuit with n input gates and let $x = x_1 x_2 \ldots x_n$ denote a binary input of length n. The function f_i associated with a gate g_i is then defined inductively as follows (we are assuming that the inputs of g_i are connected to the outputs of

---

[1]Recall that, informally, a complete basis for Boolean algebra is a set of functions able to express by suitable combinations any other Boolean function.

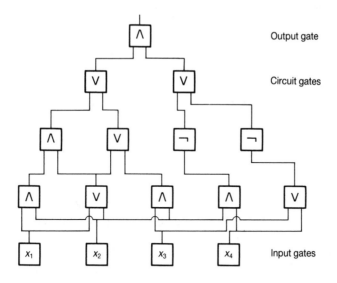

Figure 11.1 A simple example of a circuit

g_j and g_k):

$$
f_i(x) = \begin{cases}
x_i & \text{if } 1 \le i \le n, \\
\neg f_j(x) & \text{if } n+1 \le i \le n+q \text{ and } o_i = \neg, \\
f_j(x) \vee f_k(x) & \text{if } n+1 \le i \le n+q \text{ and } o_i = \vee, \\
f_j(x) \wedge f_k(x) & \text{if } n+1 \le i \le n+q \text{ and } o_i = \wedge
\end{cases}
$$

(note that in circuit notation, the Boolean constants **true** and **false** are denoted as 1 and 0, respectively).

The function f_{n+q} is said to be the function computed by c.

Example 11.1 Refer to the circuit shown in Figure 11.1. If $x = 0000$, then the value of the function computed by c is equal to 0 while if $x = 1100$ it is equal to 1.

In general, determining the value of the function computed by a circuit with a given input is a well-known problem.

Example 11.2 Given a circuit c of $n + q$ gates, its *standard encoding* denoted as $\bar{c}$ consists of q triples $\langle o_i, j, k \rangle$ with $n + 1 \le i \le n + q$ such that o_i is the Boolean function computed by g_i, and g_j, g_k are the gates connected to the inputs of g_i.

CIRCUIT VALUE: given the encoding of an $(n + q)$-gate circuit and a binary input x of length n, is $f_{n+q}(x)$ equal to 1? Clearly, this problem belongs to P (see Problem 11.5). In the next chapter we shall see that this problem is P-complete.

The previous definitions refer to *acceptor circuits*: indeed, each circuit can compute only one n-variable binary function. However, these definitions can readily be extended to *transducer circuits*. For that purpose, it suffices to consider circuits having m output gates and thus simultaneously computing m Boolean functions.

11.1.1   Circuit complexity of Boolean functions

The two most natural complexity measures of a circuit are those of size and depth which correspond roughly to the number of processors and to the time needed to compute a function.

Given a circuit c, its *size*, in symbols $SIZE(c)$, is defined as the number of circuit gates of c while its *depth*, in symbols $DEPTH(c)$, is defined as the length of the longest path from an input gate to the output gate of c (in general, the depth of an arbitrary gate is similarly defined).

Note that since each gate has, at most, two inputs, $SIZE(c) \leq 2^{DEPTH(c)}$. In contrast to $TIME$ and $SPACE$ which are dynamic measures, $DEPTH$ and $SIZE$ are static measures since they can be derived from the circuit characteristics, independently from the input value. At the same time, they can also be considered as dynamic measures since they express, respectively, the time and the amount of hardware or number of processors needed to compute a given function with a fixed number of variables. This double role of a measure is caused by the fact that circuits are a very elementary model of computation which correspond somehow to the class of programs without loops or cycles.

Returning to the evaluation of the complexity of functions, it is reasonable to consider as simple functions those which can be computed by simple circuits. The *circuit complexity* of a Boolean function f, in symbols $SIZE_f$, is then defined as

$$SIZE_f = \min\{q : \exists c \text{ with } SIZE(c) = q \text{ which computes } f\}.$$

The next theorem shows that the circuit complexity of Boolean functions is exponentially bounded by the number of their variables.

Theorem 11.1 Let f be any n-variable Boolean function. Then $SIZE_f < 2^{n+2}$.

Proof. Let us make use of the following identity between n-variable Boolean formulas:

$$f(x_1, \ldots, x_n) = (x_1 \wedge f(1, x_2, \ldots, x_n)) \vee (\neg x_1 \wedge f(0, x_2, \ldots, x_n)).$$

The previous identity ensures that a circuit for an n-variable Boolean function can always be obtained by appropriately connecting two circuits for two $(n-1)$-variable Boolean functions. This connection, in turn, requires, at most, two $\wedge$

gates, one $\lor$ gate and one $\neg$ gate, that is, four additional gates. In conclusion, for any $n \geq 1$, $SIZE_f \leq g(n)$ where

$$g(n) = \begin{cases} 2 & \text{if } n = 1, \\ 2g(n-1) + 4 & \text{otherwise.} \end{cases}$$

It is easy to verify (see Problem 11.2) that $g(n) < 2^{n+2}$ for all n. $\qquad\square$

Let us now show by a counting argument that Boolean functions exist whose circuit complexity is close to the bound set by the previous theorem.

Theorem 11.2 For n sufficiently large, an n-variable Boolean function f exists such that $SIZE_f > 2^n/n$.

Proof. Denote with $M(q, n)$ the number of distinct circuits having n input gates and q circuit gates. We make use of the circuit encoding introduced in Example 11.2. According to that encoding, a circuit is described as a word consisting of q triples. Since there are, at most, $3(n + q)^2$ 'legal' triples, the number of distinct $(n + q)$-gate circuits is thus bounded by $(3(n + q)^2)^q$. We can obtain an even better bound by partitioning the $(3(n + q)^2)^q$ possible words into classes such that all words in the same class either describe a circuit which computes the same function or they do not describe a proper circuit because the topological order implicit in the enumeration of the gates is not respected. More precisely, each class of words consists of a word w encoding a circuit together with the $q! - 1$ additional words corresponding to permutations of the triples of w where the gate indices of the triples have been suitably modified in agreement with the new enumeration of the q gates. (See the example illustrated in Figure 11.2, which describes a circuit with $n = 4$ and $q = 3$.)

We have thus proved that $M(q, n) \leq (3(n + q)^2)^q/q!$ and we are now almost finished. Indeed, according to Stirling's approximation, $q! < \sqrt{2\pi q}(q/e)^q$, that is,

$$M(q, n) < (3e(n + q)^2)^q/(\sqrt{2\pi q}q^q).$$

By choosing $q = 2^n/n$, we get $q > n$ for any $n > 4$ and thus

$$M(2^n/n, n) < (c2^n/n)^{2^n/n}$$

with c constant. Finally, for any n sufficiently large,

$$M(2^n/n, n) < (2^n)^{2^n/n} = 2^{2^n}.$$

In other words, it is not possible to compute all possible 2^{2^n} Boolean functions of n variables by making use of circuits consisting of n input gates and $q = 2^n/n$ circuit gates, hence the thesis. $\qquad\square$

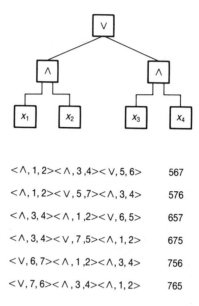

$$<\wedge, 1, 2><\wedge, 3, 4><\vee, 5, 6>\qquad 567$$

$$<\wedge, 1, 2><\vee, 5, 7><\wedge, 3, 4>\qquad 576$$

$$<\wedge, 3, 4><\wedge, 1, 2><\vee, 6, 5>\qquad 657$$

$$<\wedge, 3, 4><\vee, 7, 5><\wedge, 1, 2>\qquad 675$$

$$<\vee, 6, 7><\wedge, 1, 2><\wedge, 3, 4>\qquad 756$$

$$<\vee, 7, 6><\wedge, 3, 4><\wedge, 1, 2>\qquad 765$$

Figure 11.2 Permutations associated with the encoding of a circuit

Unbounded fan-in circuits

Define the number of input (respectively, output) lines of a gate as the gate *fan-in* (respectively, *fan-out*). According to such terminology, the circuit just described has a bounded fan-in of 2. Since the $\vee$ and $\wedge$ operations are distributive, it makes sense (at least from a theoretical point of view!) to consider $\vee$ and $\wedge$ gates with $m > 2$ input lines. Such strange circuits which are appropriately called circuits with *unbounded fan-in* are found to be useful in making some proofs clearer. The following result establishes a connection between circuits with bounded and unbounded fan-in.

Lemma 11.1 Given a circuit of size $s(n)$ and depth $d(n)$ with unbounded fan-in, an equivalent circuit with fan-in 2, size $\mathbf{O}[s^2(n)]$, and depth $\mathbf{O}[\log(s(n))d(n)]$ exists.

Proof. Since any unbounded fan-in gate can have, at most, $s(n)$ inputs, then it can be replaced by a tree of depth $\mathbf{O}[\log(s(n))]$ of fan-in 2 gates. $\square$

11.1.2   Circuit families

A single circuit cannot be considered as a parallel model of computation since it is only able to decide a finite language, that is, a language consisting of words of length n (with the obvious convention that a binary word is accepted if the output function is 1). This limitation may be overcome by considering not just one circuit but an infinite sequence of them. A *circuit family* C is a sequence of circuits $C = \{c_n : n \geq 1\}$ such that each c_n includes n input gates. A family C *decides the language* L if every $c_n \in C$ decides the language L_n. The *size of a family* C, in symbols $SIZE_C(n)$, is a function defined as $SIZE_C(n) = SIZE(c_n)$. Similarly the *depth of* C, in symbols $DEPTH_C(n)$, is a function defined as $DEPTH(C, n) = DEPTH(c_n)$. In particular, a circuit family C is said to be *polynomial* if $SIZE_C(n) \in \mathbf{O}[p(n)]$ where p denotes a polynomial.

Circuit families as defined above are also called *non-uniform circuit families* since no constraint whatsoever is put on the number of steps needed to derive, given any n, the nth circuit of the family. This broad definition leads to some contradictory results. Very hard languages which can be decided by circuit families of a negligible size do exist.

Example 11.3 Let L be a binary language such that, for all $n \geq 0$, either $L_n = \Sigma_n^*$ or $L_n = \emptyset$. Such an L can be decided by a circuit family of constant size. Indeed, each circuit of the family must only compute either the constant function 1 or the constant function 0. On the other hand, L can be a very hard language, even a non-decidable one.

The converse proposition is not true.

Theorem 11.3 Let T be a deterministic Turing machine deciding a language L in time $f(n)$. Then a circuit family C with $SIZE_C(n) \in \mathbf{O}[f^2(n)]$ can be derived which decides the same language.

Proof. Let us use a top-down approach. For any input x of length n, the entire circuit will be formed by $f(n)$ identical layers, one for each step of the computation $T(x)$ (without loss of generality, we shall assume that the computation halts after exactly $f(n)$ steps). Intuitively, each layer encodes a global state and the connections between successive layers are flexible enough to yield from one global state the next one in the computation.

Next, the yes/no answer will be derived from the output of the last layer. This can be easily done by a circuit which examines the state of the Turing machine included in the global state and ouputs 1 if and only if that state is the accepting one. The structure of the resulting circuit is shown in Figure 11.3.

We shall prove later that each of the circuit layers can be implemented by making use of $\mathbf{O}[f(n)]$ gates. Similarly, it will be easy to verify that the topmost circuit also requires $\mathbf{O}[f(n)]$ gates. Since the computation $T(x)$ consists of exactly $f(n)$

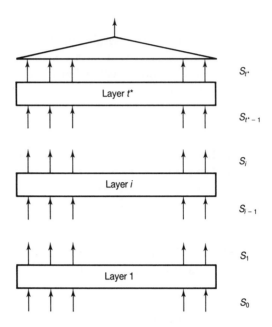

Figure 11.3 Simulation of a set of computations by a circuit

steps, the resulting circuit has size $\mathbf{O}[f^2(n)]$ and this concludes the outline of the proof.

Now, let us consider in more detail the inner structure of a layer and its connections with adjacent layers.

At any instant t of the computation $T(x)$, we can associate with each cell i a binary word w_i^t of length $2 + \lceil \log(|Q|) \rceil$ where Q denotes the set of states of T. The first two bits of w_i^t encode the symbol contained in cell i (either 0, or 1, or $\square$) while the remaining $\lceil \log(|Q|) \rceil$ bits are the binary representation of j if T is in state q_j and T's head is positioned on cell i, otherwise, they are all equal to 0. Note that the value of w_i^t depends only on the three words w_{i-1}^{t-1}, w_i^{t-1} and w_{i+1}^{t-1}. It is thus easy to derive a constant depth transducer circuit which, on input w_{i-1}^{t-1}, w_i^{t-1}, and w_{i+1}^{t-1}, computes the correct value of w_i^t (clearly, this circuit depends on the quintuples of T).

Each layer consists of $f(n)$ such transducer circuits, one for each cell potentially scanned during the computation $T(x)$, and the connection between two adjacent layers are shown in Figure 11.4. It follows immediately from the construction outlined above that each circuit layer requires $\mathbf{O}[f(n)]$ gates to be implemented. We encourage the reader to choose a simple Turing machine and to detail the structure of the corresponding layers. $\square$

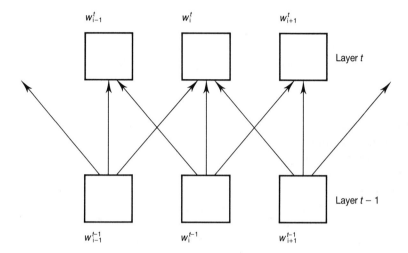

Figure 11.4 Structure of a circuit layer

11.1.3   Uniform circuit complexity

We already observed that an obvious limitation of non-uniform circuit complexity is that very difficult languages (from a 'time complexity' point of view) may have a very low circuit complexity. This problem can be avoided by considering only families of circuits that are uniformly constructible, i.e. families for which the nth circuit c_n can 'easily' be determined from n. Our choice of 'easy' obviously affects the circuit complexity of problems. If the uniformity condition is too weak, the theory may become trivial since most of the computational power lies in the circuit constructor rather than in the circuit itself (see Example 11.3). On the other hand, if it is too strong, i.e. if a requirement is made for the circuits to be computed very easily, then it is no longer possible to establish a correspondence between circuit families and realistic parallel computers. For instance, requiring the circuit to be derived in constant working space seems to be too restrictive since no handling of gate indices would be allowed.

It is therefore clear that a compromise has to be found between the weak and the strong uniformity. In fact, several plausible definitions have been proposed but

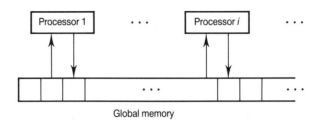

Figure 11.5 The PRAM model

no practical basis exists for choosing one instead of another. Fortunately, it has been shown that uniform circuit complexity is fairly insensitive to minor changes in the definition of uniformity (as an example, the class NC that will be defined in the next chapter is identical under several uniformity conditions).

Let us now introduce a first and rather intuitive uniformity condition. A circuit family $C = \{c_n : n \geq 1\}$ of size $s(n)$ is *logspace-uniform* if the mapping $1^n \to \bar{c}_n$ is computable by a deterministic Turing machine T in space $\mathbf{O}[\log(s(n))]$.

Alternative approaches to defining uniformity, perhaps less intuitive but more useful in obtaining proofs of uniformity have also been considered (see Notes). For the sake of uniformity (pun intended), we have preferred to present the main results on the complexity of parallel computations by referring in a consistent manner to logspace uniformity.

11.2 The PRAM model

The PRAM model is the parallel extension of the RAM model already introduced in Chapter 2. It is a synchronous model (all processors perform a step of the computation at the same time, driven by a centralized clock) and all instructions considered require the same time to be executed.[2] In particular, a PRAM consists of a potentially infinite sequence of processors able to operate on a shared global memory which, in turn, consists of a potentially infinite number of cells.

The PRAM cannot be considered a physically realizable model, since, as the number of processors and the size of the global memory increase, the assumption that any processor can access any memory word in constant time is no longer realistic. Nevertheless, the PRAM has shown to be a quite useful tool for studying the logical structure of parallel computation in a context where communications

---

[2]As for the RAM model, a non-uniform version where the instruction time varies with the logarithm of the operand values has also been considered.

costs are simply ignored. In fact, it is fair to say that algorithms developed for more realistic parallel models of computation are often based on algorithms originally designed for the PRAM.

Each processor of a PRAM executes the same program. However, two basic types of PRAMs denoted as SIMD-PRAM and MIMD-PRAM, respectively, can be distinguished, depending on whether processors are allowed to execute only the same instruction at any instant or not.

11.2.1   The SIMD-PRAM model

Each processor of a SIMD-PRAM includes two registers denoted as ID and ACC, respectively. The former is a read-only register containing the index of the processor while the latter can be viewed as a local memory cell. The set of instructions of the processors is then extended as follows:

1. $ACC \leftarrow ID$ (write the index of the processor in the register ACC).
2. The first six types of instructions of a RAM (see Section 2.1.5) are extended by allowing ACC to replace any occurrence of i, j, k, M_i, M_j, and M_k (assuming that M_{ACC} denotes the global memory cell whose index is contained in the register ACC).

Note that the above extension allows different processors to access different global memory cells, depending on the current values of ACC, at the same time. Thus, at any time in a SIMD-PRAM, all active processors execute the same instruction, although on distinct operands. Indeed, SIMD is a well-known acronym for 'Single Instruction Multiple Data'.

As for the RAM model, the input $x = x_1 x_2 \ldots x_N$ is assumed to be contained in the cells $M_1, M_2, \ldots, M_N$ of global memory, the result of the computation is stored in cell M_0 and both acceptor and transducer PRAMs will be considered.

As far as processor activation is concerned, a cell of global memory, say M_p, specifies the number of active processors at any time: if $M_p = k$, the first k processors are activated. The value of M_p can be altered by the processors to vary the number of active processors.

11.2.2   The MIMD-PRAM model

The MIMD-PRAM is similar to the SIMD-PRAM; the only difference is that processors are now allowed to execute distinct instructions at the same time. MIMD is the acronym for 'Multiple Instruction Multiple Data'. To that purpose, we extend the set of instructions of a SIMD-PRAM by allowing ACC to replace either i or M_i in the seventh type of instructions of a RAM (see Section 2.1.5). Because of this new control instruction, processors are no longer bound to execute the same instruction at every step.

Although the multiple instruction feature seems to yield more flexibility in the design of parallel algorithms, in practice it is very seldom used. Furthermore, it can be easily shown (see Problems 11.11 and 11.12) that a MIMD-PRAM can be simulated with a small overhead by a SIMD-PRAM.

Moreover, theoretical arguments to be discussed in the next chapter ensure that determining the exact complexity of efficient parallel algorithms can be done more easily when such algorithms are described by making use of a SIMD-PRAM model. For the above reasons, we shall restrict our attention to SIMD-PRAMs, which will be referred to from now on as PRAMs.

11.3   PRAM memory conflicts

PRAMs can be classified according to restrictions on global memory accesses. In fact, *memory conflicts* may occur when more than one processor attempts to read from or to write into the same global memory cell at the same time. The following four schemes describe all possible occurrences of such conflicts:

1. Exclusive Read Exclusive Write (EREW): neither read conflicts nor write ones are allowed.
2. Concurrent Read Exclusive Write (CREW): several reads can occur simultaneously on the same cell but no write conflict is allowed.
3. Exclusive Read Concurrent Write (ERCW): several writes can occur simultaneously on the same cell but no read conflict is allowed.
4. Concurrent Read Concurrent Write (CRCW): several reads or writes can occur simultaneously on the same cell.

Allowing multiple-read accesses to the same cell should in principle pose no problem: intuitively, each processor merely receives a copy of the cell's content. With multiple-write accesses, however, difficulties arise. If several processors are simultaneously attempting to write a number in a given cell, which of them should succeed? Several policies have been proposed to arbitrate such conflicts. Two popular policies are the following:

1. COMMON: all write operations must write the same (common) value into the memory cell.
2. PRIORITY: the write operation executed by the processor with smallest ID (priority) is selected as the one which will set the value of the memory cell.

The intuitive notations PRAM-EREW, PRAM-CREW, PRAM-COMMON, and PRAM-PRIORITY are used to specify which restriction on global memory access is assumed for the PRAM (for simplicity, we assume that whenever Concurrent Writes are allowed, Concurrent Reads are also allowed).

In order to describe PRAM-algorithms, we will continue to make use of the pseudo-Pascal language enriched with statements of the form

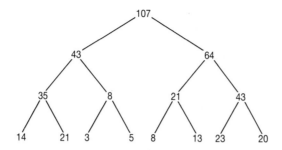

Figure 11.6 Parallel sum of eight numbers in three steps

for $i = 1$ **to** k **do in parallel** instruction;

where, as usual, i takes every integer value from 1 to k. The meaning of the above statement is the following. Each of the first k processors is active, that is, $M_p = k$ and executes the specified instruction. Since the processors work in parallel, the time-complexity of such a statement is simply that of the specified instruction. As shown in the next example, the instruction usually refers to the variable i so that different processors perform the same instruction but on different data.

Example 11.4 We wish to write a PRAM program which computes the sum of N numbers by a 'tree-like' technique as shown in Figure 11.6. For simplicity, we assume that the number of operands N is a power of 2 and is included in the input (see Problem 11.10).

program {input: $N, x_1, x_2, \ldots, x_N$}
begin
    for $j = 1$ **to** $\log(N)$ **do**
        for $i = 1$ **to** $N/2^j$ **do in parallel**
            $x_i := x_{2i-1} + x_{2i}$;
end.

    Clearly, the above algorithm requires logarithmic time. Note also that the same technique can be applied to any associative binary operation.

Less trivial examples of PRAM algorithms will be given in the next chapter.

11.4   A comparison of the PRAM models

Let us try to compare the computing power of the PRAM models introduced previously.

According to the definitions, it can immediately be verified that all programs running on a PRAM-EREW (respectively, PRAM-CREW, PRAM-COMMON) also run on a PRAM-CREW (respectively, PRAM-COMMON, PRAM-PRIORI-TY) within the same time bound.

Moreover, the following result shows that any PRAM-PRIORITY algorithm admits an equivalent PRAM-COMMON one running within the same time bound even though the number of processors must be squared.

Theorem 11.4 Any set of simultaneous concurrent write operations of p processors on a PRAM-PRIORITY can be simulated by a constant number of concurrent write operations of p^2-processors on a PRAM-COMMON.

Proof. The idea is to derive a permission array by comparing the write requests of the p processors pairwise. In particular, the ith entry of such an array will be either 1 or 0 depending on whether the ith processor is allowed to execute its write operation, if any. Assume that the jth processor wishes to write the value $v(j)$ into cell $M_{c(j)}$. The simulation can then be performed by the following algorithm:

begin {input:$c(1), v(1), \ldots, c(p), v(p)$}
    for $j = 1$ **to** p **do in parallel**
        $perm(j) := 1$;
    for any pair $i < j$ of processor indices **do in parallel**
        if $c(i) = c(j)$ **then** $perm(j) := 0$;
    for $j = 1$ **to** p **do in parallel**
        if $perm(j) = 1$ **then** $M_{c(j)} := v(j)$;
end.

It can immediately be verified that the above algorithm requires a constant number of steps. □

The last simulation result shows that the PRAM-EREW model is powerful enough to allow an efficient simulation of the three other PRAM models considered. In order to prove the theorem, we first need the following two lemmas.

Lemma 11.2 Any set of simultaneous concurrent read operations of p processors can be simulated by, at most, $\mathbf{O}[\log(p)]$ exclusive-read operations of the same p-processors.

Proof. In general, several arbitrary subsets of the p processors attempt to access different memory cells, one cell per subset. The idea of the proof is to simulate this set of concurrent read operations by a multiple broadcast technique, that is, by simultaneously broadcasting the contents of addressed cells to the processors included in the corresponding subsets.

We assume for simplicity that p is a power of 2. We then expand each memory cell M_i as a set $\{M'_j\}$ of cells corresponding to a binary tree of $p - 1$ internal nodes and p leaves. The nodes of the tree represent consecutive cells in memory.

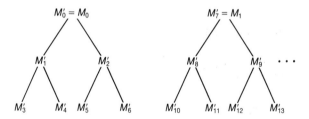

Figure 11.7 Expansion of memory cells as trees of memory cells

Figure 11.7 represents the first two trees of $2p-1 = 7$ memory cells each. Assuming $p = 4$ these trees correspond, respectively, to cells M_0 and M_1.

The simulation makes use of the following two arrays:

1. Array *level* whose ith element stores the current level of the tree reached by the ith processor read request.
2. Array *loc* whose ith element stores the current node of the tree reached by the ith processor read request.

Assume that the jth processor wishes to read from cell $M_{c(j)}$. It places its request at cell $M'_{c(j)(2p-1)+(p-1)+j-1}$, which is the jth leaf of the tree of cells corresponding to cell $M_c(j)$. This is done by initializing $level(j)$ to 0 and $loc(j)$ to $p-1+j-1$. The simulation then consists of two phases: ascent and descent. During the ascent phase, the processors execute the following. At each level, a processor occupying a left child is first given priority to advance its request one level up the tree. It does so by marking the parent cell with a special marker. It then updates its *level* and *loc* entries. In this case, a request at the right child is immobilized for the remainder of the procedure. If there is no processor occupying the left child, then the processor occupying the right child can now 'claim' the parent cell. This continues until, at most, two processors reach level $\log(p) - 1$. At this point, each of them in turn reads the value stored in the root and the descent phase starts. During this phase, the value just read goes down the tree of memory cells until every request has been honored. The above simulation can be performed by the following algorithm:

```
begin {input: c(1),...,c(p)}
    for j = 1 to p do in parallel
    begin
        level(j) := 0;
        loc(j) := (p-1) + (j-1);
        M'_{c(j)(2p-1)+loc(j)} := marker_j;
```

```
  end;
  for k = 0 to log(p) − 2 do
  begin
    for j = 1 to p do in parallel
    begin
      temp(j)  :=  ⌊(loc(j) − 1)/2⌋;
      if loc(j) is odd and level(j) = k then
      begin
        loc(j)  :=  temp(j);
        M'_{c(j)(2p−1)+loc(j)}  :=  marker_j;
        level(j)  :=  level(j) + 1;
      end;
    end;
    for j = 1 to p do in parallel
      if M'_{c(j)(2p−1)+loc(j)} is not marked then
      begin
        loc(j)  :=  temp(j);
        M'_{c(j)(2p−1)+loc(j)}  :=  marker_j;
        level(j)  :=  level(j) + 1;
      end;
  end;
  for k = log(p) − 1 down to 0 do
  begin
    for j = 1 to p do in parallel
    begin
      temp(j)  :=  ⌊(loc(j) − 1)/2⌋;
      temp2(j)  :=  2loc(j) + 1;
      if loc(j) is odd and level(j) = k then
      begin
        M'_{c(j)(2p−1)+loc(j)}  :=  M'_{c(j)(2p−1)+temp(j)} ;
        level(j)  :=  level(j) − 1;
        if M'_{c(j)(2p−1)+temp2(j)} = marker_j then loc(j)  :=  temp2(j)
        else loc(j)  :=  temp2(j) + 1;
      end;
    end;
    for j = 1 to p do in parallel
      if loc(j) is even and level(j) = k then
      begin
        M'_{c(j)(2p−1)+loc(j)}  :=  M'_{c(j)(2p−1)+temp(j)};
        level(j)  :=  level(j) − 1;
        if M'_{c(j)(2p−1)+temp2(j)} = marker_j then loc(j)  :=  temp2(j)
        else loc(j)  :=  temp2(j) + 1;
      end;
  end;
end.
```

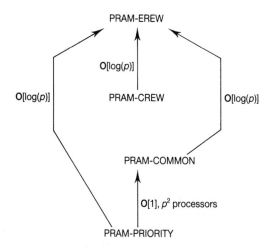

Figure 11.8 Relations between some PRAM models

Clearly, both the ascent and descent phases require $\mathbf{O}[\log(p)]$ steps. □

Lemma 11.3 Any set of simultaneous concurrent write operations of p processors can be simulated by, at most, $\mathbf{O}[\log(p)]$ exclusive-write operations of the same p-processors.

Proof. The proof is similar to that of the previous lemma and is left as an exercise (see Problem 11.14). □

Theorem 11.5 Any PRAM-CREW (alternatively, PRAM-COMMON, PRAM-PRIORITY) algorithm using p processors admits an equivalent PRAM-EREW algorithm. Moreover, t steps of the former algorithm can be simulated by the latter one in $\mathbf{O}[\log(p)t]$ steps.

Proof. The proof follows from the two previous lemmas. □

Figure 11.8 summarizes the relationships between the four PRAM models obtained so far.

The following two examples show that two of the bounds obtained in Theorem 11.5 cannot be improved. In particular, they yield separations between the PRAM-EREW and the PRAM-CREW on the one hand, and between the PRAM-COMMON and the PRAM-CREW on the other.

Example 11.5 Given N distinct keys k_i and a search key k^*, we want to determine whether k^* is equal to some k_i. Assuming a PRAM-CREW is available, a parallel search requiring constant time can be made and, at most, one processor, if any, will write a 1 in cell M_0. The concurrent read feature is necessary to allow the N processors to read in parallel the same value k^*.

A simple argument shows that without such a feature the same problem cannot be solved in constant time. The key observation is that when reads are exclusive, each step of the PRAM allows a given piece of information to be copied to, at most, one other memory cell. Thus the number of cells that can contain a given piece of information, at most, doubles with each step. After a constant number of steps, only a constant number of processors can thus know the value k^* and, clearly, a constant number of processors is not sufficient to perform the search in constant time.

Example 11.6 Given N distinct numbers n_i, we want to determine the maximum among them. Assuming that a PRAM-CRCW is available, N^2 processors can be used to compare all the pairs of numbers n_i and n_j and to 'mark' the smaller value. Successively, exactly one processor, that is, the one reading the single unmarked number, will write it in cell M_0. Clearly, the above operations require constant time. The concurrent write feature is necessary to allow concurrent mark operations. As in the previous example, the same problem cannot be solved in constant time without such a feature.

11.5   Relations between circuits and PRAMs

In this section we compare the two above parallel models of computation, namely circuits and PRAMs, by establishing a relation between size and depth on the one hand, and number of processors and time on the other.

Before proceeding, let us point out that a uniformity condition must be imposed on the family of PRAM programs dealing with inputs of length n since we do not want to specify a different program for any n. For that purpose, we shall say that a PRAM algorithm is *uniform* if the program can be derived, for any input length n, by a deterministic Turing machine requiring logarithmic space. Intuitively, all programs parameterized by n are uniform.

Theorem 11.6 A uniform circuit family of size $s(n)$ and depth $d(n)$ can be simulated by a uniform PRAM-PRIORITY algorithm using $\mathbf{O}[s(n)]$ active processors and running in time $\mathbf{O}[d(n)]$.

Conversely, a uniform PRAM-PRIORITY algorithm requiring $p(n)$ active processors and running in time $t(n)$ can be simulated by an unbounded fan-in uniform circuit family having polynomial size with respect to $p(n)$ and linear depth with respect to $t(n)$.

Proof. We assume without loss of generality (see Problem 11.1) that the $\neg$ gates of the circuits have been pushed back to the inputs and eliminated by supplying twice as many input gates. In the simulation of a circuit c_n by a PRAM, a distinct processor is assigned to each circuit line and a distinct memory cell is assigned to each circuit gate. Denote by $n + q$ the number of gates of c_n. Initially, the inputs or input gates are in memory cells M_i with $1 \leq i \leq n$ and the q circuit gates are in memory cells M_{n+j} with $1 \leq j \leq q$.

The simulation can be described by the following algorithm:

begin {input: $x_1, \ldots, x_n$}
   for $i = 1$ **to** q **do in parallel**
     if $o_{n+i} = \vee$ **then** $M_{n+i} := 0$ **else** $M_{n+i} := 1$;
   for $k = 1$ **to** $d(n)$ **do**
   begin
     for any circuit line $e = (g_i, g_j)$ **do in parallel**
       $value(e) := M_i$;
     for any circuit line $e = (g_i, g_j)$ **do in parallel**
       if $((value(e) = 0)$ **and** $(o_j = \vee))$ **or** $((value(e) = 1)$ **and** $(o_j = \wedge))$ **then**
         $M_j := value(e)$;
     for any circuit line $e = (g_i, g_j)$ **do in parallel**
       if $((value(e) = 1)$ **and** $(o_j = \vee))$ **or** $((value(e) = 0)$ **and** $(o_j = \wedge))$ **then**
         $M_j := value(e)$;
   end;
end.

Clearly, after $\mathbf{O}[d(n)]$ steps, memory cell M_{n+i} has the value of gate i for $i = 1, \ldots, n+q$ and this proves the first part of the theorem (notice how the concurrent writes in the same memory cell are needed by the above simulation).

Conversely, we note that each of the binary operations in the instruction set of a PRAM can be implemented by constant-depth, polynomial size circuit with unbounded fan-in (see Problem 11.19). It is also fairly easy to implement conditional branching by such circuits by suitably updating the program counter. The non-trivial part of the simulation lies in simulating the memory accesses. Since combinatorial circuits have no memory, the simulation retains all the values that are written in a given memory cell during the computation, and has a bit associated with each such value that indicates whether the value is current or not. With this scheme, it is not difficult to construct a constant-depth, unbounded fan-in circuit to implement reads and writes into memory (see Problem 11.18). Thus, a single step of the PRAM can be simulated by an unbounded fan-in circuit of polynomial size and constant depth and the second part of the theorem follows (we leave as an exercise to the reader the task of proving that the circuit family obtained is uniform). □

Note that, according to Lemma 11.1, the second part of the above theorem can be suitably extended to circuits with bounded fan-in.

11.6 The parallel computation thesis

Assume that a time-complexity class of languages has been defined by making use of a parallel model of computation. Is it possible to characterize the same class by a sequential model of computation, namely the deterministic Turing machine? The study of several models of parallel computation has shown that by putting suitable limitations on both the number and the power of the parallel processors a general rule seems to hold which has been called the *Parallel computation thesis*.

Denote by $\mathcal{P}$ a parallel model of computation. The thesis holds for the model $\mathcal{P}$ if two polynomials p and q exist such that

$$\text{P-TIME}[f(n)] \subseteq \text{DSPACE}[p(f(n))] \text{ and } \text{DSPACE}[g(n)] \subseteq \text{P-TIME}[q(g(n))]$$

where, as usual, the notation $\text{P-TIME}[f(n)]$ denotes the class of languages decided by model $\mathcal{P}$ in time $\mathbf{O}[f(n)]$. More concisely, the thesis states that *parallel time is polynomially related to sequential space*.

Although the above thesis does not hold for all parallel models of computation (see Notes), it does for the two models we have considered and this gives further assurance that we are dealing with models that are coherent with each other.

Theorem 11.7 PRAMs and uniform circuit families satisfy the parallel computation thesis.

Proof. According to Theorem 11.6, we need to prove the theorem for only one model, namely for the uniform circuit families.

For the first part of the thesis, consider a circuit of size $s(n)$ and depth $d(n)$. Given a description of this circuit together with an input, a deterministic Turing machine can compute its output in $\mathbf{O}[d(n)]$ space by starting from the output gates and working its way back to the input gates while using a stack to keep track of the paths taken. Since the depth of the circuit is $d(n)$, the stack has, at most, $d(n)$ entries, each of which has constant size; hence, the value computed by the circuit can be evaluated in $\mathbf{O}[d(n)]$ space. The theorem then follows from the uniformity condition.

Let us now prove the second part of the thesis, namely that sequential space is polynomially related to parallel time. Denote by g a space-constructible function bounding the space used by T. The number of global states is, at most, $m = 2^{cg(n)}$ for some constant c. Again, we assume that only one accepting global state, say $\mathcal{S}_m$, exists and we denote by $\mathcal{S}_1$ the initial global state.

The general algorithm to be implemented on a specific parallel model is the following. First, an m by m transition matrix A is constructed in parallel. An entry $A(i, j)$ is set to 1 if global state $\mathcal{S}_j$ can be reached from $\mathcal{S}_i$ by executing a 0 or 1 quintuple of T, otherwise it is set to 0. Next, the transitive closure of A, that is, the matrix $B = A^m$, is computed. It can immediately be verified that T accepts x if and only if $B(1, m) = 1$, that is, if a sequence of global states exists which allows T to evolve from $\mathcal{S}_1$ to $\mathcal{S}_m$.

It is not hard to verify (see Problem 11.20) that A can be computed in $\mathbf{O}[\log(m)]$ steps by making use of a uniform family of circuits. On the other hand, we shall see in the next chapter that B can be computed in $\mathbf{O}[\log^2(m)]$ steps, that is, in $\mathbf{O}[g^2(n)]$ steps by making use of a parallel model of computation.

Note that since the algorithm deals with matrices whose sizes are exponential with respect to the input size, there is little hope when using this approach of simulating sequential space in parallel time with realistic parallel computers.   ☐

Problems

11.1. Prove that any circuit with $\vee, \wedge$ and $\neg$ gates can be transformed into an equivalent circuit where the $\neg$ gates have been pushed back to the inputs and eliminated by supplying $2n$ input gates instead of n. Show that if the original circuit has size $s(n)$ and depth $d(n)$, the new circuit has size $\mathbf{O}[s(n)]$ and depth $\mathbf{O}[d(n)]$.

11.2. Prove that the function g defined in the proof of Theorem 11.1 is such that $g(n) < 2^{n+2}$. Show that if additional binary Boolean functions are allowed, the bound can be lowered to 2^n. [Hint: lower the value of $g(n)$ for $n = 2$ from 8 to 1 by making use of other functions and modify the recursive scheme.]

11.3. Prove that every language in P can be decided by a circuit family having a polynomial size. [Hint: recall how a Turing machine can be simulated by a circuit family.]

11.4. Consider the well-known adder circuit consisting of n smaller identical circuits, one for each bit of the operands x and y. The inputs of such circuits are the bits x_i, y_i of the operands and the carry bit c_i from the previous stage. The outputs are the sum bit z_i and the next carry bit c_{i+1}. It is easy to prove that this family of circuits is uniform and, in fact, one can immediately derive circuit c_{n+1} from circuit c_n by concatenating to it another identical circuit. From this specific example are we allowed to state that if c_{n+1} can be derived from c_n by adding a constant number of gates, then the corresponding family is logspace uniform? Justify the answer.

11.5. Give a polynomial-time algorithm to solve CIRCUIT VALUE.

11.6. Assume that two functions f and g can be computed by two logspace-uniform circuit families of depth, respectively, $d_1(n)$ and $d_2(n)$. Prove that an uniform circuit family exists which computes $f(g(x))$ and define its depth in terms of d_1 and d_2.

11.7. Show that a language $L \in \text{DSPACE}[2^{n^k}]$ for some constant k exists which cannot be decided by a circuit family having a polynomial size. [Schöning (1985)]

11.8. A language L is said to be *p-selective* if a function $f \in \text{FP}$ exists such that, for any x and y,

   1. $f(x,y) \in \{x, y\}$.

2. If $x \in L$ or $y \in L$, then $f(x, y) \in L$.

Prove that if L is p-selective then it can be decided by a circuit family having a polynomial size. [Hint: show that, for any n, a language $L' \subseteq L_n$ exists with $|L'| \leq n + 1$ such that, for any x, $x \in L_n$ if and only if $(\exists y \in L')[f(x, y) = x \vee f(y, x) = x]$.]

11.9. Show that any PRAM algorithm requiring p processors and t steps can be simulated by a RAM algorithm in time $\mathbf{O}[tp]$.

11.10. The performance of a PRAM algorithm may vary depending on whether the number of operands is part of the input or whether it must be computed dynamically. In the second case, what is the cost of determining such a number?

11.11. Describe a simulation of a MIMD-PRAM by a SIMD-PRAM which has a $\mathbf{O}[\log(p)]$ overhead where p denotes the maximum number of active processors. [Hint: since the MIMD-PRAM program has a constant length, say k, the p processors can be partitioned into k groups and all processors in a group can be run in parallel executing the same instruction. Some bookkeeping has to be done in order to update the k lists of processors after each instruction execution.]

11.12. Consider a MIMD-PRAM which has, at most, p active processors and assume that processor activation is done via a **fork** instruction whose effect is to activate a second processor in addition to the one issuing the instruction. As a result, $\mathbf{O}[\log(p)]$ steps are needed in order to activate p processors. Describe a simulation of this type of MIMD-PRAM by a SIMD-PRAM which has a constant overhead. [Hint: partition the computation of the MIMD-PRAM in $\log(p)$-step blocks and double at each step the number of processors. Then compact the p^2 SIMD-PRAM processors so that the active ones effectively correspond to the active MIMD-PRAM processors.]

11.13. Give an efficient PRAM-EREW algorithm to make n copies of the same piece of information.

11.14. Prove Lemma 11.3.

11.15. Define a *strong PRAM-CRCW* as a PRAM-CRCW in which the value written in any concurrent write is the largest of the values the processors are attempting to write. Show how to simulate such a strong PRAM-CRCW by a PRAM-COMMON with a constant overhead.

11.16. Define a *weak PRAM-CRCW* as a PRAM-CRCW in which concurrent writes are allowed only if all processors performing a concurrent write are writing the value 0. How do a weak PRAM-CRCW compare with a PRAM-COMMON?

11.17. Prove that a parallel computation which requires t steps on a strong PRAM-CRCW with, at most, p active processors can also be simulated in $\mathbf{O}[t \log(p)]$ steps by a PRAM-EREW with the same number of processors. [Nassimi and Sahni (1981)]

11.18. Describe a circuit with unbounded fan-in, polynomial size, and constant depth simulating the read/write operations relative to a memory cell. [Hint: model the instruction counter as a set of binary variables corresponding to the cell currently addressed and to the time step. Model the memory cells as sets of binary variables corresponding to the cell address and contents and to the the time step. Use an additional variable for each cell address a and for each step t which is equal to 1 only if the istruction counter at step t contains the value a.]

11.19. Show that each PRAM instruction can be implemented by a constant-depth, polynomial size, and unbounded fan-in circuit.

11.20. Describe a uniform circuit family which constructs the matrix A introduced in the proof of Theorem 11.7. Show that the depth of such a family is $\mathbf{O}[\log(m)]$. [Hint: make use of the circuit layers shown in Figure 11.4.]

11.21. Extend Theorem 11.7 by showing that nondeterministic sequential space is polynomially related to parallel time.

Notes

As stated in the introduction to this chapter, many models of parallel computers have been proposed which range from very primitve to quite sophisticated machines. We have chosen to present only two, namely the circuits and the PRAMs. For additional information on parallel models of computations we refer the reader to the survey by van Emde Boas (1990).

A large bibliography on circuits is available. To the interested reader we suggest the introductory text by Harison (1965) and that by Savage (1976) illustrating the relations existing between circuits and Turing machines.

Circuit complexity started with Shannon (1949), where the size of the smallest circuit computing a function was first proposed as a measure of complexity. Theorem 11.1 is a slightly modified version of a result appeared in Lupanov (1958) where all sixteen possible dyadic Boolean functions were considered. This result was strengthened in Harison (1965), where it was shown that for each n-variable Boolean function f,

$$SIZE(f) \leq (1 + \epsilon(n))2^n/n \text{ with } \epsilon(n) \in \mathbf{O}[n^{-1/2}].$$

The converse of Lupanov's theorem, that is, Theorem 11.2, is due to Riordan and Shannon (1942).

Circuit families were investigated in depth since the existence of lower bounds on circuit complexity imply separation results for some important complexity classes. As an example, it was shown in Karp and Lipton (1980) that if all languages in LEXP had a polynomial circuit complexity, then LEXP would coincide with Σ_2^p. Moreover, by limiting the capabilities of the computation model it may be easier to prove lower bounds on the complexity of specific problems, thus leading to lower bounds for more powerful models. However, despite many efforts, no exponential lower bound is known for the circuit complexity of a problem in NP (which, according to Theorem 11.3, would imply P $\neq$ NP). Indeed, the best of such bounds is linear and is due to Blum (1984).

The connection between circuit size and Turing machine time, that is Theorem 11.3, was first shown in Savage (1972). In Pippenger and Fischer (1979) the size of the circuit family was lowered from $f^2(n)$ to $f(n)\log(n)$.

The distinction between non-uniform and uniform circuit complexity is studied exhaustively in Ruzzo (1981). The same paper describes five different uniformity conditions and shows that uniform circuit complexity is relatively insensitive to the choice of the definition. The logspace-uniformity was introduced in Cook (1979) as an extension of the uniformity proposed by Borodin (1977). Indeed, the notation u_{BC}-uniform is also used as a mnemonic for the names of the two authors.

The PRAM model was introduced in Fortune and Wyllie (1978). Our definition of MIMD-PRAM is quite similar to the original one. The only noticeable difference is that processor activation was done via a special instruction called **fork** as described in Problem 11.12.

In the same spirit, SIMD-PRAMS are equivalent to a parallel model denoted as SIMDAG which was introduced in Goldschlager (1982). As a minor variation, we have replaced the infinite local memories of SIMDAGs with finite ones (namely, the registers IND and ACC) and we have suppressed the SIMDAG's central processor by forcing all parallel processors to execute the *same* instruction simultaneously.

Although only two CRCW models (namely, COMMON and PRIORITY) were introduced, several other interesting models were proposed, some of which have been implemented on existing parallel computers. For additional information, we refer the reader to Vishkin (1984), Groslmusz and Radge (1987) and to the survey by Eppstein and Galil (1988).

The comparison of PRAM models has been an active field of research. Theorem 11.4 is taken from Kucera (1982) while the multiple broadcast technique used to prove Lemmas 11.2 and 11.3 is attributed to Eckstein (1979) and nicely presented in Akl (1989). The separation results illustrated in Examples 11.5 and 11.6 are due to Snir (1983) and Kucera (1982), respectively. Another important separation result showing that the PRAM-CREW is strictly less powerful than the PRAM-CRCW appeared in Cook, Dwork, and Reischuk (1986). A more refined analysis of the relations among several policies to solve memory conflicts which takes into account the number of memory cells shared by the processors can be found in Fich, Radge, and Widgerson (1988).

The relations between circuits and PRAMs were investigated in Stockmeyer and Vishkin (1984).

The parallel computation thesis was successively verified by Pratt and Stockmeyer (1976) for a parallel model called a vector machine, by Borodin (1977) for circuits, and by Fortune and Wyllie (1978) for the MIMD-PRAM model. Finally, Goldschlager (1982) verified it both for the SIMD-PRAM and for another model called conglomerate. As pointed out in van Emde Boas (1990), it is easy to define parallel models of computation which do not obey the parallel computation thesis. If we allow, for instance, the PRAM to be nondeterministic, or if we add powerful arithmetic operations to its instruction set, the model becomes too powerful and the proof techniques of Theorem 11.7 no longer apply. In fact, compliance with the parallel computation thesis should be viewed not as a general rule, but rather as an insurance that the parallel model considered is reasonable.

Chapter 12

Parallel algorithms

It is now time to make use of the parallel models of computation introduced in the previous chapter. Our main objective will be to characterize the problems that are most suited for being solved by a parallel computer.

Intuitively, the main reason for our interest in parallel algorithms is the possibility of speeding up the solution of problems, that is, of obtaining algorithms whose running time is far better than that of the corresponding fastest known sequential algorithms. For instance, in Example 11.4 we were able to sum N numbers in $O[\log(N)]$ steps while it is known that no sublinear sequential algorithm exists to compute the same function. However, another important criterion in evaluating a parallel algorithm is the number of processors it requires, not only because of the communication costs mentioned in the previous chapter, but also because it costs money to purchase, maintain and run computers and the price paid to guarantee a high degree of reliability increases sharply with the number of processors.

The above two measures, namely parallel time and number of processors, are sometimes combined yielding the so-called *cost* of a parallel algorithm which is defined as the product of those two quantities. In other words, the cost equals the number of steps executed collectively by all processors in solving the problem. Clearly, the cost of a parallel algorithm cannot be less than the sequential lower bound. This is because any parallel algorithm can be simulated by a sequential computer as stated in Problem 11.9. Whenever the cost of a parallel algorithm matches the lower bound, that algorithm is usually said to be *optimal* since it cannot be improved. It may be possible, of course, to reduce the running time of an optimal parallel algorithm by using more processors (conversely, fewer processors may be used if we are willing to settle for a higher running time). We shall prefer, however, to consider the parallel time and the number of processors separately and our goal will be to develop parallel algorithms which achieve a significant speed-up while maintaining the number of processors tractable. As usual, significant denotes exponential while tractable stands for polynomial (with respect to the input size).

These considerations will lead us to introduce in Section 12.1 a new complexity class denoted as NC which includes all problems that can be efficiently solved by parallel computers. Next, an alternative characterization of NC is given showing that the definition of this new class does not depend on the type of parallel model of computation considered. The inner structure of NC is considered in Section 12.2 where a few significant fast parallel algorithms of different complexity are presented while randomized parallel algorithms are briefly discussed in Section 12.3. Finally, we conclude our study of the complexity of parallel algorithms in Section 12.4 by providing a simple characterization of problems that do not seem to admit fast parallel algorithms.

12.1 The class NC

Let us be more precise about the definition of fast parallel algorithm. Such an algorithm will be considered fast if it requires polylogarithmic parallel time, that is, $O[\log^k(n)]$ steps for some constant k, while making use of a number of processors which is polynomially bounded with respect to the input size.

Both requirements are rather stringent. The first rules out trivial parallelizations consisting of splitting the problem into simpler ones and then combining together the partial results as shown in the following example.

Example 12.1 A rather inefficient method for finding the largest among n components of a vector consists of breaking the problem into $\sqrt{n}$ subproblems of $\sqrt{n}$ elements each. First, an optimal sequential algorithm is applied in parallel to each subproblem and, in a second phase, the same algorithm is used to determine the largest among the $\sqrt{n}$ elements computed previously. The number of parallel steps required is $O[\sqrt{n}]$ while it is easy to verify that more efficient parallel algorithms requiring $O[\log(n)]$ steps do exist.

The second requirement is also essential not only from a practical point of view as already discussed in the introduction but also from a theoretical point of view since a hyperpolynomial number of processors would make the parallel model too powerful with respect to conventional Turing machines.

Example 12.2 By making use of 2^n processors, it is possible to solve any instance of NODE COVER referring to graphs of n nodes in parallel polynomial time. In the first step, each processor converts its index into a binary vector. Next, each processor checks whether the number of ones in the binary vector is, at most, k and, if so, whether the nodes associated with the ones represent a node cover for the graph. In other words, if the model includes an exponential number of processors, then it is able to solve in parallel polynomial time any NP-complete problem.

Let us now give a formal definition, based on logspace-uniform circuit families, of the class of problems which admit fast parallel algorithms.

A language L belongs to the *class NC^k* with $k = 1, 2, \ldots$ if a logspace-uniform circuit family C and a constant h exist such that

1. C decides L.
2. $SIZE_C(n) \in \mathbf{O}[n^h]$.
3. $DEPTH_C(n) \in \mathbf{O}[\log^k(n)]$.

Now the *class NC* can be defined as

$$\mathrm{NC} = \bigcup_{k \geq 1} \mathrm{NC}^k.$$

Similarly, we define the classes FNC^k and FNC as the classes of functions computable in polylogarithmic depth and in polynomial size by uniform circuit families.

The class NC includes all problems which admit fast parallel algorithms while the index k of the subclass NC^k provides further information on the inherent 'parallelizability' of problems in that class. As in the case of the class P, most 'natural' problems in NC can be placed in the first few levels.

12.1.1   Some properties of NC

As shown in the following lemma, the class NC is a subset of the class P. As we shall see in Section 12.4, it is conjectured that the inclusion is strict although no proof exists at present.

Lemma 12.1 $\mathrm{NC} \subseteq \mathrm{P}$.

Proof. Given any language $L \in \mathrm{NC}$, denote by C the uniform circuit family which decides it in polylogarithmic time. Since C is uniform, a Turing machine T exists which derives, for any input x of length n, the corresponding circuit encoding $\bar{c}_n$ in logarithmic space with respect to $SIZE_C(n)$, and thus in polynomial time with respect to n. A deterministic Turing machine T' can then be defined which first simulates T deriving the circuit c_n and then solves the corresponding CIRCUIT VALUE instance. Since the circuit has, at most, a polynomial number of nodes, this task can also be performed in polynomial time. $\square$

We have already seen in Theorem 11.7 how sequential space is polynomially related to parallel time. As an application of that theorem, we can relate the classes LOGSPACE and NLOGSPACE introduced in Chapter 8 with the first two levels of NC.

Lemma 12.2 $\mathrm{NC}^1 \subseteq \mathrm{LOGSPACE} \subseteq \mathrm{NLOGSPACE} \subseteq \mathrm{NC}^2$.

Proof. The first inclusion derives from the first part of the proof of Theorem 11.7.

The third inclusion derives from the second part of the proof of the same theorem. Although the matrices to be computed by the circuit family have an exponential size with respect to the input length, since global states have a logarithmic length, the number of gates required is polynomial with respect to the input length and the algorithm belongs to NC^2 (see also Problem 11.21). □

In addition to the logspace reducibility introduced in Chapter 8, some other reducibilities such as the FNC^1 and the FNC reducibilities denoted as $\leq_{NC^1}$ and $\leq_{NC}$, respectively, have also been considered and used to prove the membership of a problem in NC. As a consequence of the previous lemma, we may state that logspace reducibility is somehow included between the FNC^1 and the FNC reducibilities. In general, it can be shown that NC is closed with respect to any of these three reducibilities.

Lemma 12.3 NC is closed with respect to the logspace, the FNC^1 and the FNC reducibilities.

Proof. According to Lemma 12.2, it is sufficient to show that if a language L belongs to NC^k for some $k > 0$ and if $L' \leq_{NC} L$ holds, then L' belongs to NC. Indeed, $L' \leq_{NC} L$ implies that a uniform transducer circuit family having some depth, say $O[\log^h(n)]$, and transforming words of L' into corresponding words of L must exist. For any input length n, the transducer circuit c'_n of depth $O[\log^h(n)]$ and the acceptor circuit c_n of depth $O[\log^k(n)]$ can be cascaded together obtaining a new circuit of depth $O[\log^{k'}(n)]$ with $k' = \max\{h, k\}$. It is easy to verify that the cascading operation maintains the uniformity condition (see Problem 12.1). Thus the language L' belongs to $NC^{k'}$ and consequently to NC. □

12.1.2 An alternative characterization of NC

The reader may object to the fact that the previous characterization of NC is based on a rather unrealistic model of computation such as the uniform circuit family while it has been repeatedly noticed that parallel algorithms are best expressed by referring to PRAMs.

We can answer such a criticism by introducing new classes denoted as AC^k and AC whose definition is based on uniform PRAM-PRIORITY algorithms (recall that a PRAM algorithm is uniform if it can be derived, for any input length n, by a deterministic Turing machine requiring logarithmic space with respect to n). The *classes AC^k* with $k = 1, 2, \ldots$ are defined as the classes of languages decided by uniform PRAMs in $O[\log^k(n)]$ steps with a polynomial number of active processors. The *class AC* is then defined as

$$AC = \bigcup_{k \geq 1} AC^k.$$

We already know from Theorem 11.6 that the same classes AC^k can be alternatively defined as the classes of languages decidable by logspace uniform circuit families with unbounded fan-in of depth $O[\log^k(n)]$ and of polynomial size.

By combining that theorem and Lemma 11.1 we obtain a new lemma which establishes a close correlation between the classes NC^k and AC^k.

Lemma 12.4 For all $k \geq 1$, $NC^k \subseteq AC^k \subseteq NC^{k+1}$.

As stated in the next corollary, we have thus shown that a definition of NC in terms of PRAMs does exist.

Corollary 12.1 NC = AC.

12.2   Examples of NC problems

Let us begin by describing a few fast parallel algorithms which are slightly more complex than those considered in the previous chapter. The first deals with a classical problem in computer science.

Example 12.3 Sorting the n components of a vector $x = x_1, \ldots, x_n$ can be done in $\mathbf{O}[\log(n)]$ steps by an enumeration algorithm. The position in which x_j should be placed is calculated by counting the number of x_is that are no greater than x_j:

begin {input: $x = x_1, \ldots, x_n$}
   for each pair i, j of processor indices **do in parallel**
     if $x_i \leq x_j$ **then** $a[i, j] := 1$ **else** $a[i, j] := 0$;
   for $j = 1$ **to** n **do in parallel**
     $b[j] := \sum_{i=1}^{n} a[i, j]$ by algorithm of Example 11.4;
   for $i = 1$ **to** n **do in parallel**
     $y[b[i]] := x[i]$;
end.

The above algorithm makes use of n^2 processors. Note that if some x_i occurs k times, it will appear in the resulting vector y only once preceded by $k-1$ empty entries. It is easy to extend the above algorithm allowing y to include identical entries (see Problem 12.2).

The next two examples revisit from a parallel point of view problems already considered in previous chapters.

Example 12.4 The problem SHORTEST WEIGHTED PATH is similar to SHORTEST PATH already considered in Example 4.3, except that the graph is weighted, that is, each edge $\langle n_i, n_j \rangle$ is characterized by a positive integer called weight and denoted as $w(n_i, n_j)$. Clearly, the length of a path is the sum of the weights of the edges included in it and the problem consists of finding the shortest path lengths between all pair of nodes.

Let us present a fast parallel algorithm which solves SHORTEST WEIGHTED PATH in $\mathbf{O}[\log^2(n)]$ steps with n^2 processors.

Let $A^h(i,j)$ be the length of the shortest path from node i to node j containing, at most, h edges. Since a path from i to j containing, at most, $2h$ edges can be divided into two paths of, at most, h edges each, we have that

$$A^{2h}(i,j) = min_{k \in \{1,2,...,n\}} (A^h(i,k) + A^h(k,i)).$$

Taking into account that a shortest path contains, at most, $n-1$ edges, we obtain the following algorithm which makes use of the $\mathbf{O}[\log(n)]$ parallel algorithm for finding the minimum among n elements:

begin {input: $G = (N, E)$}
   $n := |N|$;
   for any pair i, j of processor indices **do in parallel**
      $A^1[i,j] := w(n_i, n_j)$;
   for $m := 1$ **to** $\lceil \log(n) \rceil$ **do**
   begin
      $h := 2^m$;
      for any pair i, j of processor indices **do in parallel**
         $A^h[i,j] := min\{A^{h/2}[i,k] + A^{h/2}[k,j] : 1 \le k \le n\}$;
   end;
end.

Example 12.5 Let us describe an efficient parallel algorithm for the problem SCHEDUL-ING FIXED JOBS introduced in Example 6.8. The algorithm consists of four distinct phases:

1. Compute the number σ_j of machines that are busy just after the start of job J_j and the number τ_j of machines that are busy just before the completion of J_j $(j = 1, \ldots, n)$.

2. For each job J_j, determine its immediate predecessor $J_{\pi(j)}$ on the same machine (if it exists). The same stacking discipline used in the sequential algorithm implies that this job must be, among the σ_j jobs to be executed after the start of J_j, the one that terminates last before the start of J_j.

3. For each job J_j, set $J_{\pi(j)}$ as its first predecessor on the same machine.

4. Use the $J_{\pi(j)}$s to perform the actual machine scheduling.

Figure 12.1 shows an application of the above algorithm to the scheduling problem illustrated in Figure 6.1.

The full parallel algorithm can then be stated as follows:

begin {input: $s_1, t_1, \ldots, s_n, t_n$}
   {phase 1}
   sort in parallel the s_j, t_j in non-decreasing order in $(u_1, \ldots, u_{2n})$,
   if $t_j = s_k$ for some j, k then insert t_j before s_k in u;
   for $k = 1$ **to** $2n$ **do in parallel**
      if $u_k \sim s_j$ **then** $\alpha_k := 1$ **else** $\alpha_k := -1$;

j:	1	2	3	4	5	6
s_j:	0	0	3	4	7	6
t_j:	2	8	6	7	9	8

σ_j:	2	2	2	3	3	3
τ_j:	2	3	3	3	1	3

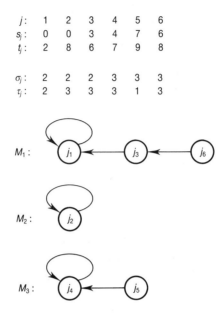

M_1 :

M_2 :

M_3 :

Figure 12.1 Parallel assignment of jobs to machines

for $k = 1$ **to** $2n$ **do in parallel**
    $\beta_k := \alpha_1 + \ldots + \alpha_k$;
for $k = 1$ **to** $2n$ **do in parallel**
begin
    if $u_k \sim s_j$ **then** $\sigma_j := \beta_k$;
    if $u_k \sim t_j$ **then** $\tau_j := \beta_k + 1$;
end;
{phase 2}
for $j = 1$ **to** n **do in parallel**
begin
    find k such that $\tau_k = \sigma_j$ and $t_k = \max\{t_m : t_m \leq s_j, \tau_m = \sigma_j\}$;
    if k exists **then** $\pi(j) := k$ **else** $\pi(j) := j$;
end;
{phase 3}
for $l = 1$ **to** $\lceil \log(n) \rceil$ **do**
    for $j = 1$ **to** n **do in parallel** $\pi(j) := \pi(\pi(j))$;
{phase 4}
for $j = 1$ **to** n **do in parallel**
    assign machine $\sigma_{\pi(j)}$ to job J_j;
end.

By making use of the maximum, sum and sorting parallel algorithms described in previous examples, it is easy to verify that this algorithm requires $\mathbf{O}[\log(n)]$ time and $\mathbf{O}[n^2]$ processors.

The next two examples deal with integer matrix computations. In particular, they refer to the widely used product and power operations.

Example 12.6 The product of two square matrices A and B of n^2 elements can be computed in $\mathbf{O}[\log(n)]$ steps by a PRAM algorithm in the following way. First, n^3 processors are used to compute the products $a_{ik}b_{kj}$ with $1 \leq i, j, k \leq n$. Next, $n^3/2$ processors are used to compute the n^2 sums of the type $c_{ij} = \Sigma_{k=1}^{n} a_{ik}b_{kj}$ by making use of the algorithm described in Example 11.4.

Example 12.7 Given an $n \times n$ matrix A, it is possible to compute the matrix power A^n in $\mathbf{O}[\log^2(n)]$ steps by making use of a PRAM with $n^3/2$ active processors. Assume for simplicity that n is a power of 2. In the first step, the product A^2 is computed by making use of the parallel algorithm described in Example 12.6; in the next step, the same algorithm is applied to compute A^4, and so on. After the $\log(n)$th step, the value A^n has been computed.

12.2.1   Inverting a matrix

A more ambitious task consists of describing a fast parallel algorithm to compute the inverse of a $n \times n$ matrix of integers. We recall that the inverse A^{-1} of a matrix A is such that $AA^{-1} = I = A^{-1}A$ where I denotes the *identity matrix*, that is, the diagonal matrix with 1s along the diagonal.

Inverting a lower triangular matrix
Let us start with a simplified case where the matrix A to be inverted is assumed to be *lower triangular*, that is, such that all elements above the central diagonal are equal to 0 ($A[i, j] = 0$ for all $i < j$).

For this purpose, a divide-and-conquer technique will be used. According to the definition, A can be block-decomposed into four matrices of half its size, as follows:

$$A = \begin{pmatrix} A_{11} & 0 \\ A_{21} & A_{22} \end{pmatrix}$$

Since A is lower triangular, it follows that the upper right-hand submatrix is the zero matrix, and that A_{11} and A_{22} are lower triangular. The inverse of A is given by

$$A^{-1} = \begin{pmatrix} A_{11}^{-1} & 0 \\ -A_{22}^{-1}A_{21}A_{11}^{-1} & A_{22}^{-1} \end{pmatrix}$$

The above formula hints a recursive parallel algorithm for computing A^{-1}. In a first phase, A_{11}^{-1} and A_{22}^{-1} are computed recursively in parallel. Next, $-A_{22}^{-1}A_{21}A_{11}^{-1}$ is computed via two matrix multiplications. It is easy to verify that $\mathbf{O}[\log^2(n)]$ steps are sufficient.

Inverting an arbitrary matrix

To extend the previous result to arbitrary matrices we first need some preliminary definitions and results. Given an $n \times n$ matrix A, the *characteristic polynomial of A* is defined as

$$\varphi_A(x) = det(xI - A).$$

Lemma 12.5 For any $n \times n$ matrix A, $\varphi_A(x)$ is a polynomial of degree n such that the coefficient of x^n is 1 and the constant term is equal to $det(-A)$.

Proof. Clearly, $\varphi_A(x)$ is a polynomial of degree n. Moreover, it is easy to verify by induction on n that the coefficient of x^n is equal to 1. Finally, by simply setting $x = 0$ we obtain that the constant term of $\varphi_A(x)$ is equal to $det(-A)$.   □

From the above lemma it follows that computing the determinant of a matrix is no harder than computing the coefficients of its characteristic polynomial (remember that $det(A) = (-1)^n det(-A)$). Once we are able to compute the determinant, we can also invert the matrix as follows. The (j,i)th entry of A^{-1} is given by $(-1)^{i+j}det(A_{ij})/det(A)$ where A_{ij} is the matrix formed by removing the ith row and the jth column from A. Since all these calculations can be done in parallel, computing the inverse takes only a few steps more than computing the coefficients of a characteristic polynomial (even though a higher number of processors is required). Therefore, it remains to find an efficient parallel algorithm for computing such coefficients.

In order to do this, we define the *trace* of a matrix to be the sum of its diagonal entries. It is a simple fact from linear algebra that the trace of a matrix is equal to the sum of the roots of its characteristic polynomial, also called *eigenvalues*. Moreover, the eigenvalues of A^k are simply the kth powers of the eigenvalues of A.

Lemma 12.6 Given an $n \times n$ matrix A, the coefficients $c_1, \ldots, c_n$ of the characteristic polynomial of A satisfy the following equations:

$$s_{i-1}c_1 + s_{i-2}c_2 + \ldots + s_1c_{i-1} + ic_i = -s_i$$

where s_i denotes the trace of A^i, for $1 \le i \le n$.

Proof. Let $\lambda_1, \ldots, \lambda_n$ denote the eigenvalues of A. Then, we have that

$$x^n + c_1x^{n-1} + \ldots + c_{n-1}x + c_n = \prod_{i=1}^{n}(x - \lambda_i).$$

We will now prove the lemma by differentiating the two sides of the above equality. The derivative of the left-hand side is given by

$$nx^{n-1} + c_1(n-1)x^{n-2} + \ldots + c_{n-1}$$

while the derivative of the right-hand side is equal to

$$\sum_{i=1}^{n} \frac{\varphi_A(x)}{x - \lambda_i}.$$

By using the series expansion

$$\frac{1}{x - \lambda_i} = \frac{1}{x(1 - \lambda_i/x)} = \frac{1}{x}\left(1 + \frac{\lambda_i}{x} + \frac{\lambda_i^2}{x^2} + \ldots\right)$$

which is valid for $|x| > |\lambda_i|$, we obtain that the derivative of the right-hand side can also be written as

$$\frac{\varphi_A(x)}{x} \sum_{i=1}^{n}\left(1 + \frac{\lambda_i}{x} + \frac{\lambda_i^2}{x^2} + \ldots\right)$$

$$= (x^n + c_1 x^{n-1} + \ldots + c_{n-1}x + c_n)\left(\frac{n}{x} + \frac{s_1}{x^2} + \frac{s_2}{x^3} + \ldots\right).$$

Since the two derivatives must be equal for all values of x satisfying $|x| > |\lambda_i|$ for any i, it follows that the coefficients of each power of x must be the same. By comparing the first n coefficients we obtain, for $1 \le i \le n$,

$$c_i(n - i) = c_i n + s_{i-1}c_1 + s_{i-2}c_2 + \ldots + s_1 c_{i-1} + s_i,$$

that is,

$$s_{i-1}c_1 + s_{i-2}c_2 + \ldots + s_1 c_{i-1} + ic_i = -s_i$$

which is the desired system of equations. $\square$

The above lemma thus suggests the following algorithm for computing the coefficients of a characteristic polynomial:

1. Compute A^k for $k = 2, \ldots, n$.
2. Compute s_k for $k = 1, \ldots, n$.
3. Solve the system of equation of the previous lemma.

Clearly the first two steps can be performed efficiently in parallel. Also the last step can also be done efficiently in parallel. Indeed, it suffices to observe that the coefficient matrix of the system is lower triangular and thus invertible by means of the algorithm described previously.

In conclusion, the problem of computing the determinant of a matrix and thus that of inverting the matrix itself belongs to FNC.

The main application of matrix inversion consists of solving a system of n linear equations in n variables. Indeed, this is quite straightforward. Given the system

$$Ax = b$$

where A is an $n \times n$ matrix, x is an n-component row vector of variables x_i and b is an n-component column vector of numbers b_j, the solution can be obtained as

$$x = A^{-1}b.$$

Since fast parallel algorithms exist both for the matrix inversion and for the matrix product, solving a linear system of equations also belongs to FNC.

12.3   Probabilistic parallel algorithms

We already know from Chapter 9 that probabilistic algorithms with bounded error probability are found to be useful in efficiently solving some decision problems. In this section we investigate whether this claim still holds when making use of parallel computers. To that end, we first need a precise definition of a probabilistic parallel model of computation.

A *probabilistic circuit* is a circuit c_n with ordinary inputs $x = x_1 \ldots x_n$ and a polynomial number (with respect to n) of 'coin tossing' inputs $y = y_1 \ldots y_{p(n)}$. For any ordinary input x, the probability that the function f_{n+q} computed by c_n has value 1 is defined to be the fraction of input combinations y such that f_{n+q} has value 1.

The acceptance criterion of probabilistic circuits is the same as that of BPP machines, that is, the error probability must be, at most, $1/2 - \epsilon$ with $0 < \epsilon \leq 1/2$.

We can thus define RNC^k as the class of languages decided by a probabilistic uniform circuit family C with polynomial size and depth $\mathbf{O}[\log^k(n)]$. As usual, the *class* RNC (random NC) shall denote the infinite union of RNC^{k}s and the definition can be readily extended to the classes of functions FRNC^k and FRNC.

It is easy to show (see Problem 12.6) that RNC is included in BPP. It is not clear, however, whether RNC is included in NC or even in P.

As in the case of sequential probabilistic algorithms with bounded error probability, the error probability of probabilistic circuit families can be made arbitrarily small while maintaining the size polynomial and the depth polylogarithmic. In particular, one can arrange many copies of the same circuit (but with different coin tossing inputs) in parallel, each computing the same function, and a majority vote can be taken to obtain a reliable value.

Similarly, a *probabilistic PRAM* can be defined as a PRAM where each processor has the capability of making random choices while executing its program based on a common sequence of coin tossing inputs.

12.3.1   Testing for matching in bipartite graphs

A number of interesting problems have been shown to be in RNC. As for most probabilistic algorithms, these results are based on some probabilistic lemmas which ensure the correctness of the proposed algorithms. To acquaint the reader with this kind of result, in this section we present a fast parallel probabilistic algorithm for the following problem.

BIPARTITE PERFECT MATCHING: given a bipartite graph G, find a perfect matching (see Section 9.1.3) if it exists.

First observe that an RNC-algorithm for deciding whether a graph admits a perfect matching can be easily derived from the results of Sections 9.1.2 and 9.1.3 (see Problem 12.7). However, this result does not directly yield an RNC-algorithm for finding a perfect matching. For that purpose, we proceed as follows.

Let $U = \{u_1, \ldots, u_n\}$ and $V = \{v_1, \ldots, v_n\}$ be the two sets of nodes of the bipartite graph G and let A be the $n \times n$ adjacency matrix of G. Let us assign random integer weights to the edges of G chosen uniformly and independently from the set $\{1, \ldots, 2m\}$ where m is the number of edges. The binary matrix A can then be transformed into an integer matrix B by replacing each entry (i, j) equal to 1 in A by $2^{w_{ij}}$ where w_{ij} is the weight assigned to the edge $\langle u_i, v_j \rangle$.

The basic idea is that if it can be assumed that a *unique* perfect matching of minimum weight exists, then it can be derived at the cost of a single matrix inversion by the following sequential algorithm ($adj(B)$ denotes the *adjoint* matrix of B whose (i, j)th entry is $det(B_{ij})$):

begin {input: G, B}
    $M := \emptyset$;
    compute $det(B)$;
    $w := \max\{k : 2^k \text{ divides } det(B)\}$;
    compute $adj(B)$;
    for all edges $\langle u_i, v_j \rangle$ **do**
       if $adj(B)[i, j]2^{w_{ij}}/2^w$ is odd **then** $M := M \cup \{\langle u_i, v_j \rangle\}$;
end.

From the results of the previous section, it is easy to derive a fast parallel version of the above algorithm. The following lemma ensures that the set M computed by the above algorithm is the unique perfect matching of minimum weight.

Lemma 12.7 Suppose that a unique minimum weight perfect matching M exists and denote with w its weight. Then,

1. $det(B) \neq 0$.
2. $w = \max\{k : 2^k \text{ divides } det(B)\}$.
3. The edge $\langle u_i, v_j \rangle \in M$ if and only if $adj(B)[i,j]2^{w_{ij}}/2^w$ is odd.

Proof. First note that each perfect matching in G corresponds to a permutation π of $\{1, \ldots, n\}$. For each π let us define $v_\pi = \prod_{i=1}^n b_{i\pi(i)}$. Clearly, $v_\pi \neq 0$ if and only if $\langle u_i, v_{\pi(i)} \rangle$ is an edge of G for all is, that is, if and only if π represents a perfect matching. By definition,

$$det(B) = \sum_\pi \sigma_\pi \prod_{i=1}^n b_{i\pi(i)} = \sum_\pi \sigma_\pi v_\pi$$

where σ_π is 1 (respectively, -1) if π is an even (respectively, odd) permutation.

Let π_M be the permutation corresponding to the minimum weight perfect matching M. Then $v_{\pi_M} = 2^w$. For any other permutation π, $v_\pi = 0$ (π does not correspond to a perfect matching) or v_π is a power of 2 greater than 2^w (since M is the unique minimum weight perfect matching). Since a power of 2 cannot be obtained as an algebraic sum of higher powers of 2, it then follows that $det(B) \neq 0$. Moreover, it is clear that 2^w is the greatest power of 2 dividing $det(B)$.

To prove the third part of the lemma, let us first note that, according to the definitions of det and of minors, for any i, j,

$$det(B_{ij})2^{w_{ij}} = \sum_{\pi \text{ with } \pi(i)=j} \sigma_\pi v_\pi.$$

If the edge $\langle u_i, v_j \rangle$ belongs to M, then exactly one permutation, that is, π_M, in the above sum will have value 2^w. The remaining permutations have a value of either 0 or a higher power of 2. Thus, $det(B_{ij})2^{w_{ij}}/2^w$ will be odd. On the other hand, if $\langle u_i, v_j \rangle$ does not belong to M, all permutations in the sum either have a value of 0 or are a power of 2 greater then 2^w, hence $det(B_{ij})2^{w_{ij}}/2^w$ will be even. The lemma follows. □

It remains to be proven that by assigning random weights to the edges of G as stated above, the probability that a unique minimum weight perfect matching exists is sufficiently large. In order to prove this, we need the following lemma.

Lemma 12.8 Let $C = \{c_1, \ldots, c_m\}$ be any non-empty collection of subsets of $X = \{1, \ldots, n\}$ and let $w_1, \ldots, w_n$ be integer weights chosen uniformly and independently from $\{1, \ldots, 2n\}$. Associate with each set $c_j \in C$ a weight $w(c_j) = \sum_{i \in c_j} w_i$. Then, with a probability of at least $1/2$, the family C contains a unique minimum weight set.

Proof. Fix the weights of all elements of X except the ith one. Let us define the threshold of i to be the number α_i such that if $w_i \leq \alpha_i$, then i is contained in some minimum weight set of C, otherwise i is not contained in any such set.

Clearly, if $w_i < \alpha_i$, then i must be in every minimum weight set of C. Indeed, suppose that two minimum weight sets c and c' exist such that $i \in c$ and $i \notin c'$.

Thus, $w(c) = w(c')$. If we now set the weight of i to $w_i + 1$, then both c and c' are still minimum weight sets but they have different weights, which is, of course, a contradiction.

Hence, ambiguity about i occurs if and only if $w_i = \alpha_i$ since in this case two minimum weight sets exist, one containing i and the other not containing it. We now make the crucial observation that the threshold of i has been defined without reference to its weight: it follows that α_i is independent of w_i. Since w_i is chosen uniformly from $\{1, \ldots, 2n\}$, it then follows that the probability that $w_i = \alpha_i$ is, at most, $1/2n$.

Since X contains n elements, the probability that an element i exists such that $w_i = \alpha_i$ is, at most, $1/2$. Thus, with a probability of at least $1/2$, no ambiguous element exists. The lemma follows from the observation that a unique minimum weight set exists if and only if no ambiguous element exists. $\qquad\square$

We can then view the set of perfect matchings in G as the family C of the previous lemma. The lemma itself thus ensures that the minimum weight perfect matching in the weighted version of G will be unique with a probability of at least $1/2$. The above algorithm will identify this perfect matching. In conclusion, BIPARTITE PERFECT MATCHING belongs to RFNC. On the other hand, no FNC algorithm is known for the same problem.

12.4   P-complete problems revisited

We know from Lemma 12.1 that NC is included in P and it is conjectured that the inclusion is strict although no proof exists at present.

According to Lemma 12.3, NC is closed with respect to logspace-reducibility. Thus, if NC $\neq$ P holds, any problem which is P-complete with respect to $\leq_{log}$, in short a P-complete problem, must belong to P − NC.

P-complete problems thus play a second important role. Besides being problems that do not seem to be solvable in logarithmic space, it also appears that they do not admit fast parallel algorithms (in fact, the parallel computation thesis discussed in the previous chapter provides some hints in this direction).

Example 12.8 The P-completeness of SOLVABLE PATH SYSTEMS has been proved in Example 8.5, thus we are allowed to state that fast parallel algorithms for such a problem are unlikely to exist. It is interesting to note that the reason for which SOLVABLE PATH SYSTEMS does not seem to belong to LOGSPACE (the algorithm must keep in its memory the list of all the nodes that have been identified as connected to some source node of X_s) is different from the reason for which the same problem does not seem to admit fast parallel algorithms (even though the problem may be divided into subproblems, logical constraints forbid solving many subproblems in parallel).

Let us present a few more significant P-complete problems arising in several fields of combinatorics.

Example 12.9 The CIRCUIT VALUE problem has been defined in Example 11.2. The P-completeness of this problem follows immediately from Theorem 11.3 and by reasoning as in the proof of the NP-completeness of SATISFIABILITY. Indeed, it is easy to verify that the construction of the circuit described in the proof of Theorem 11.3 requires logarithmic space (see Problem 11.3).

Example 12.10 LINEAR PROGRAMMING: given an $n \times m$ integer matrix A, an n integer row vector B, an m integer column vector C and an integer k, does an m non-negative rational row vector X exist satisfying both $AX \leq B$ and $CX \geq k$? This problem has been shown to belong to P (see Notes) and it is also P-complete. A straightforward reduction can be obtained from CIRCUIT VALUE in the following way (we assume without loss of generality that the circuit does not include $\vee$ gates):

1. Transform each input gate g_j with value 1 into the equation $x_j = 1$ and each input gate g_j with value 0 into the equation $x_j = 0$ (note that an equality $x = y$ can be replaced by the two inequalities $x \leq y$ and $-x \leq -y$).

2. Transform each $\wedge$ gate g_j whose inputs are from gates g_h and g_i into the inequalities $x_j \leq x_h, x_j \leq x_i, x_j \geq x_h + x_i - 1$.

3. Transform each $\neg$ gate g_j whose input is from gate g_i into the equation $x_j = x_i - 1$.

4. If g_j is the circuit output gate, then add the equation $x_j = 1$ to the previous ones.

Consider the circuit represented in Figure 12.2. Thus, the corresponding set of inequalities obtained from the above reduction is the following:

1. Input gates: $x_1 = 1, x_2 = 0, x_3 = 0, x_4 = 1$.

2. $\wedge$ gates: $x_7 \leq x_1$, $x_7 \leq x_4$, $x_7 \geq x_1 + x_4 - 1$, $x_8 \leq x_2$, $x_8 \leq x_6$, $x_8 \geq x_2 + x_6 - 1$, $x_9 \leq x_5, x_9 \leq x_8, x_9 \geq x_5 + x_8 - 1$, $x_{10} \leq x_9, x_{10} \leq x_7, x_{10} \geq x_9 + x_7 - 1$.

3. $\neg$ gates: $x_5 = x_1 - 1$, $x_6 = x_3 - 1$.

4. Output gate: $x_{10} = 1$.

We leave it to the reader to verify that each feasible solution is a 0-1 vector, that a feasible solution exists if and only if the circuit value is 1, and that the reduction requires logarithmic space.

Example 12.11 GENERIC MACHINE SIMULATION: given an input x, an encoding of a Turing machine T, and an integer t coded in unary, does T accept x within t steps?

Clearly, this problem belongs to P since the unary encoding of t gives enough time for the universal Turing machine to simulate the computation $T(x)$ in polynomial time with respect to the input length.

Reducing an arbitrary language L in P to GENERIC MACHINE SIMULATION is also easy since the reduction f must only transform x into the new word of the form

$$f(x) = \langle x, T, 1^{p(|x|)} \rangle$$

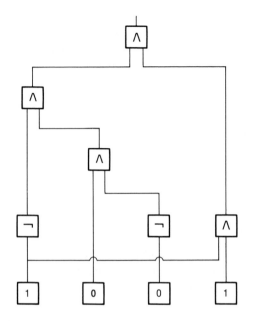

Figure 12.2 A simple circuit without ∨ gates

where T denotes the encoding of a Turing machine deciding L in polynomial time $p(n)$. This transformation is easily performed in logarithmic space, and thus GENERIC MACHINE SIMULATION is P-complete.

Let us conclude with two comments on P-complete problems.

First, since it seems unlikely that $P \subseteq RNC$, a proof that a problem is P-complete is a strong indication that the same problem does not belong to RNC.

Second, note that the set of problems which do not admit fast parallel algorithms is not necessarily limited to P-complete problems. Indeed, according to Lemma 12.2, the set $P - NC$ (assuming $P \neq NC$ holds) may also include other problems which are not P-complete. As an example, any problem (if it exists) which is complete with respect to $\leq_{NC}$ but not to $\leq_{log}$ also belongs to $P - NC$.

Problems

12.1. Complete the proof of Lemma 12.3.

12.2. Extend the algorithm described in Example 12.3 to the case where x may include components having the same value.

12.3. Derive a fast parallel algorithm to check whether a graph is connected.

12.4. A *minimum spanning tree* of a weighted connected graph $G = (N, E)$ is defined as an acyclic subgraph $G' = (N, E')$ such that the total weight of its edges is minimum. Derive a fast parallel algorithm to compute the minimum spanning tree. [Hint: 'parallelize' the well-known sequential greedy algorithm.]

12.5. Prove that computing the determinant is FNC^1-reducible to solving a system of linear equations. [Csanky (1976)]

12.6. Show that RNC is included in BPP.

12.7. Show that the problem of deciding whether a graph admits a perfect matching belongs to NC. [Hint: use Theorem 9.4.]

12.8. Consider a restriction of CIRCUIT VALUE in which the gates are only of type ∨ and ¬. Show that such a problem is P-complete. [Hint: show that CIRCUIT VALUE is logspace-reducible to the new problem.]

12.9. Given a graph $G = (N, E)$ and a node, consider the problem of determining whether that node is contained in the lexicographically first subset E' of E such that no two nodes in E' are adjacent. Show that this problem is P-complete. [Hint: refer to previous problem.]

12.10. A term is a composition of variables and function symbols. A substitution for a variable x in a term s is the replacement of all the occurrences of x in s by another term t. Given two terms s and t, consider the problem of deciding whether a series of substitutions exists that unifies s and t, that is, such that, at the end of the substitutions, the two terms coincide. Prove that this problem is P-complete. [Hint: refer to Problem 12.8.]

12.11. A weaker concept of P-completeness refers to algorithms instead of languages. Given an algorithm T, let us consider the following language:

$$L_T = \{\langle x, b, i \rangle : \text{the } i\text{th bit of } T(x) \text{ is } b\}.$$

An algorithm is said to be P-complete if the corresponding language is P-complete.

Given a graph G and a node n, find a path starting from n that cannot be extended. Consider the following greedy algorithm to solve this problem:

```
begin {input: G = (N, E), n}
    path := {n};
    m := n;
    while m has an adjacent node not in path do
    begin
        u := adjacent node of m not in path with lowest index;
        add u to path;
        m := u;
    end;
end.
```

Prove that the above algorithm is P-complete. [Hint: refer to Problem 12.8.]

Notes

The class NC was first studied in Pippenger (1979) who defined it as the class of languages decided by polynomial-time deterministic Turing machines performing a logarithmic number of tape head reversals (the reversals associated with a computation correspond to the number of times the tape heads changes direction). The definition of NC in terms of uniform circuit families is due to Cook (1979) who also coined the term NC which stands for 'Nick's Class' as a reminder of Pippenger's first name.

The class AC, and thus the characterization of NC in terms of PRAMs, was described in Stockmeyer and Vishkin (1984).

Two additional important contribution to the understanding of NC were given in Ruzzo (1981). First, several circuit uniformity conditions were considered besides the logspace-uniformity introduced in Chapter 11 and it was proved that the definition of NC remains substantially the same when referring to these other conditions. Next, a characterization of NC in terms of random access alternating Turing machines was given. This kind of alternating Turing machine does not make use of the input tape but rather of an index tape onto which the computation writes the index i of the input symbol to be read. Random access alternating machines are a convenient model to prove the inclusion in NC of some difficult problems. As an example, it was shown in Ruzzo (1980) that deciding whether an input x can be derived from a given type 2 grammar is in NC^2.

We may conclude from the above discussion that NC is a rather robust class which captures efficiently the concept of problem admitting a fast parallel algorithm.

The parallel algorithms described in Sections 12.2 and 12.3 are only a very limited and somewhat arbitrarily chosen sample. In fact, the introduction of massively parallel computers has stimulated researchers to revisit the field of sequential algorithms and provide whenever possible corresponding fast parallel algorithms. Techniques useful for designing parallel algorithms were reviewed, among many others, in the books of Gibbons and Rytter (1988) and of Akl (1989). Further surveys of parallel algorithms may be found in Kindervater and Lenstra (1986), Eppstein and Galil (1988), Karp and Ramachandran (1990).

The algorithms illustrated in Examples 12.3, 12.4, and 12.5 appeared in Muller and Preparata (1975), Dekel, Nassimi, and Sahni (1981), and Dekel and Sahni (1983), respectively.

Thanks to the results contained in Borodin (1977), a large class of natural problems have been shown to be in NC, namely, those belonging to NLOGSPACE and to *co*NLOGSPACE. Further enrichments of NC were discussed in Cook (1985).

One of the first parallel algorithms for inverting a matrix was given in Csanky (1976). Further extensions to non-numeric fields, that is, methods which do not make use of divisions, were developed in Berkowitz (1984).

The applications of matrix inversion are well known and, not surprisingly, a subclass of NC included between NC^1 and NC^2 and denoted as DET was introduced in Cook (1985) and it was shown that the problems of computing the determinant and the power of a matrix, and that of inverting a matrix are DET-complete with respect to NC^1-reducibility.

The RNC algorithm for BIPARTITE MAXIMUM MATCHING and the companion lemmas illustrated in Section 12.3.1 appeared in Mulmuley, Vazirani, and Vazirani (1987). Other problems in RNC^2 can be found in Borodin, von zur Gathen, and Hopcroft (1982). New results are still appearing and we refer the reader to the technical literature for an updated survey of additional RNC algorithms.

The P-completeness of CIRCUIT VALUE was proved in Ladner (1975b). The problem LINEAR PROGRAMMING deserves some additional comments. The simplex method commonly used cannot be considered a polynomial-time algorithm since in the worst case the execution time becomes exponential with respect to the size of the problem instance and it had been conjectured for several years that this problem does not belong to P. The work of Khachiyan (1979) and of Karmakar (1984) has shown that LINEAR PROGRAMMING does belong to P although the practical sgnificance of this result has yet to be understood. In the same work by Khachiyan and in a successive work by Dobkin and Reiss (1980), the P-completeness of LINEAR PROGRAMMING was proved.

Finally, a few comments on the problem GENERIC MACHINE SIMULATION introduced in Example 12.11. In Greenlaw, Hoover, and Ruzzo (1991), its P-completeness is used to provide evidence that NC $\neq$ P: their reasoning can be summarized as follows. First, note that the universal machine used in the proof need not be a Turing machine since it could be replaced by any interpreter written for some high-level programming language such as Pascal or Lisp. We are thus looking for a programming language interpreter that is able to achieve highly parallel execution on completely *arbitrary* programs. Since program code can be remarkably obscure, our ability to deduce (mechanically) non-trivial properties of programs given just the text of the sequential progam is severely limited. In fact, parallel compiler optimizations rarely make radical alterations to the set of intermediate values computed by a program, to the method by which they are computed, or even to the order in which they are computed, while such transformations would certainly be necessary to achieve a highly parallel generic simulation.

References

Abrahamson, K., Fellows, M. R., Langston, M. A., and Moret, B., "Constructive complexity", Technical Report, Department of Computer Science, Washington State University, 1988.

Adleman, L.M. and Huang, M.A., "Recognizing primes in random polynomial time", Technical Report, University of Southern California, 1988.

Aho, A.V., Hopcroft, J.E., and Ullman, J.D., *The design and analysis of computer algorithms*, Addison-Wesley, 1974.

Akl, S.G. *The design and analysis of parallel algorithms*, Prentice Hall, 1989.

Apsvall, B., Plass, M. F., and Tarjan, R. E., "A linear time algorithm for testing the truth of certain quantified Boolean formulas", *Information Processing Letters*, 8, 121-123, 1979.

Arora, S. and Safra, S., "Probabilistic checking of proofs; a new characterization of NP", *Proc. IEEE Symposium on Foundations of Computer Science*, 2-13, 1992.

Arora, S., Lund, C., Motwani, R., Sudan, M., and Szegedy, M., "Proof verification and the hardness of approximation problems", *Proc. IEEE Symposium on Foundations of Computer Science*, 14-23, 1992.

Ausiello, G., "Abstract computational complexity and cycling computations", *Journal of Computer and System Sciences*, 5, 118-128, 1971.

Ausiello, G., D'Atri, A., and Protasi, M., "Structure preserving reduction among convex optimization problems", *Journal of Computer and System Sciences*, 21, 136-153, 1980.

Ausiello, G., Marchetti Spaccamela, A., and Protasi, M., "Towards a unified approach for the classification of NP-complete optimization problems", *Theoretical Computer Science*, 12, 83-96, 1980.

Babai, L., Talk presented at *Proc. IEEE Symposium on Foundations of Computer Science*, 1979.

Babai, L., "Trading group theory for randomness", *Proc. ACM Symposium on Theory of Computing*, 421-429, 1985.

Babai, L., Fortnow, L., and Lund, C., "Non-deterministic exponential time has two-prover interactive protocols", *Computational Complexity*, 1, 3-40, 1991.

Babai, L., Fortnow, L., Levin, L., and Szegedy, M., "Checking computations in polylogarithmic time", *Proc. ACM Symposium on Theory of Computing*, 21-31, 1991.

Baker, B.S., "Approximation algorithms for NP-complete problems on planar graphs", *Proc. IEEE Symposium on Foundations of Computer Science*, 265-273, 1983.

Baker, T., Gill, J., and Solovay R., "Relativizations of the P=?NP question", *SIAM Journal on Computing*, 4, 431-442, 1975.

Balcazar, J.L., Diaz, J., and Gabarro, J., *Structural complexity I*, Springer-Verlag, 1988.

Balcazar, J.L., Diaz, J., and Gabarro, J., *Structural complexity II*, Springer-Verlag, 1990.

Balcazar, J.L. and Russo, D.A., "Immunity and simplicity in relativizations of probabilistic complexity classes", *Theoretical Informat. Applied*, 22, 227-244, 1988.

Beigel, R., Reingold, N., and Spielman, D., "PP is closed under intersection", Technical Report, Yale University, 1990.

Bennett, C. and Gill, J., "Relative to random oracle A, $P^A \neq NP^A \neq coNP^A$ with probability 1", *SIAM Journal on Computing*, 10, 96-113, 1981.

Berge, C. "Two theorems in graph theory", *Proc. of National Academy of Science*, 43, 842-844, 1957.

Berkowitz, S.J., "On computing the determinant in small parallel time using a small number of processors", *Information Proc. Letters*, 18, 147-150, 1984.

Berman, P., "Relationships between density and deterministic complexity of NP-complete languages", *Lecture Notes in Computer Science*, Vol. 62, Springer-Verlag, 63-71, 1978.

Berman, L. and Hartmanis, J., "On isomorphisms and density of NP and other complete sets", *SIAM Journal on Computing*, 6, 305-322, 1977.

Blass, A. and Gurevich, Y., "On the unique satisfiability problem", *Information and Control*, 55, 80-88, 1982.

Blum, M., "A machine independent theory of the complexity of recursive functions", *Journal of ACM*, 14, 322-336, 1967a.

Blum, M., "On the size of machines", *Information and Control*, 11, 257-265, 1967b.

Blum, M., "How to prove a theorem so no one else can claim it", *International Congress of Mathematicians*, 1986.

Blum, N., "A Boolean function requiring $3n$ network size", *Theoretical Computer Science*, 28, 337-345, 1984.

Book, R.V., "Tally languages and complexity classes", *Information and Control*, 26, 186-193, 1974.

Book, R.V., "Restricted relativizations of complexity classes", in: Hartmanis, J., ed., *Computational complexity theory*, Proc. Symposia in Applied Mathematics, 38, 47-74, 1989.

Book, R.V., Long T., and Selman A., "Qualitative relativization of complexity classes", *Journal of Computer and System Sciences*, 30, 395-413, 1985.

Borodin, A., "Computational complexity and the existence of complexity gaps", *Journal of ACM*, 19, 158-174, 1972.

Borodin, A., "On relating time and space to size and depth", *SIAM Journal on Computing*, 6, 733-743, 1977.

Borodin, A., von zur Gathen, J., and Hopcroft, J., "Fast parallel matrix and GCD computations", *Proc. IEEE Symposium on Foundations of Computer Science*, 65-71, 1982.

Bovet, D.P., Crescenzi, P., and Silvestri, R., "Complexity classes and sparse oracles", *Proc. IEEE Structure in Complexity Theory Conference*, 102-108, 1991.

Bovet, D.P., Crescenzi, P., and Silvestri, R., "A uniform approach to define complexity classes", *Theoretical Computer Science*, 104, 263-283, 1992.

Bruschi, D., Joseph, D., and Young, P., "A structural overview of NP optimization problems", *Algorithms Reviews*, 2, 1-26, 1991.

Cai, J., Gundermann, T., Hartmanis, J., Hemachandra, L.A., Sewelson, V., Wagner, K., and Wechsung, G., "The Boolean Hierarchy I: structural properties", *SIAM Journal on Computing*, 17, 1232-1252, 1988.

Cai, J., Gundermann, T., Hartmanis, J., Hemachandra, L.A., Sewelson, V., Wagner, K., and Wechsung, G., "The Boolean Hierarchy II: applications", *SIAM Journal on Computing*, 18, 95-111, 1989.

Cai, J. and Hemachandra, L.A., "The Boolean hierarchy: hardware over NP", *Lecture Notes in Computer Science*, Vol. 223, Springer-Verlag, 105-124, 1986.

Carmichael, R.D., "On composite numbers p which satisfy the Fermat congruence $a^{p-1} \equiv 1 \pmod{p}$", *American Mathematical Monthly*, 19, 22-27, 1912.

Chandra, A.K., Kozen, D.C., and Stockmeyer, L.J., "Alternation", *Journal of ACM*, 28, 114-133, 1981.

Chandra, A.K., Kozen, D.C., and Stockmeyer, L.J., "Alternation", *Journal of ACM*, 28, 114-133, 1981.

Chomsky, N., "On certain formal properties of grammars", *Information and Control*, 2, 137-167, 1959.

Chomsky, N., "Formal properties of grammars", in: Luce, R.D., Bush, R.R, and Galanter, E., eds., *Handbook of mathematical psychology, vol 2*, Wiley, 323-418, 1963.

Cobham, A., "The intrinsic computational difficulty of functions", *Proc. Congress for Logic, Mathematics, and Philosophy of Science*, 24-30, 1964.

Constable, R.L., "The operator gap", *Journal of ACM*, 19, 175-183, 1972.

Conway, J. and Gordon, C., "Knots and links in spatial graphs", *Journal of Graph Theory*, 7, 445-453, 1983.

Cook, S.A., "The complexity of theorem proving procedures", *Proc. ACM Symposium on Theory of Computing*, 151-158, 1971.

Cook, S.A., "An observation on time-storage trade off", *Journal of Computer and System Sciences*, 7, 308-316, 1974.

Cook, S.A., "Deterministic CFL's are accepted simultaneously in polynomial time and log squared space", *Proc. ACM Symposium on Theory of Computing*, 338-345, 1979.

Cook, S.A., "A taxonomy of problems with fast parallel algorithms", *Information and Control*, 64, 2-22, 1985.

Cook, S.A., Dwork, C., and Reischuk, R., "Upper and lower time bounds for parallel random access machines without simultaneous writes", *SIAM Journal on Computing*, 15, 87-97, 1986.

Cormen, T.H., Leiserson, C.E., and Rivest, R.L., *Introduction to algorithms*, The MIT Press, 1990.

Crescenzi, P. and Panconesi, A., "Completeness in approximation classes", *Information and Computation*, 93, 241-262, 1991.

Csanky, L., "Fast parallel matrix inverison algorithms", *SIAM Journal on Computing*, 5, 618-623, 1976.

Davis, M., *Computability and unsolvability*, McGraw-Hill, 1958.

Davis, M., ed., *The undecidable*, Raven Press, 1965.

Dekel, E., Nassimi, D., and Sahni, S., "Parallel matrix and graph algorithms", *SIAM Journal on Computing*, 10, 657-675, 1981.

Dekel, E. and Sahni, S., "Parallel scheduling algorithms", *Oper. Res.*, 31, 24-29, 1983.

de Leeuw, K., Moore, E.F., Shannon, C.E., and Shapiro, N., "Computability by probabilistic machines", in: Shannon, C.E., ed., *Automata studies*, American Mathematical Society, 183-198, 1956.

Deming, K. W., "Independence numbers of graphs - an extension of the Konig - Egervary property", *Discrete Mathematics*, 27, 23-24, 1979.

Dijkstra, E.W., "A note on two problems in connection with graphs", *Numerische Mathematik*, 1, 269-271, 1959.

Dobkin, D.P. and Reiss, S., "The complexity of linear programming", *Theoretical Computer Science*, 11, 1-18, 1980.

Eckstein, D.M., "Simultaneous memory accesses", Technical Report 79-6, Department of Computer Science, Iowa State University, 1979.

Edmonds, J.R., "Paths, trees and flowers", *Canadian Journal of Mathematics*, 17, 449-467, 1965.

Elgot, C.C. and Robinson, A., "Random access stored program machines", *Journal of ACM*, 11, 365-399, 1964.

Eppstein, D. and Galil, Z., "Parallel algorithmic techniques for combinatorial computation", *Ann. Rev. Comput. Sci.*, 3, 233-283, 1988.

Even, S. and Tarjan, R.E., "A combinatorial problem which is complete in polynomial space", *Journal of ACM*, 23, 710-719, 1976.

Feige, U., Goldwasser, S., Lovasz, L., Safra, S., and Szegedy, M., "Approximating clique is almost NP-complete", *Proc. IEEE Symposium on Foundations of Computer Science*, 2-12, 1991.

Fellows, M.R. and Langston, M.R., "Non constructive tools for proving polynomial-time decidability", *Journal of ACM*, 35, 727-739, 1988.

Fich, F.E., Radge, P., and Widgerson, A., "Relations between concurrent-write models of parallel computations", *SIAM Journal on Computing*, 17, 606-627, 1988.

Ford, L.R. Jr and Fulkerson, D.R., *Flows in networks*, Princeton University Press, 1962.

Fortnow, L. and Sipser, M., "Are there interactive protocols for co-NP languages?", *Information Processing Letters*, 28, 249-251, 1988.

Fortune, S. and Wyllie, J., "Parallelism in random access machines", *Proc. ACM Symposium on Theory of Computing*, 114-118, 1978.

Friedman, H., Robertson, N., and Seymour, P., "The metamathematics of the graph-minor theorem," *AMS Contemporary Mathematics Series*, 65, 229-261, 1987.

Furst, M., Hopcroft, J., and Luks, E., "A subexponential algorithm for trivalent graph isomorphism", *Congressus Numerantium*, 28, 421-446, 1980.

Furst, M., Saxe, J., and Sipser, M., "Parity, circuits, and the polynomial-time hierarchy", *Mathematical System Theory*, 17, 13-27, 1984.

Galil, Z., "Efficient algorithms for finding maximum matching in graphs", *ACM Computing Surveys*, 18, 23-38, 1986.

Garey, M.R. and Johnson, D.S., "Strong NP-completeness results: motivation, examples, and implications", *Journal of ACM*, 25, 499-508, 1978.

Garey, M.R. and Johnson, D.S., *Computers and intractability: a guide to the theory of NP-completeness*, Freeman, 1979.

Gavril, F., "Algorithms for minimum coloring, maximum clique, minimum covering by cliques, and maximum independent set of a chordal graph", *SIAM Journal on Computing*, 1, 180-187, 1972.

Gibbons, A.M. and Rytter, W., *Efficient parallel algorithms*, Cambridge University Press, 1988.

Gill, J., "Computational complexity of probabilistic Turing machines", *SIAM Journal on Computing*, 6, 675-695, 1977.

Goldreich, O., "Randomness, interactive proof, and zero-knowledge. A survey", in: Herken, R., ed., *The universal Turing machine. A half-century survey*, Kammerer und Unverzagt, 377-405, 1988.

Goldreich, O., Micali, S., and Wigderson, A., "Proofs that yield nothing but their validity and a methodology for protocol design", *Proc. IEEE Symposium on Foundations of Computer Science*, 174-187, 1986.

Goldschlager, L.M., "The monotone and planar circuit value problems are logspace complete for P", *SIGACT News*, 9, 25-29, 1977.

Goldschlager, L.M., "A universal interconnection pattern for parallel computers", *Journal of ACM*, 29, 1073-1086, 1982.

Goldwasser, S., Micali, S., and Rackoff, C., "The knowledge complexity of interactive proof systems", *SIAM Journal on Computing*, 18, 186-208, 1989.

Goldwasser, S. and Sipser, M., "Private coins versus public coins in interactive proof-systems", *Proc. ACM Symposium on Theory of Computing*, 59-68, 1986.

Goldwasser, S., "Interactive proof systems", *Proc. Symposia in Applied Mathematics*, 38, 108-128, 1989.

Graham, R.L., Knuth, D.E., and Patashnik, O., *Concrete mathematics*, Addison-Wesley, 1989.

Greenlaw, R., Hoover, H.J., and Ruzzo, W., "A compendium of problems complete for P", Technical Report, Department of Computer Science and Engineering, University of Washington, 1991.

Groslmusz, V. and Radge, P., "Incomparability in parallel computation", *Proc. IEEE Symposium on Foundations of Computer Science*, 89-98, 1987.

Gupta, U.I., Lee, D.T., and Leung, J.Y., "An optimal solution for the channel-assignment problem", *IEEE Transactions on Computers*, 28, 807-810, 1979.

Harison, M.A., *Introduction to switching and automata theory*, McGraw-Hill, 1965.

Hartmanis, J., "On sparse sets in NP-P", *Information Processing Letters*, 16, 55-60, 1983.

Hartmanis, J., "Gödel, von Neumann and the P=?NP problem", *EATCS Bulletin*, 38, 101-107, 1989.

Hartmanis, J. and Hopcroft, J.E., "An overview of the theory of computational complexity", *Journal of ACM*, 18, 444-475, 1971.

Hartmanis, J., Immerman, N., and Sewelson, W., "Sparse sets in NP-P: EXPTIME versus NEXPTIME", *Information and Control*, 65, 158-181, 1985.

Hartmanis, J. and Mahaney, S., "An essay about research on sparse NP-complete sets", *Lecture Notes in Computer Science*, Vol. 88, Springer-Verlag, 40-57, 1980.

Hartmanis, J. and Stearns, R.E., "On the computational complexity of algorithms", *Transactions of the American Mathematical Society*, 117, 285-306, 1965.

Hermes, H., *Enumerability, decidability, computability*, Springer-Verlag, 1969.

Hoffmann, C.M., "Group-theoretic algorithms and graph isomorphism", *Lecture Notes in Computer Science*, Vol. 136, Springer-Verlag, 1982.

Homer, S. and Maas, "Oracle-dependent properties of the lattice of NP sets", *Theoretical Computer Science*, 24, 279-289, 1983.

Hopcroft, J.E., Paul, J.W., and Valiant, L., "On time versus space", *Journal of ACM*, 24, 332-337, 1977.

Hopcroft, J.E. and Ullman, J.D., "Relations between time and tape complexities", *Journal of ACM*, 15, 414-427, 1968.

Hopcroft, J.E. and Ullman, J.D., *Introduction to automata theory, languages, and computation*, Addison-Wesley, 1979.

Hunt, J.W., "Topics in probabilistic complexity", PhD Dissertation, Stanford University, 1978.

Immerman, N., "Nondeterministic space is closed under complementation", *SIAM Journal on Computing*, 17, 935-938, 1988.

Johnson, D.S., "Approximation algorithms for combinatorial problems", *Journal of Computer and System Sciences*, 9, 256-278, 1974.

Johnson, D.S., "A catalog of complexity classes", in: van Leeuwen, J., ed., *Handbook of theoretical computer science, vol. A*, Elsevier, 67-161, 1990.

Jones, N.D., "Space-bounded reducibility among combinatorial problems", *Journal of Computer and System Sciences*, 11, 68-85, 1975.

Joseph, D. and Young, P., "Some remarks on witness functions for nonpolynomial and noncomplete sets in NP", *Theoretical Computer Science*, 39, 225-237, 1985.

Karmakar, N., "A new polynomial-time algorithm for linear programming", *Combinatorica*, 4, 373-395, 1984.

Karp, R.M., "Reducibility among combinatorial problems", in: Miller, R.E. and Tatcher, J.W., eds., *Complexity of computer computations*, Plenum Press, 85-103, 1972.

Karp, R.M., "An introduction to randomized algorithms", Technical Report, University of California, Berkeley, 1990.

Karp, R.M. and Lipton, R.J., "Some connections between nonuniform and uniform complexity classes", *Proc. ACM Symposium on Theory of Computing*, 302-309, 1980.

Karp, R.M. and Ramachandran, V., "Parallel algorithms for shared-memory machines", in: van Leeuwen, J., ed., *Handbook of theoretical computer science, vol. A*, Elsevier, 871-941, 1990.

Khachiyan, L.G., "A polynomial algorithm in linear programming", *Soviet Math. Dokl.*, 20, 191-194, 1979.

Kleene, S.C., "General recursive functions of natural numbers", *Matematische Annalen*, 112, 727-742, 1936.

Kleene, S.C., *Introduction to metamathematics*, North-Holland, 1962.

Knuth, D.E., *The art of computer programming, vol. 1: fundamental algorithms*, Addison-Wesley, 1968.

Ko, K., "Some observations on the probabilistic algorithms and NP-hard problems", *Information Processing Letters*, 14, 39-43, 1982.

Kobayashi, K., "On proving time constructibility of functions", *Theoretical Computer Science*, 35, 215-225, 1985.

Kolaitis, P.G. and Thakur M.N., "Approximation properties of NP minimization classes", *Proc. IEEE Structure in Complexity Theory Conference*, 353-366, 1991.

Kozen, D.C., *The design and analysis of algorithms*, Springer-Verlag, 1992.

Kranakis, E., *Primality and cryptography*, Wiley-Teubner, 1986.

Krentel, M., "The complexity of optimization problems", *Journal of Computer and System Sciences*, 36, 490-509, 1988.

Kucera, L., "Parallel computation and conflicts in memory access", *Information Processing Letters*, 14, 93-96, 1982.

Kuroda, S.Y., "Classes of languages and linear-bounded automata", *Information and Control*, 7, 207-223, 1964.

Kurtz, S.A., Mahaney, S.R., and Royer, J.S., "The structure of complete degrees", in: Selman, A., ed., *Complexity theory retrospective*, Springer-Verlag, 108-146, 1990.

Ladner, R.E., "On the structure of polynomial-time reducibility", *Journal of ACM*, 22, 155-171, 1975a.

Ladner, R.E., "The circuit value problem is logspace complete for P", *SIGACT News*, 7, 18-20, 1975b.

Ladner, R.E, Lynch, N.A., and Selman, A.L., "A comparison of polynomial time reducibilities", *Theoretical Computer Science*, 1, 103-124, 1975.

Landweber, L., Lipton, R., and Robertson, E., "On the structure of sets in NP and other complexity classes", *Theoretical Computer Science*, 15, 181-200, 1981.

Lewis, H.R. and Papadimitriou, C.H., *Elements of the theory of computation*, Prentice Hall, 1981.

Li, M. and Vitany, P.M.B., "Kolmogorov complexity and its applications", in: van Leeuwen, J., ed., *Handbook of theoretical computer science, vol. A*, Elsevier, 187-254, 1990.

Liskiewicz, M. and Lorys, K., "Some time-space bounds for one-tape deterministic Turing machines", *Lecture Notes in Computer Science*, Vol. 380, Springer-Verlag, 297-307, 1989.

Long, T.J. and Selman, A.L., "Relativizing complexity classes with sparse sets", *Journal of ACM*, 33, 618-628, 1986.

Lorys, K. and Liskiewicz, M., "Two applications of Fürer's counter to one-tape nondeterministic TMs", *Lecture Notes in Computer Science*, Vol. 324, Springer-Verlag, 445-453, 1988.

Lovasz, L., "On determinants, matchings, and random algorithms", in: Budach, L., ed., *Proc. Symposium on Fundamentals of Computing Theory*, Akademia-Verlag, 565-574, 1979.

Lund, C., Fortnow, L., Karloff, H., and Nisan, N., "Algebraic methods for interactive proof systems", *Journal of ACM*, 39, 859-868, 1992.

Lund, C. and Yannakakis, M., "On the hardness of approximating minimization problems", *Proc. ACM Symposium on Theory of Computing*, 1993.

Lupanov, O.B., "On the synthesis of contact networks", *Doklady Akademia Nauk SSSR*, 119, 23-26, 1958.

Machtey, M. and Young, P., *An introduction to the general theory of algorithms*, Elsevier, 1978.

Mahaney, S.R., "Sparse complete sets for NP: solution of a conjecture by Berman and Hartmanis", *Journal of Computer and System Sciences*, 25, 130-143, 1982.

Markov, A.A., "Theory of algorithms", *Trudy Mathematicheskogo Instituta imeni V.A. Steklova*, 42, 1954.

Meyer, A.R. and Stockmeyer, L.J., "The equivalence problem for regular expressions with squaring requires exponential space", *Proc. IEEE Symposium on Switching and Automata Theory*, 125-129, 1972.

Miller, G.L., "Riemann's hypothesis and tests for primality", *Journal of Computer and System Sciences*, 13, 300-317, 1976.

Miller, G.L., "On the $n^{\log n}$ isomorphism technique: a preliminary report", *Proc. ACM Symposium on Theory of Computing*, 51-58, 1978.

Minsky, M.L., *Computation: finite and infinite machines*, Prentice Hall, 1967.

Miyano, S., Shiraishi, S., and Shoudai, T., "A list of P-complete problems", Technical Report RIFIS-TR-CS-17, Kyushu University 33, 1989.

Muller, D.L. and Preparata, F., "Bounds to complexity of networks for sorting and for switching", *Journal of ACM*, 22, 195-201, 1975.

Mulmuley, K., Vazirani U.V., and Vazirani, V.V., "Matching is as easy as matrix inversion", *Proc. ACM Symposium on Theory of Computing*, 345-354, 1987.

Nassimi, D. and Sahni, S., "Data broadcasting in SIMD computers", *IEEE Transactions on Computers*, C-30, 101-107, 1981.

Norman, R.Z. and Rabin, M.O., "An algorithm for a minimum cover of a graph", *Proc. of the American Mathematical Society*, 10, 315-319, 1959.

Orponen, P. and Mannila, H., "On approximation preserving reductions: complete problems and robust measures", Technical Report, University of Helsinki, 1987.

Papadimitriou, C.H., "Games against nature", *Proc. IEEE Symposium on Foundations of Computer Science*, 446-450, 1983.

Papadimitriou, C.H. and Steiglitz, K., *Combinatorial optimization: algorithms and complexity*, Prentice Hall, 1982.

Papadimitriou, C.H. and Wolfe, D., "The complexity of facets resolved", *Journal of Computer and System Sciences*, 37, 2-13, 1988.

Papadimitriou, C.H. and Yannakakis, M., "The complexity of facets (and some facets of complexity)", *Journal of Computer and System Sciences*, 28, 244-259, 1984.

Papadimitriou, C.H. and Yannakakis, M., "Optimization, approximation, and complexity classes", *Journal of Computer and System Sciences*, 43, 425-440, 1991.

Paz, A. and Moran, S., "Non deterministic polynomial optimization problems and their approximation", *Theoretical Computer Science*, 15, 251-277, 1981.

Petreschi, R. and Simeone, B., "Experimental comparison of 2-satisfiability algorithms", *RAIRO Operation Research*, 25, 241-264, 1991.

Pippenger, N., "On simultaneous resource bounds", *Proc. IEEE Symposium on Foundations of Computer Science*, 307-311, 1979.

Pippenger, N. and Fischer, M.J., "Relations among complexity measures", *Journal of ACM*, 26, 361-381, 1979.

Post, E.L., "Formal reductions of the general combinatorial decision problem", *American Journal of Mathematics*, 65, 197-215, 1943.

Pratt, V.R., "Every prime has a succinct certificate", *SIAM Journal on Computing*, 4, 214-220, 1975.

Pratt, V.R. and Stockmeyer, L.J., "A characterization of the power of vector machines", *Journal of Computer and System Sciences*, 12, 198-221, 1976.

Rabin, M.O., "Degree of difficulty of computing a function and a partial ordering of recursive sets", Technical Report 2, Hebrew University, Jerusalem, 1960.

Rabin, M.O., "Probabilistic algorithms", in: Traub, J.F., ed., *Algorithms and complexity, recent results and new direction*, Academic Press, 21-40, 1976.

Rabin, M.O., "Probabilistic algorithm for testing primality", *Journal of Number Theory*, 12, 128-138, 1980.

Riordan, J. and Shannon, C.E., "The number of two-terminal series-parallel networks", *Journal of Mathematics and Physics*, 21, 83-93, 1942.

Robson, J.M., "N by N checkers is Exptime complete", *SIAM Journal on Computing*, 13, 252-267, 1984.

Rogers, H. Jr, *Theory of recursive functions and effective computability*, McGraw-Hill, 1967.

Ruzzo, W.L., "Tree-size bounded alternation", *Journal of Computer and System Sciences*, 21, 218-235, 1980.

Ruzzo, W.L., "On uniform circuit complexity", *Journal of Computer and System Sciences*, 22, 365-383, 1981.

Santos, E., "Probabilistic Turing machines and computability", *Proc. of the American Mathematical Society*, 22, 704-710, 1969.

Savage, J.E., "Computational work and time of finite machines", *Journal of ACM*, 19, 660-674, 1972.

Savage, J.E., *The complexity of computing*, Wiley, 1976.

Savitch, W.J., "Relationship between nondeterministic and deterministic tape complexities", *Journal of Computer and System Sciences*, 4, 177-192, 1970.

Schmidt, D., "The recursion-theoretic structure of complexity classes", *Theoretical Computer Science*, 38,143-156, 1985.

Schöning, U., "A uniform approach to obtain diagonal sets in complexity classes", *Theoretical Computer Science*, 18, 95-103, 1982a.

Schöning, U., "Relativization and infinite subsets of NP sets", unpublished manuscript, 1982b.

Schöning, U., "On the structure of Δ_2^p", *Information Processing Letters*, 16, 209-211, 1983.

Schöning, U., "Complexity and structures", *Lecture Notes in Computer Science*, Vol. 211, Springer-Verlag, 1985.

Schöning, U., "Graph isomorphism is in the low hierarchy", *Lecture Notes in Computer Science*, Vol. 247, Springer-Verlag, 114-124, 1986.

Schöning, U. and Book, R.V., "Immunity, relativizations and nondeterminism", *SIAM Journal on Computing*, 13, 329-337, 1984.

Schroeder, M.R., *Number theory in science and communication*, Springer-Verlag, 1984.

Schwartz, J.T., "Fast probabilistic algorithms for verification of polynomial identities", *Journal of ACM*, 27, 701-717, 1980.

Seiferas, J.J., "Machine-independent complexity theory", in: van Leeuwen, J., ed., *Handbook of theoretical computer science, vol. A*, Elsevier, 163-186, 1990.

Selman, A.L., "Complexity issues in cryptography", *Proc. Symposia in Applied Mathematics*, 38, 92-107, 1989.

Shamir, A., "IP=PSPACE", *Journal of ACM*, 39, 869-877, 1992.

Shannon, C.E., "The synthesis of two-terminal switching circuits", *Bell Systems Technical Journal*, 28, 59-98, 1949.

Shen, A., "IP=PSPACE: simplified proof", *Journal of ACM*, 39, 878-880, 1992.

Shepherdson,J.C. and Sturgis, H.E., "Computability of recursive functions", *Journal of ACM*, 10, 217-255, 1963.

Simon, J., "On some central problems in computational complexity", Technical Report, Cornell University, 1975.

Sipser, M., "On relativization and the existence of complete sets", *Lecture Notes in Computer Science*, Vol. 140, Springer-Verlag, 523-531, 1982.

Snir, M., "On parallel searching", Research Report 83-21, Department of Computer Science, The Hebrew University of Jerusalem, 1983.

Solovay, R. and Strassen, V., "A fast Monte-Carlo test for primality", *SIAM Journal on Computing*, 6, 84-85, 1977.

Spaan, E., Torenvliet L., and van Emde Boas, P., "Nondeterminism, fairness and a fundamental analogy", *EATCS Bulletin*, 37, 186-193, 1989.

Stearns, R.E., Hartmanis, J., and Lewis, P.M., "Hierarchies of memory limited computations", *Proc. 6th Annual Symp. on Switching Circuit Theory and Logical Design*, 179-190, 1965.

Stockmeyer, L.J., "The polynomial-time hierarchy", *Theoretical Computer Science*, 3, 1-22, 1977.

Stockmeyer, L.J., "On approximation algorithms for #P", *SIAM Journal on Computing*, 14, 849-861, 1985.

Stockmeyer, L.J. and Meyer, A.R., "Word problems requiring exponential time", *Proc. ACM Symposium on Theory of Computing*, 1-9, 1973.

Stockmeyer, L. and Vishkin, U., "Simulation of parallel random access machines by circuits", *SIAM Journal on Computing*, 13, 409-422, 1984.

Toda, S., "On the computational power of PP and $\oplus$P", *Proc. IEEE Symposium on Foundations of Computer Science*, 514-519, 1989.

Turing, A.M., "On computable numbers, with an application to the Entscheidungsproblem", *Proc. London Mathematical Society ser. 2*, 42, 230-265, 1936.

Turing, A.M., "Systems of logic based on ordinals", *Proc. London Mathematical Society ser. 2*, 45, 161-228, 1939.

Tutte, W.T., "The factors of graphs", *Canadian Journal of Mathematics*, 4, 314-328, 1952.

Valiant, L.G., "Relative complexity of checking and evaluating", *Information Processing Letters*, 5, 20-23, 1976.

van Emde Boas, P., "Machine models and simulations", in: van Leeuwen, J., ed., *Handbook of theoretical computer science, vol. A*, Elsevier, 1-66, 1990.

van Leeuwen, J., "Graph algorithms", in: van Leeuwen, J., ed., *Handbook of theoretical computer science, vol. A*, Elsevier, 525-632, 1990.

Vishkin, U. "On the choice of a model of parallel computation", manuscript, 1984.

Wechsung, G., "On the Boolean closure of NP", *Lecture Notes in Computer Science*, Vol. 199, Springer-Verlag, 485-493, 1985.

Wrathall, C., "Complete sets and polynomial time hierarchy", *Theoretical Computer Science*, 3, 23-33, 1977.

Yao, A.C., "Separating the polynomial-time hierarchy by oracles", *Proc. ACM Symposium on Theory of Computing*, 1-10, 1985.

Young, P., "Easy constructions in complexity theory: gap and speed-up theorems", *Proc. of the American Mathematical Society*, 37, 555-563, 1973.

Young, P., "Juris Hartmanis: fundamental contributions to isomorphism problems", in: Selman, A., ed., *Complexity theory retrospective*, Springer-Verlag, 28-58, 1990.

Index